Praise for *IT Systems Management, Second Edition*

IT Systems Management, Second Edition, is one of those definitive books that will serve as the foundation for a whole new breed of IT professionals. Apart from the innovative content, instructors and students will appreciate the added features such as revision questions and answers per chapter, additional reading suggestions, and real-life experiences. The supporting material for instructors makes it quick and easy to develop courses for IT Systems Management.

Prof. Les Labuschagne
Director: School of Computing
University of South Africa (UNISA)

In Rich's second edition of *IT Systems Management*, he has built a true bridge between academia and today's IT professional working in a highly complex, ever changing environment. Now both student and practitioner have a common play-book available to guide us through the 21st century technology landscape. I strongly recommend this book as mandatory reading, whether on the front lines of support or for the senior executive working on navigating a long-term strategy for an organization.

Mike Marshall
Director, MMT Production Service
Association of Retired Persons (AARP)

Managing IT infrastructures has always been a complex undertaking and most managers had to learn its ins and outs through experience. Rich Schiesser's *IT Systems Management* text offers a much more humane approach in that one can gain the breath of exposure to the topic without suffering the negative conse-quences resulting from knowledge gaps. This text offers insights into this topic that only someone who had been intimately involved over a long period of time could provide. Students and technical managers alike can profit from this treatise. I highly recommend this as a source book for academic courses in this area. It has too long been an ignored topic.

Dr. Gary L. Richardson
Program Coordinator
Graduate Technology Project Management Program
University of Houston

The 2nd edition of *IT Systems Management* uses a managerial approach to handling IT systems. The techniques described in the book are appropriate for professionals in the Telephony and Information technology industries. Schiesser offers in-depth looks at processes and procedures, and provides "how to" approaches to customer service and systems support issues. The book is an excellent reference manual for practitioners who manage enterprise or carrier-class infrastructures. I have used Schiesser's 1st and 2nd edition books in my in-person, mixed-mode, and on-line courses, and the materials and discussion questions included at the end of each chapter were well received by the students.

Robert Chow
Adjunct Professor
School of Business, Professional Studies, and On-line education
University of San Francisco
Golden Gate University
University of Phoenix - Online

In *IT Systems Management, Second Edition*, Rich Schiesser has done an exceptional job of compiling a wealth of information that is both comprehensive for the serious student and useful for the field practitioner. In addition to dozens of illustrative practical examples, many of his treatments of subjects such as executive support, staffing, customer service, and business continuity illuminate important principles that also apply to general business management. As both a former IT management instructor and systems manager, I would use the book as core material in either setting.

Michael E. Anzis, CBCP
Former CIO - Mazda North America Operations and Emulex Corp.
M.S. Business Information Systems, UCLA Anderson School of Management
Director, Global Business Continuity, Ingram Micro, Inc.

IT Systems Management is an excellent resource for understanding the "real" technology environment in today's connected organization. Schiesser's emphasis on people first, followed by processes then technology, lays the groundwork for learning how IT should be managed. Topical questions at the end of each chapter make this an ideal teaching tool for Instructors and a valuable learning experience for students who want to learn from a seasoned IT professional. I recommend *IT Systems Management* for both the classroom and as a reference book for practitioners.

David Reavis, CPP, Ph.D.
Assistant Professor of MIS
College of Business
Texas A&M University – Texarkana

One of the characteristics that make any IT management reference book so valuable in industry is its ability to transform widely-accepted best practices into real-life applications. Rich Schiesser's new version of his best-selling *IT Systems*

Management displays this ability in many ways. From updating technical areas such as ITIL and VoIP, to illuminating managerial challenges involving ethics, governance, and legislation, Schiesser deftly clarifies a variety of key issues that are of interest to both students and practitioners alike. This should be on the bookshelf of anyone seeking effective management of IT infrastructures.

Jeffery L Rohloff
IT Manager
Clark County Detention Services

There can be little disagreement about the impact that IT has had on our organizations, but getting value from these complex investments while managing the costs of delivery is a challenge for any IT professional. Rich Schiesser's *IT Systems Management* provides both the big-picture view and the essential elements of managing the people, processes, and technologies that make up world-class information systems. This book is destined to become both a well-used desk reference for seasoned IT veterans and an important textbook for soon-to-be IT professionals.

Dennis Adams, PhD
Decision and Information Sciences
Bauer College of Business
University of Houston

Change is, somewhat ironically, the only constant in the management of an IT infrastructure and the capabilities it enables. Companies and organizations are tasked with providing continuous service in an environment of continuous change. Over the years I have seen Rich apply his expertise of infrastructure processes in a number of capacities, and it's all captured in *IT Systems Management*. Rich's proven approach of People, Process, and Technology will give the reader, whether they are an IT leader, manager, technician or student, insight on how to excel in managing the seemingly juxtaposed interests of availability and change.

Mark Galligan
IT Director
Pacific Life Insurance Company

This book can be used effectively by educators and practitioners alike. It follows sound academic principles with questions and selected answers included in each chapter. Additional reading references enhance the wealth of information provided, and extensive use of real-life scenarios and case studies clarify issues and problems. A new chapter on Ethics and Legislation explores these issues now topical in IT. Various chapters have been revised to address new technologies and trends, such as outsourcing, within the IT industry. It is a well structured book focusing on the three main components of IT Management, i.e. People, Processes, and Technology.

Dr. Carl Marnewick
Head, Dept of Business IT
University of Johannesburg, South Africa

The new edition of *IT Systems Management* is current, understandable and practical. It serves well as both a practical workplace reference and as a classroom textbook, and provides electronic materials for formal instruction. Also included are a large variety of real-life examples, definitions of key terminology, and end-of-chapter materials that test and enhance comprehension. Rich's book delivers business value, which is what IT is all about these days, by enabling thousands of current and future IT professionals to make better decisions, take better actions, and deliver better results in managing IT infrastructures.

David Pultorak
President and Founder
Pultorak and Associates

IT Systems Management takes the IT professional beyond viewing IT as strictly managing technology, but to recognize data as a corporate asset and an integral part of an organization's Governance, Risk and Compliance (GRC) strategy. The concept of strategic security and safeguarding the availability, integrity, and confidentiality of designated data is essential to complying with almost every privacy and information security regulation, including HIPAA, Gramm-Leach-Bliley, FACTA, and state-level requirements. I recommend *IT Systems Management* as a valuable resource for both IT and privacy professionals.

Eric L. Nelson, CIPP
President and Senior Associate
Secure Privacy Solutions

I have used the first edition of this book for several semesters to teach an Information Systems Management course to senior MIS majors. I believe instructors will find the topics covered in this new edition to be practical, relevant, and insightful. Students will find the book informative in the classroom, and an excellent reference after they enter the workforce.

Prof. Rex Karsten
Associate Professor of Management Information Systems
University of Northern Iowa

IT Systems Management gives the new IT manager a compass for professional performance and career growth. Each topic area is a building block that combines to show IT individuals how to manage, lead, and build teams to deliver business results. Each chapter is clear, readable, and useful in dispensing advice from the author's experience. Significantly, the information in each chapter can be immediately used to systematically improve your workgroup in small, easy-to-implement doses. More importantly, the book advises you on how to refine your leadership and management skills.

Dennis M. Pinto II
Instructor Recruitment Manager
Global Knowledge

This new edition of IT Systems Management serves to introduce university students to key IT management concepts. These include updates on trends in IT such as regulatory, privacy legislation, and strategic security management. The real life examples and essay questions stimulate conversation among students, while the instructor material frees up time to provide added insight. The assessment worksheets and checklists are useful to IT practitioners conducting audits and evaluating processes. Instructors will appreciate how this book provides an excellent framework for a university level course, and experienced IT professionals will appreciate how it pulls together many various life experiences into one useful reference.

Dave Albers
Former Instructor of IT and Business Management, University of Calgary
Manager of IT Strategic Planning, Agnito Consulting

IT Systems Management

IT Systems Management

Second Edition

Rich Schiesser

PRENTICE
HALL

Upper Saddle River, NJ • Boston • Indianapolis
San Francisco • New York • Toronto • Montreal
London • Munich • Paris • Madrid • Cape Town
Sydney • Tokyo • Singapore • Mexico City

Library of Congress Cataloging-in-Publication data is on file.

ISBN-13: 978-0-137-02506-0
ISBN-10: 0-137-02506-8
Text printed in the United States on recycled paper at RR Donnelley, Crawfordsville, IN.

First printing February 2010

Cover - The Big Ben clock tower symbolizes Great Britain, where best practices for IT infrastructure processes were first formalized.

Editor-in-Chief
Mark Taub

Acquisitions Editor
Greg Doench

Development Editor
Songlin Qiu

Managing Editor
Patrick Kanouse

Project Editor
Mandie Frank

Copy Editor
Box Twelve
Communications, Inc.

Indexer
Tim Wright

Proofreader
Elizabeth Scott

Technical Reviewers
Dave Albers
Rex Karsten
Les Labuschagne

Publishing Coordinator
Michelle Housley

Book Designer
Chuti Prasertshith

Compositor
Bronkella Publishing LLC

*In Fondest Memory of
My Beloved Son Ben*

Contents

Chapter 19   Developing Robust Processes 375

Preface

Introduction to the Second Edition

Few industries have grown as rapidly or as widely as that of Information Technology (IT). What began as an infant offshoot of the accounting profession just a few generations ago has since matured into a prevalent and compelling force in nearly every segment of business, industry, and society in general. IT is the latest, and most significant, of cultural revolutions.

Futurist author Alvin Tofler, in his book on cultural phenomena, *The Third Wave*, describes three significant movements in American social development. These were the agricultural revolution of the late 1800s; the industrial revolution of the early 1900s; and the information revolution of the last two decades of the 20th century.

Some 40 years ago, Tofler correctly forecast many of today's social and technological trends. But even he could not predict the rapid rate of progress which the IT industry would sustain, nor its profound impact on living standards and business practices.

Much has been written about the various IT breakthroughs involving chip technology, compiler designs, hardware components, and programming languages. But little has been written about how to effectively manage the environment in which IT entities coexist and thrive. This environment is commonly called the IT infrastructure, and the process of managing the many attributes that contribute to a stable, responsive IT infrastructure is known as systems management.

This book offers an in-depth technical treatment of the various disciplines of systems management, from the prospective of people, process, and technology. The people discussion shows the importance of executive support, customer service, and other management aspects of delivering and supporting IT services. The process discussion of each discipline shows how to implement and manage each one effectively, regardless of the size and types of platforms or the complexity of environments. For the first time, systems management is shown as it applies to mainframe data centers, mid-range shops, client/server environments, and web-enabled systems alike.

The 12 disciplines of systems management are presented in the approximate order in which they became prevalent and integral to an infrastructure's operation. Obviously this prioritization varies slightly from enterprise to enterprise, depending on the emphasis of applications running at a particular center. The technology discussion describes several key developments that enable these disciplines to be implemented more productively. As a final discussion, three appendices offer an historical perspective of the various disciplines of systems management and an in-depth technical treatment of each of them. The historical background explains the *when* and *why* of each discipline to better explain its purpose and evolution.

Why the Second Edition was Written

When the first edition of *IT Systems Management* came out a few years ago, I could not predict what type of reception it would receive. Fortunately, thousands of readers found the book to be a practical and helpful guide for managing IT infrastructure processes. As a result, it has landed on several best-selling lists and has been translated into four languages.

During the past few years it has been in publication, a number of suggestions have been offered by readers for a possible second edition. Chief among these suggestions was to make it more university-friendly in the form of classroom materials for instructors and end-of-chapter materials for students.

This formed the primary motivation for writing a second edition. There were a number of other reasons that led to the decision to produce another version, including:

1. Enable the book to be both a useful reference for practicing IT professionals and a comprehensive textbook for university instructors and students.
2. Supply electronic classroom materials for university instructors to use in developing courses around this book.
3. Include additional material at the end of each chapter for readers to test their knowledge and understanding of the content, computational problems to make the material more interactive, and further sources of information on the chapter topic.
4. Provide additional real life examples in each chapter and highlight them in separate sections within each chapter.
5. Update information about technology and trends in most of the process areas, especially problem management, storage

management, network management, strategic security, disaster recovery, and facilities management.

6. Develop two new chapters, one covering ethics, legislation and outsourcing and a second showing the alignment of the systems management processes to the IT Infrastructure Library (ITIL).

7. Offer electronic copies of the non-weighted and the weighted assessment worksheets to readers.

How the Second Edition Differs from the First Edition

The second edition of this book differs in several ways from the first edition. First, two new chapters have been added. The first chapter deals with three timely and related topics of ethics, legislation, and outsourcing. The privacy of personal information, identity theft, falsifying financial records, and high-level corporate scandals surrounding unethical accounting procedures and over-inflated stock valuations all led to a variety of new legislation in the United States that related directly to IT. This chapter describes the ethics and legislation that resulted from these activities. It also presents the factors that lead many companies to outsource portions of their IT organization as well as the advantages and disadvantages of doing so. This chapter is inserted as the new Chapter 5, "Ethics, Legislation and Outsourcing," at the end of Part One: People.

The second new chapter describes the IT Infrastructure Library (ITIL) and how the various processes it comprises align themselves with the 12 processes covered in this edition. Many of the ITIL methodologies are similar to, but not identical to, the processes explained in Part Two of this book; any significant differences are explained in this chapter. You will find this supplement as Chapter 6, "Comparison to ITIL Processes," and it is a fitting introduction to Part Two: Processes.

IT is a rapidly changing industry and there have been a number of advances in technologies and methodologies in the six years since the first edition came out. As a result, I have updated several of the original chapters from the first edition. The first three chapters in the first edition served as an historical reference for IT infrastructures. Although many readers found these chapters interesting, they did not directly relate to infrastructures of today. As a result, these first three chapters have been dropped from the printed book but are available online at www.informit.com/title/0137025068. The topic of staffing in Chapter 3, "Staffing for Systems Management," now includes a discussion of career-pathing and suggestions on how to prepare for advancements in the field of IT.

The chapters in Part Two that have been revised include:

- Chapter 12, "Storage Management," which includes updates on more advanced methods for storage area networks (SANs).
- Chapter 13, Network Management," discusses the role of voice over the Internet protocols (VoIP).
- Chapter 16, "Strategic Security," presents the topical issues of identity theft, authentication, verification, token smart cards, single sign-on, and blogging.
- Chapter 17, "Business Continuity," includes updates to the more proactive and inclusive concept of business continuity.
- Chapter 18, "Facilities Management," now includes more contemporary issues of equipment density, data-center hot spots, maximization of floor space, and the outsourcing of environmental monitoring.

Two other chapters in Part Two have been modified extensively. Chapter 9, "Production Acceptance," now contains a major case study in which I compare how seven clients of mine dealt with their own versions of production acceptance. I also significantly expanded Chapter 11, "Problem Management," now includes its closely related process of incident management and the critical function of the service desk. This area was not included in the first edition because, strictly speaking, it is not truly an infrastructure process but rather an organizational function. But the function of the service desk in any of its various forms (such as the help desk, the trouble desk, and the Customer Service Center) has become such a vital component of problem management that it warrants being included here.

One of the most popular features of the first edition, among IT practitioners and university students alike, are the numerous real-life experiences I include in several of the chapters. In this second edition, I expand the number of these experiences throughout the book and highlight them in separate sections. Each chapter also contains terms and definitions as they occur in the text, also highlighted in separate sections.

This edition also features a number of enhancements at the end of each chapter. These include a few true and false questions to enable students and other readers to test their knowledge and understanding of the material. There are also one or two essay-type questions to provoke deeper thought and discussion about a specific aspect of the chapter topic. Finally, there are sources of further readings to provide additional perspectives and more detailed information about topic at hand.

One of the most frequent requests surrounding the first edition concerned the assessment worksheets used to evaluate the quality of infrastructure processes.

Many readers were disappointed that these useful charts were not available in electronic form. This edition affords readers the opportunity to download electronic copies of all 24 non-weighted or weighted assessment worksheets. Go to www.informit.com/title/0137025068 to download the worksheets.

Another request for electronic material often was made by professors who developed courses around the first edition. Many instructors asked for PowerPoint slides of each chapter to use in classroom presentations and for electronic versions of quizzes and essay-type questions with answers provided. This edition provides these types of materials for credentialed instructors. A test bank containing more than 400 questions and answers is also available for credentialed instructors. The questions are in the forms of true or false, multiple choice, fill in the blank, and essay-type. The requesting procedure is similar to that used to request the assessment worksheets. Lastly, this edition corrects a small number of minor typographical and formatting errors present in the first edition.

Intended Audience

This book is intended for IT professionals who are involved in designing, implementing, and managing parts or all of the infrastructure of an IT environment. It is also intended for teachers, instructors and university professors who are involved with the development of courses or the conducting of classes that focus on the topic of IT infrastructure management. An infrastructure usually consists of departments involving data and voice networks and communications, technical services, database administration, computer operations, and help desks. While the structure and composition of infrastructure groups may vary, the previously mentioned departments represent a typical organization in a medium-sized to large IT department.

Most of the concepts presented here are based on experiences with infrastructure groups varying in size from 50 to 150 individuals, but the underlying principles described here apply equally well to all sized groups. Smaller shops may have less need for implementing all of the disciplines of systems management and should focus only on those which most apply to their particular environment.

The format and content of this book are based on a fundamental belief that people, process, and technology are the three key ingredients in any successful implementation of systems management. A section of this book is dedicated to each of these three key ingredients, with primary and secondary audiences intended for each segment.

Infrastructure managers, directors, and CIOs are the intended audiences for the **People** part of this book. For purposes of brevity and simplicity, this group is referred to as *managers*.

The **Process** part of this book is especially intended for senior analysts, leads, senior systems administrators, and supervisors who are typically involved with designing and implementing systems management processes and procedures. This group is called *leads*.

The **Technology** part of this book is primarily intended for technical professionals such as systems programmers, database administrators, operations analysts, and systems administrators who are responsible for installing and maintaining systems management products. Once again, for purposes of brevity and simplicity, this group is called *technicians*.

Secondary groups of audiences will benefit from the parts of the book that are outside their primary areas of interest. For example, people issues will be of interest to technicians for topics such as communication and will be of importance to leads for the emphasis on teamwork.

The efficiency and cost savings of process improvements will be of interest to managers, while the eliminating of duplicate work should be of interest to technicians. Each chapter of the technology section contains an introduction and a summary to facilitate time-saving skimming for managers. Leads will find these chapters cross-referenced to corresponding chapters in the process section.

Topics Not Included In This Book

The term *systems management* as used in this book refers to the 12 specific processes of IT infrastructures that I have found to be the most prevalent and significant in relation to managing a world-class IT organization. As with virtually any business organization within American industry, few infrastructures are organized exactly the same. Some companies may include in their own infrastructures more or less of the 12 functions that I describe within these chapters. So it is worth noting those related areas of the infrastructure that I chose not to include in this book.

Asset management is not included here. Asset management is primarily a financial and administrative function; it isn't normally an integral part of an IT infrastructure. While it is closely related to infrastructure management, particularly in the area of desktop hardware and software, most IT organizations view it as a procurement responsibility. Some companies have their corporate procurement departments, which are outside of the IT organization, managing their IT assets. Others have a separate procurement department inside of IT, but outside of the infrastructure, to manage IT assets.

Similarly, the infrastructure functions of systems administration, network administration, and database administration are not covered here since any meaningful discussion of these important topics would require technical details that would go beyond our intended focus. Elements of systems administration are touched on in Chapter 7, "Availability," and in Chapter 8, "Performance and Tuning." Some fundamentals of network administration are covered in Chapter 13, "Network Management," and some of the basics of database administration are mentioned in Chapter 12, "Storage Management."

Desktop support is usually an infrastructure activity but it is not discussed here due to the day-to-day details of hardware and software maintenance that go beyond the emphasis of process design and management. Another more timely reason for excluding this area is that many companies are now outsourcing their desktop-support functions.

Three areas of traditional computer operations are not included because of their reduced emphasis due to automation, distributed processing, and the use of the Internet. These include batch scheduling, console operations, and output processing. Finally, I do not cover voice networks in this book in detail due to this function's highly technical nature. I do include a brief discussion of voice over Internet protocols (VoIP) in Chapter 13.

How Instructors and Students Can Use This Book

This book can be used for an upper-level undergraduate course for technology, science, or business majors or as a first-level graduate course for business majors and management majors. Courses are structured in a variety of formats, such as 12-week quarters, 15-week semesters, or six-week summer school sessions. As a general guideline, a 12-week quarter that meets three times a week (36 hours total) could develop the following course based on this book. The nine chapters that comprise Part One and Part Three could be allotted one hour each. The 13 chapters of Part Two could be allotted 1.5 hours each due to the more complex nature of the process material. This totals 28.5 hours (9 + 19.5) with 7.5 hours left for quizzes, tests, a mid-term exam, and a final exam. For courses comprising slightly more or less hours, slight adjustments to the times allotted for Part One and Part Three could be made. Homework can be assigned from the material at the end of each chapter, and quizzes, tests, and examinations can be developed from a test bank of questions provided for instructors.

How IT Practitioners Can Use This Book

IT practitioners can benefit from all three parts of this book. It is intended to be informative reading for any IT professional desiring a basic understanding of systems management.

The three major parts address the issues of people, process, and technology. Part One discusses various people issues such as executive support, staffing, retention, organization, budgets, communication, customer service, supplier partnerships, and service level agreements (SLAs). All IT professionals should read these chapters. While the emphasis is on traditional management topics, leads, technicians, and even desktop users should benefit from this enterprise-wide view of systems management. Students of business should find this section especially relevant to their field of study.

Part Two focuses on the process issues of systems management. This part consists of 13 chapters, an initial one that discusses the IT infrastructure library (ITIL) processes, and one for each of the 12 separate disciplines covered in this book. Each of these 12 chapters defines what the discipline is, which technologies within the infrastructure are involved, and what types of technical tools are commonly used to manage it.

Technicians and leads should thoroughly read all of these chapters with particular attention to the disciplines for which they are directly responsible. Managers should read the introduction and summary of each chapter to gain a basic understanding of systems management and then select those chapters which most apply to their enterprises to read more fully. Technology students should gain valuable insights from Part Three into the complex management of a modern computer center.

Part Three describes how to use technology to develop and integrate robust, bulletproof processes to support any of the disciplines of systems management. Understanding how these processes integrate with each other is critical to the success of any systems management implementation. One of today's greatest challenges is to apply the tried and true processes of traditional systems management to an open systems environment and to web-enabled applications. These topics should be of particular interest to those involved with client/server systems and Internet applications, as well as to students who may be pursuing a career in these fields.

Some of the techniques presented here are based on proven Baldrige National Quality Award (BNQA) methodologies. I became very involved with these methods and their practical applications while serving as an internal Baldrige examiner at a major aerospace company. While the emphasis on the BNQA has diminished a bit in recent years, the effectiveness of its process-improvement techniques is without question.

Leads for any of the disciplines of systems management should read all of the chapters of Part Three. This information provides them with a sound basis for applying technology tools to process improvements and communicating these improvements in detail to technicians and in summary form to managers. Technicians who are assigned responsibilities for either tactical or strategic disciplines should read those chapters applicable to their involvement. Managers should skim all these chapters to gain a good understanding of the important role of processes in managing a world-class infrastructure organization.

Because some chapters are intended to be skimmed by some readers to determine their applicability, I have prefaced each chapter with a short introduction. There is also a brief summary at the end of each chapter to capture its essential highlights.

The terms *process, function,* and *discipline* are all used synonymously throughout this book, as in a systems management function of availability being compared to the systems management discipline of security. Similarly, the terms *infrastructure* and *systems management* are used interchangeably when referring to the above three terms, as in the infrastructure process of availability being compared to the systems management process of security.

Acknowledgments

One of the reasons for offering a second edition of this book is to accommodate the many requests I received from university professors to make the first edition more academia-friendly. While this was not the only factor—others are cited in the Introduction—in deciding to put forth the effort of a second version, it was a primary one.

In light of this, I would like to thank several of the professors whose suggestions and encouragement helped to bring this second edition into existence.

First, there is Professor Les Labuschagne, who heads up the School of Computing at the University of South Africa in Pretoria, South Africa. This is the largest distance-education university in all of Africa. Prof. Labuschagne was among the earliest to use the first edition in a classroom setting. He developed courses around each edition of the book and offered several helpful recommendations for the second edition. Prof. Labuschagne also invited me to Johannesburg as the keynote speaker at the international conference on Information Security of South Africa (ISSA). This afforded me the opportunity to solicit input from a host of highly regarded international experts on IT infrastructures.

Second, there is Professor Robert Chow, who is currently an adjunct professor at Golden Gate University and the University of San Francisco in San Francisco, California. He is also a faculty member teaching online courses at the University of Phoenix. Professor Chow used both the first edition and a draft of the second edition to structure an effective classroom experience for his students at Golden Gate University. He uses his many years of experience working in the IT and communications industries to supplement his lectures with practical examples and he offered several valuable suggestions for the second edition.

Next, there is Dr. Carl Marnewick, who heads up the Department of Business Information Technology for the University of Johannesburg in South Africa. He offered helpful opinions about the second edition, particularly how questions and answers could be presented.

Others include Professor Karl Schwarzenegger, who heads up the Computing Department of the State University of New York (SUNY) at Cobleskill. He met with me to discuss how he would be using the book in a computer curriculum course he was developing. Professor David Reavis, of Texas A&M University at Texarkana, also developed a course around the first edition of this book and conferred with me about its use. The University of Calgary offered a course using the initial version of this book under the sponsorship of Professor Dave Albers, who provided useful feedback about it.

Professor Gary Richardson of the University of Houston requested use of several excerpts from the first edition for papers he was working on and, in the process, he offered several helpful comments. And at the University of Northern Iowa, Professor Rex Karsten developed an undergraduate course around the first edition. He also provided critiques of some of the classroom material I was developing at the time. To all of these professors I extend my heartfelt thanks for their interest in this second edition and their support of my efforts.

In addition to the eight universities previously named, there are at least two others that developed IT courses around the first edition of this book. These schools are the Swiss Management Center in Zurich, Switzerland, and the Open University of Hong Kong in Hong Kong, China. There are also several universities which keep copies of the first edition in their science and engineering libraries as recommended reading. These include Virginia Tech, the University of Texas at Austin, Southern Methodist University, North Carolina State University, and the Catholic University of Melbourne, Australia. To each of these schools I express my appreciation for their interest in the use of the first edition of this book.

I would also like to thank several key members of the team associated with Prentice Hall. Their diligent work made this second edition possible. Development editor Songlin Qiu and production copy editor Jeff Riley each offered dozens of helpful and insightful suggestions. Project manager Mandie Frank and editorial assistant Michelle Housley both used their organization skills to maximum benefit. And bringing all the efforts together was acquisitions editor Greg Doench.

After the first edition arrived, there were dozens of reviews posted on major bookseller websites such as Amazon.com, Barnes and Noble, and Safari. Although the majority of these reviews were positive, several offered constructive criticisms and valuable suggestions for improvement. Many of these suggestions, such as making the assessment worksheets available electronically, were applied to this version. I want to express my appreciation to all of the numerous online reviewers who provided practical and useful feedback. I also want to thank the thousands of IT professionals, managers, project leads, engineers, technicians, and those just entering the field of IT infrastructures whose support of the first edition helped to make it a best seller.

While some of the material in this second edition is new and much of it is changed, much of it is not, and for this reason I would again like to acknowledge all of those individuals who contributed to the success of the first edition. The easiest way I know of to do this is simply to repeat the recognitions I made in the first edition. The following are those initial acknowledgements.

This book covers a wide variety of technical topics and could not have been completed without the capable assistance of several talented colleagues and friends. First and foremost, I want to thank Harris Kern for his unwavering support, suggestions, and encouragement. I appreciate his patience and perseverance, which helped make this book a reality.

I am grateful to my colleague Joerg Hallbauer for his technical expertise and keen insight into a variety of topics. He was particularly helpful with the chapter on capacity planning. Next, I want to thank my long-time associate, Jim Adzema. His knowledge of process improvements and efficiencies were valuable offerings, especially in the area of problem management.

Fred Middleton is another long-time colleague who graciously extended his expertise and experience in operations management. He especially contributed to the topic of managing the physical environment. Another talented professional with whom I have worked is Ted Gresham who offered suggestions on the training of operations personnel.

Thanks to Natalie Tournat, who offered several contributions in the complicated arena of databases. I am also very grateful to my good friend Marcus Howery for reviewing several parts of this book and for upgrading the image of motorcycle riders everywhere.

A writer is only as good as the proofreaders and editors who can transform vague ideas into coherent sentences. No one I know does this better than my former mentor, Sarah Provost. I am indebted to her for her many suggestions to improve clarity and enhance the manuscript.

Many thanks go to Ruth Frick for her tireless effort and countless enhancements during the editing process. Her keen insight and quick responses to questions were very helpful during the final stages.

Last, but certainly not least, I must acknowledge the many contributions of the love of my life, my wife Ann. She offered support and understanding when I needed it the most. Her dedication and loyalty to my efforts served as a constant inspiration, for which I will always be grateful.

About the Author

In his service of numerous clients nationwide, infrastructure expert Rich Schiesser combines the experiences of a senior IT executive, professional educator, acclaimed author, and highly regarded consultant.

During the past three decades, Rich has headed up major computer centers at firms as diverse as Hughes Aircraft Company, the City of Los Angeles, and Twentieth Century Fox. For nearly 10 years he managed the primary computer center at Northrop Grumman Corporation, considered at the time to be one of the largest and most advanced in the world.

For the past several years, Rich has consulted on designing and implementing world-class infrastructures through his company, RWS Enterprises, Inc. Among his numerous clients are The Weather Channel, Emory Air Freight, Amazon.com, DIRECTV, Las Vegas Police, Option One Mortgage, Lionsgate Entertainment, and St. Joseph Health Systems.

Rich has also consulted at a variety of colleges, including Corinthian Colleges, Victor Valley College, Pasadena City College, University of Montana, and Kern County College District. He has taught a variety of IT classes at California State University, Los Angeles (CSULA), the University of California at Los Angeles (UCLA), and Phoenix University.

In addition to writing the first edition of *IT Systems Management*, Rich coauthored the best-selling book *IT Production Services*. He has also written more than 200 articles on IT management for leading trade journals and websites, including InformIT.com.

Rich holds a Bachelor of Science degree from Purdue University, a Master of Science degree from the University of Southern California (USC), and has completed graduate work in business administration from UCLA. He and his wife, Ann, live in Southern California, where they contribute time to their two favorite charities, the Olive Crest home for abandoned and abused children and the Legacy One organization for organ transplants.

CHAPTER 1

Acquiring Executive Support

Introduction

Regardless of how well we design and implement systems management processes, they will likely fail without the approval and support of senior management. At some point in time, almost all requests for systems management hardware, software, or staffing need approval by IT executives or their superiors. That, in essence, is where the budget buck usually stops. This chapter discusses ways to acquire executive support and approvals, as well as how to ensure their ongoing endorsement.

Before we attempt to gain executive support for systems management processes, we need to be clear on exactly what the expression means. The words *systems management* may have different meanings for different people. So we begin with a proposed definition for this term.

Among the other topics covered in this chapter will be techniques to build surefire business cases to demonstrate the true value of systems management. Also included will be methods to educate executives on technical issues without alienating them; in addition, you will learn how to develop and use one of the most powerful weapons available in the ongoing battle for budget dollars.

Systems Management: A Proposed Definition

The term *systems management* may have different meanings for different people. In order to establish a consistent meaning throughout this book, I propose the following definition.

Systems Management

Systems Management is the activity of identifying and integrating various products and processes in order to provide a stable and responsive IT environment.

What does this mean? First, as the name implies, this entity is a management activity. It does not mean we will be creating new hardware and software products in and of themselves. It does not mean we will be separately installing some products or services at the exclusion of others. It *does* mean we will be looking at a group of products and processes which interact with each other to bring stability and responsiveness to an IT environment.

For example, an enterprise may choose to enact a thorough business resumption plan by contracting with one of the major disaster recovery service providers. For the plan to be executed successfully, however, there must be an extensive and flawless data backup and restore process in place. In other words, the overall goal of business resumption depends on both the disaster recovery component and the backup/restore component.

Each of these components, or disciplines, will be addressed at length in separate chapters. The point here is that no one discipline is as effective individually as it is when integrated with complementary disciplines. This is one of the key cornerstones of effective systems management: the integration of separate but related products and processes.

The overall objective of systems management is to bring stability and responsiveness to an IT infrastructure. Stability means that systems are always up and accessible as scheduled. This can present enormous challenges when systems need to be up 24 hours a day, 7 days a week. These challenges will be discussed in detail in the chapter on availability.

Stability is normally measured as a percentage of available uptime for both online and batch applications. Other related gauges include the amount of actual downtime, measured in minutes per day or hours per month; the elapsed time between outages, commonly referred to as the mean time between failures (MTBF); and the average time spent in recovering from an outage, usually called the mean time to recover (MTTR).

Responsiveness refers to how quickly batch jobs or, more commonly, online transactions can be processed and completed. For the batch environment, throughput is measured as the number of jobs processed per hour; turnaround is the average time required to complete a job. For the online environment, response time is measured as the number of completed transactions per second, or the average time in seconds to complete a single transaction. These concepts are all covered extensively in the chapter on performance and tuning.

Why Executive Support Is Especially Critical Today

There are two reasons why executive support is more important today than it has ever been. The first is that more critical functions of systems management are necessary to run contemporary data centers effectively, requiring more key resources and more management support to acquire them. During the initial growth of the use of computers several decades ago, systems management was not as significant a factor in the success of a data center as it is today. In the early 1970s, availability and online response times were key measures of an effective data center. Functions such as storage management, capacity planning, change management, problem management, and disaster recovery were not major factors in the equation for effective computer centers. Fewer functions meant fewer resources were required and less management support was needed to acquire them.

Second, the infrastructure support groups of computer centers from two or three decades ago focused primarily on technical issues. Internal support groups were relatively isolated from outside influences such as executive management, end-users, and to some extent even application software developers. What little contact many internal support personnel had outside of IT was with hardware service engineers or software marketing representatives. Today these internal support groups are frequently bombarded with requests from a user community that is far more technically educated and computer-literate. This includes executives who are much more likely to be technically astute than their counterparts from several years back.

The modern IT executive's technical knowledge can be a double-edged sword. Many executives have just enough technical knowledge to be budgetarily dangerous, but not enough technical experience to fully appreciate the requirements and importance of a well-implemented infrastructure. That is why executive support for systems management is so critical today.

Building a Business Case for Systems Management

By the time most IT supervisors reach senior executive positions, they are more oriented toward the goals of the business than they are toward the intricacies of technology. Their peers are typically chief operating officers (COOs), chief financial officers (CFOs), and the heads of various departments such as engineering, manufacturing, operations, distribution, and marketing. Consequently, the focus of most chief information officers (CIOs) is on the application of cost-effective technology, rather than on the technology itself.

Many CIOs insist that well-developed business cases be presented to ensure the cost-effectiveness of IT systems. In its simplest form, a business case is a clear and succinct cost justification for the funds to be expended for new systems or for upgraded support of existing systems. An effective and thorough business case will itemize all of the associated costs of a new system or process and compare it to the expected benefits. One of the major hurdles with this approach is that it is often very difficult to predict accurately the true benefits of a new system or process. Even when the estimated benefits are reasonably accurate, they are seldom described in terms of cost savings. This is because in many instances the paybacks are more qualitative then quantitative.

Business Case

A business case is a clear and succinct cost justification for the funds to be expended for new systems or for upgraded support of existing systems. A business case will itemize all of the associated costs of a new system or process (including hardware, software and labor) and compare it to the expected benefits.

Dollar costs and dollar savings are the common denominators used by business professionals in making technology decisions. Yet they are the measures least offered by IT professionals in presenting the benefits of a process improvement. This is especially true when estimating the benefits of a particular systems management function. For example, it may be relatively easy to show how an effective availability process reduces downtime by, say, 10 hours per month, but it is much more difficult to quantify the downtime into actual dollars lost. This difficulty stems from the variety of hidden impacts that an outage may have—lost productivity in terms of labor time; rework due to errors or lack of restarts; time lost due to users not knowing exactly when the system comes back up; and lowered morale due to interrupted services.

One way to be effective with business cases is to develop them for the appropriate systems management function. Understanding which functions are the most beneficial to a company at any point in time is critical to acquiring the necessary management support. One aspect sometimes overlooked is that an organization's dependency on a specific systems management discipline may change to reflect a company's changed goals. The maturity cycle of a typical Internet, or dotcom, company will serve to illustrate this point.

During the start-up phase of many dotcom companies, the infrastructure function most frequently emphasized is availability. As the number of visitors to a dotcom's website increases, performance and tuning gain in importance. When the growth of the website starts to accelerate, capacity planning will likely take precedence. Then the maturing of both the company and its infrastructure usually requires more formalized processes for storage management, security, and disaster recovery.

It pays to know exactly which systems management disciplines are most significant to your company at any particular point in time and to be aware that these functions will likely change over time. It is also important to understand which IT business goals are most critical to meeting the business goals of the company. Then you can determine which infrastructure functions are most critical to meeting those IT business goals.

The next step in building an effective business case for selected disciplines of systems management is to meet and confer with senior IT executives to confirm that the infrastructure functions thought to be critical are in fact the correct ones. This meeting should also include prioritizing these functions in the event that multiple functions end up competing for scarce budget dollars.

The most challenging step comes next, in terms of estimating all associated costs of implementing a particular function and doing so with reasonable accuracy. The obvious costs for items such as software licenses and the labor for implementation and operation are easy to identify and quantify. But some costs are occasionally overlooked when implementing a systems management function, and these expenses are summarized as follows:

1. Recruiting
2. Training
3. Office space
4. Software enhancements
5. Software maintenance
6. Hardware upgrades
7. Hardware maintenance
8. Scheduled outages

By the same token, all associated benefits need to be thoroughly itemized and converted to dollar savings. Like some of the less obvious costs of a function, there are several benefits of implementing a systems management function that are occasionally overlooked:

1. Being able to predict capacity shortages before they occur
2. Avoiding lost labor time of users by reducing both the frequency and duration of outages
3. Increasing productivity by improving response times
4. Ensuring business continuity during disaster recovery
5. Avoiding the cost of rebuilding databases and reissuing transactions

A final step—one that is seldom pursued, but is capable of adding invaluable credibility to your business case—is to solicit testimonials from customers in other companies about a particular systems management software product. Customers should be selected who are using the product in an environment as similar as possible to your own. It is surprising that this simple technique is not used more frequently—it usually requires little effort, and yet it can strengthen a justification immensely by demonstrating real-life benefits of a product in an actual business setting.

The following list summarizes the basic steps used to develop an effective business case for any number of systems management functions:

1. Understand which IT business goals are most critical to a company's business goals.
2. Determine which systems management functions are most critical to meeting the IT business goals that are aligned to those of the company.
3. Meet and confer with IT senior management to confirm and prioritize the systems management functions to be acquired.
4. Accurately estimate all costs associated with the implementation and maintenance of a particular function.
5. Itemize all benefits associated with the function.
6. Convert benefits to dollar savings to the extent possible.
7. Solicit customer references for the product being proposed.

Educating Executives on the Value of Systems Management

The best way to talk to executives is in a language with which they are comfortable and familiar. For most senior managers this means presenting information and proposals in commonly used business terms, not technical jargon. IT personnel in infrastructure organizations sometimes become so enthused about the technical merits of a product that they fail to showcase its business benefits effectively. Yet these business benefits are often the very factors that will decide whether a package is approved. Executives need to be educated about the value of systems management in general and about the benefits of individual functions and products in particular.

No matter how compelling your reasons may be for additional IT expenditures, they may fall short of a convincing argument if not expressed in the language of senior management. Your job is to determine exactly what that language is. Some decision makers may speak purely in bottom-line terms, such as the ultimate total cost of ownership. Others may be more financially oriented and focus on items such as depreciation, tax implications, or lease-versus-buy comparisons. Some may prefer descriptive narratives while others choose graphs, charts, and pictures. Regardless of their preference, the closer you can align your proposal to their comfort zone, the more likely you will be to acquire their approval.

Real Life Experience—A Business Picture Worth 1,000 Words

I experienced firsthand the value of effective executive education while heading up the infrastructure department at a major motion picture studio. Similar to many large, established companies, this shop had relied for years on mainframe computers for the processing of their critical corporate business systems. By the mid-1990s it was apparent that this company's long-established legacy systems were approaching the end of their useful life. A major migration project plan was initiated to replace the outdated mainframe applications with more modern client-server applications. The functionality and scalability of these new systems would better meet the current and future needs of the corporation.

The first of several business applications was successfully implemented a short time after initiating the project plan. The payroll and human resources departments were due to be installed next, but we first needed to add more server capacity. We discussed this necessary increase in capacity with the executive managers who would decide on whether to approve of the additional dollars. We explained how the expansion of the database to provide the extra required fields would result in more channel traffic on the system. We showed how the expected increase in concurrent users would push processor utilizations close to full capacity during peak periods. Other technical information involving security and automated backup software also helped to build a solid justification for more servers. Or so we thought.

While the foregoing arguments were strong and legitimate, a slightly different approach is what finally prompted the senior managers to approve our request. We had instituted a formal capacity planning process several months earlier (described in detail in Chapter 15, "Capacity Planning"). A cornerstone of the process involved discussions with non-IT users and their managers about future workload projections. When we presented our information to senior management, we included the data that we had collected from these user departments.

The executives immediately identified with the terms and projections that the user department managers had given us. Graphs indicating current and future workloads were readily interpreted by our senior-level audience, as were the correlations between increased headcounts and larger numbers of concurrent users. While our technical facts presented a solid case for capacity increases, the business picture we painted with the help of our user departments was even more persuasive.

Three Universal Principles Involving Executive Support

During my many years working among IT executives, I have observed three universal principles involving executive support:

1. Managers love alternatives.
2. Managers hate surprises.
3. Managers thrive on metrics.

Since one of the primary responsibilities of managers is to make decisions, they appreciate when you simplify the decision-making process for them by presenting viable alternatives. For infrastructure decisions, these could involve choices among products, vendors, platforms, or levels of support.

Most managers do not like to be blindsided by business surprises, such as hidden costs, unpredicted delays, or unscheduled outages. The third principle deals with the use of meaningful business metrics. This topic is of such importance that we'll take some time to explore it here.

Developing a Powerful Weapon for Executive Support—Business Metrics

A prudent use of meaningful business metrics is a budgetary weapon that offers powerful persuasive capabilities when proposing systems management implementations. To understand more clearly what this weapon is and how to use it to its optimal benefit, it is first worth looking at how many of today's IT executives ended up in their current positions.

Most of today's IT executives have risen to positions of senior management from one of four primary career paths (see Table 1-1). The oldest and most traditional path originates from financial departments. In this scenario, senior accountants, controllers, or CFOs ended up running the IT organization of a company since, early on, IT was considered essentially an accounting function of a firm.

Table 1-1   Origins of CIO Career Paths

Timeframe	CIO Origin	Examples
Prior to 1980s	Finance	Senior accountants, financial controllers, CFOs
1980s and early 1990s	IT	IT managers, directors, vice presidents
Mid-1990s	Customer service	Customer service directors and vice presidents
Late 1990s	IT consulting	Senior consultants and partners of the then-Big 5 consulting firms

A second path became more prevalent in the 1980s and early 1990s, as IT managers became better trained as business leaders to head up IT organizations. In this case, talented IT professionals who had shifted over to a supervisory career path succeeded in transforming their technical expertise into business savvy.

The third alternative started almost as an experiment in the early 1990s. A key external customer with sound business practices and excellent customer service techniques was selected as head of IT despite limited exposure to the technology. This movement was motivated by IT departments finally realizing that they were first and foremost service organizations. Consequently, to survive the growing trends toward outsourcing, downsizing, mergers, and acquisitions, IT organizations needed to make customer service their top priority. What better way to demonstrate this than to assign a qualified customer representative as the head of IT? Some of the risk of this approach was eased by the fact that many user departments had become very computer literate in recent years, particularly as it related to client-server, desktop, and Internet applications.

Toward the end of the 1990s, CIOs also emerged from the IT consulting industry. Though much more limited in numbers than the other types of IT executives, these IT leaders nonetheless made their influence felt, particularly in smaller companies. Three factors contributed to the increased occurrence of consultants becoming CIOs:

- **Expanded use of consultants.** There was an overall increase of the use of consultants due the expanding growth, complexity, and integration of IT systems worldwide. This gave many senior consultants key access and valuable exposure to IT shops. Thus they could see how the shops should and should not be managed, allowing them to become candidates for the top job.

- **The Y2K problem.** The unprecedented rush to upgrade or replace Y2K-noncompliant systems gave those consultants who came into companies to do this work access and exposure to most aspects of IT environments, enabling some of them to contend as CIO candidates.

- **The rapid rise of dotcom companies.** Many of these start-ups hired consultants out of necessity to develop their fledgling IT departments; some stayed on as permanent CIOs.

Regardless of the diversity of their career origins, most CIOs share some important common characteristics in their decision-making process. One of these is to rely on a small number of key ingredients as the basis for critical technical decisions. One of the most common and effective of these ingredients is the use of meaningful business metrics. By this I mean metrics that clearly demonstrate the business value of a decision.

Real Life Experience—Speaking a Language Executives Understand

During my time in the aerospace industry, I was managing one of the largest data centers in the country for a major defense contractor. The data center supported a highly classified military program. This particular defense venture required huge amounts of processing power to drive, among other applications, advanced 2- and 3-dimensional (2-D and 3-D) graphic systems. As with many high-cost defense projects that involve cutting-edge technologies, cutbacks eventually began to reduce department budgets, including that of IT. But to keep the program on budget and within schedule, IT needed to invest more in high availability and response time resources for the online graphical computer systems.

Traditional availability metrics such as the percentage of uptime or hours per week of downtime were not presenting a very convincing argument to the budget approvers. Two of the most critical measures of productivity of the program were the number of engineering drawings released per day and the number of work orders completed per hour. The former was tied directly to the availability of the online engineering systems, and the latter was directly influenced by the uptime of the online business systems.

We knew that senior management relied heavily on these two metrics to report progress on the program to their military customers. Since our traditional IT availability metrics correlated so closely to these two critical business metrics, we decided to use versions of these business metrics to report on system uptime. Prior to this we would have shown how we improved availability from, say, 98.7 percent to 99.3 percent, and response time per transaction from 1.2 seconds to 0.9 seconds. Instead, we charted how our improvements increased the number of released drawings daily and completed work orders per hour. Furthermore, when the data showed daily drawing releases improving from 18 to 20, we extrapolated the increases, based on a 24-day work month, to a monthly total of 48 drawings and a yearly total of 576 drawings.

These improvements caught the attention of the executives and eventually led to approval of the requested IT expenditures. Not only were the quantities of improvement impressive and substantiated, but they were presented in the type of meaningful business metrics with which most managers could identify. Never underestimate the power of these kinds of metrics in securing executive support.

Ensuring Ongoing Executive Support

Today's IT executives work in a fast-paced world of ever-changing technology and ever-increasing demands from customers. They may be faced with dozens of decisions on a daily basis and an even larger number of tasks to juggle and prioritize. Strategies and events that do not require immediate attention are often put on the back burner in favor of those that do. Similarly, executive support for key systems management processes is quickly forgotten and needs to be continually reinforced.

One way to provide this reinforcement is to showcase the successes of your processes. In the case of availability, this could mean showing improvements in system uptime over the course of weeks and months. For tuning processes, it could involve showing increased productivity of users. Remember to speak in the language of your executives and to present information in charts, graphs, or tables. If you are not well versed in exhibiting data in high-level business formats, try scanning business publications such as *The Wall Street Journal* or *USA Today* for examples of simple but effective presentation of trends, forecasts, and performance.

Executives tend to be very goal-oriented and results-driven. Their time is valuable and limited. Use it to your best advantage in securing ongoing support for systems management disciplines. Do not assume that because approval was given for previous resources required by an infrastructure process, it will be granted automatically in the future. Just as an IT environment changes rapidly in terms of direction, scope, and focus, so also may the environment of the entire enterprise. The best strategy to ensure ongoing executive support for systems management is to stay informed about the strategies and trends of your enterprise and to keep your senior managers apprised of the synergistic strategies and trends of IT.

Summary

This chapter has discussed some techniques to use in capturing and maintaining executive support for the implementation of systems management disciplines. These included building and presenting business cases, educating executives on necessary technical issues without alienating them, and developing and using meaningful, business-oriented metrics—one of the most effective weapons in your arsenal for budget battles.

Test Your Understanding

1. In a business case, all associated costs of a new system are itemized and compared to other expected costs in the organization. (True or False)
2. IT professionals frequently offer dollar costs and dollar savings when presenting the benefits of a process improvement. (True or False)
3. A cost occasionally overlooked when implementing a systems management function is:
   a. software development
   b. desktop hardware
   c. software maintenance
   d. network connectivity
4. An important step in building a business case is to solicit testimonials from_____.
5. How can a modern IT executive's technical knowledge be a double-edged sword?

Suggested Further Readings

1. *Inside the Minds: Leading Executives on Managing Costs, Negotiating Pricing, and Reducing Overall Technology Spending: Ways to Reduce IT Spending,* Aspatore Books, 2004
2. *Does IT Matter? Information Technology and the Corrosion of Competitive Advantage,* Carr, Nicholas, 2004
3. www.gao.gov/special.pubs/ai94115.pdf (*Improving Mission Performance Through Strategic Information Management and Technology,* United States General Accounting Office)

CHAPTER 2

Organizing for Systems Management

Introduction

The second important people issue to address after acquiring executive support is organizing your IT infrastructure for optimal efficiency and effectiveness of systems management processes. This chapter presents several alternative scenarios for structuring the various groups that comprise an infrastructure. If an infrastructure is organized improperly, it can lead to stifling inaction between departments. We begin by discussing why IT departments need to evolve their organizational structures to succeed; then we examine three factors used in determining these structures. We go on to propose alternative organizational structures for several common scenarios within an IT infrastructure.

We next develop a table of desired attributes for the eventual owner of each of the 12 system management processes. The intent is to provide a technique that any infrastructure manager can use to identify those attributes most desirable for each process. This methodology also shows how some traits may compliment or conflict with others should a process owner assume responsibility for more than one process at a time. Identifying the optimal attributes for each process owner can then become a factor in organizing the overall infrastructure.

Factors to Consider in Designing IT Organizations

Few employees enjoy departmental restructuring, and IT professionals are no exception. Although IT professionals are involved in one of the most rapidly changing technical industries, they still tend to be creatures of habit that, like everyone else, prefer stable and unchanging environments. Newly assigned executives and managers are notorious for proposing a partial or total reorganization of their entire department as one of their first official acts.

But, in the case of IT, restructuring is often necessary to support company growth, increased customer demand, changing business requirements, acquisitions, mergers, buyouts, or other industry changes. The question then becomes: on which factors should we base the restructuring of IT organizations, particularly infrastructures? In my experience there are three key factors on which to base these decisions: departmental responsibilities, planning orientation, and infrastructure processes. These factors tend to follow the normal evolution of an IT organization from company start-up to full corporate maturity.

For example, most start-up companies initially structure their IT departments with a very basic organization such as that shown in Figure 2–1. As the company grows and IT begins expanding its services, an administrative department is added to the base structure as shown in Figure 2–2. The administrative department is responsible for billing, invoices, asset management, procurement, human resources, and other tactically oriented support activities. During a corporation's early building years, IT usually structures its organization by departmental responsibilities. As the departmental responsibilities in each of the three groups reporting to the CIO continue to grow, they will likely evolve into an organization similar to that shown in Figure 2-3. The applications department is split out between application development and application maintenance. The infrastructure department is organized between technical and network services and computer operations. The administration department has added planning to its charter of responsibilities. This is a key event—it marks the first formal initiation of a planning responsibility within IT, although much of its early emphasis is on tactical, short-term planning.

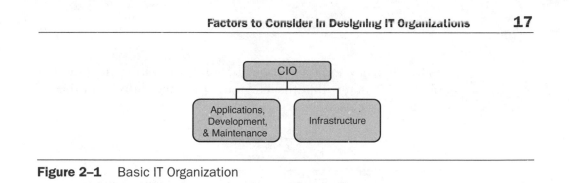

Figure 2–1   Basic IT Organization

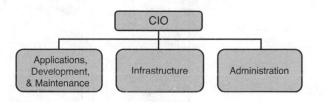

Figure 2–2   Basic IT Organization with Administration

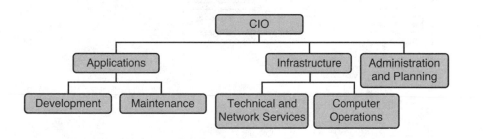

Figure 2–3   IT Organization with Dual Management Levels

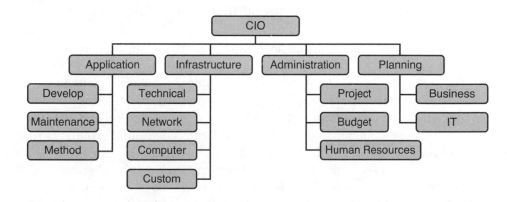

Figure 2–4   IT Organization with Three Management Levels

As the company and the IT organization both continue to grow, the planning orientation within the IT group gradually shifts from that of tactical to strategic planning.

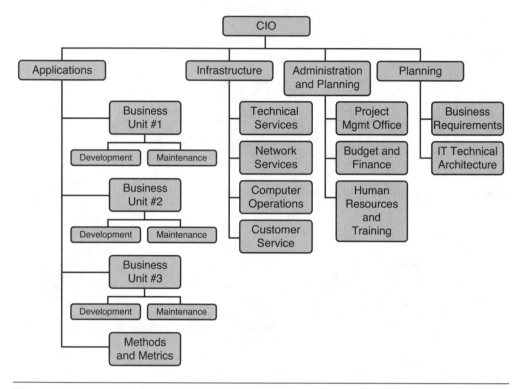

Figure 2–5   IT OrganizationThree Management Levels with Business Units

Eventually, all strategic planning activities can be centralized in a separate department. Over time this department will likely subdivide into two groups along the lines of business requirements planning and IT architecture planning. The ongoing growth of the company and its customers would cause the applications, infrastructure, and administration departments to similarly subdivide into dedicated groups. This further evolution of the IT organization is shown in Figure 2–4. A final modification to the IT organizational structure is the alignment of the applications areas along business units as shown in Figure 2–5. The intent of this increasingly popular refinement is to foster greater empathy between end-users and developers, as well as to increase their understanding of user requirements. At this stage of a company's maturity, the IT organizational structure is based on the two factors of departmental responsibilities as well as planning orientation. A third factor that influences IT departmental design is how the responsibility for infrastructure processes is integrated into the organizational structure. We will examine key elements of this design in the next several sections.

Factors to Consider in Designing IT Infrastructures

There are various ways to organize an infrastructure, but there is no single structure that applies optimally to all situations. This is due, in part, to factors such as size, maturity, and orientation of a firm and its IT organization. These factors vary widely from company to company and directly influence how best to design the IT infrastructure.

Where some enterprises may combine the voice and data network groups, others may keep them totally separate. Some firms incorporate IT-wide functions such as security, planning, quality assurance, procurement, and asset management directly into the infrastructure organization; others keep these functions outside of the infrastructure.

Locating Departments in the Infrastructure

Sometimes the organizational position of a department can play an important role in distinguishing a world-class infrastructure from a mediocre one. Four departments where this is particularly the case are the service desk, database administration, network operations, and systems management.

Alternative Locations for the Service Desk

The proper location of the service desk is critical to the success of almost any IT infrastructure. There are many reasons for this. Paramount among these is that the level 1 service desk is the first encounter most users have with an IT organization. Placing the service desk higher in the organization or merging it with other service desks can increase its effectiveness, visibility, and stature. The initial impression that customers form when they first dial the service desk number is often long lasting.

Service desk specialists refer to this critical interaction as *the moment of truth*: the point at which customers form their initial, and—in the case of poor encounters—often irreversible opinions about the quality of IT services. The number of rings before answering, the setup of the menu system, and especially the attitude of the service desk agent responding to the caller are all factors that influence a user's perception of the effectiveness of a service desk. The following lists in order of preference 10 things users want when they call a service desk.

1. Answer incoming calls within two rings.
2. Whenever possible, a service desk agent answers the call; users don't want an automated telephone menu to select from.
3. If you must use automated telephone menus, design them to be as simple to understand and use as possible.
4. Sequence most commonly used automated telephone menu items first.
5. Allow for the bypass of some or all automated telephone menu items.
6. Calculate and report to callers average hold times in real time.
7. Practice good telephone etiquette by being polite, patient, courteous, and helpful to callers.
8. When handing a call off to level 2 support, give the caller a reliable time estimate for follow-up and resolution.
9. Follow up with level 2 support to ensure the problem is being worked.
10. Follow up with callers to ensure problems are resolved to their satisfaction.

Another reason the location of the service desk is so important is that it defines to what degree multiple service desks may eventually integrate into fewer service desks or into one fully integrated service desk usually referred to as a Customer Service Center (CSC). During periods of initial growth, many IT organizations increase the number of service desks in response to expanding services and a growing user base. Several clients of mine would institute a new service desk number whenever they implemented a new, major application. Eventually, a large number of service desks—or service desk numbers—becomes unwieldy and unmanageable. Sooner or later, most shops realize that a consolidated service desk is the most efficient way to structure a customer service department. Many shops today fold their desktop support unit into the customer services department as a peer to the service desk. This configuration often facilitates handing off of desktop problems from the service desk directly to desktop support. The organization of this type of infrastructure is shown in Figure 2–6.

Real Life Experience—Where Service is its Middle Name

One of my prior clients had no less than seven service desks: applications, operations, desktop support, technical services, database administration, data network services, and voice network services. The client asked me to assess the feasibility of integrating some, if not all, of the multiple help desks into a much smaller quantity. After assembling a cross-functional team, I worked with team members to design and implement a single, totally integrated help desk, or customer service center (CSC). Much discussion centered on where to locate this new centralized service desk. Some thought it best to have it outside of the infrastructure, or to outsource it, but the majority saw there were more benefits in regard to control, staffing, and measurement by keeping it within the infrastructure.

Some of the team members suggested that it go under computer operations in the structure. The strongest argument for this alternative was that computer operations was the only other group at the time being staffed 24/7 and this was the direction we wanted to take the CSC. But most of the calls coming into the CSC were desktop oriented rather than computer operations oriented. In the end we elected to locate the CSC of the infrastructure as a peer to the desktop support department. A major advantage of this configuration was that it put the level 1 (CSC) and level 2 (desktop support) support groups both in the same organization. This facilitated handoffs between levels 1 and 2, drastically cut down on the finger pointing between these two groups, and held each of them to higher levels of accountability.

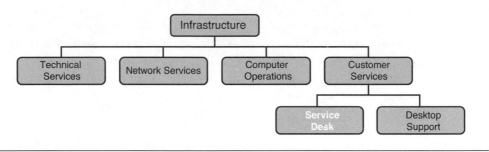

Figure 2–6   IT Organization Highlighting Service Desk

Alternative Locations for Database Administration

Many IT shops locate their database administration group in the applications development department. The argument here is that the structure and design of the database is more closely aligned to the requirements of the users with whom the applications group works directly. But once the database is designed, most of the ongoing maintenance involves performance and tuning issues; these issues are more closely aligned with the technical services group in the infrastructure.

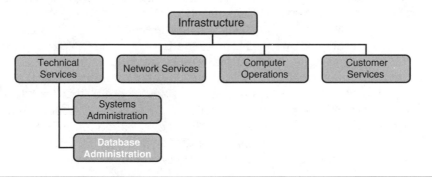

Figure 2–7   IT Organization Highlighting Database Administration

Some IT organizations have the database administration group reporting directly to the head of the infrastructure group, but I have seen this work successfully only when the database unit is unusually large and most all mission-critical applications are running on sophisticated databases. Another alternative I have seen work well with large database administration groups is to put the architecture portion of the group, which is primarily strategic and user oriented, in the applications development group, and to put the administration portion, which is primarily tactical and technically oriented, in the infrastructure's technical services group. See Figure 2–7 for an example of database administration location.

Alternative Locations for Network Operations

To many it would seem obvious that the network operations group belongs in the network services department. After all, both groups are involved with providing reliable, responsive, real-time network services. It makes perfect sense to initiate this type of network organization during the start-up of an IT department. But as the network operations group grows, and particularly as network and computer operations assume critical 24/7 responsibilities, a compelling case can be made to have network operations report to computer operations. Both groups have around-the-clock monitoring and troubleshooting responsibilities, both can benefit technically from cross-training each other, and both could give each other more backup support. I recommend that IT organizations with mature infrastructures locate their network operations group within computer operations (see Figure 2-8).

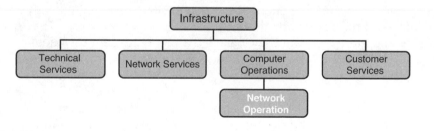

Figure 2–8   IT Organization Highlighting Network Operations

Alternative Locations for Systems Management

The existence and location of a systems management group is one of the key characteristics that make an infrastructure world class. Many shops do not include such a dedicated process group within their infrastructure, but those that do usually benefit from more effective management of their key processes. The systems management group is a separate department solely responsible for those infrastructure processes determined to be most critical to a particular IT environment. At a minimum, these processes include change management, problem management, configuration management, and production acceptance. Depending on the maturity and orientation of the infrastructure, additional systems management processes—such as capacity management, storage management, security, and disaster recovery—may be a part of this department.

Real Life Experience—Mirror, Mirror On the Wall

One of my responsibilities at a major defense contractor was to upgrade the quality of service on the IT help desk. Telephone etiquette by the call takers needed improvement, so I brought in a highly-regarded company that specialized in this type of training. The instructors were very helpful and within weeks we were all enjoying numerous accolades on the quality of our help desk personnel.

One of the methods these trainers used to invoke empathy with callers sounded a bit peculiar but ended up being extremely effective. Their technique involved presenting each call-taker with a facial mirror that they were to look at while answering the phone. On the bottom of the mirror was the inscription: What You See Is What They Hear. A few thought it sounded a bit lame, but in reality it totally changed the tone and demeanor of the call takers as they answered the phones. The expressions reflected back to them in the facial mirror completely mirrored the mood of their voice. They quickly realized the more pleasant they looked, the more pleasant they sounded.

This department usually reports to one of three infrastructure groups, depending on the processes receiving the most emphasis. When change management or production acceptance is the key process, this group often reports to computer operations. In a traditional mainframe environment, this department would have been called production support and could have included batch scheduling, batch processing, and output processing. When problem management is the key process, this group usually reports to the customer services or help desk department. In a world-class infrastructure, all of the key processes are managed out of a single systems management group that reports directly to the head of the infrastructure. This arrangement gives systems management the visibility and executive support needed to emphasize integrated process management. This optimal organization scheme is shown in Figure 2–9.

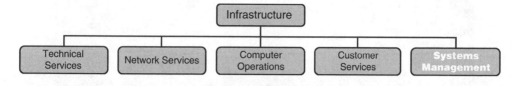

Figure 2–9   IT Organization Highlighting Systems Management

Recommended Attributes of Process Owners

One of the most critical success factors in implementing any of the 12 systems management processes is the person you select as the process owner. This individual is responsible for assembling and leading the cross-functional design team; for implementing the agreed-upon process; for communicating it to all appropriate parties; for developing and maintaining the process's documentation; for establishing and reporting on its metrics; and, depending on the specific process involved, for administering other support tasks such as chairing change review boards or compiling user-workload forecasts.

Knowing which owner attributes are most important for a given process can help in selecting the right individual for this important role. Table 2-1 lists 19 attributes that the owners of each of the 12 processes should have—in varying degrees—to manage their discipline effectively. Reading the table across identifies disciplines for which a given attributes applies and to what degree. This can help in assigning potential process owners to those disciplines for which they have the greatest number of matching attributes. Reading the table down identifies which attributes apply most for a given discipline. This can help identify potential process owners by matching a discipline to candidates who demonstrate the greatest number of attributes most needed.

Table 2-1   Recommended Attributes of Process Owners

Attribute	AV	PT	PA	CM	PM	SM	NM	CF	CP	SE	BC	FM
1. Knowledge of applications	Low	Med	High	Low	Low	High	Low	Med	Med	High	Med	N/A
2. Ability to rate documentation	N/A	N/A	High	Med	N/A	N/A	Med	High	N/A	N/A	High	Med
3. Knowledge of company's business model	N/A	N/A	Med	Low	N/A	N/A	Low	N/A	N/A	Med	High	Low
4. Ability to work effectively with IT developers	Low	Med	High	Med	Low	Med	High	Low	High	Med	Low	Low
5. Ability to meet effectively with customers	N/A	Low	Med	N/A	Med	N/A	High	N/A	Med	Low	Med	N/A
6. Ability to talk effectively with IT executives	Low	N/A	Med	Low	N/A	N/A	N/A	N/A	Med	Med	High	Med
7. Ability to inspire teamwork and cooperation	N/A	Low	Med	High	High	N/A	N/A	Low	Med	N/A	N/A	Med
8. Ability to manage diversity	Low	Low	Med	High	Med	Low	Low	Low	N/A	N/A	N/A	Med
9. Knowledge of system software and components	High	High	Low	Low	Low	Med	Med	High	High	High	Med	N/A
10. Knowledge of network software and components	High	High	Low	Low	Low	Low	High	High	High	High	High	Low
11. Knowledge of software configurations	Med	High	Med	Low	N/A	Med	Med	High	Med	Med	Med	Low
12. Knowledge of hardware configurations	Med	High	Low	Low	N/A	High	Med	High	Med	Low	Med	High

Attribute	AV	PT	PA	CM	PM	SM	NM	CF	CP	SE	BC	FM
13. Knowledge of backup systems	Med	N/A	Med	N/A	Low	High	Low	N/A	N/A	Med	High	High
14. Knowledge of database systems	High	N/A	N/A	Low	Low	High	N/A	N/A	Low	N/A	Low	High
15. Knowledge of desktop systems	Med	Med	Med	Low	Low	Low	Med	Med	Low	Med	Low	N/A
16. Ability to analyze metrics	N/A	N/A	Med	Low	High	N/A	Med	Med	Low	High	N/A	N/A
17. Knowledge of power and air conditioning systems	High	Med	N/A	Med	High	Low	N/A	N/A	Low	N/A	N/A	High
18. Ability to think and plan strategically	Low	N/A	High	Med	Low	Med	Low	N/A	High	High	High	High
19. Ability to think and act tactically	High	High	N/A	Med	High	High	High	Med	N/A	Low	Low	Low

Legend

AV – Availability Management
PT - Performance/Tuning
PA – Production Acceptance
CM – Change Management
PM – Problem Management
SM – Storage Management

NM – Network Management
CF – Configuration Management
CP – Capacity Planning
SE – Security
BC – Business Continuity
FM – Facilities Management

Summary

This chapter covered the second important people issue of organizing an infrastructure for optimal systems management. We began with a look at how an IT environment evolves and matures from a basic reporting structure into a more expansive, sophisticated organization. We next identified three key factors by which infrastructures can be organized: departmental responsibilities, planning orientation, and systems management processes.

We then discussed alternative locations of four departments that greatly influence the effectiveness of an infrastructure. These departments are the help desk, database administration, network operations, and systems management. Finally, we listed the key attributes of process owners for each of the 12 systems management disciplines.

Test Your Understanding

1. Newly assigned executives and managers are usually reluctant to reorganize any parts of their new areas of responsibility. (True or False)
2. Size, maturity, and the orientation of a company directly influence how best to organize the IT infrastructure. (True or False)
3. Which of the following is not a factor on which to base a reorganization decision?
   a. departmental responsibilities
   b. expertise of employees
   c. planning orientation
   d. infrastructure processes
4. One of the most critical success factors in implementing any of the 12 systems management processes is the person you select as the process_____.
5. What are some of the pros and cons of outsourcing a company's Service Desk function?

Suggested Further Readings

1. *Information Technology Organizations and People, Advances in Management and Business Studies Series #6*; Watkins, Jeff, 1998
2. *Transforming Organizations with Information Technology: Proceedings of the IFIP WG 8.2 Working Conference on Information Technology and New Emergent Forms of Organization*; Ann Arbor, MI; Baskerville, Richard; 1994
3. *Information and Organizations*; Stinchombe, Arthur L.; 1990
4. *Information and Organizations*; Lilley, Simon/Lightfoot, Geoff; 2004
5. *IT Organization: Building a Worldclass Infrastructure*; Kern, Harris/Galup, Stuart D./Nemiro, Guy; 2000

6. www.inastrol.com/Articles/990511.htm;*Structuring Organizations;* Moriarity, Terry; May 1999

7. http://leadership.wharton.upenn.edu/structure/Tools_for_ design_and_ change/information_technology_and_organ.shtml; *Information Technology and Organizations*

CHAPTER 3

Staffing for Systems Management

Introduction

It is often said that people are the most important resource in any organization. This is certainly true as it applies to systems management. Smooth-running infrastructures are built with robust processes and reliable technologies. But before procedures and products are put in place, first must come the human element. Skilled professionals are needed at the outset to develop plans, design processes, and evaluate technologies; then they are needed to transform these ideas from paper into realities.

This chapter describes various methods you can use to staff an IT infrastructure with appropriately skilled individuals. We start out by looking at how to qualify and quantify the diversity of skill sets required. Next we discuss ways to assess the skill levels of current onboard staff and some not-always-obvious alternative sources for staffing you can use if needed. We then move on to some helpful tips on using recruiters, landing the ideal candidate, and retaining highly sought-after individuals.

Competent IT professionals who are both well-trained and highly experienced in the disciplines of systems management are in short supply and large demand. This chapter offers effective approaches to meet this ever-increasing challenge.

Determining Required Skill Sets and Skill Levels

Most newly proposed IT projects begin with a requirements phase. Staffing for systems management also has a requirements phase in the sense that necessary skill sets and skill levels need to be identified and prioritized early on. A *skill set* is defined as technical familiarity with a particular software product, architecture, or platform. For example, one enterprise may use primarily IBM mainframes with IBM's information management system (IMS) databases while another may use mostly Sun Solaris platforms with Oracle databases. The skill sets needed to implement systems management functions in these two environments are significantly different.

Skill Set

A skill set is defined as technical familiarity with a particular software product, architecture, or platform.

Within a skill set there is another attribute known as the skill level. The *skill level* is simply the length of experience and depth of technical expertise an individual has acquired and can apply to a given technology. The process of determining and prioritizing the required skill sets and levels has several benefits:

1. Quantifying the skill sets that will be needed to implement selected functions forces you to more accurately reflect the diversity of technical experience your environment will require.
2. Estimating necessary skill levels within each required skill set will reflect the amount of technical depth and expertise that will be needed.
3. The quantifying and qualifying required skill sets and levels are valuable aids in building the business cases we discussed in the previous chapter.

Skill Level

A skill level is defined as the length of experience and depth of technical expertise and variety of platform familiarity an individual has acquired and can apply to a given technology.

Developing a skill set matrix that is customized for your particular environment can help simplify this process. Table 3–1 shows an example of a skill set matrix for a relatively typical mainframe environment. The first column describes the major areas of focus for which systems management functions would apply and for which staffing would need to be considered. These major groupings would obviously differ from company to company depending on their own particular area of focus. Similarly, the platforms may be different for different enterprises. Next are the five groupings of skill levels, starting with the least experienced intern level and progressing to the senior and lead levels. The value of a table such as this is that it helps to visually qualify the skills that will be needed to implement selected systems management disciplines. The table can also be used to quantify how many individuals will be needed for each skill set and level. Occasionally a skill set and skill level requirement may amount to less than one full-time person. In this case, a decimal portion of a full-time equivalent (FTE) is commonly used to represent the staffing need.

Table 3–1   Mainframe Environment Skill Set Matrix

		Skill Level				
Area of Focus	**Platform**	**Intern**	**Junior**	**Associate**	**Senior**	**Lead**
Operating Systems	IBM					
	Support Products					
	Other					
Database Management Systems	IMS					
	CICS					
	Support Products					
	Other					
Network Systems	LAN					
	WAN					
	Support Products					
	Other					

Table 3–2 is similar to Table 3–1 except that it applies to a midrange environment rather than a mainframe one. Several of the platforms have consequently changed, reflecting the difference in environments.

Table 3–3 applies to a client-server environment. The two major platforms are UNIX and Microsoft NT; each platform is delineated by manufacturer. The manufacturer entry for NT is designated as "various" because the skill set for NT tends to be independent of the supplier.

Table 3–2   Midrange Environment Skill Set Matrix

Area of Focus	Platform		Skill Level				
		Intern	Junior	Associate	Senior	Lead
Operating Systems	IBM/AS400					
	HP/3000					
	Support Products					
	Other					
Database Management Systems	IBM					
	HP					
	Support Products					
	Other					
Network Systems	LAN					
	WAN					
	Support Products					
	Other					

Table 3–3   Client-Server Environment Skill Set Matrix

Area of Focus	Platform	Manufacturer		Skill Level			
			Intern	Junior	Associate	Senior	Lead
Operating Systems	UNIX	IBM/AIS					
		Sun/Solaris					
		HP/HPUNIX					
		REDDOG/LINUX					
		Support Products					
		Other					
	NT	Various					
		Support Products					
	Other						

			Skill Level				
Area of Focus	**Platform**	**Manufacturer**	**Intern**	**Junior**	**Associate**	**Senior**	**Lead**
Database Management Systems	UNIX	Oracle					
		Sybase					
		Informix					
		Support Products					
		Other					
	NT	MS SQL Server					
		Support Products					
		Other					
Network Systems	LAN	Various					
	WAN	Various					
	Support Products	Various					
	Other	Various					

Assessing the Skill Levels of Current Onboard Staff

Once we have determined the level and set of skills essential to supporting a particular systems management function, we need to identify potential candidates who have acquired the necessary experience. The first place to look is within your own company. Surprising as it may sound, some firms immediately look outside to fill many IT infrastructure openings rather than pursuing internal staff. Some believe the positions may be too specialized for someone who has not already obtained the skills. Others may feel that the cost and time to retrain is not acceptable.

The fact of the matter is that many companies enjoy unexpected success by redeploying onboard personnel. Potential candidates who are already on board usually are proficient in one or more technologies, but not necessarily in the systems management function being implemented. The more similar the new skill sets are to a person's existing ones, the more likelihood of success. For instance, the discipline being implemented may involve the performance and tuning of servers running a new flavor of UNIX. Onboard system administrators may be very capable in the performance and tuning of a different, but similar, version of UNIX and thus could easily transition to the new flavor. Redeploying a database administrator into the role of a systems administrator or as a network analyst may be a more challenging.

Being able to predict which onboard candidates can successfully transition into a new infrastructure role can be an invaluable skill for IT managers facing staffing needs. I developed a rather simple but effective method to help do this while filling staffing requirements at a major motion picture studio. The method evolved from lengthy analyses that I conducted with the human resources department to identify attributes most desirable in a transitioning employee. After sorting through literally dozens of very specific characteristics, we arrived at four basic but very pertinent qualities: attitude, aptitude, applicability, and experience. While the definition of these traits may seem obvious, it is worth clarifying a few points about each of them.

In my opinion, **attitude** is the most important feature of all in today's environment. It implies that the outlook and demeanor of an individual closely matches the desired culture of the enterprise. Some of the most brilliant IT programmers and analysts have become hampered in their careers because they have poor attitudes.

Exactly what constitutes an acceptable or proper attitude may vary slightly from firm to firm, but there generally are a few traits that are common to most organizations. Among these are the following:

- **Eagerness** to learn new skills
- **Willingness** to follow new procedures
- **Dedication** to being a team player

This last trait contrasts with that of aptitude, which emphasizes the *ability* to learn new skills as opposed to simply the *desire* to do so.

Applicability refers to an individual's ability to put his or her skills and experience to effective use. Employees may have years of experience with certain skill sets, but, if lack of motivation or poor communication skills prevent them from effectively applying the knowledge, it is of little value to an organization.

Experience is normally thought of as the total number of years a person has worked with a particular technology. An adage refers to distinguishing between someone who has 10 years of actual experience in an area of expertise versus someone who has one year of experience 10 times over. Depth, variety, and currency are three components of experience that should be factored into any assessment of a person's skill level.

- **Depth** refers to the level of technical complexity a person has mastered with a given product or process. An example of this would be the ability to configure operating systems or modify them with software maintenance releases as opposed to simply installing them.

- **Variety** describes the number of different platforms or environments an individual may have worked in with a certain technology. For example, one person may have familiarity with a multi-platform storage backup system but only in a single version of UNIX environment. Another individual may have a deeper understanding of the product from having used it in several different platform environments.

- **Currency** refers to how recent the person's experience is with a given product or technology. IT in general is a rapidly changing industry, and specific technologies within it may become outdated or even obsolete within a few years. A database administrator (DBA), for example, may have extensive familiarity with a particular version of a database management system, but if that experience took place longer than four to five years ago, it may no longer be relevant.

Table 3–4 summarizes the four key characteristics used to assess an individual's skill potential in transitioning from one infrastructure to another. Additional descriptions are shown for each characteristic to assist in clarifying differences between them.

Table 3–4 Skill Assessment Attributes and Characteristics

Attribute	Characteristics
Attitude	Empathy, patience, team player, active listener
	Polite, friendly, courteous, professional
	Helpful, resourceful, persevering
	Eagerness to learn new skills
	Willingness to follow new procedures

Table 3–4   Skill Assessment Attributes and Characteristics Continued

Attribute	Characteristics
Aptitude	Ability to learn new skills
	Ability to retain new skills
	Ability to integrate new skills with appropriate old ones
Applicability	Ability to apply knowledge and skills to appropriate use
	Ability to share knowledge and skills with others
	Ability to foresee new areas where skills may apply
Experience	Number of years of experience in a given skill
	How recent the experience has been
	Degree of variety of the experience

We can take a more analytical approach to this assessment by applying numerical weights to each of the four key characteristics. These weights may be assigned in terms of their relative importance to the organization in which they are being used. Any magnitude of number can be used, and in general the greater the importance of the attribute the higher the weight. Naturally these weights will vary from company to company. The attribute of an individual is then assessed and given a numerical rating. For example, the rating could be on a 1-to-5 basis with 5 being the best. The weight and rating are then multiplied to compute a score for each attribute. The four computations are then summed for an overall score. This approach is certainly not foolproof. Other factors such as personality, chemistry, and communication skills may override mere numerical scores. But the technique can be useful to narrow down a field of candidates or as additional assessment data. Table 3–5 shows an example of how this method could be used. With a rating range from 1 to 5, the range of overall scores could vary between 10 and 50.

Table 3–5   Skill Assessment Weighting and Rating Matrix

Attribute	Weight	Rating	Score	Characteristics
Attitude	4	3	12	Empathy, patience, team player, active listener
				Polite, friendly, courteous, professional
				Helpful, resourceful, persevering
				Eagerness to learn new skills
				Willingness to follow new procedures

Attribute	Weight	Rating	Score	Characteristics
Aptitude	3	4	12	Ability to learn new skills
				Ability to retain new skills
				Ability to integrate new skills with appropriate old ones
Applicability	2	2	4	Ability to apply knowledge and skills to appropriate use
				Ability to share knowledge and skills with others
				Ability to foresee new areas where skills may apply
Experience	1	5	5	Number of years of experience in a given skill
				How recent the experience has been
				Degree of variety of the experience

Alternative Sources of Staffing

Several alternative sources for infrastructure staffing are available inside most reasonably sized enterprises. One source involves cross-training existing infrastructure personnel in related skill sets. For example, if a company decides to change from one type of UNIX platform to another, a systems administrator who is familiar with only one variation of UNIX may be cross-trained in the alternative version. Similarly, an NT systems administrator may be cross-trained on UNIX.

A more challenging transition, though no less viable, may be between systems administration, database administration, and network administration. In some instances, suitable candidates may be found outside of the infrastructure group. Application departments may be able to supply DBA prospects or performance specialists, and planning groups may offer up metrics analysts. In certain cases, even business units outside of IT may have personnel qualified for selected positions within an IT infrastructure.

Recruiting Infrastructure Staff from the Outside

Not all infrastructure positions can be filled from inside a company. The introduction of new technologies, company growth, or simple attrition can necessitate the need to go outside a firm to meet staffing requirements.

Larger companies normally have human resources departments to assist in recruiting, scheduling interviews, and clarifying benefits and compensation issues. Smaller firms may need to recruit from the outside directly or use professional recruiters to fill IT infrastructure openings. Recruiting directly saves costs but requires more time and effort on the part of managers; additionally, it may take longer to locate qualified candidates this way.

Several direct recruiting methods exist to aid in this approach. Word-of-mouth recruiting by coworkers and staff can be surprisingly effective. Many companies now offer lucrative incentives for job referrals. Advertising in leading trade publications and local newspapers can also attract qualified talent. Perhaps the quickest and simplest method today is to use the Internet, which businesses of all sizes are now using to post job openings.

The use of outside recruiters is a common practice today, particularly when filling positions requiring critical or advanced technical skills. Recruiters are becoming much more specialized, enabling managers to pick and choose firms that best meet their particular recruiting needs. Care should be taken to ensure that recruiters have a proven track record; references should be requested and checked whenever possible.

Once you have selected your recruiter, you should provide them with very specific information about the type of individual you are seeking. Most reputable recruiting firms have a sizable database of prospective candidates and should be able to match most of your requirements. The more detailed the job description, the more likely they will find a desirable candidate. Do not specify merely the skill set and level of experience required. Describe the specific kind of work you anticipate the new hire to perform, the types and versions of software products and platforms involved, and the amount of recent practical experience you expect. For leads and supervisors, request how many individuals were under their leadership and for how long.

Real Life Experience—Relying on Spousal Support

I needed to staff a critical position for a senior Oracle database administrator. I selected a recruiting firm that specialized in these kinds of candidates and within a few days had the resume of what appeared to be the ideal person for the job. This individual stated recent extensive experience with the exact levels of Oracle needed. But upon interviewing the candidate, it quickly came out that most of the recent Oracle experience had come from training classes that the prospect's spouse—a professional Oracle instructor—had provided. The recruiter was even more surprised than we were to learn of this development; needless to say, all three parties involved ended up the wiser and parted ways.

A final suggestion on the use of recruiters: Always clarify with the recruiting firm any questions you might have on specific points of a candidate's resume prior to calling that candidate for an interview.

Selecting the Most Qualified Candidate

Once a perspective candidate has been identified, a relatively formal interview process should follow. Both the employer and the potential employee should ask sufficient questions to make sure a good fit is likely. For key positions it may be appropriate to have several key staff members interview the candidate to ensure that a variety of viewpoints are covered and to arrive at a consensus about the candidate.

Real Life Experience—Questioning Questionable Decision-Making

Sometimes selecting the best candidate becomes a process of eliminating those who are not quite the best. Recently, a colleague used a slight variation of this technique to narrow his field of prospects. This manager needed a senior-level systems administrator who, among other things, would be willing to respond to periodic calls outside of normal working hours and to occasionally come in to work on weekends. After the field had been narrowed down to two finalists, one of them failed to show up for his interview at the appointed time. The next day he explained that, on the way in to his interview, traffic had been so bad from an accident that he decided to turn around, go home, and call back the next day to schedule a new interview. His apparent lack of a sense of urgency and his questionable decision-making skills were all that my colleague needed to see. The manager promptly extended an offer to the alternate candidate.

Telephone interviews sometimes are necessary to accommodate conflicting schedules, especially if multiple people will be involved in the interview process. Whenever possible, however, face-to-face interviews should be conducted to evaluate personality, body language, and other nonverbal cues not apparent over a telephone. Most companies have unique job benefits as well as drawbacks, and all of these should be discussed thoroughly and openly during the interview process. The fewer surprises in store for both the employer and the new hire once employment begins, the better for everyone involved.

For positions involving leadership and supervisory roles, you should almost always require references. Request a minimum of two and preferably three or four, and then thoroughly follow up on them. When company benefits are explained to prospective candidates, the explanation should be very thorough; it is usually best handled by a person in the company's human resources department.

Real Life Experience—What's In a Name? Everything

A few years ago I was on a consulting assignment at a progressive Internet start-up company. This firm was becoming a very successful e-commerce and licensing company for pop culture merchandise and trends. The executives there had worked very hard to grow and expand their firm and took pride in branding their company name, called WhatsHotNow.com. While looking through a stack of applications for a key management position, the hiring executive immediately rejected one of the resumes, even though the candidate had impressive credentials. His reason was direct and succinct: The applicant had inadvertently rearranged the letters in the company's name and in doing so changed the firm's image of ultra hip to just the opposite. The applicant referred to his prospective employer as WhatsNotHot.com.

Retaining Key Personnel

Once a candidate has accepted the job offer, the challenge of staffing now shifts to retaining this person (along with all the other highly talented personnel). IT departments and human resources groups have been struggling with this phenomenon for years. As a result, some creative approaches have been used to stem the tide of turnover and attrition.

Some of these new approaches involve creative compensation such as supplying personnel with free cell phone use, remote Internet access from home, laptop computers, or compensating them for business mileage. Recent research suggests that several nonmonetary factors often are just as important as cash salary. These nonmonetary incentives include the amount of on-the-job training to be provided, the currency of technology used, attendance at conferences and seminars, the meaningfulness and significance of the work being performed, promotion opportunities, and the stability of the management staff.

More often than not, skilled technical professionals change jobs because of some key ingredient missing in the relationship they have with an immediate manager. We have all heard about the importance of communication, but it is hard to overstate its significance. Over the years I have come to know several highly skilled IT professionals who left an otherwise excellent job opportunity simply because of poor communication with their managers. Lack of recognition, little career planning, and their managers' inabilities to convey an organization's vision, direction, and goals are some other common reasons employees cite when discussing a poor management relationship.

A few years ago I headed up an outsourcing effort at a major film studio. One of the unfortunate circumstances of the project was that a number of good employees would need to be redeployed by the prospective outsourcer. To mitigate the adverse effect of this displacement, we requested that each prospective outsourcing bidder itemize the employee benefits that they would offer to our former employees. The quantity and quality of these benefits would become part of our evaluation criteria in selecting an eventual winner of the contract.

To ensure that we were evaluating the proposed benefits appropriately, I also worked with our human resources department to survey our employees to determine which benefits meant the most to them. We jointly comprised what we all felt was a comprehensive list of typical employee benefits, including those that would likely come into play during a change in companies. We then asked each employee to indicate the level of importance they would give to each benefit. The rating was to be made on a 1 to 5 scale; 1 indicated the least important benefit and 5 indicated the most important benefit

The results of the employee benefit survey were surprising, even to some of the more seasoned human resources representatives. The responses (see Table 3-6) provide some interesting insight into employee priorities. Each benefit is ranked from most important to least important according to its average score. As shown in the table, salary was not the highest priority benefit, although it was close to the top. Medical care was first.

Table 3–6   Survey of Traditional Employee Benefits

Rank	Benefit	Score
1	Medical coverage	4.76
2	Dental coverage	4.59
3	Base salary	4.53
4	Training in client-server	4.24
5	Vacation	4.23
6	Vision care	4.12
7	Career advancement	4.12
8	Company matching 401k	4.06
9	Training in networking	4.05
10	Sick leave	4.00
11	Proximity to home	3.88
12	Medical leaves	3.71
13	Training in PCs/Intranet/Web	3.65
14	Flexible work hours	3.53
15	Flexible work week	3.47
16	Training in operations	3.12
17	Personal leaves	3.11

Rank	Benefit	Score
18	Personal time off	3.06
19	Compensation time for overtime	2.65
20	Distance to workplace	2.64
21	Opportunity for overtime pay	2.47
22	Van pools or car pools	2.35
23	Bonuses	2.29
24	Absence of overtime	1.17

Even more surprising was the list of additional benefits that we asked employees to propose. We felt we had compiled a fairly thorough list of traditional benefits and were not expecting to receive more than two or three newly proposed benefits. As shown in Table 3–7, we underestimated the creative talents of our staff as they proposed an additional 13 benefits. Each benefit is ranked from most important to least important according to the total number of respondents who selected it.

Table 3–7 Newly Proposed Employee Benefits

Rank	Description of Benefit	Respondents
1	Long-term disability	6
2	Life insurance	5
T-3	Floating or additional holidays	4
T-3	Bereavement leave	4
T-3	Direct deposit of paycheck	4
T-6	Pension plans	3
T-6	Attendance at conferences	3
T-6	Education reimbursement	3
T-9	Early retirement	2
T-9	Quality management	2
T-11	High degree of teamwork	1
T-11	Respect for all ideas and abilities	1
T-11	Training in mainframes	1

Using Consultants and Contractors

Another alternative available to infrastructure managers needing to fill positions is the use of consultants and contractors. Their use in IT environments in general, and in IT infrastructures in particular, is increasing at a rapid rate for a variety of reasons. Outsourcing, company downsizing, acquisitions and mergers, and global competition are leading to significant reductions in full-time IT staff.

This trend toward reduced IT staffing—especially in larger, more established shops—is also feeding the supply of ready consultants. Many of the previously displaced IT personnel elect to become independent consultants. Frequently many of these former workers enter into service contracts with their previous employers. Others market their skills to companies with IT environments similar to their previous company to ensure a good fit between the skills they can offer and the technical requirements needing to be met.

The explosive growth of the Web and the flood of Internet start-up companies have also contributed to unprecedented demand for IT consulting services. Integrating dissimilar architectures—database software, desktop operating systems, and networking technologies, for example—often requires specialized skills. In many cases managers find it easier to contract with a consultant for these specialized skills than to attempt to grow them from within. A heightened awareness of the benefits of new, replaced, or migrated systems is pushing implementation schedules forward. Accelerated schedules are well suited for the immediate availability and short-term commitments offered by consultants and contractors. The shortened project life cycles of open system applications, the rapid deployment of Web-enabled systems, and the intensifying of global competition are some of the forces at work today that fuel this demand for accelerated implementations.

Consultants come in a variety of types, and they contrast slightly with the notion of a contractor. Understanding the differences between the two can help ensure a better fit between the skills being offered and the business requirements needing to be met. The term *consultant* normally refers to someone hired to do an analytical task, such as a capacity study, a security audit, or a re-engineering assignment. This contrasts with the term *contractor*, which generally refers to someone hired to perform a more specific task, such as coding an interface or developing a software enhancement.

Consultants are commonly supplied from one of the major accounting firms or from major computer hardware or software suppliers. Contractors, on the other hand, are more likely to come from software development companies or they are in business for themselves. Consultants tend to be oriented toward issues of strategy, service process, and management. Contractors tend to be oriented towards issues of coding, documentation, technology, and deliverables. These orientations then determine the specific type of consultant or contractor to be hired.

Knowing the specific type of person to be hired helps in one other important area—that of teaming with onboard employees. For example, a consultant hired to develop IT customer service levels needs to show empathy toward the customers that he or she is dealing with. Similarly, a contractor hired to work with an existing team of onboard developers must be able to fit in with the members of the group.

Benefits of Using Consultants and Contractors

One immediate benefit of using consultants and contractors is that they provide readily available technical expertise. Since they are under contract, you pay only for the time they expend. As the demand for IT services continues to increase, it often becomes difficult—if not impossible—to attract and retain personnel that is skilled, knowledgeable, and highly motivated. This requirement becomes even more challenging as the diversity of IT environments continues to grow. Shops are migrating from one hardware platform to another or from one software architecture to another—be it applications, databases, or operating systems—at ever increasing rates. In the midst of these many transitions, there often may not be the necessary level of technical expertise onboard at the time to perform the migration, support, or maintenance of these systems. Highly specialized consultants can help alleviate this by providing technical expertise needed in these diverse areas.

Another benefit that consultants and especially contractors offer to an enterprise is that they can assist in accelerating critical development schedules. The schedule to implement some major applications is often dictated by specific needs. For example, a critical distribution system for a major toy company may have been cost-justified because it absolutely had to be in place before the Christmas rush. New systems that were designed to correct the Y2K problem obviously had to be in place prior to the start of the new millennium. Organizations may have the necessary quality of skilled employees onboard, but simply not an adequate quantity of them to meet critical schedules. In these instances, consultants and contractors may quickly be brought in to assist in keeping projects on schedule.

Real Life Experience—Project Tricks Delay the Treats

One of the most highly publicized examples of an IT development effort missing its critical deadline involved the Hershey Chocolate Corporation. A totally new and highly advanced distribution system was slated to be implemented during the summer of 1999. Teams of consultants and contractors were brought in to assist in this effort, but a series of missteps undermined the progress of the project. Unanticipated problems, untimely miscommunications, and a possibly overaggressive deployment plan all contributed to a six-month delay in the launch of the system. Unfortunately for Hershey, the majority of their annual sales come during the month of October in preparation for Halloween. The system was eventually implemented successfully, but long after the lucrative holiday buying season, costing Hershey a substantial amount in lost sales.

Occasionally a highly unique technical requirement may arise. Even a fully staffed and highly diversified IT department may not possess the unique technical expertise required for such a task. Consultants may be a more cost-effective alternative to hiring full-time personnel, particularly if the implementation of the project is relatively short-lived. Interfacing an NT-based application with a UNIX/Oracle database environment may be an example of this.

Drawbacks of Using Consultants and Contractors

One of the primary drawbacks of using consultants and contractors is that they are often much more expensive than onboard staff. The rates of critically skilled consultants from key suppliers or major accounting firms can easily exceed multiple thousands of dollars per day per individual. But if the need is of a high enough urgency, expense may not be a prime factor.

Another drawback that occasionally occurs in larger shops is that it has an adverse effect on employee morale. Consultants and contractors who are highly skilled in a critical technical area may dismiss the need to be good team players. Their extremely high rates may justify in their minds the insistence for priority treatment in order to optimize their time on the clock. Thorough interviewing and reference checks can usually mitigate this concern.

Since most consultants and contractors bill on an hourly or daily basis, there is always the concern that some may not work as efficiently as possible. The more time a consultant spends on a project, the more revenue they generate for themselves. Three areas that are prone to inefficiencies are email, voicemail, and meetings. Email is an excellent mechanism for distributing simple, one-way information to many recipients. It typically does not lend itself to activities such as brainstorming, problem-solving, or personnel issues; with email, tone, emotion, and reactions can easily be misinterpreted. When consultants or contractors use emails for these latter activities instead of limiting the use email for simple communication, a task that may have taken only a few hours can often drag on for days or even weeks.

Voicemail is another area where consultants and contractors can be inefficient. They neglect to employ a simple technique of leaving detailed messages on voicemail about the nature of the call when a called party is not available and instead ask only to have the call returned. This usually results in numerous rounds of time-wasting telephone tag. Efficiency-minded consultants and contractors often can actually resolve issues with voicemail by simply providing specific questions, information, or responses.

Meetings can be time-wasters for consultants and contractors from two standpoints. The first is simple mismanagement of meetings. You can significantly improve a meeting's efficiency and effectiveness by using commonly accepted meeting practices, such as sending advance online invitations; providing agendas, objectives, action items, and minutes; and assigning a scribe, a timekeeper, and a facilitator. Although contractors (and consultants, especially) need to conduct numerous meetings as part of the performance of their duties, few follow many of these common meeting practices. The second way to waste time with meetings is to hold them when they're not needed. Often a brief face-to-face discussion or even a telephone call may accomplish the same result as a costly and time-consuming meeting.

A final drawback of using consultants and contractors is the issue of hidden costs. The total cost of employing a consultant or contractor is not always apparent when the initial contract is drawn up. Some of these hidden costs include costs for office space, parking, and long-distance telephone calls. Most consultants today have their own laptop computers or access to a desktop. But an independent contractor who is employed primarily to do coding work may require access to a company desktop computer, login authority to the company network, and printing services. All of these activities require setup time, administration work, and other expenses not specifically spelled out in the initial contract.

Table 3–8 summarizes the benefits and drawbacks of using consultants and contractors.

Table 3–8   Summary of Benefits and Drawbacks of Using Consultants and Contractors

Benefits	Drawbacks
Immediate availability	High costs
Pay only for effort expended	Potential source of morale problems
Ability to accelerate schedules	Occasional inefficiencies
Can supply rare or unique technical expertise	Hidden expenses

Steps for Developing Career Paths for Staff Members

The opportunity for career advancement is one of the most important considerations that perspective candidates factor into their decisions to accept employment offers. Table 3-6 shows a prioritized listing of benefits that candidates prefer the most. The opportunity for advancement and training in current technologies (such as client-servers, networking, PCs, the Internet, and Web design) are among the most desired. Surprising, managers and employees alike often lose sight of this important aspect once the employment contract is signed and work quickly begins. The nature of IT work, particularly within IT infrastructures, is usually so fast-paced that even well-intentioned plans of career-pathing are often relegated to lower priority status. It is the responsibility of both the manager and the employee to ensure this does not happen.

The following three steps can help managers ensure that career-pathing does not become de-emphasized:

1. Conduct a skills assessment of each member of your staff. This should determine what technical or managerial skills each member currently has or aspires to obtain.
2. Match the future needs of your organization to those individuals who express similar goals.

3. Plan out a career program of training, assignments, and mentoring to help the employee and the organization obtain the desired results.

There are also three steps for employees to enable career-pathing to stay on the front burner of priorities:

1. Determine your short-term career goals (3 to 5 years) and long-term career goals (10 to 20 years).

   If you are fresh out of college or a technical institution, you likely will be pursuing a technical career path. Decide which area of IT appeals to you the most and in which area you feel you have the most aptitude. Some students like programming, some enjoy analysis, some prefer translating business problems into technical solutions, while others lean more toward networking or web design. Taking a variety of IT courses in school can help you set an initial path, but do not be reluctant to change course once you are out working in a business environment. Just as an incoming college freshman may change majors a few times during the course of his college career, an IT professional may change his preferred area of IT expertise.

   If you have worked in the industry for some time, but never in IT, your short-term goals may include supervisory or managerial positions. This will depend on the type and amount of experience you have and what policies and available positions an employer may have. In any event, long-term goals should also be decided in terms of a technical career, a managerial career, or something in–between (such as project management). Knowing your current short- and long-term career goals keeps you focused on where you want to be and how to stay on course to get there.

2. Discuss your short- and long-term career goals with your manager and request his or her assistance in attaining them.

3. This suggestion goes hand-in-hand with the second one. Take the initiative to stay abreast of current developments in your chosen area of preference. Investigate websites, join industry organizations, look into certification programs. For example, there are organizations such as the Help Desk Institute, the Service Management Forum, and the Disaster Recovery Institute that deal with the issues of help desks, service management and disaster recovery, respectively.

These suggestions help managers and employees alike keep career advancement and employment development in the forefront. In the long run, that improves the welfare of employees and managers alike—which means it eventually helps the customers.

Summary

This chapter presented effective ways to staff your infrastructure organization, presenting techniques to assess a variety of groups of onboard personnel who may be qualified to work in systems management. For those instances where outside hiring is required, we discussed effective ways to attract candidates from other organizations, including the use of recruiters. We then looked at the selection process itself, along with several suggestions for how to retain key personnel. Finally, the chapter concluded with a treatment of the benefits and drawbacks of using consultants and contractors.

Test Your Understanding

1. A skill set is defined as technical familiarity with a particular software product, architecture, or platform. (True or False)
2. Cross-training is typically ineffective as an alternative source of staffing. (True or False)
3. Which of the following is not a component of experience?
   a. depth
   b. ability
   c. variety
   d. currency
4. Most newly proposed IT projects begin with a _____ phase.
5. Describe several of the benefits of cross-training within an IT organization.

Suggested Further Readings

1. *House of Lies: How Management Consultants Steal Your Watch and Then Tell You the Time*; Business Plus; Kiln, Martin; 2005
2. www.mwoodco.com/value/stratstaff.html; *Are You Strategic When It Comes To Staffing?*; John Poracky, 2000

CHAPTER 4

Customer Service

Introduction

No discussion about the important role people play in systems management would be complete without looking at the topic of customer service. This chapter details the full spectrum of customer service within an infrastructure organization. It begins by describing how IT has evolved into a service industry and how this influences the culture and hiring practices of successful companies.

Next, we present techniques on how to identify who your real customers are and how to effectively negotiate realistic service expectations. Toward the end of the chapter we describe the four cardinal sins that almost always undermine good customer service in an IT environment.

How IT Evolved into a Service Organization

Most IT organizations began as offshoots of their company's accounting departments. As companies grew and their accounting systems became more complex, their dependency on the technology of computers also grew. The emphasis of IT in the 1970s was mostly on continually providing machines and systems that were bigger, faster, and cheaper. During this era, technological advances in IT flourished. Two factors led to very little emphasis on customer service.

1. In the 1970s, the IT industry was still in its infancy. Organizations were struggling just to stay abreast of all the rapidly changing technologies, let alone focus on good customer service.

2. Within most companies the IT department was the only game in town, so to speak. Departments that were becoming more and more dependent on computers—finance, engineering, and administration, for example—were pretty much at the mercy of their internal IT suppliers, regardless of how much or how little customer service was provided.

By the 1980s, the role of IT and customer service began changing. IT was becoming a strategic competitive advantage for many corporations. A few industries, such as banking and airlines, had long before discovered how the quality of IT services could affect revenue, profits, and public image. As online applications started replacing many of the manual legacy systems, more and more workers became exposed to the power and the frustration of computers. Demand for high availability, quick response, and clear and simple answers to operational questions gave rise to user groups, help desks, service level agreements (SLAs), and eventually customer service representatives—all within the confines of a corporate structure.

Good customer service was now becoming an integral part of any well-managed IT department. By the time the 1990s rolled around, most users were reasonably computer literate; PCs and the Internet were common fixtures in the office and at home; and the concept of customer service transitioned from being hoped for to being expected. Demands for excellent customer service grew to such a degree in the 1990s that the lack of it often led to demotions, terminations, and outsourcing.

SLA

SLA is short for service level agreement and refers to a documented, negotiated agreement between a representative from an IT department and a representative from an end-user department concerning the quality of service delivered. Common SLA metrics include percent uptime availability, average response times, and escalation procedures for problems.

Whether IT professionals were prepared for it or not, IT had evolved from a purely accounting and technical environment into a totally service-oriented one. Companies hiring IT professionals now often require employees to have traits such as empathy, helpfulness, patience, resourcefulness, and a sense of teamwork. The extent to which these traits are in evidence frequently determines an individual's, or an organization's, success in IT today.

The Four Key Elements of Good Customer Service

There are four elements of good customer service:

- Identifying your key customers
- Identifying key services of key customers
- Identifying key processes that support key services
- Identifying key suppliers that support key processes

We'll discuss the first two at length and briefly describe the last two.

Identifying Your Key Customers

One of the best ways to ensure you are providing excellent customer service is to consistently meet or exceed the expectations of your key customers. In transitioning to a service-oriented environment, infrastructure professionals sometimes struggle with identifying who their key customers are. I frequently hear this comment:

> Since most all company employees in one way or another use IT services, then all company employees must be our key customers.

In reality, there are usually just a small number of key representative customers who can often serve as a barometer for good customer service and for effective process improvements. For example, you may design a change management process that dozens or even hundreds of programmers may be required to use. But you would probably need to involve only a handful of key programmer representatives to assist in designing the process and measuring its effectiveness.

There are various criteria to help in determining which of your numerous customers qualify as key customers. An IT department should identify those criteria that are the most suitable for identifying the key customers in their particular environment. The following list summarizes characteristics of key customers of a typical infrastructure:

1. Someone whose success critically depends on the services you provide.
   Infrastructure groups typically serve a variety of departments in a company. Some departments are more essential to the core business of the company than others, just as some applications are considered mission critical while others aren't. The heads or designated leads of these departments are usually good candidates for key customers.

2. Someone who, when satisfied, assures your success as an organization.
   Some individuals hold positions of influence in a company and can help market the credibility of an infrastructure organization. These customers may be in significant staff positions, such as those found in legal or public affairs departments. The high visibility of these positions may afford them the opportunity to highlight IT infrastructure achievements to other non-IT departments. These achievements could include high availability of online systems or the reliable restorations of inadvertently deleted data.

3. Someone who fairly and thoroughly represents large customer organizations.
   The very nature of some of the services provided by IT infrastructures results in these services being used by a large majority of a company's workforce. These highly used services include email, Internet, and intranet services. An analysis of the volume of use of these services by departments can determine which groups are using which services the most. The heads or designated leads of these departments would likely be good key customer candidates.

4. Someone who frequently uses, or whose organization frequently uses, your services.
   Some departments are major users of IT services by nature of their relationship within a company. In an airline company, it may be the department in charge of the reservation system. For a company supplying overnight package deliveries, the key department may be the one overseeing the package tracking system. During the time I headed the primary IT infrastructure groups at a leading defense contractor and later at a major motion picture studio, I witnessed firsthand the key IT user departments—design engineering (defense contractor) and theatrical distribution (motion picture company). Representatives from each group were solid key-customer candidates.

5. Someone who constructively and objectively critiques the quality of your services.

   It's possible that a key customer may be associated with a department that does not have a critical need for or high-volume use of IT services. A noncritical and low-volume user may qualify as a key customer because of a keen insight into how an infrastructure could effectively improve its services. These individuals typically have both the ability and the willingness to offer candid, constructive criticism about how to improve IT services.

6. Someone who has significant business impact on your company as a corporation.

   Marketing or sales department representatives in a manufacturing firm may contain key customers of this type. In aerospace or defense contracting companies, it may be advanced technology groups. The common thread among these key customers is that their use of IT services can greatly advance the business position of the corporation.

7. Someone with whom you have mutually agreed-upon reasonable expectations.

   Most any infrastructure user, both internal and external to either IT or its company, may qualify as a key customer if the customer and the IT infrastructure representative have reasonable expectations that are mutually agreed upon. Conversely, customers whose expectations are not reasonable should usually be excluded as key customers. The adage about the squeaky wheel getting the grease does not always apply in this case—I have often seen just the reverse. In many cases, the customers with the loud voices insisting on unreasonable expectations are often ignored in favor of listening to the constructive voices of more realistic users.

Identifying Key Services of Key Customers

The next step after identifying your key customers is to identify their key services. This may sound obvious but in reality many infrastructure managers merely presume to know the key IT services of their key customers without ever verifying which services they need the most. Only by interacting directly with their customers can these managers understand the wants and needs of their customers.

Infrastructure managers need to clearly distinguish between services their customers *need* to conduct the business of their departments and services that they *want* but may not be able to cost-justify to the IT organization. For example, an engineering department may need to have sophisticated graphics software to design complex parts and may want to have all of the workstation monitors support color. The IT infrastructure may be able to meet their expectations of the former but not the latter. This is where the importance of negotiating realistic customer expectations comes in.

Negotiating and Managing Realistic Customer Expectations

The issue of reasonable expectations is a salient point and cuts to the heart of sound customer service. When IT people started getting serious about service, they initially espoused many of the tenets of other service industries. Phrases such as the following were drilled into IT professionals at several of the companies where I was employed:

> The customer is always right.
>
> Never say no to a customer.
>
> Always meet your customers' expectations.

As seemingly obvious as these statements appear, the plain and simple fact is that rarely can you meet all of the expectations of all of your customers all of the time. The more truthful but less widely acknowledged fact is that customers sometimes are unreasonable in their expectations. IT service providers may actually be doing more of a disservice to their customers and to themselves by not saying no to an unrealistic demand. This leads to the first of two universal truths I have come to embrace about customer service and expectations.

> An unreasonable expectation, rigidly demanded by an uncompromising customer and naively agreed to by a well-intentioned supplier, is one of the major causes of poor customer service.

I have observed this scenario time and time again within IT departments throughout various industries. In their zest to please customers and establish credibility for their organizations, IT professionals agree to project schedules that cannot be met, availability levels that cannot be reached, response times that cannot be obtained, and budget reductions that cannot be reached. Knowing when and how to say no to a customer is not an easy task, but there are techniques available to assist in negotiating and managing realistic expectations.

While heading up an extensive IT customer service effort at a major defense contractor, I developed with my team a simple but effective methodology for negotiating and managing realistic customer expectations. The first part involved thorough preparation of face-to-face interviews with selected key customers; the second part consisted of actually conducting the interview to negotiate and follow up on realistic expectations.

Changing the mindset of IT professionals can be a challenging task. We were asking them to focus very intently on a small number of customers when for years they had emphasized doing almost the exact reverse. The criteria covered in the previous section helped immensely to limit their number of interviews to just a handful of key customers.

Real Life Experience—Preparing for the General's Question

The reluctance of managers to interview people face-to-face reminds me of an incident back in the mid 1980s, when I was managing a highly classified computer environment for a major American defense contractor. During the startup of a huge classified program, we had a need to hire close to 100 computer operations personnel. Because they had to clear strict security background checks prior to hiring, many applicants did not make it through the initial screening. Any experimentation with banned drugs, including marijuana, was grounds for disqualification. This fact alone accounted for many disqualifications of young applicants who had come of age during the more pot-lenient years of the early 1970s.

As a result, several of my managers interviewed 5-to-10 candidates for each one hired. So, after the hundreds of interviews they collectively conducted, I could almost understand their reluctance to interview potentially unsupportive customers.

Soon after the managers had hired all of the computer operations personnel, the Air Force asked for a tour of our large, sophisticated computer facility. A two-star general with a background in military security was the primary focus of the tour. My managers and I had prepared for most any question the general might ask during or after the tour. He had little to say while on the tour, but during the de-briefing, he leaned toward me and said he had just one question. I braced in anticipation as my superiors and subordinates looked on. Then the general—, a father of three youthful sons,—asked, "How did you ever find so many young people who have never tried marijuana?"

Getting the IT leads and managers to actually schedule the interviews was even more of a challenge for us. This reluctance to interview key customers was puzzling to our team. These IT professionals had been interviewing many new hires for well over a year and had been conducting semiannual performance reviews for most all of their staffs for some time. Yet we were hearing almost every excuse under the sun as to why they could not conduct a face-to-face interview with key customers. Some wanted to conduct it over the phone, some wanted to send out surveys, others wanted to use email, and many simply claimed that endless phone tag and schedule conflict prevented successful get-togethers.

We knew that these face-to-face interviews with primary customers were the key to successfully negotiating reasonable expectations that, in turn, would lead to improved customer service. So we looked a little closer at the reluctance to interview. What we discovered really surprised us. Most of our managers and leads believed the interviews could easily become confrontational unless only a few IT-friendly customers were involved. Many had received no formal training on effective interviewing techniques and felt ill-equipped to deal with a potentially belligerent user. Very few thought that they could actually convince skeptical users that some of their expectations may be unrealistic and yet still come across as being service-oriented.

This turn of events temporarily changed our approach. We immediately set up an intense interview training program for our lead and managers. It specifically emphasized how to deal with difficult customers. Traditional techniques (such as open-ended questions, active listening, and restatements) were combined with effective ways to cut off ramblers and negotiate compromise, along with training on when to agree to disagree. We even developed some sample scripts for them to use as guidelines.

Real Life Experience—Unexpected Benefit of Interviewing System

The thought of interviewing a less than supportive customer face-to-face proved to be almost unbearable for one of my managers. He had an extensive programming background and developed a very elaborate online interview survey to send out to his six key customers. As I was about to chastise him for bypassing the personal encounter, I received a call from one of his key customers. It seems the customer had a bit of a programming background of his own and was duly impressed with my manager's online survey. I thanked him for his call and suggested he thank my manager himself—in person—which he did. That led to several successful face-to-face meetings for these two.

The training went quite well and proved to be very effective. Leads and managers from all across our IT department began to conduct interviews with key customers. From the feedback we received from both the IT interviewers and our customers, we learned what the majority felt were the most effective parts of the interview. We referred to them as *validate*, *negotiate*, and *escalate*:

- **Validate.** Within the guidelines of the prepared interview scripts, the interviewers first validated their interviewees by assuring them that they were, in fact, key customers. They then told the customers that they did indeed critically need and use the services that we were supplying. Interviewers then went on to ask what the customers' current expectations were for the levels of service provided.

- **Negotiate.** If customers' expectations were reasonable and obtainable, then the parties discussed and agreed upon the type and frequency of measurements to be used. If the expectations were not reasonable, then negotiations, explanations, and compromises were proposed. If these negotiations did not result in a satisfactory agreement, as would occasionally occur, then the interviewer would politely agree to disagree and move on to other matters.

- **Escalate.** Next the interviewer would escalate the unsuccessful negotiation to his or her manager, who would attempt to resolve it with the manager of the key customer.

The validate/negotiate/escalate method proved to be exceptionally effective at negotiating reasonable expectations and realistic service levels. The hidden benefits included clearer and more frequent communication with users, improved interviewing skills for leads and managers, increased credibility for the IT department, and more empathy of our users for some of the many constraints under which most all IT organizations work.

This empathy that key customers were sharing with us leads me to the second universal truth I embrace concerning customer service and expectations:

> Most customers are forgiving of occasional poor service if reasonable attempts are made to explain the nature and cause of the problem and what is being done to resolve it and prevent its future occurrence.

As simple and as obvious as this may sound, it still amazes me to see how often this basic concept is overlooked or ignored in IT organizations. We would all be better served if it was understood and used more frequently.

Identifying Key Processes that Support Key Services

Negotiating realistic expectations of service leads into the third element of good customer service: identifying key processes. These processes comprise the activities that provide and support the key services of the customers. For example, a legal department may need a service to retrieve records that have been archived months previously. In this case, the activities of backing up the data, archiving and storing it offsite, and retrieving it quickly for customer access would be the key processes that support this key service.

Similarly, a human resources department may need a service that safeguards the confidentiality of payroll and personnel data. In this case, the processes that ensure the security of the data involved would be key.

Identifying Key Suppliers that Support Key Processes

Identifying key suppliers is the fourth element of good customer service. Key suppliers are those individuals who provide direct input, in terms of products or support, to the key processes. In our example in the prior section regarding the legal department, some of the key suppliers would be the individuals responsible for storing the data offsite and for retrieving it back to make it accessible for users. Similarly for the human resources example, the developers of the commercial software security products and the individuals responsible for installing and administering the products would be key suppliers for the data-security processes.

Integrating the Four Key Elements of Good Customer Service

As we have discussed, the four key components of good customer service are identifying key customers, identifying key services of these customers, identifying key processes, and identifying key suppliers. Understanding the relationships between these four entities can go a long way to ensuring high levels of service quality.

Figure 4-1 shows the traditional model of a basic work-flow process. Suppliers provide input of some type into a process. In the case of an IT production control department this could be data being fed into a program stream that is part of a job execution process, or it could be database changes being fed into a quality-assurance process. The output of the first process may be updated screens or printed reports for users; the output of the second process would be updated database objects for programmers.

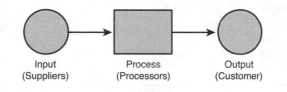

Input
(Suppliers)

Process
(Processors)

Output
(Customer)

Figure 4-1 Traditional Work-Flow Process Model

The problem with the traditional work-flow model is that it does not encourage any collaboration between suppliers, processors, and customers, nor does it measure anything about the efficiency of the process or the effectiveness of the service.

In Figure 4-2, the model is revised in several aspects to improve the quality of customer service. First, a key services box has been added to emphasize that the output of the process should result in a deliverable and measurable service that is critical to the success of the customer. Second, the flow of work between all four elements is shown going both ways to stress the importance of two-way communication between the individuals involved with each element. Third, each of the elements are designated as key elements to highlight the fact that, while many customers and suppliers may be involved in a particular work-flow process, there are usually only a handful that significantly affect the quality of input and output.

A narrative interpretation of the Figure 4-2 work-flow model in each direction may serve to clarify its use and importance. We will start first in the right-to-left direction. Key suppliers provide high-quality input into a key process. The streamlined key process acts upon the high-quality input, ensuring that each step of the activity adds value to the process; this results in delivering a key service to a key customer.

Next we will go in the left-to-right direction. We start by identifying a key customer and then interviewing and negotiating reasonable expectations with this customer. The expectations should involve having key services delivered on time and in an acceptable manner. These services are typically critical to the success of the customer's work. Once the key services are identified, the key processes that produce these services are next identified. Finally, having determined which key processes are needed, the key suppliers that input to these processes are identified.

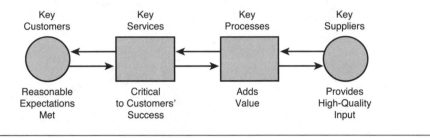

Figure 4-2   Revised Work-Flow Process Model

The revised work-flow model shown in Figure 4-2 serves as the basis for a powerful customer service technique we call a customer/supplier matrix. It involves identifying your key services, determining the key customers of those services, seeing which key processes feed into the key services, and identifying the key suppliers of these key processes. A more succinct way of saying this is:

Know **who** is using **what** and **how** it's being **supplied.**

The *who* refers to your key customers. The *what* refers to your key services. The *how* refers to your key processes. The *supplied* refers to your key suppliers.

Table 4-1 shows how a matrix of this type could be set up. The matrix comprises four partitions, each representing a key element of the relationship. The leftmost partition represents customers whose use of IT services is critical to their success and whose expectations are reasonable. The partition to the right of the customer box contains the IT services that are critical to a customer's success and whose delivery meets customer expectations. The next partition to the right shows the processes that produce the key services required by key customers. The last partition represents the suppliers who feed into the key processes.

Table 4-1   Customer/Supplier Matrix

Key Customers	Key Services	Key Processes	Key Suppliers
Customers whose use of IT services is critical to their success and whose expectations are reasonable	IT services that are critical to a customer's success and whose delivery meets customer expectations	Processes that produce the key services required by key customers	Suppliers who feed into the key processes

Table 4-2 shows how the matrix is divided into two major partitions. The left half represents the customer-oriented phases and the right half represents the supplier-oriented phases.

Table 4-2   Customer-Oriented and Supplier-Oriented Phases

Key Customers	Key Services	Key Processes	Key Suppliers
Customer-oriented phases of the Customer/supplier matrix		Supplier-oriented phases of the Customer/supplier matrix	

Table 4-3 shows the two phases representing the human interaction phases. These are sometimes referred to as the external phases of the matrix.

Table 4-3   External Human Interaction Phases

Key Customers	Key Services	Key Processes	Key Suppliers
Human interaction phase			Human interaction phase

Table 4-4 shows the two nonpersonal phases of the matrix representing process, technology, and automation. These are sometimes referred to as the internal phases of the matrix.

Table 4-4   Internal Nonpersonal Phases

Key Customers	Key Services	Key Processes	Key Suppliers
	Internal	Nonpersonal	
	Phases	of the	
	Customer/Supplier	Matrix	

A worthwhile enhancement to the basic customer/supplier matrix is shown in Table 4-5. Here we add service and process metrics. The service metrics are negotiated with key customers to measure the quality of the services delivered as seen through the eyes of the customer. The process metrics are negotiated with key suppliers to measure the quality of the input they provide into key processes.

Table 4-5   Customer/Supplier Matrix with Service and Process Metrics

Key Customers	Service Metrics	Key Services	Key Processes	Process Metrics	Key Suppliers
	Measure quality of services delivered			Measure quality of input suppliers provide	

The Four Cardinal Sins that Undermine Good Customer Service

During my many years directing and consulting on infrastructure activities, I often lead teams in search of how to improve the quality of good customer service. While these efforts produced many excellent suggestions on what to do right, including the use of the customer/supplier matrix, they also uncovered several common tendencies to avoid. I refer to these inadvertent transgressions as the four cardinal sins that undermine good customer service:

1. Presuming your customers are satisfied because they are not complaining.
   No news is good news? Nothing could be further from the truth when it comes to customer service. Study after study has shown—and my own personal experience has confirmed—that the overwhelming majority of customers do *not* complain about

poor service. They usually go elsewhere, find alternate means, complain to other users, or suffer silently in frustration. That is why proactively interviewing your key customers is so important.

2. Presuming that you have no customers.

   IT professionals working within their infrastructure sometimes feel they have no direct customers because they seldom interact with outside users. But they all have customers who are the direct recipients of their efforts. In the case of the infrastructure, many of these recipients are internal customers who work within IT, but they are customers nonetheless and need to be treated to the same high level of service as external customers.

   The same thinking applies to internal and external suppliers. Just because your direct supplier is internal to IT does not mean you are not entitled to the same high-quality input that an external supplier would be expected to provide. One final but important thought on this is that you may often be an internal customer and supplier at the same time and need to know who your customers and suppliers are at different stages of a process.

3. Measuring only what you want to measure to determine customer satisfaction.

   Measurement of customer satisfaction comes from asking key customers directly just how satisfied are they with the current level of service. In addition to that, service and quality measurements should be based on what a *customer* sees as service quality, not on what the *supplier* thinks.

4. Presuming that written SLAs will solve problems, prevent disputes, and ensure great customer service.

   A written SLA is only as effective as the collaboration with the customer that went into it. Effective SLAs need to be developed jointly with customer and support groups; they must be easily, reliably, and accurately measured; and they must be followed up with periodic customer meetings.

Summary

This chapter showed the importance of providing good customer service and the value of partnering with key suppliers. It presented how to identify key customers and the key services they use. I discussed how to negotiate realistic service levels and looked at two universal truths about customer service and expectations. Next I showed how to develop a customer/supplier matrix. Finally, I provided a brief discussion about the four cardinal sins that undermine good customer service.

Test Your Understanding

1. By the start of the 1990s, most users were still not very computer literate. (True or False)
2. Service providers typically need just a small number of key representative customers to serve as a barometer of good customer service. (True or False)
3. Which of the following is not a key element of good customer service?
   a. identifying your key customers
   b. identifying key complaints of key customers
   c. identifying key services of key customers
   d. identifying key processes that support key services
4. The decade in which the primary roles of IT and customer service began changing was the _____.
5. Develop reasons why the adage about the squeaky wheel always getting the grease is either good or bad for high-quality customer service.

Suggested Further Readings

1. *Managing the IT Service Process*; Computer Weekly Professional Services; Bruton, Noel; 2004
2. *Effective Computer User Support: How to Manage the IT Help Desk*; McGraw-Hill; Bruton, Noel; 1996
3. *Customer Liaison*; IT Infrastructure Library Services; BT Stationary Office Books (The Stationary Office of the Government of the United Kingdom); CCTA; 2001

CHAPTER 5

Ethics, Legislation, and Outsourcing

Introduction

This last chapter of Part One presents three separate but related elements of managing today's complex IT environments. These are the important aspects of ethics, legislation, and outsourcing, and they all involve highly intertwined human characteristics. The reason these are significant and timely is because each has come to influence how companies in general, and IT organizations in particular, are managed today.

The chapter begins with clear definitions of personal and business ethics. Next is a look at how several major corporations in the United States drastically compromised their business ethnics just after the turn of the new millennium. These breaches in ethical business behavior led to the prosecution and conviction of several chief executives and to the enactment of several pieces of far-reaching legislation.

The next segment of this chapter discusses some of these new laws that directly affect the accountability of corporate officers and their financial reporting; we also look at the IT systems that produce these reports. One of the results of these new ethical and legislative trends is that companies are considering the outsourcing of some or all of their IT processing. Finally, this chapter covers the implications of outsourcing.

Ethics

This section describes the important role business ethics plays in managing complex organizations today and how this role impacts the management and delivery of IT offerings. Before initiating any discussion on ethics, it is helpful to first distinguish between personal ethics and business ethics. The following two definitions provide this distinction.

Personal Ethics

Personal ethics are the set values an individual uses to influence and guide his or her personal behavior.

The personal ethics of an individual are usually developed early in one's life. The values of honesty, trust, responsibility, and character are typically instilled in a person during childhood. But the degree to which these values are reinforced and strengthened during the trying years of adolescence and early adulthood vary from person to person. In some cases these early life traits may not always win out over the temptations of power, greed, and control.

Business Ethics

Business ethics are the set values an individual uses to influence and guide his or her business behavior.

Business ethics tend to focus on the behaviors of an individual as it pertains to his or her work environment. The differences between personal and business ethics may be at once both subtle and far-reaching.

For example, individuals who are unfaithful to their spouses will have compromised their personal ethics of trust and honesty. The number of people affected by such discretions may be few but the intense impact of the actions may very well be devastating, life altering, and even life-threatening. But if these same individuals embezzle huge sums of money from a corporation, the impact on a personal level may be felt less while the number of people affected—employees, investors, stockholders—could be substantial. Table 5-1 summarizes some of the major differences between a breach of personal ethics and a breach of business ethics.

Table 5-1 Summary of Differences Between Breaches of Personal and Business Ethics

Category	Breach of Personal Ethics	Breach of Business Ethics
Relative number of people impacted	Few	Many
Nature of relationship to people impacted	Personal or family-oriented	Business or professionally-oriented
Type of legal offense	Civil	Criminal
Examples	Substance-abuse	Embezzlement
	Excessive gambling	Falsified accounting
	Infidelity	Tax fraud

Following the boom-and-bust dotcom craze of the first few years of the new millennium, a record number of major business scandals occurred in the United States. Tempted with over-inflated stock values, a lack of close government regulation, and a booming, optimistic economy, executives with questionable ethics took advantage of their situations. In 2002 alone, 28 Fortune 500 companies were found to be engaged in significant corporate scandals. The downfalls of the executives from these firms became very public in their coverage, devastating in their effect, and, in a few cases, stunning in their scope. As details of the criminal acts of these individuals emerged, it became apparent that corporate officers used a wide variety of accounting irregularities to enact their illegal schemes. The following list shows some of the more common of these uncommon practices:

- Overstating revenues
- Understating expenses
- Inflating profits
- Underreporting liabilities
- Misdirecting funds
- Artificially inflating stock prices
- Overstating the value of assets

Any number of fraudulent firms from this time period could be held up as instances of unethical business practices, but the following four serve as especially good examples: RadioShack, Tyco, WorldCom, and Enron.

The RadioShack Case

The RadioShack Corporation, headquartered in Fort Worth, Texas, offers consumer electronics through hundreds of its retail stores. In May 2005, David Edmondson became RadioShack's Chief Executive Officer (CEO) after having been groomed for the job for several years prior. The company did not fare well under Edmondson. Sales and stock prices both dropped. Employee morale was low, both for non-supervisory personnel whose employee stock purchase plan was cancelled and for managers who were subjected to a controversial 'Fix 1500' initiative in which the lowest-rated 1,500 store managers (out of 5,000) were on notice to improve or else.

Edmondson's final undoing was due less to his corporate performance and more to a personal lack of ethics. Police arrested Edmondson for driving under the influence in early 2006 at about the same time reporters learned he had misstated his academic record on his resume. Edmondson claimed he had earned degrees in theology and psychology from the Heartland Baptist Bible College when, in fact, school records showed he had attended only two semesters and was never even offered a course in psychology. On February 20, 2006, a company spokesperson announced that David Edmondson had resigned over questions raised by his falsified resume. The company struggled through all of 2006 attempting to recover its financial health.

Edmondson's civil indiscretions are small in comparison to the criminal behavior of other executives described in this section. Still, it points out how unethical behavior by even one key individual can have far-reaching effects on a company and its employees, including all those working in the IT department.

The Tyco Case

The scandal at Tyco International, a diversified manufacturing conglomerate whose products include toys, plastics, and household goods, was far more significant than that experienced by RadioShack and eventually led to criminal prosecutions. CEO L. Dennis Kozlowski and Chief Financial Officer (CFO) Mark Swartz had both enjoyed highly regarded business reputations before their fall from grace. In its January 14, 2002 edition, *Business Week* magazine even listed Kozlowski as one of the top 25 corporate managers of 2001. By September 2005 both were being led away in handcuffs to begin serving 8-1/3 to 25 years in prison.

On June 17, 2005, a Manhattan jury found Kozlowski and Swartz guilty of stealing more than US$150 million from Tyco. Specific counts included grand larceny, conspiracy, falsifying business records, and violating business law. Judge Michael J. Obus, who presided over the trial, ordered them to pay $134 million back to Tyco. In addition, the judge fined Kozlowski $70 million and Swartz $35 million.

The case came to represent the pervasive impression of greed and dishonesty that characterized many companies which enjoyed brief periods of prosperity through devious means. When some of Kozlowski's extravagances came to light during trial, they served only to fuel this notion. Kozlowski had purchased a shower curtain for $6,000 and had thrown a birthday party for his wife on an Italian island for $2 million— all paid for with Tyco funds.

The WorldCom Case

On November 10, 1997, WorldCom and MCI Communications merged to form the $37 billion company of MCI WorldCom, later renamed WorldCom. This was the largest corporate merger in U.S. history. The company's bankruptcy filing in 2003 arose from accounting scandals and was symptomatic of the dotcom and Internet excesses of the late 1990s.

After its merger in 1997, MCI WorldCom continued with more ambitious expansion plans. On October 5, 1999, it announced a $129 billion merger agreement with Sprint Corporation. This would have made MCI WorldCom the largest telecommunications company in the U.S., eclipsing AT&T for the first time. But the U.S. Department of Justice and the European Union (EU), fearing an unfair monopoly, applied sufficient pressure to block the deal. On July 13, 2000, the Board of Directors of both companies acted to terminate the merger; later that year, MCI WorldCom renamed itself WorldCom.

The failure of the merger with Sprint marked the beginning of a steady downturn of WorldCom's financial health. Its stock price was declining and banks were pressuring CEO Bernard Ebbers for coverage of extensive loans that had been based on over-inflated stock. The loans financed WorldCom expansions into non-technical areas, such as timber and yachting, that never proved to be profitable. As conditions worsened, Ebbers continued borrowing until finally WorldCom found itself in an almost untenable position. In April 2002, Ebbers was ousted as CEO and replaced with John Sidgmore of UUNet Technologies.

Beginning in 1999 and continuing through early 2002, the company used fraudulent accounting methods to hide its declining financial condition, presenting a misleading picture of financial growth and profitability. In addition to Ebbers, others who perpetuated the fraud include CFO David Sullivan, Controller David Myers, and the Director of General Accounting Buford Yates.

In June 2002, internal auditors discovered some $3.8 billion of fraudulent funds during a routine examination of capital expenditures and promptly notified the WorldCom board of directors. The board acted swiftly: Sullivan was fired, Myers resigned, and Arthur Anderson (WorldCom's external auditing firm) was replaced with KPMG. By the end of 2003, it was estimated that WorldCom's total assets had been inflated by almost $11 billion.

On July 21, 2002, WorldCom filed for Chapter 11 bankruptcy protection in the largest such filing in U.S. history. The company emerged from bankruptcy as MCI in 2004 with approximately $5.7 billion in debt and $6 billion in cash. On February 14, 2005, Verizon Communications bought MCI for $7.6 billion. In December 2005, Microsoft announced MCI would join them by providing Windows Live Messenger customers with voice over the Internet protocol (VoIP) service for calls around the world. This had been MCI's last totally new product, called MCI Web Calling, and has since been renamed Verizon Web Calling. It continues to be a promising product for future markets.

CEO Bernard Ebbers was found guilty on March 15, 2005, of all charges and he was convicted of fraud, conspiracy, and filing false documents with regulators. He was sentenced to 25 years in prison. He began serving his sentence on September 26, 2006, in Yazoo City, Mississippi. The other executives who conspired with Ebbers all pled guilty to various charges and were given slightly reduced sentences.

There are many lessons to be learned from this case, but two elements especially stand out:

1. The fraudulent accounting was found during a routine examination of company records, indicating a fair degree of arrogance on the part of the conspirators as little was done to conceal the irregularities.
2. It marked a rare instance of a reputable external accounting firm being involved, at least peripherally, with suspicious activities. But the tarnishing of Arthur Anderson's reputation was only beginning (as we will see in the next section).

The Enron Case

The most famous case of corporate fraud during this era was that of the Enron Energy Corporation headquartered in Houston, Texas. The fraud put both Enron and its external auditing firm out of business. Never before in U.S. business have two major corporations fallen more deeply or more quickly. This case epitomizes how severe the consequences can become as a result of unethical business practices.

Enron enjoyed profitable growth and a sterling reputation during the late 1990s. It pioneered and marketed the energy commodities business involving the buying and selling of natural gas, water and waste water, communication bandwidths, and electrical generation and distribution, among others. *Fortune* magazine named Enron "America's Most Innovative Company" for six consecutive years from 1996 to 2001. It was on *Fortune's* list of the "100 Best Companies to Work for in America" in 2000.

By 2001, however, Enron's global reputation was becoming undermined by persistent rumors of bribery and strong-armed political tactics to secure contracts in Central America, South America, Africa, and the Philippines. In July 2001, Enron admitted to incurring a $102 million loss; in November of the same year, Enron admitted to hiding hundreds of millions more. By the end of 2001 the financial collapse of Enron was in full effect and its stock price plummeted to less than one dollar per share.

In 2002, a complex network of suspicious offshore partnerships and questionable accounting practices surfaced. The mastermind behind these activities was Enron CFO Andrew Fastow. He was indicted on November 1, 2002, by a federal grand jury in Houston on 78 counts, including fraud, money laundering and conspiracy. He and his wife, Lea Fastow, Enron's former assistant treasurer, accepted a plea agreement on January 14, 2004. Andrew Fastow agreed to serve a 10-year prison sentence and pay $23.8 million in fines and his wife agreed to a five-month prison sentence. In exchange for their pleas, both would testify against other Enron corporate officers.

Federal prosecutors issued indictments against dozens of Enron executives. Key among these were Kenneth Lay, the former Chairman of the Board and CEO and Jeffrey Skilling, former CEO and Chief Operating Officer (COO). They were served in July 2004 with a 53-count, 63-page indictment covering a broad range of financial crimes. Among these were bank fraud, making false statements to banks and auditors, securities fraud, wire fraud, money laundering, conspiracy, and insider trading.

Lay pled not guilty to his 11 criminal charges, claiming he had been misled by those around him. His wife, Linda Lay, also claimed innocence to a bizarre set of associated circumstances. On November 28, 2001, Linda Lay sold approximately 500,000 shares of her Enron stock (when its value was still substantial) some 15 minutes before news was made public that Enron was collapsing, at which time the stock price plummeted to less than one dollar per share.

After a highly visible and contentious trial of Lay and Skilling, the jury returned its verdicts on May 25, 2006. Skilling was convicted on 19 of 28 counts of securities fraud and wire fraud and was acquitted on the remaining nine, including insider trading. He was sentenced to 24 years, 4 months in prison, which he began serving on October 23, 2006. Skilling was also ordered to pay $26 million of his own money to the Enron pension. Kenneth Lay was convicted of all six counts of securities and wire fraud and sentenced to 45 years in prison. On July 5, 2006, he died at age 64 after suffering a heart attack the day before.

Corporate officers from Enron were not the only ones to suffer the consequences of the scandal. On June 15, 2002, Arthur Andersen was convicted of obstruction of justice for shredding documents related to its audit of Enron. On May 31, 2005, the Supreme Court of the United States unanimously overturned Andersen's conviction due to flaws in the jury obstructions. Despite this ruling, it is highly unlikely Andersen will ever return as a viable business.

Arthur Andersen was founded in 1913 and enjoyed a highly regard reputation for most of its history. But the firm lost nearly all of its clients after its Enron indictment and there were more than 100 civil suits brought against it related to its audits of Enron and other companies, including WorldCom. From a peak of 28,000 employees in the United States and 85,000 worldwide, the firm now employs roughly 200 people, most of whom are based in Chicago and still handle the various lawsuits. Andersen was considered one of the Big Five large international accounting firms (as listed below); with Andersen's absence, this list has since been culled to Big Four.

- Arthur Andersen
- Deloitte & Touche
- Ernst & Young
- KPMG
- PricewaterhouseCoopers

Real Life Experience—Moths Drawn Too Close to the Flame

In 2000, I briefly worked for a small start-up consulting firm during the height of the dotcom boom. To raise money for expansion, the owners appealed to venture capitalists and these venture capitalists were all too happy to oblige. Like moths attracted to a flame, these investors succumbed to the temptation of quick-and-easy fortune by sinking tens of millions of U.S. dollars into the venture. Unfortunately, the company expanded too fast and based much of their future revenue on dotcom companies that failed. The consulting firm was out of business within 18 months, leaving the investors scorched by the flame.

What made the Enron scandal particularly galling to its victims and its observers was that only a few months prior to Enron's collapse, corporate officers assured employees that their stock options, their benefits, and their pensions were all safe and secure. Many employees were tempted to pull their life savings out of what they felt was a failing investment. But the convincing words of Kenneth Lay and the employees' own misplaced loyalty to their company dissuaded them from doing so. In the end, thousands of employees lost most, if not all, of their hard-earned savings.

Legislation

In response to these various accounting scandals and other concerns of the consuming public, the U.S. Congress and state legislators passed a series of laws to place greater governance on corporations. Lawmakers passed dozens of bills to address these concerns and three of these laws (see Table 5-2) had particular impact on IT organizations: The Sarbanes-Oxley Act, the Graham-Leach-Bliley Act, and California Senate Bill 1386.

Table 5-2 Key Legislation Passed in Response to Major Corporate Scandals

Name of Law	Year Enacted	Key Provisions
Sarbanes-Oxley Act	2002	CEOs and CFOs certify financial reports
Graham-Leach-Bliley Act	1999	Regulates how firms share personal data
California Senate Bill 1386	2002	Discloses security breaches to NPI

Sarbanes-Oxley Act

If there is one single act of U.S. legislation that is known for its direct response to the various scandals of the early 21st century, it is the Sarbanes-Oxley Act. The name comes from the sponsors of the legislation, Senator Paul Sarbanes (Democrat-Maryland) and Representative Michael G. Oxley (Republican-Ohio). The law is also known by its longer name, The Public Company Accounting Reform and Investor Protection Act of 2002, or by its more common shorter name of SOX. The numerous corporate scandals caused a decline of public trust in accounting and reporting practices; SOX was intended to restore that trust. The Enron scandal was not the only impetus behind this law, but it certainly served as its catalyst. The law passed overwhelmingly on July 30, 2002, with a House vote of 423 to 3 and a Senate vote of 99 to 0.

The Act contains 11 titles, or sections, ranging from additional corporate board responsibilities to criminal penalties and it requires the Securities and Exchange Commission (SEC) to implement rulings on requirements to comply with the new law. The following list details some of the other major provisions of SOX.

- Creation of a Public Company Accounting Oversight Board (PCAOB)
- Stronger penalties for fraud
- Public companies cannot make loans to management
- Report more information to the public
- Maintain stronger independence from external auditors
- Report on and have audited financial reporting controls

Two of the more controversial parts of SOX are sections 302 and 404.

Section 302 mandates that companies establish and maintain a set of internal procedures to ensure accurate financial reporting. The signing officers must certify that such controls are in existence and are being used, and within 90 days of the signing, they must certify that they have evaluated the effectiveness of the controls.

Section 404 requires corporate officers to report their conclusions in the annual Exchange Act report about the effectiveness of their internal financial reporting controls. Failure of the controls being effective, or failure of the officers to report on the controls, could result in criminal prosecution. For many companies, a key concern is the cost of updating information systems to comply with the control and reporting requirements. Systems involving document management, access to financial data, or long-term data storage must now provide auditing capabilities which were never designed into the original systems.

The financial reporting processes of most companies are driven by IT systems, and the Chief Information Officer (CIO) is responsible for the security, accuracy, and reliability of the systems that manage and report on financial data. Systems such as enterprise resource planning (ERP) and customer relationship management (CRM) are deeply integrated with the processing and reporting of financial data. As such, they are intertwined with the overall financial reporting process and fall under the requirement of compliance with SOX. Many companies now require not only the CEO and CFO to sign-off on SOX compliance reports, but CIOs as well. Several CIOs are also asking subordinate managers to sign off on SOX reports. Many of the processes discussed in this book—such as availability, production acceptance and security—have direct bearing on SOX compliance.

Other countries have now begun instituting SOX-like legislation to prevent the type of accounting scandals experienced in the United States. For example, CSOX is the Canadian version of SOX. In line with Sarbanes-Oxley, South Korea has begun debating the establishment a separate, regulatory body similar to the PCAOB (Public Company Accounting Oversight Board). Foreign countries doing business with American companies have learned it is prudent to be both knowledgeable and compliant with SOX provisions.

Graham-Leach-Bliley Act

The Graham-Leach-Bliley Act, also known as the Financial Modernization Act, regulates the sharing of personal information about individuals who are doing business with financial institutions. The law requires financial companies to inform their customers about the company's privacy policies and practices, especially as it relates to non-public information (NPI). Based on these policies and practices, customers can then decide whether or not they want to do business with the company.

NPI

NPI stands for non-public information and pertains to the private, personal information of an individual not readily available in public records. Customers typically disclose such information to private or public companies to transact business. Examples of NPI are social security numbers, unlisted telephone numbers, and credit card account numbers.

The law also gives consumers additional control over how financial institutions will use and share the personal information of consumers. It does this by requiring a financial company to offer consumers an 'opt-out' clause. This clause empowers consumers to choose whether or not they want to have their personal information shared with other companies. If consumers elect to exercise their opt-out clause, the financial institution with whom they are doing business cannot share their personal information with any other organization.

California Senate Bill 1386

California Senate Bill 1386 is also known as California SB 1386. It requires that any business, individual, or state agency conducting business in the state of California disclose any breaches of security of computerized NPI to all individuals with whom they conduct business. Because of the large numbers of companies that process and store the NPI of customers, this law has far-reaching effects. It also places a high premium on the security processes used by IT to ensure the likelihood of such a breach is kept to an absolute minimum. The law also means information systems must be readily able to contact all customers on a moment's notice should even a single compromise of NPI occur.

If a bank, for example, unintentionally discloses a customer's credit card number, the bank must disclose to all of its customers the nature of the security breach, how it happened, the extent of exposure, and what is being done to prevent its reoccurrence. This very scenario happened to Wells Fargo bank in 2003. Sensitive customer information was put at risk when an employee's laptop on which it resided was stolen. The CEO of the bank sent out a letter to the bank's tens of thousands of customers explaining what happened, how it happened, and what was being done to prevent it from happening again.

Outsourcing

Because of this increased accountability of corporate executives and their IT reporting systems, many organizations consider outsourcing some or all of their IT functions. There certainly are other factors that come in to play when making an IT outsourcing decision. Chief among these are the overall cost savings and other benefits to be realized versus some of the drawbacks to outsourcing. The following list describes some of the more common factors. But the additional responsibilities of legislation, such as those mandated by Sarbanes-Oxley, cause many a CEO to look seriously at outsourcing their IT environments.

- Overall cost savings
- Scalability of resources
- Potential loss of control
- Total cost of maintaining an outsourcing agreement
- Credibility and experience of outsourcer
- Possible conflicts of priority
- Geographic and time-zone differences
- Language barriers
- Cultural clashes

The effects of outsourcing an IT organization varies from company to company. The effects also depend on whether all or only parts of the IT department are outsourced. Many companies today outsource their call centers or service desks to locations such as India or the Philippines. Other companies keep service-oriented functions (such as call centers) but outsource programming or web development to countries such as Vietnam or South Korea.

Regardless of how much of an IT organization is outsourced, there remain benefits of maintaining high ethical standards. When evaluating which particular outsourcer to use, many companies today include compliance to SOX-like legislation involving corporate governance as part of the selection criteria. One key lesson the recent business scandals taught very well was that violating basic business ethics seems to always result in far greater long-term losses than whatever short-term gains they may have provided.

Summary

This chapter described the significance and the relationships of ethics, legislation, and outsourcing in managing today's complex IT environments. The chapter offered definitions of personal and business ethics and described how the lack of them led to the undoing of several executives and the corporations they ran. Further discussions showed how these breaches of corporate ethics led to the enactment of several pieces of far-reaching legislation.

The second segment of this chapter explained some of these new laws and how they impact the accountability of corporate officers and of the reporting of their company's finances. This additional accountability and governance directly affects the IT organization, its managers, and the systems that produce the financial reports. The chapter concluded with the topic of outsourcing and how it is sometimes considered as a response to these new laws of accountability.

Test Your Understanding

1. The differences between personal and business ethics are both subtle and far-reaching. (True or False)
2. CIOs play only a very small role in ensuring compliance to the Sarbanes-Oxley Act. (True or False)
3. Corporate business scandals of U.S. companies between 2002 and 2007:
    a. were neither civil nor criminal in nature
    b. were only civil in nature
    c. were only criminal in nature
    d. were both civil and criminal in nature
4. The Graham-Leach-Bliley Act regulates the sharing of _____ .
5. What are some of the advantages and disadvantages of outsourcing?

Suggested Further Readings

1. http://en.wikipedia.org/wiki/Accounting_scandals
2. http://en.wikipedia.org/wiki/RadioShack
3. www.usatoday.com/money/industries/manufacturing/2005-06-17-tyco-timeline_x.htm
4. www.cheatingculture.com/tyco.htm
5. www.usatoday.com/money/industries/manufacturing/2005-06-17-tyco-timeline_x.htm
6. http://money.cnn.com/2005/09/19/news/newsmakers/kozlowski_sentence/
7. http://en.wikipedia.org/wiki/Worldcom
8. http://en.wikipedia.org/wiki/Enron
9. http://en.wikipedia.org/wiki/Sarbanes_oxley
10. www.consumerprivacyguide.org/law/glb.shtml

CHAPTER 6

Comparison to ITIL Processes

Introduction

Part Two of this book presents 12 key infrastructure processes used in IT systems management. There is a separate chapter dedicated to each process. Each chapter contains a formal definition of the process, desirable traits for a process owner, steps on how to develop and implement the process, and worksheets to use in evaluating the quality of each process.

But in today's environment, no discussion of IT infrastructure processes is complete without mention of the Information Technology Infrastructure Library (ITIL). The first edition of *IT Systems Management* offered practical, proven practices on how to improve infrastructure processes. It was based on my many years of managing IT infrastructures in a variety of environments. I wrote about what I knew and what I had experienced. And this is what I continue to emphasize in this second edition.

Several of the professional reviewers who critiqued the first edition commented on how closely the book aligned itself with the IT Infrastructure Library (ITIL). At that time, I had little knowledge of what ITIL was and even less on the specifics about what it entailed. The version of ITIL available at the time was not widely used in the United States until 2002, three years after I started work on the first edition and a year after it was first published.

As a result of the first edition being compared to ITIL, I decided to learn all about this new framework (which really wasn't so new after all).

I wanted to compare the processes I had written about to the ITIL processes, and I wanted to know to what degree the similarities existed. That is the primary purpose of this chapter: to compare and contrast the processes in this book with those of ITIL. We will see that there are many similarities and a few noteworthy differences. ITIL has become the de facto world standard for best practices of IT infrastructure processes and warrants a brief summary here of its framework.

My education about this new framework led me to becoming certified as an ITIL practitioner and instructor, heading up several ITIL implementations, speaking on ITIL at various conferences and seminars around the world, and certifying over 1000 IT professionals on the fundamentals of the ITIL framework. Still, the emphasis of this book is on practical implementation and management of what I consider key infrastructure processes, and we will see that while they are close to ITIL, they are not identical.

This chapter begins with some of the developments that led to ITIL and a discussion of the cornerstone of ITIL: IT service management. This is followed with a brief look at the history of ITIL. We then describe the six service delivery processes of ITIL followed by its six service support processes (this includes the service desk function). Next we compare and contrast the ITIL processes in this chapter with those presented in Part Two. The chapter closes with descriptions of some of the myths surrounding the implementation of the ITIL framework based on my experiences as an ITIL consultant and instructor.

Developments Leading Up To ITIL

Over the past 25 years, IT managers in the United States have sponsored a number of initiatives to improve the overall efficiency of their infrastructures. Some of these efforts ended almost as soon as they started, leading some detractors to label them as 'the management fad of the month'. Initiatives that fell into this category included:

- Quality circles
- Focus groups
- Work simplification programs

Other initiatives geared themselves toward the more effective management of personnel. This included:

- Mentoring programs
- Employee empowerment
- Cross-training
- Rotation of staff assignments

While these initiatives were worthwhile and effective, they required ongoing executive support to sustain their existence. Unfortunately, when executive turnover occurred (as it inevitably does), many of these personal development initiatives turned over as well.

In the late 1980s and early 1990s, a new series of process-management initiatives took hold in American industry. Fueled by intense foreign competition, these American initiatives focused on various methods to improve the quality of products and services. Total quality management, continuous process improvement, statistical process controls, and the Malcolm Baldrige National Quality Award were part of a movement to improve the quality of American output in the global economy. Only remnants of these programs are still evident today, with the Six Sigma defect reduction initiative the one notable exception.

What this tells us is that process-improvement programs are easy to start, difficult to sustain, and prone to very short life cycles. So what is it about ITIL that has made it last longer than the others? One of the primary reasons for the longevity of ITIL is that it is built on a foundation of IT service management. The next section describes the basics of IT service management, including the evolution of IT into a more service-oriented organization and the three primary objectives of IT service management.

IT Service Management

When IT professionals began developing the original ITIL framework, they quickly realized that IT service management was the common link on which the numerous best practices of IT infrastructure management was based. Service management in general focuses the quality of products and services on the reasonable expectations of customers. When applied to an IT environment, service management focuses the quality of its IT services on the reasonable business expectations of its customers and end-users.

IT Service Management (ITSM) bridges the gap between the business goals of a company and the technology used to accomplish those goals. It sets up formalized and regular communications channels to allow requirements, requests, and difficulties to be expressed and dealt with. This serves the very important function of ensuring IT aims are correctly aligned to the business.

This notion of IT service management was not always prevalent within IT. In fact, the first decade or so of the IT industry had little or no emphasis on service management. Eventually, IT environments evolved from being totally technical entities into service-oriented organizations, as was described in Chapter 4, "Customer Service."

This evolution to a service-oriented IT organization leads us to the three primary objectives of IT service management:

1. To ensure that the organization's business needs are supported by high-quality, cost-effective, value-adding IT services
2. To improve the quality of IT service provision
3. To reduce the long-term cost of IT service provision

These objectives were very much in the minds of the developers of the original version of ITIL. The next section describes how ITIL came into existence and led to world-wide acceptance of its framework.

The Origins of ITIL

ITIL began in Great Britain in the mid-1980s. The British government saw that its vast bureaucracy was depending more and more on computers to process the huge amounts of numeric and text data required of its various agencies. It also realized that the more dependent they became on computers, the poorer the job they were doing at providing reliable, responsive service to its users.

The British government was not the first to notice that users were not always satisfied with the quality of IT services they were receiving. The dominant supplier of computer hardware and software at the time was the International Business Machines Corporation (IBM). IBM attempted to address this problem in part with a series of books in 1981 that came to known as the IBM Yellow Books. They touched on issues of infrastructure performance, programming standards, and service levels. But the books never really caught on in the United States and were barely even heard of in Europe, although some of the infrastructure issues were similar to what ITIL would eventually address.

In 1986, the British government authorized its Centralized Telecommunications and Computing Agency (CTCA) to sponsor a program to promote improved management of IT services. The CTCA put out a call for IT experts from the public, private, and academic sectors to come forward and establish a framework of best practices for managing the ever-expanding IT environment. Approximately 40 individuals from the public sector of government, the private sector of business, and the academia sector participated in the effort. In 1989, they completed a set of 42 books that comprised the initial set of books covering the first version of ITIL.

In 1991, a user forum for ITIL was formed in the Netherlands and called the Information Technology Service Management Forum (itSMF). The itSMF logo is now recognized world-wide, and the forum acts as a clearinghouse and sounding board for discussions and suggestions on how to implement and improve ITIL. In 1997, the first U.S. chapter of itSMF was started in Dallas, Texas. There are hundreds of itSMF chapters in existence around the world today.

By 1995, the total number of ITIL books had grown to more than 60 and that volume was becoming more than a bit unwieldy. Based on input from the itSMF, work began in 1998 on a second, more condensed version of ITIL known as version 2 (V2). This reduced the list of available books to the following seven books, presented herein the order they were published:

1. *Service Support*
2. *Service Delivery*
3. *Security Management*
4. *Application Management*
5. *ICT* Infrastructure Management*
6. *Planning to Implement Service Management*
7. *The Business Perspective*

---

* ICT is Information and Communications Technology

The two books that proved to be most beneficial to IT infrastructure managers were those of *Service Delivery* and *Service Support*. Perhaps coincidentally, also in 1998, the itSMF issued its first version of the widely popular Pocket Guide, which condensed the basic elements of the *Service Delivery* and *Service Support* books to a pocket-sized booklet of only 70 pages.

The Service Delivery and Service Support books comprise the bulk of the infrastructure processes on which certifications are based (along with a small portion from Security Management). Table 6-1 lists the processes associated with each of these two books.

Table 6-1   Service Delivery and Service Support Processes

Service Delivery	Service Support
Service level management	Service desk°°
Financial management for IT services	Incident management
Capacity management	Problem management
Availability management	Configuration management
IT service continuity management	Change management
Security management°	Release management

° Part of a separate book on Security Management but included in certification exams.
°° Considered by ITIL to be a function, not a process, but closely related to Service Support

In 2000, several ITIL-related events occured. In the United Kingdom, the CCTA merged into the Office of Government Commerce, reinforcing the notion that technology should serve business rather than the other way around. Microsoft became one of the first American companies to embrace ITIL and developed an operations architecture on top of it called the Microsoft Operations Framework (MOF). MOF added the roles of teams and risk discipline to the implementation of ITIL. And the first book of ITIL V2 was published: Service Support.

In 2001, the *Service Delivery* and *Security Management* books of ITIL V2 were published with the other four books following by 2002. A new version 3 (V3) of ITIL became available in June 2007. As was the case with ITIL V2, the itSMF provided many practical suggestions from ITIL users for the development of V3. Hundreds of companies from around the world that either utilize the ITIL framework or provide products and services in support of it also contributed greatly to V3.

The most significant change between ITIL V2 and V3 is the introduction of the concept of a *Service Lifecycle*. This notion describes an IT service as having five distinct stages throughout its life:

- Service strategy
- Service design
- Service transition
- Service operation
- Continual service improvement.

The six processes of V2 service delivery are included in the V3 lifecycle stages of service strategy and service design, along with four new processes. The six processes of V2 service support are included in the V3 lifecycle stages of service transition and service operation, along with three new processes and three new functions. Table 6-2 lists a timeline of major events in the evolution of ITIL.

Table 6-2 Timeline of Major Events in Evolution of ITIL

Year	Event
1981	IBM Yellow Books published
1986	Work begins on ITIL version 1 (V1)
1989	First books of ITIL V1 published
1991	Service Management Forum formed
1995	itSMF issues ITIL Pocket Guide
1997	First chapter of itSMF in United States
1998	Work begins on ITIL version 2 (V2)
2000	CCTA merges into OGC
2000	Microsoft creates MOF to work with ITIL
2000	ITIL V2 Service Support book published
2001	ITIL V2 Service Delivery book published
2001	ITIL V2 Security book published
2002	ITIL V2 remaining ITIL books published

Table 6-2   Timeline of Major Events in Evolution of ITIL Continued

Year	Event
2005	ISO 2000 published, based on ITIL
2005	Work begins on ITIL version 3 (V3)
2007	ITIL V3 books published
2008	Microsoft releases MOF version 4 (V4)

The use of the ITIL framework was primarily confined to European nations up through the late 1990s. ITIL did not start gaining acceptance (and later prominence) in the United States until just after the turn of the new century. There were several reasons for the timing of this increased American interest in ITIL, including:

- **Expanded use of the Internet**. Companies were expanding their e-commerce over the Internet and required best practices for infrastructure management.

- **Legislation**. New laws in response to accounting scandals, such as Sarbanes Oxley (SOX), mandated documented controls and processes on how data was being managed.

- **9/11**. After the tragedy of the New York World Trade Center on September 11, 2001, many companies wanted to invest in proven, world-class processes to improve the management and protection of their infrastructures.

- **Globalization**. American companies were starting to set up data centers in Europe and vice versa; infrastructure managers of American companies noticed the superior use of ITIL processes in data centers of their European counterparts and became interested.

Although ITIL has experienced a number of refinements over the years, it remains at its roots a set of publications that provides guidance for service management. It has emerged as the international de facto standard framework of best practices for IT service management. It is a public domain framework. It is not proprietary. You have to pay for the publications, but you do not have to pay to use them; you can apply them freely in your organization. It is a best-practice framework, and that means it is not an academic or theoretical view of how to manage IT services; it is actually culled from practitioners out in the field.

Quality Approach and Standards

ITIL focuses on providing high-quality services and supports quality systems such as ISO 9000, total quality frameworks such as the European Framework for Quality Management (EFQM), and major quality recognition programs such as the Malcolm Baldrige National Quality Award (MBNQA). The British Standards Institute (BSI) published *A Code of Practice for IT Service Management* (PD0005), which was based on ITIL. There is now a standard BS15000 in support of IT service management. The International Standards Organization (ISO) published in December 2005 a standard for IT Service Management, ISO20000, that is based heavily on the ITIL processes.

ITIL constitutes codes of practice for quality management of IT services and infrastructure processes in which the services are matched to business needs. There are a number a unique characteristics and benefits of ITIL, including:

- **Best practice guidance**. ITIL was written by practitioners, for practitioners. It is not an academic or theoretical framework of how IT processes should be or could be; it is a methodology of what works in actual practice derived from what practitioners around the world have indicated truly works.

- **Non-proprietary**. ITIL is not a single vendor view of IT processes. Although you must purchase the publications to own them, you can apply ITIL in your organization without paying a fee to use it.

- **Comprehensive**. The value of IT service management processes is in their interaction and interdependence. Rather than focusing on just one process domain, ITIL captures all of the essential service support and services delivery processes and integrates them to work together. Infrastructure professionals may call them something else, and in all likelihood a version of some of the ITIL Service Management processes are operating in their organizations, whether they recognize them or not.

- **Consistent terminology**. One of the greatest benefits of ITIL is that it uses consistent terminology throughout its implementation across all of the Service Management processes. It gives everyone a common vernacular for terms of reference. This is a huge advantage, especially in large organizations where various individuals may refer to something as an incident, error, issue, problem, event, or fault—and they think they are all talking about the same thing but they are actually referring to different entities.

Criteria to Differentiate Infrastructure Processes

Now that we have learned some of the background of ITIL, it is time to compare its processes to those covered here in *IT Systems Management*. As mentioned previously, the processes here differ slightly from the ITIL framework because they are based on my personal application of key infrastructure processes and because ITIL did not gain prominence in the United States until after the turn of the new century.

There are far more similarities than differences between the *IT Systems Management* processes and those of ITIL. One of these differences is the manner in which processes are categorized as either strategic or tactical. Table 6-3 shows the criteria I use to make this distinction and the infrastructure processes that pertain to each of these two groupings. In comparison, Table 6-4 shows the criteria ITIL uses to distinguish its two groupings of processes, how this criteria is used, and the processes that pertain to each grouping. It is worth noting that ITIL uses the term 'tactical' to describe what many may refer to as strategic, and it uses the term 'operational' to describe what some may refer to as tactical. These terms should not be confused when used among the various sets of processes. An easy way to distinguish the groupings is to think of one group as always being 'long-term' in nature and the other as always being 'short-term'.

There are other notable similarities and differences between these two tables. Aside from the difference in terms, the criteria used to distinguish the two groupings is very similar. The total number of processes in both groups is identical at 12. The number of processes is evenly divided six-to-six with the ITIL criteria and closely divided five-to-seven with the *IT Systems Management* criteria. The specific processes named in each grouping are identical for only seven of the 12 processes in each group. But as we will see in the next section, even in this regard there are more similarities than differences.

Table 6-3   Differentiating Processes Using IT Systems Management Criteria

Strategic Process Characteristics	Tactical Process Characteristics
1 Long range in nature	1 Short range in nature
2 Two- to three-year focus	2 Day-to-day focus
3 Supports long-term business goals	3 Supports short-term SLAs
4 May require months to produce results	4 Should produce results within a few days or weeks
5 May require new budget approvals to implement	5 Should already be in the existing budget
Applicable Strategic Processes	**Applicable Tactical Processes**
1 Production acceptance	1 Availability management
2 Capacity planning	2 Performance and tuning
3 Strategic security	3 Change management
4 Business continuity	4 Problem management
5 Facilities management	5 Storage management
	6 Network management
	7 Configuration management

Table 6-4   Differentiating Processes Using ITIL Criteria

Tactical Process Characteristics	Operational Process Characteristics
1 Service delivery	1 Service support
2 Customer-facing	2 User-facing
3 Weeks-to-months planning	3 Hours-to-days planning
4 Management-oriented	4 End-user-oriented
5 Budget likely a factor	5 Budget not likely a factor
Applicable Tactical Processes	**Applicable Operational Processes**
1 Service level management	1 Service desk **
2 Financial management for IT services	2 Incident management
3 Capacity management	3 Problem management

Table 6-4 Differentiating Processes Using ITIL Criteria Continued

Applicable Tactical Processes	Applicable Operational Processes
4 Availability management	4 Configuration management
5 IT service continuity management	5 Change management
6 Security management°	6 Release management

° Part of a separate book on Security Management but included in certification exams.
°° Considered by ITIL to be a function, not a process, but closely related to Service Support

Comparison of Infrastructure Processes

Table 6-5 shows how the 12 processes in *IT Systems Management* compare to the 12 processes of the ITIL framework. As previously noted, ITIL treats the service desk as a function rather than a process but includes it with the other 11 processes because of its key role of integration with many of the other processes. For simplicity, I refer to the ITIL service desk as one of the 12 ITIL processes.

As shown in Table 6-5, there are far more similarities than differences. Of the 12 processes covered here in *IT Systems Management*, only three of them do not directly correspond to ITIL: storage management, network management, and facilities management. Most anyone who has ever managed a data center will attest to the importance of these processes, which is why they are included in both editions of this book.

Some of the processes take on different names or forms in ITIL. For example, performance and tuning is a separate process here but is part of capacity management within the ITIL framework. Similarly, production acceptance in this book is part of release management in ITIL.

Table 6-5 Comparison of Processes in IT Systems Management to Those of ITIL

No.	*IT Systems Management* Processes	Corresponding ITIL Processes
1	Availability management	Availability management
2	Performance and tuning	(Part of capacity management)
3	Production acceptance	(Part of release management)
4	Change management	Change management

No.	*IT Systems Management* Processes	Corresponding ITIL Processes
5	Problem management	Problem management
6	Storage management	(Not specifically covered by ITIL)
7	Network management	(Not specifically covered by ITIL)
8	Configuration management	Configuration management
9	Capacity planning	Capacity management
10	Strategic security	Security management
11	Business continuity	IT service continuity
12	Facilities management	(Not specifically covered by ITIL)

In a similar manner, Table 6-6 shows how the 12 ITIL processes compare to the 12 of *IT Systems Management*. As expected, there are more processes that are similar than there are processes that are different. The only two ITIL processes not covered in this book are service level management and financial management for IT services. Three other ITIL processes are addressed in one way or another with processes not identically named. These are the service desk and incident management (covered under problem management) and release management (covered under production acceptance).

Table 6-6   Comparison of ITIL Processes to Those in Part Two

No.	ITIL Processes	Corresponding *IT Systems Management* Processes
1	Service desk	Availability management
2	Performance and tuning	(Covered under problem management)
3	Incident management	(Covered under problem management)
4	Configuration management	Configuration management
5	Change management	Change management
6	Release management	(Covered under production acceptance)
7	Service level management	(Not specifically covered here)
8	Financial management for IT services	(Not specifically covered here)
9	Capacity management	Capacity planning
10	Availability management	Availability management
11	IT service continuity	Business continuity
12	Security management	Strategic security

Ten Common Myths Concerning the Implementation of ITIL

During the past several years I have certified more than 200 IT professionals on the fundamentals of ITIL. Before and during that time I have also offered consulting services to dozens of clients who wanted to implement some or all of the ITIL processes. These experiences have offered me the opportunity to witness first-hand a number of myths about the implementation of ITIL. This section describes 10 common myths about implementing ITIL that I have encountered with organizations in recent years:

1. You must implement all ITIL or no ITIL at all
2. ITIL is based on infrastructure management principles
3. ITIL applies mostly to data center operations
4. Everyone needs to be trained on ITIL fundamentals
5. Full understanding of ITIL requires purchase of library
6. ITIL processes should be implemented only one at a time
7. ITIL provides detailed templates for implementation
8. ITIL framework applies only to large shops
9. ITIL recommends tools to use for implementation
10. There is little need to understand ITIL origins

Real Life Experience—Credit Given When Credit Is Due

One of the reviewers of the first edition of this book gave it four stars out of five. The reviewer indicated that part of the reason he did not give the full five stars was because I did not give any credit for basing the book on the ITIL framework. The reviewer perhaps was not aware that when I wrote the first edition, I was not familiar with the ITIL set of best practices for infrastructure processes. Still, I was flattered that the reviewer thought my best-selling first edition was so closely aligned to such a well-founded framework.

Myth #1: You Must Implement All ITIL or No ITIL at All

Many individuals who first learn of the ITIL set of processes believe that all 10 of them, in addition to the function of the service desk, need to be implemented at the same time in order to gain the full benefit of the framework. This is not only false, it is not even recommended by many of those who specialize in assisting with ITIL implementations. The ITIL framework is an extensive series of IT management best practices, and few believe that it can be effectively implemented all at the same time. While it is true that all of the processes interact and integrate well with each other and should be designed with that in mind, many shops implement only what they need at the outset to ensure a successful early win.

Myth #2: ITIL is Based on Infrastructure Management Principles

Because ITIL is a library of books describing best management practices for infrastructure processes, many erroneously believe that ITIL is based primarily on the principles of sound infrastructure management. Responsible IT management certainly plays an important role when ITIL processes are being designed and implemented. But in fact, ITIL is based primarily on the principles of IT service management. The business value of basing IT support and delivery on service management may seem obvious today. But that was not the case 15-20 years ago, when originators developed the first version of ITIL.

The premise of having IT managers partner with customers to solve *their* business problems, and to offer them service levels that *they* negotiated and agreed to with IT representatives, was a fairly radical notion at the time. Not everyone is aware that this was the real basis for the development of the IT Infrastructure Library (ITIL).

Myth #3: ITIL Applies Mostly to Data Center Operations

The fact that ITIL is involved with infrastructure processes and the management of them leads some to presume that ITIL pertains primarily to data center operations. In reality, ITIL pertains to all areas of IT in which deliverables are provided. This includes the service desk, database administration, applications deployment, hardware upgrades, and network provisions. ITIL also goes far beyond the data center in terms of SLAs and financial management. Service-level management involves regular meetings and sometimes extensive negotiations between customers and the service-level manager. In many shops, the service-level manager is not even a member of the data center staff but instead may be on staff to the CIO.

Myth #4: Everyone Needs to be Trained on ITIL Fundamentals

This myth applies to some infrastructure managers and several of the engineers reporting to them. IT professionals occasionally feel that to take advantage of the benefits of ITIL, all personnel must be trained on its fundamentals. I know of some IT organizations that have implemented the ITIL framework very successfully with only a handful of their staff formally trained on ITIL fundamentals. The key here is to ensure that everyone involved with the design, implementation, use, and maintenance of ITIL processes is familiar with the fundamental concepts of the framework. These concepts include the principles of IT service management, the integration of processes, and the use of metrics and management reporting. Not everyone needs to be formally trained on ITIL fundamentals to gain an understanding of these key concepts.

Myth #5: Full Understanding of ITIL Requires Purchase of Library

The IT infrastructure library is, in fact, a set of books prescribing best practices for managing an IT infrastructure. The intent of these books is to maximize the quality and value of IT services and to ultimately reduce their costs. Some believe that to acquire a thorough understanding of ITIL and to realize its full benefits, all of the books in its library need to be purchased, read, understood, and applied.

This is a myth in that many organizations acquire a deep understanding of ITIL and profit from its benefits without ever purchasing a single book. An understanding of ITIL and how to apply it can be obtained in a variety of ways. Some of these methods include searching the Internet, attending user forums, participating in seminars, having discussions with other ITIL shops, signing up for training, and contracting with subject-matter experts.

The initial version of ITIL contained 42 books and covered areas in far greater detail than what many felt were practical. Many of the books, such as those that described how to install power supplies and how to design fire suppression systems, were dropped when later versions of ITIL were published. There currently are seven books in the library, of which the two on *Service Delivery* and *Service Support* contain the majority of information needed to effectively utilize the ITIL framework.

Myth #6: ITIL Processes Should be Implemented Only One at a Time

This myth is essentially the opposite of Myth #1. Myth #1 suggested that to obtain any of the benefits of ITIL, all of its processes should be implemented at the same time or not at all. Myth #6 suggests that the proper method of implementation is to install each process separately and serially. The basis for this myth is that each process is considered to be so intricate, so structured, so far-reaching, and so complicated.

In reality, the ITIL processes are all intertwined with each other and work best when implemented in an integrated manner. This does not mean that all of the processes must be implemented at once (as we saw with Myth #1), but it does mean that some groups of processes could and should be implemented together. Some examples of optimal groupings are Incident and Problem Management; Configuration, Change and Release Management; Availability and Security Management; and Service Level and Financial Management. Several ITIL consulting companies and software vendors now offer services and software suites of two or three of these processes combined.

Myth #7: ITIL Provides Detailed Templates for Implementation

At its core, ITIL is a framework of best practices for managing IT infrastructures. Nothing more and nothing less. By design, ITIL is a generalized, non-specific, process-oriented framework. As such, it does not include detailed templates for processes. When I am teaching certification classes to IT infrastructure personnel, students often inquire about checklists, worksheets, and assessment documents they hope to use when implementing ITIL processes. They are usually disappointed to learn that no such documents are available. One student became so indignant he questioned the real value of ITIL and threatened to leave the class.

The student fell victim to this common myth about ITIL by failing to realize that the absence of templates is one of the features that make ITIL so powerful. It is what allows ITIL to apply equally effectively to IT environments of various size, scope, and complexity. Templates are normally customized to a specific environment with specific requirements. I am often asked why ITIL does not provide forms for tracking incidents in incident management or for submitting change requests in change management. My response is that ITIL offers suggestions of what fields to include on both of these forms, but ITIL intentionally steers clear of specifics so that templates can be tailored to the needs of the specific environment.

Myth #8: ITIL Framework Applies Only to Large Shops

When authors of ITIL developed the original version of their framework in the mid and late 1980s, mainframes in large shops were the order of the day. Personal computers (PCs) were just starting to come on the scene, client/server applications were few and far between, and very few people were using or had even heard of the Internet. So it's not surprising that some 20 years ago many may have associated ITIL with large mainframe shops.

But the framers of ITIL understood that their mission was to develop management guidelines that were based on process rather than function, on service rather than size and scope, and on being independent rather than dependent on specific platforms. The structure and principles of ITIL apply to all environments regardless of size, scope, complexity, or platforms.

Myth #9: ITIL Recommends Tools to Use for Implementation

One of the most frequently asked questions I receive from IT professionals concerning ITIL is "What tools does ITIL recommend for implementation?" The answer is simple, "None." It was never the intention of ITIL to recommend specific tools to use when implementing its framework. ITIL is process-oriented library of best practices. It is not technically-oriented, which is what it would become if it was involved with evaluating and recommending specific products. There are forum groups available—itSMF, for one—that offer guidance in this regard. But it is a myth to think that the ITIL framework itself will recommend tools for implementation.

Myth #10: There Is Little Need to Understand ITIL Origins

I have met a number of managers who debated with their staffs about the merits of ITIL before finally deciding to get involved with this framework. The essence of their discussions usually centered on the amount of time and costs they would need to commit to in order to implement ITIL. Once they committed to the implementation of the processes, they focused on moving forward with ITIL rather than looking back at how ITIL got started. They erroneously believe that there is little to be gained by expending time and effort to learn of ITIL's past.

What these managers do not realize is that understanding the origins of ITIL can actually help with future implementations. Integration and collaboration are two of the key cornerstones of ITIL and these were prevalent from the start. When the government of the UK commissioned a framework of best practices to be developed, it fostered a collaborative effort among specialists from private industry, academia, and government. The final product was very much an integrated work among three very diverse groups of people. But it reinforced the notion of cooperation and communication, much like today's version reinforces the same among IT service providers, customers, and suppliers. So there can be value in understanding the origins of ITIL and applying those principles when implementing ITIL processes.

Summary

This chapter introduced the IT Infrastructure Library (ITIL). It began with some of the developments that led up to ITIL and a discussion of IT service management. Next was presented a brief summary of how ITIL came into existence. We then described the six service delivery processes of ITIL followed by its six service support processes. Then we offered a comparison of the ITIL processes with those presented in Part Two. The chapter concluded with descriptions of the 10 common myths surrounding the implementation of the ITIL framework.

Test Your Understanding

1. IT Service Management bridges the gap between the business goals of a company and the technology used to accomplish those goals. (True or False)

2. ITIL service delivery processes are considered user-facing while service support processes are considered customer-facing. (True or False)

3. Which one of the following is not considered an objective of IT Service Management?

    a. to ensure that the organization's business needs are supported by high-quality, cost-effective, value-adding IT services

    b. to maximize the performance of IT hardware and software resources

    c. to improve the quality of IT service provision

    d. to reduce the long-term cost of service provision

4. The new standard for IT Service Management from the International Standards Organization (ISO) that is heavily based on ITIL processes is _____ .

5. What are some of the cultural changes an IT organization would have to make to transition from being technology-oriented to becoming more service-oriented?

Suggested Further Readings

1. *IT Infrastructure Library (ITIL) Service Delivery Book (2001)*; The Stationary Office, Government of the United Kingdom

2. *IT Infrastructure Library (ITIL) Service Support Book (2001)*; The Stationary Office, Government of the United Kingdom

3. www.itsmf.com

4. www.itsmfusa.org

CHAPTER 7

Availability

Introduction

We start our journey through the various disciplines of systems management with one of the most commonly known characteristics of any computer system—availability. As with any term that is widely used but often misunderstood, a good place to begin is with a clear definition of the word. Discussions about availability often include several words or phrases closely associated with this process, and it is important to understand the differences in meanings of these expressions. We differentiate the term availability from other terms like uptime, downtime, slow response, and high availability. This leads to showing the benefits of a single process owner and prioritizing some of the desirable traits in a candidate for the position of availability process owner.

We then describe effective techniques to use to develop and analyze meaningful measurements of availability. The main thrust of this chapter centers around methods to achieve high availability, which are presented in the form of the seven Rs of high availability. An offshoot of this is a discussion on how to empirically analyze the impact of component failures. We close the chapter by showing how customized assessment sheets can be used to evaluate the availability process of any infrastructure.

Definition of Availability

Before we present techniques to improve availability, it is important to define exactly what we mean by the term. You may think that this should be a fairly simple concept to describe, and to most end-users, it normally is. If the system is up and running, it is available to them. If it is not up and running, regardless of the reason, it is not available to them.

We can draw a useful analogy to any telephone system. When you pick up the receiver of a desk telephone or activate a mobile phone you generally expect an immediate connection. In those rare instances when a connection cannot be made, the entire telephone system appears to be down, or unavailable, to the user. In reality, it may be a problem with the central office, the switching station, or any one of a number of other components that have failed and are causing the outage. In the case of a mobile phone, it may simply be searching for an available cell.

As a customer you typically are less concerned with the root cause of the problem and more interested in when service will be restored. But the telephone technician who is responsible for maximizing the uptime of your service needs to focus on cause, analysis, and prevention, in addition to restoring service as quickly as possible.

By the same token, infrastructure analysts focus not only on the timely recovery from outages to service, but on methods to reduce their frequency and duration to maximize availability. This leads us to the following formal definition of availability.

Availability

Availability is the process of optimizing the readiness of production systems by accurately measuring, analyzing, and reducing outages to those production systems.

There are several other terms and expressions closely associated with the term availability. These include uptime, downtime, slow response, and high availability. A clear understanding of how their meanings differ from one another can help bring the topic of availability into sharper focus. The next few sections will explain these different meanings.

Differentiating Availability from Uptime

The simplest way to distinguish the terms *availability* and *uptime* is to think of availability as oriented toward customers and the uptime as oriented toward suppliers. Customers, or end-users, are primarily interested in their system being up and running—that is, available to them. The suppliers (meaning the support groups within the infrastructure), by nature of their responsibilities, are interested in keeping their particular components of the system up and running. For example, systems administrators focus on keeping the server hardware and software up and operational. Network administrators have a similar focus on network hardware and software, and database administrators do the same with their database software.

Uptime

Uptime is a measure of the time that individual components within a production system are functionally operating. This contrasts to availability, which focuses on the production system as a whole.

What this all means is that the terms sometimes draw different inferences depending on your point of view. End-users mainly want assurances that the application system they need to do their jobs is available to them when and where they need it. Infrastructure specialists primarily want assurances that the components of the system for which they are responsible are meeting or exceeding their uptime expectations. Exactly which components' individual uptimes influence availability the most? The following list shows 10 of the most common. This list is by no means exhaustive. In fact, for purposes of clarity I have included within the list selected subcomponents. For example, the server component has the subcomponents of processor, memory, and channels. Most of the major components shown have multiple subcomponents, and many of those have subcomponents of their own. Depending on how detailed we wish to be, we could easily identify 40-50 entities that come into play during the processing of an online transaction in a typical IT environment.

1. Data center facility
2. Server hardware (processor, memory, channels)
3. Server system software (operating system, program products)
4. Application software (program, database management)
5. Disk hardware (controllers, arrays, disk volumes)
6. Database software (data files, control files)
7. Network software

8. Network hardware (controllers, switches, lines, hubs, routers, repeaters, modems)
9. Desktop software (operating system, program products, applications)
10. Desktop hardware (processor, memory, disk, interface cards)

The large number of diverse components leads to two common dilemmas faced by infrastructure professionals in managing availability:

- **Trading the costs of outages against the costs of total redundancy**. Any component acting as a single source of failure puts overall system availability at risk and can undermine the excellent uptime of other components. The end-user whose critical application is unavailable due to a malfunctioning server will care very little that network uptime is at an all-time high. We will present some techniques for reducing this risk when we discuss the seven Rs of high availability later in this chapter.

- **Multiple components usually correspond to multiple technical owners.** This can be a formula for disaster when it comes to managing overall availability. One of the first tenets of management says that when several people are in charge, there is no one in charge. This is why it is important to distinguish availability—what the end-user experiences when all components of a system are operating—from uptime, which is what most owners of a single component focus on. The solution to this dilemma is an availability manager, or availability process owner, who is responsible for all facets of availability, regardless of the components involved. This may seem obvious, but many shops elect not to do this for technical, managerial, or political reasons. Most robust infrastructures follow this model. The overall availability process owner needs to exhibit a rare blend of traits—we will look at them shortly.

Differentiating Slow Response from Downtime

Slow response can infuriate users and frustrate infrastructure specialists. The following factors can contribute to slow response times:

- Growth of a database
- Traffic on the network
- Contention for disk volumes
- Disabling of processors or portions of main memory in servers

Each of these conditions requires analysis and resolution by infrastructure professionals. Understandably, users are normally unaware of these root causes and sometimes interpret extremely slow response as downtime to their systems. The threshold of time at which this interpretation occurs varies from user to user. It does not matter to users whether the problem is due to slowly responding software (slow response) or malfunctioning hardware (downtime). What does matter is that slow or non-responsive transactions can infuriate users who expect quick, consistent response times.

Slow Response

Slow response refers to unacceptably long periods of time for an online transaction to complete processing and return results to the user. The period of time deemed unacceptable varies depending on the type of transaction involved. For simple inquiries, a one-second response may seem slow; for complex computations, two- or three-second responses may be acceptable. Slow response is usually a performance and tuning problem requiring highly-trained personnel with specialized expertise.

But *slow response* is different from *downtime*, and the root cause of these problems does matter a great deal to infrastructure analysts and administrators. They are charged with identifying, correcting, and permanently resolving the root causes of these service disruptions. Understanding the nature of the problem affects the course of action taken to resolve it. Slow response is usually a performance and tuning issue involving personnel, processes, and process owners which are different than those involved with downtime, which is an availability issue.

Downtime

Downtime refers to the total inoperability of a hardware device, a software routine, or some other critical component of a system that results in the outage of a production application.

Differentiating Availability from High Availability

The primary difference between *availability* and *high availability* is that the latter is designed to tolerate virtually no downtime. All online computer systems are intended to maximize availability, or to minimize downtime, as much as possible.

High Availability

High availability refers to the design of a production environment such that all single points of failure are removed through redundancy to eliminate production outages. This type of environment is often referred to as being fault tolerant.

In high-availability environments, a number of design considerations are employed to make online systems as fault tolerant as possible. I refer to these considerations as the seven Rs of high availability and discuss them later in this chapter. Figure 7-1 shows an example of a fault-tolerant computer manufactured by Stratus Technologies.

Fault Tolerant

Fault tolerant refers to a production environment in which all hardware and software components are duplicated such that they can automatically fail-over to their backup component in the event of a fault.

Figure 7-1 Stratus Model 4600 Mid-range Fault Tolerant Server (Photo courtesy of Stratus Technologies, Inc)

Desired Traits of an Availability Process Owner

As we mentioned previously, managers of robust infrastructures select a single individual to be the process owner of availability. Some shops refer to this person as the availability manager. In some instances, it is the operations managers; in others, it is a strong technical lead in technical support. Regardless who these individuals are, or to whom they report, they should be knowledgeable in a variety of areas, including systems, networks, databases, and facilities; they also must be able to think and act tactically. A slightly less critical, but desirable, trait of an ideal candidate for availability process owner is a knowledge of software and hardware configurations, backup systems, and desktop hardware and software. Table 7–1 lists these traits and others, in priority order, for a likely applicant for the position of availability process owner.

Table 7–1 Prioritized Characteristics of an Availability Process Owner

Characteristic	Priority
1. Knowledge of systems software and components	High
2. Knowledge of network software and components	High
3. Knowledge of database systems	High
4. Knowledge of power and air conditioning systems	High
5. Ability to think and act tactically	High
6. Knowledge of software configurations	Medium
7. Knowledge of hardware configurations	Medium
8. Knowledge of backup systems	Medium
9. Knowledge of desktop hardware and software	Medium
10. Knowledge of applications	Low
11. Ability to work effectively with developers	Low
12. Ability to communicate effectively with IT executives	Low
13. Ability to manage diversity	Low
14. Ability to think and plan strategically	Low

Methods for Measuring Availability

The percentage of system availability is a very common measurement. It is found in almost all service-level agreements and is calculated by dividing the amount of actual time a system was available by the total time it was scheduled to be up. For example, suppose an online system is scheduled to be up from 6 a.m. to midnight Monday through Friday and from 7 a.m. to 5 p.m. on Saturday. The total time it is scheduled to be up in hours is $(18 \times 5) + 10 = 100$ hours. When online systems first began being used for critical business processing in the 1970s, availability rates between 90 percent and 95 percent was common, expected, and reluctantly accepted. In our example, that would mean the system was up 90-95 hours per week or, more significantly, down for 5-10 hours per week and 20-40 hours per month. The formula for calculating the percent availability, or *percent uptime* as it is sometimes referred, is:

> Percent Availability (Uptime) = (Hours Agreed Up - Hours Down)/Hours Agreed Up

Table 7-2 shows in a tabular form how this calculation is performed.

Table 7-2   Tabular Calculation for Availability

Days	Timeframes	Hours
Monday - Friday	6:00am – Midnight	$(5 \times 18) = 90$
Saturday	7:00am – 5:00pm	10
		Total Hours = $(90 + 10) = 100$
	Lower level of availability = 90% x 100 hours = 90 hours	
	Upper level of availability = 95% x 100 hours = 95 hours	

Customers quickly realized that 10 hours a week of downtime was unacceptable and began negotiating service levels of 98 percent and even 99 percent guaranteed availability. As companies expanded worldwide and 24/7 systems became prevalent, the 99 percent level was questioned. Systems needing to operate around the clock were scheduled for 168 hours of uptime per week. At 99 percent availability, these systems were down, on average, approximately 1.7 hours per week. Infrastruc-

ture groups began targeting 99.9 percent uptime as their goal for availability for critical business systems. This target allowed for just more
than 10 minutes of downtime per week, but even this was not acceptable
for systems such as worldwide email or e-commerce websites.

Another method of measuring availability or uptime is to use a
rolling average, similar to that described in the following Real Life Experience. Table 7-3 shows how this calculation and others are performed.

Table 7-3   Sample Percent Uptime Calculations

Percent Uptime Goal/ Period	Weekly Agreed Uptime (Hrs x Days)	Rolling Weeks/ Period	Total Agreed Uptime/ Period	Total Down- time/ Period	Percent Uptime/Period	Goal Met?
99.9%	24x7=168h	4	672	3.0	(672-3.0)/672=99.6%	No
99.5%	10x5=50h	6	300	1.5	(300-1.5)/300=99.5%	Yes
99.0%	(12x5) + (8x2)=76h	8	608	2.0	(608-2.0)/608=99.7%	Yes

So the question becomes: Is the percentage of scheduled service
delivered really the best measure of quality and of availability? An incident at Federal Express several years ago involving the measurement of
service delivery illustrates some points that could apply equally well to
the IT industry. FedEx had built its reputation on guaranteed overnight
delivery. For many years its principal slogan was:

> When it positively, absolutely has to be there overnight, Federal
> Express.

FedEx guaranteed a package or letter would arrive on time, at the
correct address, and in the proper condition. One of its key measurements of service delivery was the percentage of time that this guarantee
was met. Early on, the initial goals of 99 percent and later 99.9 percent
were easily met. The number of letters and packages they handled on a
nightly basis was steadily growing from a few thousand to more than
10,000; less than 10 items were lost or delivered improperly.

Real Life Experience—Giving It the Old College Try

A 24x7 critical engineering design system at a major U.S. aerospace company required 99.5 percent availability. This figure was negotiated into a service-level agreement (SLA) with the IT department. A few weeks later, heated disagreements about the SLA arose between the heads of the Engineering and IT departments after a new release of the application resulted in three 1-hour outages during a 10-day period. To add fuel to the fire, the Engineering VP was from Notre Dame University and the CIO from the University of Southern California (USC), bitter college rivals in American football.

Engineering claimed IT was not providing the 99.5 percent availability it had contractually promised. IT countered that since there had been no previous outages for the past six weeks (1008 hours), the total period of seven and one-half weeks (1248 hours) could allow 0.5 percent downtime, or 6.24 hours—well beyond the three 1-hour outages.

Engineering was clearly not pleased and re-negotiated the contract to 99.9 percent availability and a rolling four-week average to compute the most current availability percentage. This incident taught everyone an important lesson about agreeing to sampling periods ahead of time when computing availability percentages and negotiating SLAs.

The VP of Engineering may have enjoyed the final revenge when his Notre Dame team soundly defeated USC that year in the annual Fall football classic.

A funny thing happened as the growth of their company started to explode in the 1980s. The target goal of 99.9 percent was not adjusted as the number of items handled daily approached one million. This meant that 1,000 packages or letters could be lost or improperly delivered every night and their service metric would still be met. One proposal to address this was to increase the target goal to 99.99 percent, but this goal could have been met while still allowing 100 items a night to be mishandled. A new set of deceptively simple measurements was established in which the number of items lost, damaged, delivered late, and delivered to the wrong address was tracked nightly regardless of the total number of objects handled.

The new set of measurements offered several benefits. By not tying it to percentages, it gave more visibility to the actual number of delivery errors occurring nightly. This helped in planning for anticipated customer calls, recovery efforts, and adjustments to revenue. By breaking incidents into three subcategories, each incident could be tracked separately as well as looked at in totals. Finally, by analyzing trends, patterns, and relationships, managers could pinpoint problem areas and recommend corrective actions. In many ways, this experience with service delivery metrics at Federal Express relates closely to availability metrics in IT infrastructures. A small, start-up shop may initially offer online services only on weekdays for 10 hours and target for 99 percent availability. The 1 percent against the 50 scheduled hours allows for 0.5 hours of downtime per week. If the company grows to the point of offering similar online services 24/7 with 99 percent availability, the allowable downtime grows to approximately 1.7 hours.

A better approach is to track the quantity of downtime occurring on a daily, weekly, and monthly basis. As was the case with FedEx, infrastructure personnel can pinpoint and proactively correct problem areas by analyzing the trends, patterns, and relationships of these downtimes. Robust infrastructures also track several of the major components comprising an online system. The areas most commonly measured are the server environment, the disk storage environment, databases, and networks.

The tendency of many service suppliers to measure their availability in percentages of uptime is sometimes referred to as the rule of nines. Nines are continually added to the target availability goal (see Table 7–4). The table shows how the weekly minutes of allowable downtime changes from our example of the online system with 100 weekly hours and how the number of allowable undelivered items changes from our FedEx example.

Table 7–4   Rule of Nines Availability Percentage

Number of Nines	Percentage of Availability	Weekly Hours Down	Weekly Minutes Down	Daily Packages Not Delivered (out of 10K)	Daily Packages Not Delivered (out of 1M)
1	90.000%	10.000	600.00	1,000.0	100,000.0
2	99.000%	1.000	60.00	100.0	10,000.0
3	99.900%	0.100	6.00	10.0	1,000.0
4	99.990%	0.010	0.60	1.0	100.0
5	99.999%	0.001	0.06	0.1	10.0

Real Life Experience—Exaggeration Not the Height of Flattery

A persistent hardware salesperson kept pestering me for a meeting during which he could proudly present his new line of disk drives. During the presentation, he boasted of his product's high reliability, claiming they measured it at seven 9's availability. My availability manager pointed out that such a high degree of reliability could not be measured practically.

A bit flustered, the salesperson backtracked a bit by saying that the measurements did not include four hours of scheduled downtime per month. When the availability manager explained how the scheduled maintenance time would make capturing the reliability measurement even more difficult, the product spokesman finally admitted he had been exaggerating his claim. Industry reports later showed the product to be between a respectable four and five 9's level of availability. (See the problem at the end of the chapter.)

Improving levels of availability often involves capital expenditures which most companies are reluctant to invest in unless a strong, convincing business justification is offered. Calculating and presenting the cost of a single hour of downtime can be a very convincing business justification. The costs should be verified with representatives from both the user community and the finance committee. Table 7-5 lists the cost of a single hour of downtime for various businesses.

Table 7-5   Cost of Downtime for Various Businesses

Nature of Business	Cost per Hour of Downtime (USD)
Automated teller machines (medium-sized bank)	$14,500.00
Package shipping services	$28,250.00
Telephone ticket sales	$69,000.00
Airline reservation center (small airline)	$89,500.00
Catalogue sales center	$90,000.00

The Seven Rs of High Availability

The goal of all availability process owners is to maximize the uptime of the various online systems for which they are responsible—in essence, to make them completely fault tolerant. Constraints inside and outside the IT environment make this challenge close to impossible. Some of the factors working against that elusive goal of 100 percent availability—the ultimate expression of high availability—include the following:

- Budget limitations
- Component failures
- Faulty code
- Human error
- Flawed design
- Natural disasters
- Unforeseen business shifts (such as mergers, downturns, political changes)

There are several approaches that can be taken to maximize availability without breaking the budget bank. Each approach starts with the same letter, so we refer to them as the seven Rs of high availability (see the following list). We will explain each one separately.

1. **R**edundancy
2. **R**eputation
3. **R**eliability
4. **R**epairability
5. **R**ecoverability
6. **R**esponsiveness
7. **R**obustness

Redundancy

Manufacturers have been designing this into their products for years in the form of redundant:

- Power supplies
- Multiple processors
- Segmented memory
- Redundant disks

Real Life Experience—The Department of Redundancy Department

Testing for redundancy became a little too close for comfort when a vendor of hot backup servers set up a demonstration for a client of mine. The client was already using a smaller pair of the vendor's hot backup servers but had never needed to use them as a failover in production. The salesperson confidently announced he would pull the plug on one of his test servers and show how it would failover to its redundant server with no loss of data or transactions.

The IT manager looked in horror as he realized the salesperson had just pulled the plug on one of the smaller production servers running a highly critical application. Fortunately, the system performed as designed and failed-over perfectly to its redundant server. There was no loss of data and no loss of transactions. The greatly relieved IT manager finally caught his breath, but wasn't sure whether he should congratulate the embarrassed salesperson...or reprimand him.

This can also refer to entire server systems running in a hot standby mode. Infrastructure analysts can take a similar approach by configuring disk and tape controllers, and servers with dual paths, splitting network loads over dual lines, and providing alternate control consoles—in short, eliminate as much as possible any single points of failure that could disrupt service availability.

The next three approaches—reputation, reliability, and repairability—are closely related. Reputation refers to the track record of key suppliers. Reliability pertains to the dependability of the components and the coding that go into their products. Repairability is a measure of how quickly and easily suppliers can fix or replace failing parts. We will look at each of these a bit more closely.

Reputation

The reputation of key suppliers of servers, disk storage systems, database management systems, and network hardware and software plays a principle role in striving for high availability. It is always best to go with the best. Reputations can be verified in several ways, including the following:

- Percent of market share
- Reports from industry analysts such as Gartner Group
- Publications such Wall Street Journal and ComputerWorld
- Track record of reliability and repairability
- Customer references

Customer references can be especially useful when it comes to confirming such factors as cost, service, quality of the product, training of service personnel, and trustworthiness.

Reliability

The reliability of the hardware and software can also be verified from customer references and industry analysts. Beyond that, you should consider performing what we call an *empirical component reliability analysis*. The following list describes the seven steps required to accomplish this.

1. Review and analyze problem management logs.
2. Review and analyze supplier logs.
3. Acquire feedback from operations personnel.
4. Acquire feedback from support personnel.
5. Acquire feedback from supplier repair personnel.
6. Compare experiences with other shops.
7. Study reports from industry analysts.

An analysis of problem logs should reveal any unusual patterns of failure and should be studied by supplier, product, using department, time and day of failures, frequency of failures, and time to repair. Suppliers often keep onsite repair logs that can be perused to conduct a similar analysis. Table 7-6 shows a sample supplier repair log.

Table 7-6   Sample Supplier Repair Log

Company XYZ Supplier Repair Log - 2009

Supplier: Dell <u>Date</u> <u>Time</u>
Component: Server A. Component Failed 7/13 4:41pm
Model/Version: 8100 B. Supplier called 7/13 4:15pm
<u>Description of Failure</u> C. Supplied responded 7/13 4:15pm
Circuit board D. Supplier onsite 7/13 4:30pm
#432 failed E. Component repaired 7/13 4:55pm
F. Service restored 7/13 5:00pm
<u>Description of Repair</u>
Circuit board
#432 replaced
Supplier Engineer_____ Co. XYZ Analyst_____

Feedback from operations personnel can often be candid and revealing as to how components are truly performing. This can especially be the case for offsite operators. For example, they may be doing numerous resets on a particular network component every morning prior to start-up, but they may not bother to log it since it always comes up. Similar conversations with various support personnel such as systems administrators, network administrators, and database administrators may solicit similar revelations. You might think that feedback from repair personnel from suppliers could be biased, but in my experience they can be just as candid and revealing about the true reliability of their products as the people using them. This then becomes another valuable source of information for evaluating component reliability, as is comparing experiences with other shops. Shops that are closely aligned with your own in terms of platforms, configurations, services offered, and customers can be especially helpful. Reports from reputable industry analysts can also be used to predict component reliability.

A common metric for reliability of components, applications or systems is the average or *mean time between failures (MTBF)*. This is a measure of the average length of time an entity is expected to stay up and operational over a given period of time; this timeframe is often a year and it's known as the *sampling interval*. The formula used to compute MTBF is:

MTBF = sampling interval / # of failures during sampling interval

Table 7-7 shows how the MTBF of three months would be computed (along with MTTR described in next section) for the reliability of a component during calendar year (CY) 2009.

Table 7-7   Example of Computing MTBF and MTTR

Component Failure History—CY2008		
Failure Occurrence	**Date of Failure**	**Time to Repair in Minutes**
1	April 21	27
2	June 16	49
3	November 4	16
4	November 30	72
	Total Repair Time	164
		MTTR = 164 / 4 = 41 Minutes
		MTBF = 12 Months / 4 Failures = 3 Months

Repairability

This refers to is the relative ease with which service technicians can resolve or replace failing components. A common metric used to evaluate this trait is the average or *mean time to repair (MTTR)*. MTTR is sometimes interpreted as the mean time to *recover*, the mean time to *restore*, or the mean time to *resolve*. It measures the average time it takes to do the actual repair. The formula used to compute MTTR is:

MTTR = sum of repair times / # of failures

For example, if a component failed four times in the last year with repair times (see Table 7-6), the average—or mean—time to repair would be 41 minutes. In more sophisticated systems, repairs can be done from remote diagnostic centers where failures are detected and circumvented, and arrangements are made for permanent resolution with little or no involvement of operations personnel.

Recoverability

The next characteristic of high availability is recoverability. This refers to the ability to overcome a momentary failure in such a way that there is no impact on end-user availability. It could be as small as a portion of main memory recovering from a single-bit memory error; it can be as large as having an entire server system switch over to its standby system with no loss of data or transactions. Recoverability also includes retries of attempted reads and writes out to disk or tape, as well as the retrying of transmissions down network lines.

Recoverability was a major design factor when the communication protocols for the Internet were being developed, especially the two major ones of the Transmission Control Protocol (TCP) and the Internet Protocol (IP). TCP receives 8-bit bytes of data from an application and segments them into packets. TCP then passes the packets on to the IP, which delivers them through a network of networks (the Internet) to their destination, where a receiving TCP module accepts them. TCP checks to make sure that no packets are lost by giving each packet a sequence number, which is also used to make sure that the data are delivered in the correct order. The TCP module at the far end sends back an acknowledgement for packets which have been successfully received. If a set of packets is not received properly, no acknowledgement is returned and the whole set is re-transmitted. This aspect of recoverability adds greatly to network availability.

Responsiveness

This trait is the sense of urgency all people involved with high availability need to exhibit. This includes having well-trained suppliers and in-house support personnel who can respond to problems quickly and efficiently. It also pertains to how quickly the automated recovery of resources such as disks or servers can be enacted. Escalation is another aspect of responsiveness that ensures higher levels of technical expertise and management support are involved to restore availability as quickly as possible. Escalation guidelines are usually documented in service-level agreements between IT and business customers.

Robustness

This is the final characteristic of high availability and it describes the overall design of the availability process. A robust process will be able to withstand a variety of forces—both internal and external—that could easily disrupt and undermine availability in a weaker environment. Robustness puts a high premium on documentation and training to withstand the following:

- Technical changes as they relate to:

  Platforms

  Products

  Services

  Customers
- Personnel changes as they relate to:

  Turnover

  Expansion

  Rotation
- Business changes as they relate to:

  New direction

  Acquisitions

  Mergers

These seven Rs of high availability all contribute in a unique way to extending uptime, minimizing downtime, and improving the overall level of service provided by online systems.

Assessing an Infrastructure's Availability Process

Over the years, many clients have asked me for a quick and simple method to evaluate the quality, efficiency, and effectiveness of their systems management processes. In response to these requests, I developed the assessment worksheet shown in Figure 7-2. Process owners and their managers collaborate with other appropriate individuals to fill out this form. Along the left column are 10 categories of characteristics about a process. The degree to which each characteristic is put to use in designing and managing a process is a good measure of its relative robustness.

The categories that assess the overall **quality** of a process are:

- Executive support
- Process owner
- Process documentation

Categories assessing the overall **efficiency** of a process consist of:

- Supplier involvement
- Process metrics
- Process integration
- Streamlining/automation

The categories used to assess **effectiveness** include:

- Customer involvement
- Service metrics
- The training of staff

The evaluation of each category is a very simple procedure. The relative degree to which the characteristics within each category are present and being used is rated on a scale of 1 to 4, with 1 indicating no presence and 4 indicating a large presence of the characteristic. Although the categories are the same for each of the 12 processes, the type of specific characteristics within each category varies from process to process. I address these differences by customizing the worksheet for each process being evaluated.

Availability Process—Assessment Worksheet					
Process Owner_____ Owner's Manager_____ Date_____					
Category	Questions for Availability	None 1	Small 2	Medium 3	Large 4
Executive Support	To what degree does the executive sponsor show support for the availability process with actions such as analyzing trending reports of outages and holding support groups accountable for outages?	-	2	-	-
Process Owner	To what degree does the process owner exhibit desirable traits and ensure timely and accurate analysis and distribution of outage reports?	-	-	-	4
Customer Involvement	To what degree are key customers involved in the design and use of the process, including how availability metrics and service level agreements will be managed?	-	-	-	4
Supplier Involvement	To what degree are key suppliers, such as hardware firms, software developers, and service providers, involved in the design of the process?	-	-	3	-
Service Metrics	To what degree are service metrics analyzed for trends such as percentage of downtime to users and dollar value of time lost due to outages?	-	-	-	4
Process Metrics	To what degree are process metrics analyzed for trends such as the ease and quickness with which servers can be re-booted?	-	-	3	-
Process Integration	To what degree does the availability process integrate with other processes and tools such as problem management and network management?	-	2	-	-
Streamlining/ Automation	To what degree is the availability process streamlined by automating actions such as the generation of outage tickets and the notification of users when outages occur?	1	-	-	-
Training of Staff	To what degree is the staff cross-trained on the availability process, and how well is the effectiveness of the training verified?	-	2	-	-
Process Documentation	To what degree is the quality and value of availability documentation measured and maintained?	1	-	-	-
	Totals	2	6	6	12
Grand Total = 2 + 6 + 6 + 12 = 26 Nonweighted Assessment Score = 26 / 40 = 65%					

Figure 7-2   Sample Assessment Worksheet for Availability Process

For example, suppose the executive sponsor for the availability process demonstrated some initial support for the process by carefully selecting and coaching the process owner. However, presume that over time this same executive showed no interest in analyzing trending reports or holding direct report managers accountable for outages. I would consequently rate the overall degree to which this executive showed support for this process as little and rate it a 2 on the scale of 1 to 4. On the other hand, if the process owner actively engages key customers in the design and use of the process, particularly as it pertains to availability metrics and service level agreements, I would rate that category a 4.

Each category is similarly rated (see Figure 10–6). Obviously, a single column could be used to record the ratings of each category; however, if we format separate columns for each of the four possible scores, categories scoring the lowest and highest ratings stand out visually. I have filled in sample responses for each category to show how the entire assessment might work. We now sum the numerical scores within each column. In our sample worksheet this totals to 2 + 6 + 6 + 12 = 26. This total is then divided by the maximum possible rating of 40 for an assessment score of 65 percent.

Apart from its obvious value of quantifying areas of strength and weakness for a given process, this rating provides two other significant benefits to an infrastructure. One is that it serves as a baseline benchmark from which future process refinements can be quantitatively measured and compared. The second is that the score of this particular process can be compared to those of other infrastructure processes to determine which ones need most attention.

In my experience, many infrastructures do not attribute the same amount of importance to each of the 10 categories within a process, just as they do not all associate the same degree of value to each of the 12 systems management processes. I refined the assessment worksheet to account for this uneven distribution of category significance—I allowed weights to be assigned to each of the categories. The weights range from 1 for least important to 5 for most important, with a default of 3.

Figure 7-3 shows an example of how this works. I provide sample weights for each of the rated categories from our sample in Figure 7-2. The weight for each category is multiplied by its rating to produce a final score. For example, the executive support category is weighted at 3 and rated at 2 for a final score of 6. We generate scores for the other nine categories in a similar manner and sum up the numbers in each column. In our sample worksheet, the weights add up to 30, the ratings add up to 26 as before, and the new scores add up to 90.

Availability Process—Assessment Worksheet					
Process Owner_____ Owner's Manager_____ Date _____					
Category	Questions for Availability	Weight	Rating	Score	
Executive Support	To what degree does the executive sponsor show support for the availability process with actions such as analyzing trending reports of outages and holding support groups accountable for outages?	3	2	6	
Process Owner	To what degree does the process owner exhibit desirable traits and ensure timely and accurate analysis and distribution of outage reports?	3	4	12	
Customer Involvement	To what degree are key customers involved in the design and use of the process, including how availability metrics and service level agreements will be managed?	5	4	20	
Supplier Involvement	To what degree are key suppliers, such as hardware firms, software developers, and service providers, involved in the design of the process?	5	3	15	
Service Metrics	To what degree are service metrics analyzed for trends such as percentage of downtime to users and dollar value of time lost due to outages?	5	4	20	
Process Metrics	To what degree are process metrics analyzed for trends such as the ease and quickness with which servers can be re-booted?	1	3	3	
Process Integration	To what degree does the availability process integrate with other processes and tools such as problem management and network management?	3	2	6	
Streamlining/ Automation	To what degree is the availability process streamlined by automating actions such as the generation of outage tickets and the notification of users when outages occur?	1	1	1	
Training of Staff	To what degree is the staff cross-trained on the availability process, and how well is the effectiveness of the training verified?	3	2	6	
Process Documentation	To what degree is the quality and value of availability documentation measured and maintained?	1	1	1	
	Totals	30	26	90	
	Weighted Assessment Score = 90 / (30 x 4) = 75%				

Figure 7-3   Sample Assessment Worksheet for Availability Process with Weighting Factors

The overall weighted assessment score is calculated by dividing this final score of 90 by the maximum weighted score (MWS). By definition, the MWS will vary from process to process and from shop to shop, since it reflects the specific weighting of categories tailored to a given environment. The MWS is the product of the sum of the 10 weights % 4, the maximum rating for any category. In our example, the sum of the 10 weights is 30, so our MWS = 90 / (30 % 4) = 75 percent.

Your next questions could well be: Why is the overall weighted assessment score of 75 percent higher than the nonweighted assessment score of 65 percent? And what is the significance of this? The answer to the first question is quantitative; the answer to the second one is qualitative. The weighted score will be higher whenever categories with high weights receive high ratings or categories with low weights receive low ratings. When the reverse occurs, the weighted score will be lower than the nonweighted one. In this case, the categories of customer involvement, supplier involvement, and service metrics were given the maximum weights and scored high on the ratings, resulting in a higher overall score.

The significance of this is that a weighted score will reflect a more accurate assessment of a process because each category is assigned a customized weight. The more frequently the weight deviates from the default value of 3, the greater the difference will be between the weighted and nonweighted values.

Measuring and Streamlining the Availability Process

We can measure and streamline the availability process with the help of the assessment worksheet shown in Figure 7-2. We can measure the effectiveness of an availability process with service metrics such as the percentage of downtime to users and time lost due to outages in dollars. Process metrics—such as the ease and quickness with which servers can be re-booted—help us gauge the efficiency of the process. And we can streamline the availability process by automating actions such as the generation of outage tickets whenever an online system goes down (rather than having service desk staff doing this) and by notifying users with automated voicemails and emails (if email is up) when outages occur.

Summary

This chapter described the first of our 12 systems management processes—availability. We began with a formal definition of the process and differentiated it from the related terms of uptime, downtime, slow response, and high availability. This led us to the benefits of a single process owner, for which we prioritized a list of desirable traits this individual should possess. We next discussed methods to measure and analyze availability and included an example from Federal Express to help illustrate these points.

The main portion of this chapter centered on approaches we can use to strive for high availability. We called these the seven Rs of high availability: redundancy, reputation, reliability, repairability, recoverability, responsiveness, and robustness. Each was described at some length. We concluded this chapter with a detailed discussion on how to quickly assess the quality, efficiency, and effectiveness of an infrastructure's availability process. We presented two assessment worksheets along with an explanation of how to perform such an assessment.

Test Your Understanding

1. With so many components influencing system uptime, it is usually preferred to have several individuals responsible for availability. (True or False)
2. A 24x7 system contracted to be available 99.0 percent can be down for 1.5 hours per week and still be in compliance. (True or False)
3. One of the most effective measurements of availability is:
   a. percent of uptime
   b. percent of downtime
   c. amount of time up
   d. amount of time down
4. For a 24x7x365 product or service, how much annual down time would result from seven 9's availability? _____ four 9's?_____ five 9's? _____
5. If you were providing Internet services and availability was one of its major features, how would you market it?

Suggested Further Readings

1. www.bitpipe.com/rlist/term/HighAvailability.html
2. www.ieeetfcc.org/high-availability.html
3. Association for Computer Operations Managers (AFCOM); www.afcom.com
4. *High Availability: Design, Techniques, and Processes*; Hawkins, M., Piedad, F.; Prentice Hall, Upper Saddle River, New Jersey; 2001
5. http://en.wikipedia.org/wiki/Transmission_Control_Protocol

CHAPTER 8

Performance and Tuning

Introduction

The systems management discipline of performance and tuning differs in several respects from other infrastructure processes, and this chapter begins by explaining these differences. The first difference is that—as this chapter title implies—these are actually two related activities normally combined into one process. We continually tune infrastructure hardware and software, as well as their interrelationships, to improve the performance of systems. The discussion of differences leads to a definition of the performance and tuning process followed by a listing of desirable traits of an ideal process owner.

Next we look at how the performance and tuning process applies to each of the five major resource environments found within a typical infrastructure:

- Servers
- Disk storage
- Databases
- Networks
- Desktop computers

In keeping with our focusing first on people and processes ahead of technology, we identify and examine issues associated with performance and tuning rather than provide a shopping list of the plethora of technology products and tools used to actually do the tuning. Performance specialists often find many ways to successfully tune each of the five major resource environments by deploying appropriate staff and by implementing proper procedures before applying technology.

Within each of the five areas, we discuss some of the meaningful metrics that world-class infrastructures use to measure and improve performance and tuning. We conclude the chapter by offering assessment worksheets for evaluating a company's performance and tuning process, both with and without weighting factors.

Differences between the Performance and Tuning Process and Other Infrastructure Processes

All 12 of the systems management processes that we present in Chapters 7 through 18 in Part Two differ in one way or another from each other. That is what distinguishes one from the other and led, in part, to our arrival at this even dozen of disciplines. But the performance and tuning process has more differences from the others than is typical, and the differences themselves are more significant than usual. Understanding these differences can help to define the overall process and select suitable process owners. Table 8-1 summarizes these differences.

Table 8–1 Summary of Performance and Tuning Process Differences

Performance and Tuning	Other Processes
1. Consists primarily of two major activities	1. Consists primarily of one major activity
2. Normally has multiple subprocess owners	2. Normally has one overall process owner
3. Shares ownership across multiple departments	3. Centralizes ownership in a single department
4. Tasks have a continuous and ongoing nature	4. Tasks have definitive start and end dates
5. Process is highly iterative	5. Processes are seldom iterative
6. Process tools vary widely among the resource environments	6. Process tools are usually shared across departments
7. Process utilizes a large number of diversified metrics	7. Processes utilize a small number of similar metrics

The first difference references the dual nature of performance and tuning—they are actually two related activities normally combined into one process. The performance activity has as its cornerstone the reporting of real-time performance monitoring and reporting as well as periodic management trend reports on a daily, weekly, or less-frequent basis. The tuning activity consists of a variety of analyses, adjustments, and changes to a whole host of parameters. All other systems management processes consist of primarily one major activity and they have one overall process owner. Because performance and tuning activities normally occur in five separate areas of the infrastructure, there is usually more than one subprocess owner depending on the degree to which the five areas are integrated. These multiple subprocess owners share ownership across several departments, whereas the other systems management processes have a centralized ownership within one infrastructure department.

The nature of the tasks differs in that performance and tuning is continuous and ongoing. Performance monitoring occurs for all of the time that networks and online systems are up and running. The other infrastructure processes tend to have definitive start and end dates for their various tasks. Changes are implemented, problems are resolved, and new applications become deployed.

Tuning a portion of the infrastructure environment to correct a performance problem can be a highly iterative activity, often requiring numerous trials and errors before the source of the problem is found. Other processes are seldom iterative because most of the tasks associated with them are of a one-time nature.

Processes such as change and problem management normally use a single database-oriented system to manage the activities. This becomes their main process tool. Process tools used with performance and tuning are large in number and diverse in application. This is due to the eclectic tuning characteristics of the various infrastructure resources. No single tool exists that can fine-tune the operating systems of mainframes, midranges, servers, networks, and desktop computers. Similarly, there are separate and highly specialized tools for defining databases, as well as for maintaining, reorganizing and backing up and restoring them.

Finally, there is the issue of metrics. The performance activity of this process relies heavily on a large variety of metrics and reports to identify, both proactively and reactively, trouble spots impacting online response, batch throughput, and web activity. Other processes use metrics to be sure, but not quite to the extent that performance and tuning does.

These differences are what sets this process apart from others and influences how the process is designed, implemented, and managed.

Definition of Performance and Tuning

The previous discussion on what sets the performance and tuning process apart from other infrastructure processes leads us to the following formal definition of performance and tuning.

Performance and Tuning

Performance and tuning is a methodology to maximize throughput and minimize response times of batch jobs, online transactions, and Internet activities.

Our definition highlights the two performance items that most IT customers want their systems to have: maximum throughput and minimal response times. These two characteristics apply to all platforms and to all forms of service, whether batch jobs, online transactions, or Internet activities.

The five infrastructure areas most impacted by performance and tuning are:

1. Servers
2. Disk storage
3. Databases
4. Networks
5. Desktop computers

The methodologies used to tune for optimum performance vary from one area to the other, lending to subprocesses and subprocess owners. But there are some generic characteristics of performance and tuning that apply to all five areas.

One of these is the false notion that the quickest and simplest way to solve a performance problem is to throw more hardware at it—the system is running slow, so upgrade the processors; if swap rates are too high, just add more memory; for cache hits too low or disk extents too high, simply buy more cache and disk volumes. These solutions may be quick and simple, but they are seldom the best approach. The relief they may offer is seldom permanent and usually not optimal, and it is often hard to justify their cost in the future. The fallacy of a limited hardware solution lies in the fact that it fails to address the essence of performance management: that tuning is an ongoing activity in which the performance bottleneck is never truly eliminated, it's only minimized or relocated.

To further illustrate this point, consider the following scenario. Hundreds of new desktop computers have been added to a highly used application. The resulting slow response is attributed to lack of adequate bandwidth on the network, so bandwidth is added. However, that leads to increased transaction arrival rates, which now clog the channels to the disk array. More channels are added, but that change now causes major traffic contention to the disk volumes. Volumes are added, but they saturate the cache, which, in turn, is increased. That increase saturates main memory, which is then increased and fully saturates the processors, which are upgraded to handle this, only to have the entire cycle start over in reverse order.

I admit that this is an exaggerated example, but it serves to reinforce two key points:

1. Performance and tuning are ongoing, highly iterative processes. Shops that treat them as occasional tasks usually end up with only occasionally good performance.
2. Overall planning of the type and volume of current and future workloads is essential to a robust process for performance and tuning.

Tuning is sometimes likened to trying to keep a dozen marbles on a piece of plate glass you are holding. You must constantly tilt the glass one way and then quickly to another to keep all the marbles on the surface. Distractions, unplanned changes, and unforeseen disruptions in the environment can easily cause a marble to fall off the glass, similar to what can happen with performance and tuning.

Preferred Characteristics of a Performance and Tuning Process Owner

Table 8-2 lists in priority order many of the preferred characteristics of a performance and tuning process owner. In reality, there may be two or more subprocessors whose high-priority characteristics vary depending on the area in which they are working. For example, an individual selected as the process owner for only the network area should have as a high priority knowledge of network software and components, but knowledge of systems software and components need only be a medium priority. The reverse would apply to an individual selected as the process owner for only the server area.

Knowledge of software and hardware configurations is of a high priority regardless of the area in which a process owner works, as is the ability to think and act tactically. The relationships of the process owners to the application developers can be key ones in that performance problems sometimes appear to be infrastructure related only to be traced to application coding problems, or vice versa. A good working knowledge of critical applications and the ability to work effectively with developers is at minimum a medium priority for process owners working with application systems.

Table 8–2   Prioritized Characteristics for a Performance and Tuning Process Owner

Characteristic	Priority
1. Knowledge of systems software and components	High
2. Knowledge of network software and components	High
3. Knowledge of software configurations	High
4. Knowledge of hardware configurations	High
5. Ability to think and act tactically	High
6. Knowledge of applications	Medium
7. Ability to work effectively with developers	Medium
8. Knowledge of desktop hardware and software	Medium
9. Knowledge of power and air conditioning	Medium
10. Ability to meet effectively with customers	Low
11. Ability to promote teamwork and cooperation	Low
12. Ability to manage diversity	Low

Performance and Tuning Applied to the Five Major Resource Environments

Now let's look at how the performance and tuning process applies to each of the five major resource environments found within a typical infrastructure: servers, disk storage, databases, networks, and desktop computers. Since we are focusing first on people and processes ahead of technology, we will identify and examine issues associated with performance and tuning rather than talk about all of the technology products and tools used to actually do the tuning.

Server Environment

The first of the five infrastructure areas affected by performance and tuning covers all types and sizes of processor platforms, including mainframe computers, midrange computers, workstations, and servers. For simplicity, we refer to all of these platforms as servers. The following list details the major performance issues in a server environment:

1. Processors
2. Main memory
3. Cache memory
4. Number and size of buffers
5. Size of swap space
6. Number and type of channels

The number and power of **processors** influence the rate of work accomplished for processor-oriented transactions. Processors are the central components (also called the *central processing units*) of a digital computer that interpret instructions and process data. At its core, a processor adds and compares binary digits. All other mathematical and logical functions stem from these two activities.

For optimal performance, processor utilization rates should not exceed 80 percent. Tools are available to measure real-time utilizations of processors, **main memory**, and channels. **Cache memory** is available on most mainframe computers and on some models of servers, offering an additional means of tuning transaction processing. Cache memory differs from main memory in the following manner. Main memory is extremely fast circuitry (directly attached to the processor) that stores instructions, data, and most of the operating system software, all of which are likely to be used immediately by the processor. Cache memory is slightly slower memory (directly attached to main memory) that stores instructions and data about to be used. Cache is much faster (and more expensive) than secondary storage such as disks and tape.

Real Life Experience—Swapping Club Requires an Explanation

A CIO at a major defense contractor took an active interest in online response times for his customers and wanted to know exactly when and why performance might be degrading. It was a tough sell for systems analysts to explain to him why response times increased beyond service levels whenever only a few users were signed on yet seemed to improve with more users.

The cause of this performance paradox was the way main memory swap space was set up. When many online users were signed on, almost all the available memory would be used for online transactions and very little swapping out to disk storage occurred. When only a few users signed on, much of memory was used for batch jobs and the online users would frequently get swapped out, causing slower response times.

The **number and size of buffers** assigned for processing of I/O operations can trade off the amount of memory available for processor-oriented transactions. Buffers are high-speed registers of main memory that store data being staged for input or output.

The concept of virtual storage is used to temporarily store small, frequently used portions of large programs in part of main memory to reduce time-consuming I/O operations to secondary storage. The portion of main memory set aside for this is called *swap space* because the program segments get swapped in and out of main memory. The **size of swap space** can be adjusted to match the profiles of application and database processing.

The rate of processing I/O operations is also determined by the **number and speed of channels** connecting servers to external disk equipment. Channels are physical cables that connect the main memory to external I/O devices such as disk drives, tape drives, and printers.

Performance metrics commonly collected in a server environment include:

1. Processor utilization percentages
2. The frequency of swapping in and out of main memory

3. Percentage of hits to main memory cache
4. The length and duration of processing queues
5. The percentage of utilization of channels
6. The amount of processor overhead used to measure performance

Disk Storage Environment

The second type of infrastructure resources impacted by performance and tuning is disk-storage equipment. The following list indicates the major performance issues in a disk-storage environment:

1. Cache memory
2. Volume groups
3. Striping
4. Storage area networks
5. Network-attached storage
6. Extents
7. Fragmentation

Along with the configuration of the network and the design of databases, disk storage has a huge influence on the overall performance of an online system. If your disk environment is well-tuned, the resulting response times of your online applications are more likely to be acceptable. This is because it's a relative eternity in computer time to seek for a specific track on a data volume, to search for a specific piece of data on that track, to read or write it back out to the controller, to prepare it for transport along a channel, to transmit it down the channel, and then to finally have it arrive at its destination. Anything that can be done to shorten these steps and reduce this time significantly improves online response times.

One of the most effective ways to improve disk-storage performance is to utilize **cache memory** in RAID-type disk arrays. (RAID stands for redundant array of independent—originally, inexpensive—disks; see Chapter 12, "Storage Management," for a detailed description of the configurations and architectures of RAID disk arrays.) The reason cache is so effective at improving disk performance is that, for an overwhelming number of input or output transactions to and from disks, it eliminates the time-consuming steps of seeking and searching for data out on disk volumes. It accomplishes this through the use of ingenious pre-fetch algorithms that anticipate which data will be requested next and then preload it into the high-speed cache memory.

Pre-fetch algorithms—algorithms that analyze patterns of fetch activity to more intelligently anticipate requests—have become much more sophisticated in recent years. For example, a particular application may be accessing a database in such a way that every third record is being read. After a few of these requests are handled, the pre-fetch algorithm pre-loads every third record into the high-speed cache. The number and the complexity of pre-fetch algorithms vary from supplier to supplier, so you should thoroughly research what is available and what best suits your particular environment prior to investing large capital costs into an expensive asset.

Pre-Fetch Algorithm

A pre-fetch algorithm is a set of software instructions that analyzes the patterns of disk storage read-request activity to anticipate and pre-load, or pre-fetch, expected records of data.

The reason pre-fetch algorithms are so important is that they directly affect the likelihood of finding, or hitting, the desired record in cache. The percentage of these hits to the total number of requests—called *hit ratio*—is tracked very closely and is one of the best indicators of how well-tuned a cache disk array is to a particular application. Highly tuned cache memories can have hit ratios exceeding 90 percent, which is a remarkable percentage given the millions of requests coming into the array. Some high-performance disk systems always read the cache first to check for the desired record. Having the data pre-loaded in the cache drastically reduces the time necessary to retrieve and process the data because the relatively long amount of time needed to seek and search for data out on disk is eliminated. Some manufacturers reduce this time even further by reading the cache first on every operation.

Mapping out **volume groups** is another effective way to improve performance. Volume groups are a logical grouping of physical disk drives. The intent is to improve performance with reduced seek-and-search times by combining frequently used groups of physical volumes into one logical group. Suppose, for example, a large customer database spans across dozens of physical disk drives and you want to optimize performance for the most frequently used parts of the database. Analysis determines that customer spending habits and payment history are the two most frequently used tables in the database. Database administrators could re-configure the database so that these tables are spread across several physical drives instead of all of them being on a single drive. More of the desired data can be accessed quicker because of multiple paths to the multiple physical drives. This also facilitates pre-loading of anticipated data into cache.

Striping is a performance-improvement technique in which long blocks of data that are to be read or written sequentially are stored across multiple drives, usually within a logical volume group. This is done to increase the number of data paths and transfer rates and to allow for the simultaneous reading and writing to multiple disks.

Tuning the blocksizes of the striping to the blocksizes of the databases and the application can also improve performance. For example, a common blocksize for relational databases is 8 kilobytes; for a typical disk storage array, it is 32 kilobytes; for disk-volume utilities used for striping, it is 64 kilobytes. These three sizes accommodate each other efficiently because they are all even multiples of each other. But if some application were to use an uneven multiple of blocksize, the blocksizes would need some tuning to prevent spending costly and time-consuming overhead to reconcile the differences.

A **storage area network** (SAN) is a configuration enhancement that places a high-speed fiber-optic switch between servers and disk arrays (see Figure 8-1). The two primary advantages are speed and flexibility. The fiber channel can transmit data between the servers and the arrays at speeds of up to 1 or 2 terabytes per second (as opposed to 6 to 10 megabytes per second on standard channels). This greatly improves data-transfer rates and online response times. Parameters within the switch can help to improve performance by controlling buffers, contention, and load-balancing. The switch also allows a greater number of input paths to the switch than what might be available on the array. This ratio of server paths to array paths is known as the *fan-in ratio*. A properly tuned, two-to-one fan-in ratio can result in twice as much data being transmitted between the server and the arrays as would be possible with a one-to-one conventional ratio. The major downside to SAN is that it is expensive, primarily due to the fiber channels and its associated switch.

Storage Area Network (SAN)

A storage area network (SAN) consists of a high-speed subnetwork of shared storage devices. The configuration of a SAN enables all storage devices to connect to all servers within a local or wide area network (WAN).

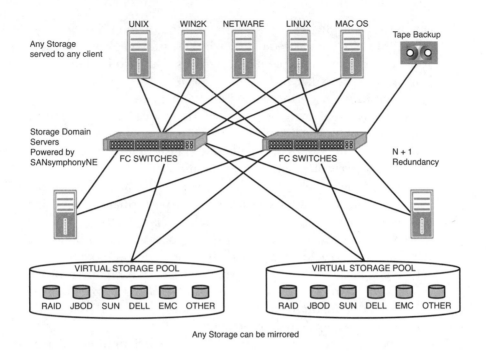

Figure 8-1 Diagram of a Storage Area Network (SAN) (Diagram courtesy of Nikita Kozlovskij)

Another storage configuration enhancement is **network-attached storage** (NAS), in which the disk array, along with the servers and the clients, is attached directly to the network. A disk-array server connects to the network with special-purpose interface devices or by using multipurpose operating systems running on multipurpose servers. The result is that data can travel from a NAS device over the network directly to the server or the client requesting the data. One common application of NAS is to use it for the network drives in a PC client network. The one drawback of using NAS rather than SAN in this way is that NAS tends to run slower. The speed of data transfer in a NAS environment is limited by the speed of the network. This normally runs between 10 and 100 megabitsper second. Gigabit Ethernet is now widely available with speeds between 10 to 100 gigabits per second.

Network Attached Storage (NAS)

A network attached storage (NAS) device is a server that is dedicated solely to file sharing. This enables other servers to be dedicated to processing activities while the NAS device is dedicated to storage activities.

The final two performance issues in a disk-storage environment involve the utilization of individual disk drives. **Extents** occur when the amount of data needing to be written exceeds the amount of original contiguous disk space allocated. Rather than abnormally terminating the request, the operating system looks for additional available space on the disk volume and extends the original contiguous space. Up to 16 extents are allowed per file, but the larger the number of extents, the longer it takes to seek and search for the data due to the fragmented nature of the data. **Fragmentation** can occur by other means as well, with the similar result of longer disk-access times and slower response times. Reallocating files and compressing them to reduce extents and fragmentation are good tuning methods to improve response.

Database Environment

The physical layout of a database can greatly influence the eventual response times of inquiries or updates. Databases in large companies can grow to hundreds of columns and millions of rows, and e-commerce databases can grow even larger. The placement of critical files such as system, data, log, index, and rollback files within the database can spell the difference between acceptable responses and outright lockups.

Eight of the most common performance issues associated with a database environment are shown in the following list:

1. Placement of table files
2. Initialization parameters
3. Placement of data files
4. Indexes and keys
5. Locks
6. Balance of system resources
7. Access patterns
8. Database fragmentation

First on the list is the **placement of table files**. A table file, which describes the various tables that reside within the database, is a critical navigational map of a database that serves as its data dictionary. Most database requests are first channeled through the table file. The placement of this file is extremely important to delivering acceptable online performance. The optimal location for this file is in the main memory of the server where fetch times are the quickest. However, the size of this file often prevents its being located there. In that case, as much of it as possible should be loaded into the cache memory of the disk array when space is available. When accessing data on disk drives, proper placement on the volume—as well as the volume's placement within a volume group—influences the amount of time it takes to complete database-access requests; this, in turn, affects online response times.

Initialization parameters for database management software have a direct impact on performance. Depending on the software being used, there can be dozens of these parameters from which to select and specify values. Some of the more common of these are database blocksize, the shared pool size for locating the data dictionary in memory, the system global area (SGA) for selected shared table files, log buffers, and the database block buffers for data files. The **placement of the data files** is crucial for minimizing access times and optimizing online response, just as it is for table files.

The judicious use of **indexes and keys** is another performance and tuning aid that can drastically reduce table lookup times. **Keys** are used to identify records in certain sequences by designating one or more unique fields in a table. The **indexes** are tree structures that hold the keys along with a pointer to the remainder of the data. Searching for a particular record is typically much quicker using an index, key, and pointer scheme because it eliminates the need to search the entire database.

Keys

Keys are a designated field within a record of a file or a database that enables the quick and secure searching or sorting of records within a table.

The keys offer another benefit as well. Since multiple keys are allowed for a given table, that table can, in effect, be sorted in multiple orders. This results in complex queries with multiple constraints that can be retrieved, in most cases, much more quickly with the use of keys. In cases where the resulting set is extremely large, it may actually be quicker to perform a single pass through the entire table. Keys can also be used to chain together groups of transactions that are normally executed sequentially. This improves transaction response times and user productivity by reducing keystrokes.

Indexes

Indexes are lists of keys within a database that enable the fast searching of a particular record or groups of records. Indexes also allow for multiple sorting of records within groups of tables or keys.

The use of indexes and keys must be balanced with the expense of additional storage, the overhead of processing and maintaining the indexes, and the updating and merging of keys. The greater the number of indexes, the greater the overhead. Performance specialists need to consider the trade-off between the benefit of fast retrievals and the cost of overhead for index maintenance.

Locks

Locks protect the integrity of a record of data by making it inaccessible to unauthorized users. Locks often are used with multi-user files and databases to ensure multiple updates are not made simultaneously.

Locks are sometimes used to protect the integrity of data records and to ensure single, sequential updates. Similar to keys, their implementation needs to be carefully planned since the overuse of locks can extend both disk space and access times. **Balancing system resources** of processors, memory, channel, and disk is necessary to ensure no single resource becomes saturated or grossly under-utilized in the quest for good performance. Monitoring the usage of these various resources to ensure none becomes under- or over-utilized is a proactive way to ensure balance among the devices. For example, once a server approaches 80 percent utilization, action should be taken to add capacity or, if possible, to re-distribute the workload to under-utilized servers.

Enterprise Resource Planning (ERP)

Enterprise resource planning refers to a set of applications that offers use and benefits across an entire corporation, rather than to just isolated departments. Finance, payroll, and personnel systems are examples of ERP systems.

Understanding the **access patterns** into a database is one of the best ways to optimize an application's performance. Anticipating what the read and write sequences are likely to be, and to which parts of the database they will likely occur, allows database administrators to map out the physical database in an optimal configuration. At the same time, performance specialists can configure disk-volume groups to align as closely as possible to the expected disk-access patterns. Measuring end-to-end response times is the best to verify the validity of these adjustments.

Extensive testing of a new database layout should be performed prior to production deployment to ensure cache hits are maximized, contention bottlenecks are minimized, and overall response times are optimized. Major hardware and software suppliers of enterprise resource planning (ERP) platforms and applications have comprehensive performance centers that can and should be utilized for testing prior to putting these systems into production.

Real Life Experience—A Chain With No Weak Links

An aerospace company instituted an extensive program to measure online response of transactions in a critical engineering application with multiple databases. The customers insisted that 90 percent of all transactions complete in less than a second. During the first few months this service-level objective was met, but even more improvements were sought.

A database consultant was brought in to suggest ways to optimize performance even more. He suggested that several of the commands frequently used sequentially could be chained together internally to save on keystrokes. The response times would slightly exceed the one-second objective since multiple commands would be processed. It took some considerable marketing efforts to convince some of the engineering customers that processing up to 10 commands in just under four seconds was more productive than entering each command manually, getting a response back in 0.9 seconds, then taking another second or two to enter the next command.

Over time, database records are rewritten in locations that are different from their optimal starting points. This causes two problems:

1. The data is no longer optimally placed for its anticipated access pattern.
2. The data records are now **fragmented**, causing less than efficient use of the disk space.

Periodically defragmenting the database with software utilities corrects both problems. Performance reports and trending statistics are available to help predict when it is best to schedule the running of defragmenting utilities.

Network Environment

There are a variety of factors that influence the performance of a network, beginning with its overall design and topology. In this section we discuss some of the more common issues:

1. Bandwidth
2. Line speed
3. Protocols
4. Single sign-ons
5. Number of retries
6. Nonstandard interfaces
7. Broadcast storms

Primary among these is network **bandwidth**. Calculating sufficient bandwidth is often more of an art than it is a science, but there are several planning aids available to help quantify these estimates. A robust capacity planning forecast is a good place to start. It should include a reasonable forecast of the number of concurrent users, the peak transaction traffic loads, and an estimate of transaction arrival patterns and types. This information should help determine the appropriate amount of bandwidth required for a given application. Network workload simulators can be used to test transaction response times under varying loads with different amounts of bandwidth.

Line speed is another key parameter affecting network performance. Obviously, the faster the speed, the greater the performance. Just as in a server and disk environment, resources need to be balanced and cost-justified, so simply upgrading lines from a T1 (1.544 megabits per second) to a T3 (43 megabits per second) may not be the best solution possible. It certainly may not be the most cost-effective solution. If lines must be upgraded for performance reasons, it pays to compare suppliers, shop around, and negotiate for terms such as maintenance, tariffs, and add-ons.

Network **protocols** are usually dictated by business, programming, and application requirements. In instances where alternatives are possible, give consideration to potential performance impacts, especially when running diagnostic programs such as traces and sniffers. Many shops struggle with the issue of **single sign-ons**—there is a trade-off between performance and security. The convenience and performance savings of logging on only once instead of multiple times for access to the network, operating system, database management system, and a particular application must be weighed against the potential security exposures of bypassing normal password checks. Most applications have robust security features designed into them to mitigate this risk.

Transmission errors occur periodically on all network lines. In most instances, the errors are quickly detected, the network request is retried, and—since most errors are temporary in nature—the retransmission is successful. If the retransmission is not successful, multiple retries are attempted. After a certain number of unsuccessful retries, the error is designated as permanent and more sophisticated diagnostics are activated. The number of retries to be attempted impacts performance and should be monitored and adjusted appropriately. Suppliers should be involved when retries originate from the line side of the network.

Connecting devices with **nonstandard interfaces** to the network can cause major performance problems such as locking up lines, introducing interference, or, in extreme cases, flooding the network with non-stop transmissions called **broadcast storms**. This becomes another trade-off between performance and security. In many shops, executives may approve the temporary use of a nonstandard device for testing, evaluation, or special business needs. Suppliers can sometimes offer interfaces to increase the compatibility of these devices with a network. Caution should be exercised and a heightened awareness of network performance put in place whenever an exception to network standards is permitted.

Desktop Computer Environment

The final area of performance that we will cover involves the desktop computing environment. While there are far fewer issues to deal with in this environment, they can still have serious impact on end-users. The following lists the six issues we will discuss:

1. Processors
2. Memory
3. Disk storage space
4. Network connections
5. Diagnostic tools
6. Administrative tools

The size and power of the **processing chip** (see Figure 8-2) required by a desktop computer is influenced by the number and type of applications that will be run. Spreadsheets, statistical analysis programs, and highly graphical routines need much more processing power to deliver acceptable response than word-processing applications. The amount of processing power and **memory** needed to ensure acceptable performance depends on the number and types of windows expected to be open simultaneously. Two windows consisting of email and textual documents need far fewer resources than six windows that include compound documents and multimedia streaming videos.

Another factor impacting desktop performance is the number of applications that run in the background that are automatically loaded during start-up. These background applications include:

- Automatic updaters for applications
- Automatic updaters for operating systems
- Anti-virus software
- Restriction software to protect children
- Anti-spam software
- Personal firewalls
- Anti-spyware

These various applications can consume half of the processing capability of the desktop without the user even being aware of it. New and advanced features of modern desktop operating systems may also use large amounts of capacity. Microsoft's Vista operating system is functionally impressive in terms of security and ease of use. But its advanced, 3-D graphics (refined from its video game experiences), while at times dazzling in their displays, requires a lot of memory and processing power to operate satisfactorily.

The amount of **disk storage space** has a less direct effect on the performance of desktop computers than either the processor or memory. In this regard, it differs from the role external disk storage plays in servers and mainframes. External desktop disks do impact performance in the sense that retrieving data locally rather than over the network usually shortens response times.

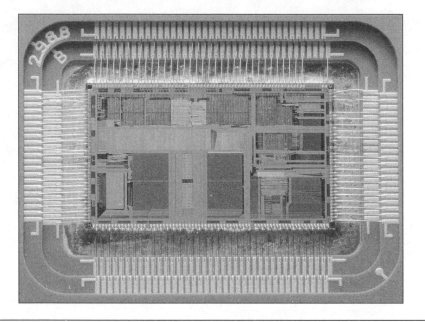

Figure 8-2   Intel Microprocessor (12x6.75mm)

Desktop devices are attached to LANs and WANs through **network connections.** The speed of the lines and of the modems that utilize these network connections obviously impact performance at the desktop; line speed and modems should be tuned to meet requirements at reasonable costs. The number of desktops on the networks, and the corresponding number of hubs and routers that interconnect the various network segments and devices, also influences desktop performance.

Diagnostic tools that enable a remote technician to take control of a desktop computer to troubleshoot problems can adversely impact performance if parameters are not initialized properly. Some diagnostic tools also are capable of running in real-time on the desktop. If these tools are inadvertently left running, they can easily impact desktop performance adversely.

Performance can also be impacted by **administrative tools**, such as those that automatically inventory the configuration of the desktop through an asset-management system. Sophisticated tools of this type can interpret and process large amounts of detailed information about the internal specifications of the desktop, which can slow down normal operations.

Real Life Experience—Tap Dancing in Real Time

A CEO at a dot.com start-up was eager to show his staff how he could display their company website in real-time at his staff meetings. Unfortunately for his IT performance team, he picked the one day when a new operating system release was installed improperly, which slowed response time to a crawl. The technical support manager had to do some quick tap-dancing when he was called into the meeting to explain what happened. Ironically, this was the same manager who had set up the displayable website in the first place.

Assessing an Infrastructure's Performance and Tuning Process

The worksheets shown in Figures 8-3 and 8-4 present a quick-and-simple method for assessing the overall quality, efficiency, and effectiveness of a performance and tuning process. The worksheet shown in Figure 8-3 is used without weighting factors, meaning that all 10 categories are weighted evenly for the assessment of a performance and tuning process. Sample ratings are inserted to illustrate the use of the worksheet. In this case, the performance and tuning process scored a total of 21 points for an overall nonweighted assessment score of 53 percent. Completely coincidentally, the weighted assessment score results in an identical value of 53 percent based on the sample weights that were used.

One of the most valuable characteristics of these worksheets is that they are customized to evaluate each of the 12 processes individually. The worksheets in Figures 8-3 and 8-4 apply only to the performance and tuning process. However, the fundamental concepts applied in using these evaluation worksheets are the same for all 12 disciplines. As a result, the detailed explanation on the general use of these worksheets presented near the end of Chapter 7, "Availability," also applies to the other worksheets in the book. Please refer to that discussion if you need more information.

Performance and Tuning Process—Assessment Worksheet						
Process Owner_____ Owner's Manager_____ Date _____						
Category	Questions for Performance and Tuning	None 1	Small 2	Medium 3	Large 4
Executive Support	To what degree does the executive sponsor show support for the performance and tuning process with actions such as budgeting for reasonable tools and appropriate training?	-	2	-	-
Process Owner	To what degree does the process owner exhibit desirable traits and know the basics of tuning system, database, and network software?	-	2	-	-
Customer Involvement	To what degree are key customers involved in the design and use of the process, including how response time metrics and SLAs will be managed?	-	-	3	-
Supplier Involvement	To what degree are key suppliers such as software performance tools providers and developers involved in the design of the process?	1	-	-	-
Service Metrics	To what degree are service metrics analyzed for trends such as response times and the number and complexity of chained transactions?	-	-	-	4
Process Metrics	To what degree are process metrics analyzed for trends such as the amount of overhead used to measure online performance, the number of components measured for end-to-end response, and the cost to generate metrics?	-	2	-	-
Process Integration	To what degree does the performance and tuning process integrate with other processes such as storage management and capacity planning?	-	-	3	-
Streamlining/ Automation	To what degree is the performance and tuning process streamlined by automating actions—such as the load balancing of processors, channels, logical disk volumes, or network lines—and by notifying analysts whenever performance thresholds are exceeded?	1	-	-	-
Training of Staff	To what degree is the staff cross-trained on the performance and tuning process, and how well is the effectiveness of the training verified?	-	2	-	-
Process Documentation	To what degree is the quality and value of performance and tuning documentation measured and maintained?	1	-	-	-
Totals		**3**	**8**	**6**	**4**

Grand Total = 3 + 8 + 6 + 4 = 21
Nonweighted Assessment Score = 21 / 40 = 53%

Figure 8-3   Sample Assessment Worksheet for Performance and Tuning Process

Performance and Tuning Process—Assessment Worksheet				
Process Owner_____ Owner's Manager_____ Date _____				
Category	**Questions for Performance and Tuning**	**Weight**	**Rating**	**Score**
Executive Support	To what degree does the executive sponsor show support for the performance and tuning process with actions such as budgeting for reasonable tools and appropriate training?	1	2	2
Process Owner	To what degree does the process owner exhibit desirable traits and know the basics of tuning system, database and network software?	3	2	6
Customer Involvement	To what degree are key customers involved in the design and use of the process, including how response time metrics and service level agreements will be managed?	3	3	9
Supplier Involvement	To what degree are key suppliers such as software performance tools providers and developers involved in the design of the process?	5	1	5
Service Metrics	To what degree are service metrics analyzed for trends such as response times and the number and complexity of chained transactions?	3	4	12
Process Metrics	To what degree are process metrics analyzed for trends such as the amount of overhead used to measure online performance, the number of components measured for end-to-end response, and the cost to generate metrics?	5	2	10
Process Integration	To what degree does the performance and tuning process integrate with other processes and tools such as storage management and capacity planning?	3	3	9
Streamlining/ Automation	To what degree is the performance and tuning process streamlined by automating actions—such as the load balancing of processors, channels, logical disk volumes, or network lines—and by notifying analysts whenever performance thresholds are exceeded?	3	1	3
Training of Staff	To what degree is the staff cross-trained on the performance and tuning process, and how well is the effectiveness of the training verified?	1	2	2
Process Documentation	To what degree is the quality and value of performance and tuning documentation measured and maintained?	1	1	1
Totals Weighted Assessment Score = 59 / (28 x 4) = 53%		28	21	59

Figure 8-4   Sample Assessment Worksheet for Performance and Tuning Process with Weighting Factors

Measuring and Streamlining the Performance and Tuning Process

We can measure and streamline the performance and tuning process with the help of the assessment worksheet shown in Figure 8-3. We can measure the effectiveness of a performance and tuning process with service metrics such as response times and the number and complexity of chained transactions. Process metrics—such as the amount of overhead used to measure online performance, the number of components measured for end-to-end response, and the cost to generate metrics—help us gauge the efficiency of this process. And we can streamline the performance and tuning process by automating certain actions—the load-balancing of processors, channels, logical disk volumes, or network lines, for example—and by notifying analysts when performance thresholds are exceeded.

Summary

We began this chapter by identifying and explaining the differences between the performance and tuning process and other infrastructure processes. The discussion of these differences led us to a formal definition of performance and tuning, followed by a prioritized list of desirable traits in a performance and tuning process owner.

The heart of this chapter centered on key performance issues in each of the major resource environments in a typical infrastructure: servers, disk storage, databases, networks, and desktop computers. The chapter ends with assessment worksheets to use in evaluating a performance and tuning process.

Test Your Understanding

1. The two primary advantages of a SAN are speed and flexibility. (True or False)
2. Connecting devices with nonstandard interfaces to the network usually enhances network performance. (True or False)
3. Which of the following is not related to managing the performance of a database?
   a. encryption codes
   b. indexes
   c. keys
   d. locks
4. The number and size of _____ can trade off the amount of memory available for processor-oriented transactions.
5. Some organizations use multiple performance managers based on their fields of expertise, such as servers, storage equipment or networks. What are some of the advantages and disadvantages of this approach?

Suggested Further Readings

1. www.redbooks.ibm.com/pubs/pdfs/redbooks
2. *Storage Area Networks for Dummies*: 2003; Poelker, Christopher and Nikitin, Alex; For Dummies Publishing
3. www.microsoft.com/technet/prodtechnol
4. *Using SANs and NAS*: 2002; Preston, Curtis; O'Reilly Media
5. www.emc.com/products/networked/san

CHAPTER 9

Production Acceptance

Introduction

No matter how well designed and well tested an application may be, the first—and often lasting—impressions that users form about that application come from how successfully it is deployed into production. Developers and operations personnel sometimes let unnecessary obstacles take their eyes off the goal of a successful deployment. This chapter defines the process of production acceptance and describes many of the benefits this process provides to a variety of groups both inside and outside of IT. The middle sections of this chapter discuss each of the 14 steps required to design and implement an effective production acceptance process. The chapter closes with a case study involving the assessment of production acceptance processes for seven diverse companies.

Definition of Production Acceptance

The primary objective of systems management is to provide a consistently stable and responsive operating environment. A secondary goal is to ensure that the production systems themselves run in a stable and responsive manner. The function of systems management that addresses this challenge is production acceptance.

> **Production Acceptance**
>
> Production acceptance is a methodology used to consistently and success-fully deploy application systems into a production environment regardless of platform.

The following key words from this definition are worth noting.

- **Consistent methodology**. While the methodology is consistent, it is not necessarily identical across all platforms. This means there are essential steps of the process that need to be done for every production deployment, and then there are other steps that can be added, omitted, or modified depending on the type of platform selected for production use.

- **Deploying into a production environment**. This implies that the process is not complete until all users are fully up and running on the new system. For large applications, this could involve thousands of users phased in over several months.

- **Application system**. This refers to any group of software programs necessary for conducting a company's business—the end-users of which are primarily, but not necessarily, in departments outside of IT. This excludes software still in development, as well as software used as tools for IT support groups.

The Benefits of a Production Acceptance Process

An effective production deployment process offers several advantages to a variety of user groups. These beneficiaries include the applications department, executive management, various groups within the IT infrastructure, customers, and suppliers (see Table 9-1).

Table 9-1 Beneficiaries and Benefits of Production Acceptance

Beneficiary	Benefits
Applications	1. Ensures that adequate network and system capacity is available for both development and production
	2. Identifies desktop upgrade requirements in advance to ensure sufficient budget, resources, and time frame
	3. Specifies detailed hardware and software configurations of both the development and production servers to ensure identical environments are used for testing and deployment
	4. Ensures infrastructure support groups (systems, networks, solution center) are trained on supporting the application weeks prior to cutover
Executive Management	1. Quantifies total ongoing support costs prior to project start-up
	2. Reduces overtime costs by identifying upgrade requirements early on
	3. Increases the likelihood of deploying production systems on schedule by ensuring thorough and timely testing
Infrastructure	1. Identifies initial system and network requirements early on
	2. Identifies future infrastructure requirements enabling more cost-effective capacity planning
	3. Identifies ongoing support requirements early on
Customers	1. Involves customers early in the planning phase
	2. Ensures customer equipment upgrades are identified early and scheduled with customer involvement
	3. Ensures satisfactory user testing
Suppliers	1. Involves key suppliers in the success of the project
	2. Identifies and partners key suppliers with each other and with support groups
	3. Provides suppliers with opportunities to suggest improvements for deployment

Implementing a Production Acceptance Process

The following list details the 14 steps necessary for implementing an effective production acceptance process. Along with our detailed discussion of each of these steps, we will look at actual experiences from industry, where appropriate, to highlight suggestions to pursue and obstacles to avoid.

1. Identify an executive sponsor
2. Select a process owner
3. Solicit executive support
4. Assemble a production acceptance team
5. Identify and prioritize requirements
6. Develop policy statements
7. Nominate a pilot system
8. Design appropriate forms
9. Document the procedures
10. Execute the pilot system
11. Conduct a lessons-learned session
12. Revise policies, procedures, and forms
13. Formulate marketing strategy
14. Follow up on ongoing enforcement and improvements

Step 1: Identify an Executive Sponsor

Production acceptance is one of a handful of systems management processes that directly involve departments outside of the infrastructure group. In this case it is the applications development area that plays a key role in making this process effective. An executive sponsor is necessary to ensure ongoing support and cooperation between these two departments. Depending on the size and scope of the IT organization, the sponsor could be the CIO, the head of the infrastructure group, or some other executive in the infrastructure. (We should note that an application manager could be an excellent sponsor providing the head of the infrastructure agrees with the selection. In this case, the executives from both departments should concur on the choice of process owner, who needs to be from the infrastructure group.)

In general, the higher the level of executive sponsor, the better. It should be noted that senior executives are usually more time constrained than those at lower levels, so support sessions should be well planned, straightforward, and to the point.

The executive sponsor must be a champion of the process, particularly if the shop has gone many years with no structured turnover procedure in place. He or she needs to be able to persuade other executives both inside and outside of IT to follow the lead. This individual is responsible for providing executive leadership, direction, and support for the process. The executive sponsor is also responsible for selecting the process owner, for addressing conflicts that the process owner cannot resolve, and for providing marketing assistance.

Step 2: Select a Process Owner

One of the first responsibilities of the executive sponsor is to select the production acceptance process owner. The process owner should be a member of the infrastructure organization since most of the ongoing activities of operating and supporting a new production application fall within this group. This person will be interacting frequently with the programmers who developed and will be maintaining the system.

This continual interaction with applications makes a working knowledge of application systems an important prerequisite for the process owner. Being able to evaluate applications documentation and to communicate effectively with program developers are two additional characteristics highly recommended in a process owner. Several other medium-priority and lower-priority characteristics (see Table 9-2) assist in selecting the process lead. These attributes and priorities may vary from shop to shop, but they are intended to emphasize the importance of predetermining the traits that best suit your organization.

Table 9-2   Prioritized Characteristics for a Production Acceptance Process Owner

Characteristic	Priority
Knowledge of applications	High
Ability to evaluate documentation	High
Ability to communicate effectively with developers	High
Knowledge of company's business model	Medium
Ability to meet effectively with users	Medium
Ability to communicate effectively with IT executives	Medium
Ability to promote teamwork and cooperation	Medium

Table 9-2 Prioritized Characteristics for a Production Acceptance Process Owner Continued

Characteristic	Priority
Ability to manage diversity	Medium
Knowledge of backup systems	Medium
Knowledge of database systems	Medium
Knowledge of desktop hardware and software	Medium
Knowledge of software configurations	Medium
Knowledge of systems software and components	Low
Knowledge of network software and components	Low
Knowledge of hardware configurations	Low

Step 3: Solicit Executive Support

Production acceptance requires much cooperation and support between the applications development and infrastructure departments. Executive support from both of these departments should be solicited to ensure that policies and decisions about the design of the process are backed up and pushed down from higher levels of management.

Step 4: Assemble a Production Acceptance Team

The process owner should assemble a cross-functional team to assist in developing and implementing a production acceptance process. The team should consist of key representatives from the development organization as well as those from operations, technical support, capacity planning, the help desk, and database administration. In cases where the development group is larger than a few hundred programmers, multiple development representatives should participate.

It is important that all key areas within development are represented on this team to ensure support and buy-in for the process. Appropriate development representatives also ensure that potential obstacles to success are identified and resolved to everyone's satisfaction. An effective executive sponsor and the soliciting of executive support (steps 1 and 3) can help to ensure proper representation.

At one company where I managed a large infrastructure group, there were more than 400 programmers in the development department grouped into the four areas of finance, engineering, manufacturing, and logistics. A representative from each of these four areas participated in the development of a production acceptance procedure; each brought unique perspectives, and together they helped to ensure a successful result to the process.

Step 5: Identify and Prioritize Requirements

Early in my career I participated on a number of production acceptance teams that fell short in providing an effective production turnover process. In looking for common causes for these failed attempts, I noticed that in almost every case there were no agreed-upon requirements at the start; when there were requirements, they were never prioritized.

Later on, as I led my own production acceptance design teams, I realized that having requirements that were prioritized and agreed upon by all participants added greatly to the success of the efforts. Requirements vary from company to company, but some are common to almost all instances. Table 9-3 lists some of the more common requirements I have witnessed in successful implementations of production acceptance, along with their typical priorities.

Table 9-3 Sample of Prioritized Requirements

Requirement	Priority
1. Ensure that operations, technical support, help desk, network services, and database administration are all involved early on in implementing a new application.	High
2. Ensure capacity-gathering requirements are compatible with the capacity planning process.	High
3. Provide application documentation to operations prior to production turnover.	High
4. Develop and enforce management policy statements.	High
5. Ensure adequate service desk support from applications during the first week of production.	Medium
6. Implement a pilot subset for very large applications.	Medium
7. Do not set up a separate help desk for a new application.	Medium
8. Ensure that a user test plan is developed and executed.	Medium

Table 9-3 Sample of Prioritized Requirements Continued

Requirement	Priority
9. Ensure that a user acceptance plan is developed and executed.	Medium
10. Analyze daily the types and frequencies of service desk calls during the first two weeks of production; then weekly thereafter.	Medium
11. Leverage the use of existing tools and processes.	Medium
12. Simplify forms as much as possible for ease of use.	Low
13. Involve appropriate groups in the design and approval of forms.	Low
14. Ensure that developers estimate the type and volume of service desk calls during the first week of production.	Low
15. Include desktop capacity requirements.	Low
16. For systems being upgraded, ensure that all impacts to end-users are identified up front.	Low

Step 6: Develop Policy Statements

The cross-functional team should develop policy statements for a production acceptance process. These statements should then be approved by the executive sponsor. Policy statements help ensure that issues such as compliance, enforcement, and accountability will be supported by senior management and communicated to the applicable levels of staffs. The following lists some sample policy statements:

1. All new mainframe- or server-based applications are to go through the formal production acceptance process prior to deployment into production.
2. All major new versions of existing production applications are to go through the formal production acceptance process prior to deployment into production.
3. Process owner ([insert name]) is responsible for coordinating and maintaining the production acceptance process and has authority to delay an application's deployment into production pending full compliance with the process.
4. Key support groups such as operations, technical support, network services, database administration, and the help desk are to be informed about the application from its start and involved

with its development as prescribed by the production acceptance process.

5. Development owners of applications that are deployed through the production acceptance process are expected to regularly update the capacity plan for their applications to ensure adequate resource support in the future.

6. Any applications deployed through the production acceptance process that require substantial desktop capacity upgrades are to provide specific requirements to capacity planners with sufficient lead time for planning, ordering, delivering, and installing all upgrades.

Pilot System

A pilot system is a small-scale version of an application used to try out new processes, functions, or features associated with the application. A single purchasing module of a comprehensive enterprise-wide financial system is an example of a pilot system.

Step 7: Nominate a Pilot System

When a production acceptance process is designed and implemented, particularly in environments that have never had one, there is normally a major change in the manner in which application systems are deployed. Therefore, it is usually more effective to introduce this new method of production turnover on a smaller scale with a minimal-impact pilot system. If a small system is not available as a pilot, consider putting only an initial portion of a major system through the new process.

Step 8: Design Appropriate Forms

During the requirements step, the cross-functional team normally discusses the quantity, types, and characteristics of forms to be used with a production acceptance process. The following list details some of the forms that are typically considered here. Some shops elect to combine some or all of these forms, depending on their complexity.

1. Primary production acceptance form
2. Capacity planning form
3. Customer-acceptance form
4. Service desk form
5. Testing plan
6. Lessons-learned form

- The capacity form is for periodic updates to resource requirements.
- The customer-acceptance form is for user feedback prior to deployment.
- The service desk form is for anticipated calls during start-up.
- The test plan is for developers to show function and performance of the new system.
- The lessons-learned form is for follow-up and improvements after full deployment of a new system.

The forms are proposed, designed, and finalized by the team. Figure 9-1 shows a production acceptance form used by one of my clients. Specific requirements of the form vary from shop to shop, but the form should always be simple, thorough, understandable, and accessible. Many shops today keep forms like these online via their company intranets for ease of use and access.

Step 9: Document the Procedures

The documentation of any systems management process is important, but it is especially so in the case of production acceptance because such a large number of developers will be using it. The documentation for these procedures must be effective and accessible (see Chapter 20 for ways to ensure that documentation is both of high quality and of high value).

Step 10: Execute the Pilot System

With a pilot system identified, forms designed, and procedures in place, it is time to execute the pilot system. User testing and acceptance plays a major role in this step, as does the involvement of support groups such as technical support, systems administration, and the help desk.

Production Acceptance Request Form
Part One: <u>Actions Required at Time of Project Approval</u>

I. General Information about the Application

A. Customer/Supplier Information (To be completed by the Project Manager)

Full system name/acronym_____

Brief description of the system:_____

_____

Current Date _____ Planned Pilot Date _____Full Deployment Date_____

Risk Assessment and Analysis_____

_____

_____ Mission Critical: Yes___ No___ Prty: A___ B___

Prim Proj Mgr _____Alt Proj Mgr _____ _____IT Dept_____

Prim Cust Contact _____Alt Cust Contact _____Cust Dept_____

Prim Ops Support _____Alt Ops Support _____Soln Ctr Rep_____

B. Service Level Information (To be completed by the Project Manager)

Tech Ctr Hrs of Oprtn _____Soln Ctr Hrs of Oprtn_____ Monitoring Hrs:_____

Expected prime-shift % avail/wk: _____ Expected off-shift % avail/wk: _____

For _____type transactions, expected response time is_____

For _____type transactions, expected response time is_____

Batch requirements:_____

C. Minimum System Requirements (To be completed by the Project Manager)

DB System _____ Appl Vendor (if applicable)_____ Appl

Lang_____ Server Platform: _____ Client Platform:

_____

D. Actual Development and Production Environment (To be completed by the Manager of Systems Administration)

DB System, Ver/Rel_____ Appl Vendor, Ver/Rel (if applicable)_____

Server O/S Ver/Rel: _____Dev Hostname_____ Prod Hostname_____

List any dependencies between server O/S, DB, and appl ver/rel_____

List any differences between Dev & Prod server, O/S, DB, appl, utilities, etc. _____

_____

E. Local Area Network Architecture (To be completed by the Manager of Network Operations)

Server Topology Required (10BaseT/100BaseT/FDDI/GB-Fiber/Other):_____

Client Topology Required (10BaseT/100BaseT/FDDI/GB-Fiber/Other):_____

Protocols Required (TCPIP/Other):_____ Estimated Bandwidth:_____

Ntwk Class: On-air_____ Business_____Internet Access (Yes/No)_____

Prod Loc: Data Ctr_____ Other_____Switch Location:_____

F. Wide Area Network Architecture (To be completed by the Manager of Network Operations)

Comments_____

G. Remote Network Access (To be completed by the Manager of Network Operations)

Remote access needed (Yes/No)_____ Method of Connectivity_____

Comments_____

Figure 9-1 Sample Production Acceptance Form (page 1 of 3)

II. Capacity, Support, and Costs

	Time at Start-Up	6 Mos after Start-Up	12 Mos after Start-Up
A. Application Usage Information (To be completed by the Project Manager)			
1. Concurrent LAN users			
2. Total LAN users			
3. Concurrent WAN users			
4. Total WAN users			
5. Concurrent remote users			
6. Total remote users			
7. Total concurrent users (sum of 1,3,5)			
8. Total overall users (sum of 2,4,6)			
B. Application Resource Information (To be completed by the Project Manager)			
1. Disk storage (GB)			
2. New/upgraded desktops			
3. Peak update transactions/hour			
4. Peak inquiry transactions/hour			
5. Peak data throughput/hour			
6. Avg. data throughput/hour			
C. Technical Center Capacity Requirements (To be completed by the Manager of Systems Administration)			
1. Additional server required			
2. Type of server required			
3. Server processor upgrades			
4. Server memory upgrades			
5. Server software upgrades			
6. Disk resource upgrades			
7. Tape resource upgrades			
8. Backup media required			
9. Physical floor space			
10. Racks, cabinets, furniture			
11. Facilities (electrical, a/c, etc.)			
D. Operations Support Requirements (To be completed by the Manager of Systems Administration)			
1. FTE Computer Operator			
2. FTE Systems Administrator			
3. FTE Database Administrator			
4. FTE Network Operator			
5. FTE Call Center Analyst			

Project Manager	Date	Customer Contact	Date	Primary Operations Support	Date

Systems Administrators Manager	Date	Network Operations Manager	Date	Solution Center Manager	Date

Figure 9-1   Sample Production Acceptance Form (page 2 of 3)

Part Two: Actions Required during Month Prior to Start-Up

I. Documentation from Applications (From Project Manager)	No	In Progress	Yes	N/A
System Architecture Diagram	___	___	___	___
System Flow Diagram	___	___	___	___
Operator Run Instructions	___	___	___	___
Backup Requirements	___	___	___	___
Disaster Recovery Requirements	___	___	___	___
Project Plan with all current infrastructure tasks	___	___	___	___
User Acceptance Test Plans	___	___	___	___
User Guide	___	___	___	___
DBA Documents (data model, dictionary, scripts, etc.)	___	___	___	___

II. Status of Testing (From Project Manager)

	No	In Progress	Yes	N/A
A. Unit Tests	___	___	___	___
B. Systems Tests	___	___	___	___
C. Integration Tests (when applicable)	___	___	___	___
D. Regression Tests (when applicable)	___	___	___	___
E. Stress Tests	___	___	___	___
F. User Acceptance Tests	___	___	___	___
G. Parallel Tests	___	___	___	___

III. Training Plans (From Project Manager)

	No	In Progress	Yes	N/A
A. Operations Support Training	___	___	___	___
B. Solution Center Training	___	___	___	___
C. User Training	___	___	___	___

_____	_____	_____	_____	_____	_____
Project Manager	Date	Customer Contact	Date	Primary Operations Support	Date

Part Three: Actions Required during Week Prior to Start-Up

I. Documentation Follow-Up

   A. Review, correct, and update as needed

II. Execution of Training Plans

   A. Operator Training
   B. Call Center Training
   C. User Training

III. Service Level Agreements

   A. Signed Service Level Agreements with Customers and Operations Support

_____	_____	_____	_____	_____	_____
Project Manager	Date	Customer Contact	Date	Primary Operations Support	Date

Figure 9-1   Sample Production Acceptance Form (page 3 of 3)

Step 11: Conduct a Lessons-Learned Session

In this step, the process owner conducts a thorough, candid lessons-learned session with key participants involved in executing the pilot system. Participants should include representatives from the user community, development area, support staff, and help desk.

Step 12: Revise Policies, Procedures, and Forms

The recommendations resulting from the lessons-learned session may include revisions to policies, procedures, forms, test plans, and training techniques for users and support staff. These revisions should be agreed to by the entire cross-functional team and implemented prior to full deployment.

Step 13: Formulate Marketing Strategy

Regardless of how thoroughly and effectively a cross-functional team designs a production acceptance process, the process does little good if it is not supported and applied by development groups. Once the final policies, procedures, and forms are in place, the process owner and design team should formulate and implement a marketing strategy. The marketing plan should include the benefits of using the process; the active support of the executive sponsor and peers; examples of any quick wins as evidenced by the pilot system; and testimonials from users, service desk personnel, and support staff.

Step 14: Follow-up for Ongoing Enforcement and Improvements

Improvement processes such as production acceptance often enjoy much initial support and enthusiasm, but that is sometimes short-lived. Changing priorities, conflicting schedules, budget constraints, turnover of staff or management, lack of adequate resources, and a general reluctance to adopt radically new procedures all contribute to the de-emphasis and avoidance of novel processes. One of the best ways to ensure ongoing support and consistent use is to follow up with reviews, post-mortems, and lessons learned to constantly improve the overall quality, enforcement, and effectiveness of the process.

Full Deployment of a New Application

By this point, the production acceptance process should be designed, approved, documented, tested, and implemented. So when does the new application become deployed? The answer is that the process of developing the process does not specifically include the deployment of a new application. When the production acceptance process is applied, it will include the use of a form such as the one previously described in Figure 9-1, which includes all of the activities leading up to the actual deployment. In other words, if all of the tasks outlined by the form in Figure 9-1 are completed on time for any new application, its successful deployment is all but guaranteed.

One of the key aspects of this entire process is the involvement of the infrastructure group early on. The development manager who owns the new application should notify and involve the production acceptance process owner as soon as a new application is approved. This ensures infrastructure personnel and support staff are given adequate lead time to plan, coordinate, and implement the required resources and training prior to deployment. Just as important are the follow-up and lessons-learned portions of the process, which usually occurs two to three weeks after initial deployment.

Real Life Experience—Celebrating Process Independence Every Day

The IT department of a company offering satellite services to residential users contracted with a consultant to implement a production acceptance process. They selected a financial module of PeopleSoft as their perfect pilot. Everything went flawlessly and the team consisting of the project manager, developers, operations, and other support groups celebrated their modest success. Two months later, several additional modules of PeopleSoft were planned to be installed. But the CIO and development manager had now both moved on and their replacements did not see the immediate value in a production acceptance process. Without it, the implementation of the three additional modules took far longer, and with far more disruption, then the original pilot module.

The new CIO and development manager eventually agreed to follow the process for all future production application implementations. But it came at a price. The original consultant had moved on to his next client and was unavailable for a short follow-up. The development group was familiarized with the original production acceptance process, but it took longer and cost more than if it had been followed through from the start. The important lesson learned here was to commit to a new process for the long-haul, and to make it independent of key personnel changes.

Distinguishing New Applications from New Versions of Existing Applications

Users of a new process understandably will have questions about when and how to apply it. One of the most frequent questions I hear asked about production acceptance is: Should it be used only for new applications, or is it for new versions of existing applications as well? The answer lies in the overall objective of the process, which is to consistently and successfully deploy application systems into production.

A new version of an existing application often has major changes that impact customers and infrastructure groups alike. In this case, deploying it into production is very similar to deploying a new application. Test plans should be developed, customer acceptance pilots should be formulated, and capacity requirements should be identified well in advance. The guideline for deciding when to use production acceptance is this: Determine how different the new version of the system is from its predecessor. If users, support staff, and service desk personnel are likely to experience even moderate impact from a new version of an existing application, then the production acceptance process should be used.

Distinguishing Production Acceptance from Change Management

Another question I frequently hear is: How does one distinguish production acceptance from change management, since both seem to be handling software changes? The answer is that production acceptance is a special type of change that involves many more elements than the typical software modification. Capacity forecasts, resource requirements, customer sign-off, service desk training, and close initial monitoring by developers are just some of the usual aspects of production acceptance that are normally not associated with change management. The other obvious difference between the two processes is that, while production acceptance is involved solely with deploying application software into production, change management covers a wide range of activities outside of production software, such as hardware, networks, desktops, and facilities.

Case Study: Assessing the Production Acceptance Process at Seven Diverse Companies

All the theory in the world about designing world-class infrastructures is of little use if it cannot be applied to real-life environments. In this section, I present real-life applications of infrastructure processes in general and applications of the production acceptance process in particular. All of the material in this part of the book is taken from work involving the production acceptance process that I performed in recent years at seven separate companies. The companies vary significantly in size, age, industry, orientation, and IT maturity. As a result, they offer a wide diversity of real-life experiences in how companies recognize, support, and improve the quality of their production acceptance environments.

In addition to the general company attributes previously mentioned, this initial part of the case study describes several key IT characteristics of each firm. This is to show both the amount and range of diversity among these organizations. I then discuss each company in more detail with emphasis on its particular strengths and weaknesses in its approach to infrastructure processes. Included in this section is a unique feature of this book: a completed assessment worksheet measuring the relative quality and robustness of each company's production acceptance process. The last part of this section summarizes and compares the attributes, relative strengths, weaknesses, and lessons learned from each of the seven companies studied.

The Seven Companies Selected

These seven companies were selected based on my familiarity with each one either as a client of my professional services or as a client whose infrastructure I personally managed. It is fortunate that these companies provided such a wide variety of IT environments. To gain further insight from studying the relative strengths and weaknesses of numerous production acceptance processes, it is helpful to draw from a variety of IT environments.

The seven companies studied here could not have been more diverse. They each consisted primarily of one of the four major platform environments: mainframe, midrange, client/server, or web-enabled. No two were in the same industry. They covered a wide spectrum of businesses that included aerospace, broadcast content, motion pictures, defense contracting, dotcom e-tailor, broadcast delivery, and financial services.

The age of the oldest company, 50 years, was more than 10 times the age of the youngest one. Even more striking was the variation by a factor of 1,000 from the largest number of total employees (and the number of IT employees specifically) to the smallest. Despite the diversity of these companies, they all had production applications to deploy, operate, maintain, and manage. They all shared a common production goal to run these systems as reliably and as efficiently as possible. The degree to which they accomplished that goal varied almost as widely as the environments that described them. Studying what each company did well or not so well when managing its applications provides important lessons as to how to implement a truly world-class production services department.

Types of Attributes

In setting out to study and analyze the production services function of these companies, I first identified attributes of each company that fell into one of three categories: business-oriented, IT-oriented and production services-oriented. The following characteristics were associated with each category.

Business-oriented attributes:
- Type of industry of the company
  Manufacturing
  High technology
  Entertainment
  Services

- Total number of its employees at the time of the study
  Largest had 80,000 workers
  Smallest had 75
  Average number was 17,300
- Number of years it had been in business
  Oldest was 70 years
  Youngest was 4 years
  Average was 31 years

IT-oriented attributes:

- Number of IT workers
  Largest had 2000 employees
  Smallest had 25 employees
  Average was 457 employees
- Number of processors by platform
- Number of desktops

Production services-oriented attributes:

- Total number of applications in production
- Number of production applications deployed per month
- Existence of a production services department
- To which group the production services department reported

The largest IT department in our sample skews the data slightly since the average is a more reasonable 200 with it removed.

Table 9-4 lists all of these attributes for each of the seven companies. We identify these seven firms simply as Company A, Company B and on through Company G. A few observations are worth noting aside from the obvious diversity of the companies. One is that the size of the company does not necessarily dictate the size of the IT department. For example, Company A has 80,000 employees, with 400 of them in IT; Company D has 30,000 workers, with 2,000 of them in IT. This is because Company A has many manufacturing workers not directly tied to IT, whereas Company D has major defense programs requiring huge investments in IT.

Table 9-4   Summary Comparison of Case Study Companies

Attribute	Company A	Company B	Company C	Company D	Company E	Company F	Company G
Industry:	Aerospace	Broadcast content	Motion pictures	Defense contractor	Dot-com e-tailor	Broadcast delivery	Financial services
Number of Employees:	80,000	1,500	3,000	30,000	75	4000	2,500
Age of Company:	50	15	70	60	4	10	8
Employees Within IT:	400	125	200	2,000	25	300	150
Mainframes:	4	0	0	8	0	2	0
(Midranges):	4	0	2	10	0	2	0
(Servers)	4	40	50	20	10	30	200
Desktops	1,200	600	2,000	5,000	80	1,800	1,500
# of Prod. Applications	350	125	150	500	25	700	250
Applications Deployed/Month:	2	2	3	4	1	3	5
Prod. Services Dept.:	Yes	No	No	Yes	No	Yes	No
Dept. to Which PS Reported:	Ops	N/A	N/A	Ops	N/A	Application Support	N/A
Quality Assurance Dept.:	No	No	Yes	Yes	No	Yes	Yes
Dept. to Which QA Reported:	N/A	N/A	Enterprise Planning	Apps Dev.	N/A	Apps Dev.	Apps Dev.
Change Mgmt. Formality	Medium	Low	Medium	High	None	Low	None
Prod. Acceptance Formality	Medium	None	Low	High	None	None	None

We will next look at each of the seven companies in more detail, focusing on their use, or non-use, of a production services function. We will also discuss each IT organization's relative strengths and weaknesses and what they learned from their experiences with attempting to implement robust infrastructure processes.

Company A

Company A is a large, well-established aerospace firm. The company is more than 50 years old and enjoys a reputation for researching, developing, and applying cutting-edge technology for both the military and commercial sectors. At the time of our assignment, it employed 80,000 workers—of whom 400 resided in IT. The IT platform environment of its main corporate computer center consisted primarily of four huge mainframes, with the same number of midrange computers and servers and approximately 1,200 desktops.

The IT operations department of Company A had a well-established production services function that ran 350 production applications daily (slightly more during month-end processing) and deployed on average two new production applications per month. There was no quality-assurance group at this company, although they did have the beginnings of a formal change management and production acceptance process.

The production services department was staffed by two very competent individuals who thoroughly knew the ins and outs of running virtually every production application in the company, though little of it was documented. They were very technically knowledgeable, as was most all of the staff in IT. This reflected part of the company's mission to develop highly technical expertise throughout the enterprise. Another part of the company's mission was to dedicate every department to continuous process improvement. The production services function was still very manually oriented and consequently somewhat inefficient. No automated scheduling systems were in place here at this time, but the company was willing to try new techniques and try new technologies to improve their processes.

Production services was also very segregated from other processes, such as change and problem management. There was only the start of a production acceptance process, which was not tied to production services at all. This segregation occasionally strained communications between operations and applications development. The fact that they were 25 miles apart sometimes added to the lack of face-to-face meetings.

Operations did a good job of collecting meaningful metrics such as outages, abnormal terminations, reruns, reprints, and reports delivered on time. There was an inconsistent emphasis on how often or how deeply their metrics should be analyzed, which sometimes undermined their usefulness.

To summarize Company A's strengths, they were willing to try new techniques and new technologies, they committed to continuous process improvement, they hired and developed a technically competent staff, and they were willing to collect meaningful metrics. To summarize their weaknesses, they tended to not interact with members of other IT staffs, they provided little documented training, they did not always have effective communications with the development group (due, in part, to a 25-mile separation), and they did not always analyze the metrics they collected.

Eventually, the operations department implemented a more formal production acceptance process. One of the most important lessons we learned was to ensure the operations department was involved very early with a new application project. This helps ensure that the appropriate operation's group provides or receives the proper resources, capacity, documentation, and training required for a successful deployment. The other important lesson we learned was that the other infrastructure support groups (such as network services, the help desk, storage management, and desktop applications) need to provide their full support to the production services function. Because this function had worked in an isolated manner in the past, other infrastructure support groups were initially reluctant to support it. They eventually did as improved processes, automation, and increased communication became more prevalent.

The nonweighted worksheet shown in Figure 9-2 presents a quick-and-simple method for assessing the overall quality, efficiency, and effectiveness of the production acceptance process at Company A. As mentioned previously, one of the most valuable characteristics of a worksheet of this kind is that it can be customized to evaluate each of the 12 processes individually. The worksheet in the following sections of this chapter applies only to the production acceptance process for each of the seven companies studied. However, the fundamental concepts applied in using these evaluation worksheets are the same for all 12 disciplines. As a result, the detailed explanation on the general use of these worksheets presented near the end of Chapter 7 also applies to the other worksheets in the book. Please refer to that discussion if you need more information on how weights are computed.

Process owners and their managers collaborate with other appropriate individuals to fill out this form. Along the left-hand column are 10 categories of characteristics about a process. The degree to which each of these characteristics is put to use in designing and managing a process is a good measure of its relative robustness.

Production Acceptance Process - Assessment Worksheet						
Process Owner: Employee A Owner's Manager: Manager A				Date: N/A		
Category	Questions About Production Acceptance	None 1	Small 2	Medium 3	Large 4
Executive Support	To what degree does the executive sponsor show support for the production acceptance process with actions such as engaging development managers and their staffs in this process?			3	
Process Owner	To what degree does the process owner exhibit desirable traits and understand application development and deployment?				4
Customer Involvement	To what degree are key customers, especially from development, operations and the help desk, involved in the design and use of the process?		2		
Supplier Involvement	To what degree are key suppliers, such as 3 rd party vendors, trainers and technical writers, involved in the design of the process?			3	
Service Metrics	To what degree are service metrics analyzed for trends such as the amount of positive feedback from users and the number of calls to the help desk, immediately after deployment?		2		
Process Metrics	To what degree are process metrics analyzed for trends such as the frequency and duration of delays to deployment and the accuracy and timeliness of documentation and training?	1			
Process Integration	To what degree does the production acceptance process integrate with other processes and tools such as change management and problem management?	1			
Streamlining/ Automation	To what degree is the production acceptance process streamlined by automating actions such as the documentation of a new application and online training for it by means of the intranet?	1			
Training of Staff	To what degree is the staff cross-trained on the production acceptance process, and how well is the effectiveness of the training verified?	1			
Process Documentation	To what degree is the quality and value of production acceptance documentation measured and maintained?		2		
	Totals	4	6	6	4
	Grand Total = 20				
	Assessment Score = 20/40 = 50%				

Figure 9-2   Assessment Worksheet for Company A

The categories that assess the overall quality of a process are executive support, process owner, and process documentation. Categories assessing the overall efficiency of a process consist of supplier involvement, process metrics, process integration, and streamlining/automation. The categories used to assess effectiveness include customer involvement, service metrics, and the training of staff.

The evaluation of each category is a very simple procedure. The relative degree to which the characteristics within each category are present and being used is rated on a scale of 1 to 4, with 1 indicating no or barely any presence and 4 representing a large presence of the characteristic. For example, at this particular company, the executive sponsor for the production acceptance process demonstrated some initial support for the process by carefully selecting and coaching the process owner. However, over time, this same executive showed only mild interest in engaging all of the necessary development managers and staffs in the process. We consequently rated the overall degree to which this executive showed support for this process as small, giving it a 3 on the scale of 1 to 4. On the other hand, the process owner was extremely knowledgeable on all of the critical applications and their deployments, so we rated this category a 4.

We similarly rated each of the categories as shown in Figure 9-2. Obviously, a single column could be used record the ratings of each category; however, if we format separate columns for each of the four possible scores, categories scoring the lowest and highest ratings stand out visually. The next step is to sum the numerical scores within each column. For Company A, this totals to 4 + 6 + 6 + 4 = 20. This total is then divided by the maximum possible rating of 40, for an assessment score of 50 percent.

Company B

Company B is a satellite broadcast venture featuring informational programming. It is a relatively young firm at 15 years old. When it began, the technology of digital informational broadcasting was in its early refinement stages. This, among other reasons, resulted in them being very willing to employ cutting-edge technology. They did this almost to a fault, using very advanced but questionably tested technology at the outset for their satellites. They learned from their experiences, improved their technology, and eventually applied to their IT department by implementing cutting-edge but proved infrastructure processes.

Company B employs 1,500 workers, of whom 125 resided in IT. Their IT platform environment consists of 40 servers and approximately 600 desktops. There was no production services function at Company B nor was there a quality assurance group. They ran 125 production applications daily and deployed on average two new production applications per month. There was only a start of a change management process and no production acceptance process.

With the company poised to implement major enterprise applications, senior IT management realized they needed a formal production acceptance process. While preferring to do the work with their own staffs, they acknowledged limited in-house process expertise and hired professional consultants to run a pilot program. The IT executives were also very helpful in supplying qualified staff members from both applications development and operations to support the pilot program.

Since this was the first formal implementation of any infrastructure process, there was no integration to other processes and no immediate plans to do so. While applications development was extremely helpful in designing the production acceptance process and testing it with a perfect pilot application, they did not provide adequate training and documentation to the operations help desk. This was partly due to a re-shuffling of applications priorities, which also delayed the implementation of the process with a fully deployed application.

In summary of Company B's strengths, they saw the need for professional support for designing a Production Acceptance processes, they started out with pilot programs, and they staffed the pilot programs with qualified staff. For their weaknesses, the company did not provide adequate training and documentation to the help-desk group for their pilot program; they allowed support for the production acceptance process to weaken.

In a manner similar to that described for Company A, we performed an initial assessment of the production acceptance environment for Company B (see Figure 9-3). Their points totaled 18, for a final assessment score of 45 percent.

Production Acceptance Process - Assessment Worksheet						
Process Owner: Employee B **Owner's Manager:** Manager B				**Date:** N/A		
Category	**Questions About Production Acceptance**	None 1	Small 2	Medium 3	Large 4
Executive Support	To what degree does the executive sponsor show support for the production acceptance process with actions such as engaging development managers and their staffs in this process?			3	
Process Owner	To what degree does the process owner exhibit desirable traits and understand application development and deployment?			3	
Customer Involvement	To what degree are key customers, especially from development, operations, and the help desk, involved in the design and use of the process?		2		
Supplier Involvement	To what degree are key suppliers, such as 3rd party vendors, trainers, and technical writers, involved in the design of the process?		2		
Service Metrics	To what degree are service metrics analyzed for trends such as the amount of positive feedback from users and the number of calls to the help desk, immediately after deployment?	1			
Process Metrics	To what degree are process metrics analyzed for trends such as the frequency and duration of delays to deployment and the accuracy and timeliness of documentation and training?	1			
Process Integration	To what degree does the production acceptance process integrate with other processes and tools such as change management and problem management?	1			
Streamlining/ Automation	To what degree is the production acceptance process streamlined by automating actions such as the documentation of a new application and online training for it by means of the intranet?	1			
Training of Staff	To what degree is the staff cross-trained on the production acceptance process, and how well is the effectiveness of the training verified?		2		
Process Documentation	To what degree is the quality and value of production acceptance documentation measured and maintained?		2		
	Totals	4	8	6	0
		Grand Total = 18			
		Assessment Score = 18/40 = 45%			

Figure 9-3   Assessment Worksheet for Company B

Company C

Our third company is one of the seven major motion picture studios in southern California. Studios in Hollywood tend to be an interesting paradox. On the one hand, they are some of the most creative companies for which one could ever hope to work. This applies to the writing, directing, acting, special effects, and other artistic pursuits that go into the production of a major motion picture. But when it comes to the traditional, administrative support of the company, they are as conservative as can be. This was especially true in their IT departments, and Company C was certainly no different in this regard. By the late 1990s, its IT department needed to be significantly upgraded to meet aggressive new business expansions.

Company C employs 3,000 workers, of whom 200 resided in IT. Their IT platform environment consists of two key midrange computers, 50 servers, and approximately 2,000 desktops. The company outsourced its mainframe processing, which still runs many of its core financial systems. There was no production services function at Company C, but there was a quality-assurance department that reported to an enterprise-planning group. Operations ran 150 production applications daily and deployed on average three new production applications per month. There was a formal, though not robust, change management process and an informal production acceptance process.

The IT executives at Company C conducted a studio-wide business assessment and determined that its current IT architecture would not support the future growth of the company. Many of the IT business systems would have to be upgraded or replaced and there would have to be a major overhaul of the IT infrastructure and its processes to support the new application environment. Among the processes needing improving was production acceptance. IT managers recognized the need and the opportunity to re-engineer their systems development life cycle (SDLC) methodology at the same time, and they committed the resources to do so. Software suppliers played key roles in these upgrades and re-engineering efforts. Managers also ensured that users, both internal and external to IT, received sufficient training on these new processes.

The IT quality assurance group at Company C worked closely with operations and developers in chartering a productions services function and in designing a production acceptance process. Since QA reported to the applications development department, IT executives elected to have the production services function report to them as well. This proved to be problematic in that the infrastructure group was often excluded from key deployment decisions. Another result of this arrangement was that it provided little documentation or training to the service desk and computer operations teams.

Summing up Company C's strengths, they recognized the need to upgrade their antiquated processes, they committed resources to re-engineer the SDLC process, and they provided considerable training to users on new processes. As to their weaknesses, they did not involve the infrastructure when designing the production acceptance process, they moved the control of production acceptance into applications development and out of operations, and they provided little or no training and documentation for the help desk and operations.

Eventually, the production services function became little more than an extension of the QA department, which still reported to applications development. As a result, although the company did now have a production acceptance process in place, the lack of infrastructure ownership of it made it less robust and less effective. The key lesson learned here was that IT executives must ensure that operations control the production acceptance process and that development be involved in the process design from the start.

Similar to the previous companies, we performed an initial assessment of the production acceptance environment for Company C (see Figure 9-4). Their points totaled 19, for a final assessment score of 48 percent.

Company D

This company is a major defense contractor which has supplied major weapons systems to the United States and foreign governments for more than 60 years. Its customers are primarily the five branches of the U.S. armed forces and secondarily the militaries of foreign governments. The company manages both classified and non-classified programs, putting an additional premium on fail-safe security systems. It also supplies limited commercial aviation products.

At the time of our involvement, Company D employed 30,000 workers, of whom 2,000 resided in IT. Their IT platform environment consists of eight mainframes, 10 midrange computers, 20 servers, and 5,000 desktops. There was a relatively formal production services function at Company D that reported to operations and a quality-assurance group that reported to applications development. They ran 500 production applications daily (dozens more on weekends) and deployed on average four new production applications per month. The company had very formal change management and production acceptance processes and was very committed to the practices of total quality and continuous process improvement.

Production Acceptance Process - Assessment Worksheet						
Process Owner: Employee C **Owner's Manager:** Manager C				**Date:** N/A		
Category	**Questions About Production Acceptance**	None 1	Small 2	Medium 3	Large 4
Executive Support	To what degree does the executive sponsor show support for the production acceptance process with actions such as engaging development managers and their staffs in this process?		2		
Process Owner	To what degree does the process owner exhibit desirable traits and understand application development and deployment?		2		
Customer Involvement	To what degree are key customers, especially from development, operations, and the help desk, involved in the design and use of the process?		2		
Supplier Involvement	To what degree are key suppliers, such as 3rd party vendors, trainers, and technical writers, involved in the design of the process?			3	
Service Metrics	To what degree are service metrics analyzed for trends such as the amount of positive feedback from users and the number of calls to the help desk, immediately after deployment?	1			
Process Metrics	To what degree are process metrics analyzed for trends such as the frequency and duration of delays to deployment and the accuracy and timeliness of documentation and training?	1			
Process Integration	To what degree does the production acceptance process integrate with other processes and tools such as change management and problem management?	1			
Streamlining/ Automation	To what degree is the production acceptance process streamlined by automating actions such as the documentation of a new application and online training for it by means of the intranet?		2		
Training of Staff	To what degree is the staff cross-trained on the production acceptance process, and how well is the effectiveness of the training verified?			3	
Process Documentation	To what degree is the quality and value of production acceptance documentation measured and maintained?		2		
	Totals	3	10	6	0
	Grand Total = 19				
	Assessment Score = 19/40 = 48%				

Figure 9-4   Assessment Worksheet for Company C

The company also emphasized the use and analysis of meaningful metrics. By meaningful, we mean metrics that our customers and our suppliers can both use to improve the level of our services. One of the most refreshing aspects of this company was their support of our pre-scribed process improvement sequence of integrating first, standardiz-ing second, streamlining third, and automating last.

As with many government defense contractors, Company D found itself rushing to meet program milestones and this sometimes under-mined infrastructure processes such as production acceptance. High-priority projects were allowed to bypass the process to meet critical deadlines. Plans to streamline and automate the production acceptance process became a victim of unfortunate timing. Just as they were about to be put into place, cutbacks in personnel prevented the plans from being implemented. Subsequent mergers and acquisitions brought about some temporary turf wars that further delayed the standardization of processes across all divisions.

To summarize Company D's strengths, they were committed to total quality and continuous process improvement criteria, they were com-mitted to doing excellent analysis of metrics, and they were striving sequentially to integrate, standardize, streamline, and then automate processes. To summarize their weaknesses, they were undermining the production acceptance process by rushing to meet deadlines, they were allowing high-priority projects to bypass the process, they were not allowing the process to be streamlined due to cutbacks, and they were experiencing occasional turf wars between IT departments.

Eventually, the standardization, streamlining, and automating of processes did occur among departments and across divisions and remote sites, and it brought with it significant operation and financial benefits. The standardization also helped facilitate future company acquisitions and the merging of remote sites.

As we did with our prior companies, we performed an initial assess-ment of the production acceptance environment for Company D (see Figure 9-5). They scored one of the highest initial assessments we had ever seen. Their points totaled 33, for a final assessment score of 83 percent.

Production Acceptance Process - Assessment Worksheet						
Process Owner: Employee D **Owner's Manager:** Manager D				**Date:** N/A		
Category	Questions About Production Acceptance	None 1	Small 2	Medium 3	Large 4
Executive Support	To what degree does the executive sponsor show support for the production acceptance process with actions such as engaging development managers and their staffs in this process?			3	
Process Owner	To what degree does the process owner exhibit desirable traits and understand application development and deployment?				4
Customer Involvement	To what degree are key customers, especially from development, operations, and the help desk, involved in the design and use of the process?				4
Supplier Involvement	To what degree are key suppliers, such as 3rd party vendors, trainers, and technical writers, involved in the design of the process?			3	
Service Metrics	To what degree are service metrics analyzed for trends such as the amount of positive feedback from users and the number of calls to the help desk, immediately after deployment?			3	
Process Metrics	To what degree are process metrics analyzed for trends such as the frequency and duration of delays to deployment and the accuracy and timeliness of documentation and training?			3	
Process Integration	To what degree does the production acceptance process integrate with other processes and tools such as change management and problem management?		2		
Streamlining/ Automation	To what degree is the production acceptance process streamlined by automating actions such as the documentation of a new application and online training for it by means of the intranet?				4
Training of Staff	To what degree is the staff cross-trained on the production acceptance process, and how well is the effectiveness of the training verified?				4
Process Documentation	To what degree is the quality and value of production acceptance documentation measured and maintained?			3	
	Totals	0	2	15	16
	Grand Total = 33				
	Assessment Score = 33/40 = 83%				

Figure 9-5   Assessment Worksheet for Company D

Company E

Our next company is a dot-com victim, but fortunately not a casualty. Like many dot-com start-ups before it, this company began with a simple idea. The idea was to offer pop culture merchandise from television, motion pictures, sports, and other forms of entertainment. It had been in existence barely four years and was poised for significant growth. A shrinking national economy coupled with fierce competition on the Internet forced dramatic cutbacks in the company. It did survive, but on a much smaller scale.

Company E employs 75 workers, of whom 25 resided in IT. Their IT platform environment consists of 10 servers and 80 desktops. There was no production services function at Company E nor was there a quality-assurance group. They ran 25 production applications daily and deployed on average one new production application per month. The initial priorities of the company were to get their website up and operational and to start producing revenue. As a result, there was no change management or production acceptance processes in place. As the company started to grow, the need for these processes became more apparent.

Since the company was starting with a clean slate, there were no previous processes to undo, replace, or re-engineer. There were many young, energetic individuals who were eager to learn new skills and methods. The relatively small profile of applications meant that we had a large number from which to select for a pilot program. A willing staff and a select group of pilot applications could not overcome the problems and changing priorities of the company's rapid growth. Just as a process was about to be implemented, a new crisis would arise, putting the new procedure on hold.

A larger challenge common to many dot-com companies was the culture clashes that arose between the entrepreneurial spirit of those behind the company's initial success and the more disciplined approach of those charged with implementing structured processes into the environment. The clash was especially evident between the technical gurus who were used to having free reign when deploying new applications, installing upgrades, or making routine maintenance changes. Those of us tasked with implementing infrastructure processes spent a fair amount of time negotiating, compromising, and marketing before achieving some positive results.

In summarizing Company E's strengths, they were a high-energy start-up with no prior processes needing to be re-engineered, they had only a small profile of existing applications with many new ones planned (allowing for a number of pilot programs), and they had a young staff eager to learn new methods. For their weaknesses, their rapid growth hindered the use of processes, their entrepreneurial culture clashed with disciplined processes, and their influential technical gurus were at times unwilling to support new processes.

Despite these drawbacks, we were able to design and pilot an initial production acceptance process. The process was much more streamlined than normal due to the accelerated nature of web-enabled applications. This streamlining actually helped to integrate it with a pilot change management process also being developed. The frequency of new applications builds in this Internet environment at times made change management and production acceptance almost indistinguishable. This integration also facilitated much cross-training between infrastructure groups and applications development to ensure each area understood the other as changes and deployments were being planned.

As we did with our prior companies, we performed an initial assessment of the production acceptance environment for Company E (see Figure 9-6). As you might expect with a start-up, the assessment was relatively low (although they did score well for cross-training). Their points totaled 16, for a final assessment score of 40 percent.

Company F

This company did everything right—almost. It broke off from a relatively rigid, conservative parent company and vowed to be more flexible, progressive, and streamlined. The IT executives understood the importance of robust infrastructure processes and committed the resources to make them a reality. Their only flaw was in diving headfirst into production acceptance before any semblance of a change management process was put in place.

Company F employs 4,000 workers, of whom 300 resided in IT. Their IT platform environment consists of two mainframe processors, two midrange computers, 30 servers, and approximately 1,800 desktops. There was a production services department at Company F that reported to an applications-support group, and there was a quality-assurance group that reported to applications development. They ran 700 production applications daily, a dozen or so more on weekends and during month-end closings, and deployed on average three new production applications per month. There was only a start of change management process and no production acceptance process.

Production Acceptance Process - Assessment Worksheet						
Process Owner: Employee E **Owner's Manager:** Manager E **Date:** N/A						
Category	**Questions About Production Acceptance**	**None** 1	**Small** 2	**Medium** 3	**Large** 4	
Executive Support	To what degree does the executive sponsor show support for the production acceptance process with actions such as engaging development managers and their staffs in this process?		2			
Process Owner	To what degree does the process owner exhibit desirable traits and understand application development and deployment?	1				
Customer Involvement	To what degree are key customers, especially from development, operations, and the help desk, involved in the design and use of the process?		2			
Supplier Involvement	To what degree are key suppliers, such as 3rd party vendors, trainers, and technical writers, involved in the design of the process?		2			
Service Metrics	To what degree are service metrics analyzed for trends such as the amount of positive feedback from users and the number of calls to the help desk, immediately after deployment?	1				
Process Metrics	To what degree are process metrics analyzed for trends such as the frequency and duration of delays to deployment and the accuracy and timeliness of documentation and training?	1				
Process Integration	To what degree does the production acceptance process integrate with other processes and tools such as change management and problem management?	1				
Streamlining/ Automation	To what degree is the production acceptance process streamlined by automating actions such as the documentation of a new application and online training for it by means of the intranet?		2			
Training of Staff	To what degree is the staff cross-trained on the production acceptance process, and how well is the effectiveness of the training verified?			3		
Process Documentation	To what degree is the quality and value of production acceptance documentation measured and maintained?	1				
	Totals	5	8	3	0	
				Grand Total = 16		
				Assessment Score = 16/40 = 40%		

Figure 9-6   Assessment Worksheet for Company E

When the company first asked us to upgrade their IT environment by implementing robust infrastructure processes, they suggested we begin with production acceptance. They reasoned that this would be a natural place to start because they were planning to deploy several new critical applications during the upcoming year and already had an application-support group in place. We conducted an initial assessment of their infrastructure and concluded that a change management process was more urgently needed than production acceptance. We based this conclusion on the number and variety of changes being made to their production environment locally and remotely and that both were increasing at an accelerated rate.

The IT executives were very receptive to our recommendation about change management and were very supportive of our efforts to involve various departments within IT. They suggested that we include the remote sites as part of our strategy and committed time and resources to the process. Including the remote sites was a key addition since it allowed us to standardize and integrate the process across all locations. Even though a partial change management process was already in place, the IT managers realized its disjointed nature and its lack of metrics and were willing to design a new process from scratch. They had not realized much need in the past to collect or analyze metrics, but they were won over after seeing how effective they could be in managing changes and new deployments.

One downside during our involvement at Company F was the frequent reorganizations, especially concerning operations, applications support, and our new production services function. This delayed some of the process approvals and made some of the managers unwilling to select a pilot project for production acceptance because responsibilities for certain applications were likely to change.

As to Company F's strengths then, they recognized that change management needed to be implemented prior to any other infrastructure processes, their IT executives provided strong support for these processes, they included their remote sites as part of the strategy, and they were willing to start with a clean slate. As to its weaknesses, Company F saw little need for the use of metrics, they had no recognition of the need to analyze metrics, they reorganized frequently, which undermined attempts at process improvements, and they were unwilling to nominate a pilot production acceptance project.

Despite these hurdles, a very effective change management process was implanted at Company F. There was total standardization among three sites despite the fact each site was separated from the other by more than 1,000 miles. There were service and process metrics in place that were regularly collected, analyzed, and distributed. And it laid the foundation for a production acceptance process that would shortly follow. The most significant lesson learned was how important it was to implement key processes in the proper sequence. We would not have been as successful with either change management or production acceptance if we had not implemented them in the order we did.

As we did with our prior companies, we performed an initial assessment of the production acceptance environment for Company F (see Figure 9-7). Their prior establishment of an application-support group resulted in them having good services metrics, which were collected and analyzed on a regular basis. Their points totaled 27, for a final assessment score of 68 percent.

Company G

Company G is a relatively young financial services establishment that began eight years ago. It is successfully transitioning from that of a small start-up to a medium-sized enterprise. We have seen many a company at a similar time in their development struggle to transform from a novice firm into a mature organization. Company G does not seem to be struggling in this transformation. They have effectively promoted a culture of empowerment, honesty, and change; it is very much in evidence in their everyday manner of doing business.

Company G employs 2,500 workers, of whom 150 reside in IT. Their IT platform environment consists of 200 servers and approximately 1,500 desktops. The reason they have such a large number of servers in relation to desktops is that for several years, each new application was given its own server. This was one of several reasons for instituting a production acceptance process. There was no production services function at Company G, although there was a quality-assurance group that reported to applications development. They run 250 production applications daily and deploy an average of five new production applications per month. There was only the start of a change management process and no production acceptance process at the time we initiated our involvement.

Because the company was so young, it had few infrastructures processes in place. The upside to this was that there were few poor processes that needed to be re-worked. IT executives recognized the need to implement robust infrastructure processes and were willing to hire full-time staff to help implement and maintain them, particularly change management, production acceptance, and business continuity. They also saw the huge benefits from integrating these processes and stressed the need to design and implement these processes in a coordinated fashion.

Production Acceptance Process - Assessment Worksheet					
Process Owner: Employee F **Owner's Manager:** Manager F			**Date:** N/A		
Category	**Questions About Production Acceptance**	None 1	Small 2	Medium 3	Large 4
Executive Support	To what degree does the executive sponsor show support for the production acceptance process with actions such as engaging development managers and their staffs in this process?			3	
Process Owner	To what degree does the process owner exhibit desirable traits and understand application development and deployment?			3	
Customer Involvement	To what degree are key customers, especially from development, operations, and the help desk, involved in the design and use of the process?			3	
Supplier Involvement	To what degree are key suppliers, such as 3rd party vendors, trainers, and technical writers, involved in the design of the process?			3	
Service Metrics	To what degree are service metrics analyzed for trends such as the amount of positive feedback from users and the number of calls to the help desk, immediately after deployment?				4
Process Metrics	To what degree are process metrics analyzed for trends such as the frequency and duration of delays to deployment and the accuracy and timeliness of documentation and training?			3	
Process Integration	To what degree does the production acceptance process integrate with other processes and tools such as change management and problem management?		2		
Streamlining/ Automation	To what degree is the production acceptance process streamlined by automating actions such as the documentation of a new application and online training for it by means of the intranet?		2		
Training of Staff	To what degree is the staff cross-trained on the production acceptance process, and how well is the effectiveness of the training verified?			3	
Process Documentation	To what degree is the quality and value of production acceptance documentation measured and maintained?	1			
	Totals	1	4	18	4
				Grand Total = 27	
				Assessment Score = 27/40 = 68%	

Figure 9-7   Assessment Worksheet for Company F

The company did have a few hurdles to overcome. Audits are a fact of life in the banking and financial services industry and Company G had their share of them. This sometimes caused them to focus more on the results of audits than on the quality of their processes and services. Another hurdle was the lack of experience of critical team leads. This was no fault of the leads. The company believed strongly in promoting from within, and with such a young organization, this meant the leads needed some time to grow into their jobs. The company did invest well in training and mentoring to address this.

The rapid growth of the company also caused many shifts in priorities. This caused some pilot applications for production acceptance to change, causing the pilot to be re-started more than once. The production acceptance process did integrate well into their system development life cycle (SDLC) methodology, although an exorbitant amount of detail went into the analyses of these processes.

In review of Company G's strengths, they provided a highly empowering environment, they were a relatively young firm with few poor processes, they integrated their processes well, and they were willing to hire full-time staff to implement a production acceptance process. As to their weaknesses, they sometimes placed more emphasis on audits than on results, they lacked experienced team leads, their rapid growth caused frequent priority changes, and their production acceptance analysis was overly detailed.

This company used three excellent strategies in its process-improvement efforts

1. They used a simple design in their processes.
2. They used widely accepted tools.
3. They had wide-spread involvement and agreement by multiple groups to ensure the required buy-in from all required areas.

These strategies worked very well in fashioning processes that were efficient, effective, and widely used.

As we did with our prior companies, we performed an initial assessment of the production acceptance environment for Company G (see Figure 9-8). Their points totaled 24, for a final assessment score of 60 percent.

Selected Companies Comparison in Summary

This concludes our discussion of our process experiences at seven client companies. Table 9-5 presents a summary comparison of each company's overall assessment scores, their relative strengths and weaknesses, and the lessons they and we learned from our process-improvement efforts.

Production Acceptance Process - Assessment Worksheet						
Process Owner: Employee G	**Owner's Manager:** Manager G			**Date: N/A**		
Category	Questions About Production Acceptance	None 1	Small 2	Medium 3	Large 4
Executive Support	To what degree does the executive sponsor show support for the production acceptance process with actions such as engaging development managers and their staffs in this process?		2		
Process Owner	To what degree does the process owner exhibit desirable traits and understand application development and deployment?		2		
Customer Involvement	To what degree are key customers, especially from development, operations, and the help desk, involved in the design and use of the process?		2		
Supplier Involvement	To what degree are key suppliers, such as 3rd party vendors, trainers, and technical writers, involved in the design of the process?			3	
Service Metrics	To what degree are service metrics analyzed for trends such as the amount of positive feedback from users and the number of calls to the help desk, immediately after deployment?		2		
Process Metrics	To what degree are process metrics analyzed for trends such as the frequency and duration of delays to deployment and the accuracy and timeliness of documentation and training?	1			
Process Integration	To what degree does the production acceptance process integrate with other processes and tools such as change management and problem management?				4
Streamlining/ Automation	To what degree is the production acceptance process streamlined by automating actions such as the documentation of a new application and online training for it by means of the intranet?		2		
Training of Staff	To what degree is the staff cross-trained on the production acceptance process, and how well is the effectiveness of the training verified?			3	
Process Documentation	To what degree is the quality and value of production acceptance documentation measured and maintained?			3	
	Totals	1	10	9	4
				Grand Total = 24	
				Assessment Score = 24/40 = 60%	

Figure 9-8   Assessment Worksheet for Company G

Table 9-5 Summary of Strengths, Weaknesses, and Lessons Learned for All Companies

AS	Company A 50%	Company B 45%	Company C 48%	Company D 83%	Company E 40%	Company F 68%	Company G 60%
Strengths	- willing to try new techniques and new technologies - Committed to continuous process improvement - technically competent staff - willing to collect meaningful metrics	- saw need for professional support for designing PA processes - started out with pilot programs - staffed pilot programs with qualified staff	- recognized need to upgrade antiquated processes - committed resources to re-engineer SDLC - provided much training to users on new processes	- committed to Baldrige quality award criteria - analyzed metrics well - strived to integrate, standardize, streamline, and then automate	- high-energy start-up with no prior processes to re-engineer - small profile of applications allowed for many pilots - young staff eager to learn	- recognized that change management must come first - total support of IT executives - remote sites part of strategy - willing to start with clean slate	- highly empowering environment - relatively young firm with few poor processes - willing to hire full-time staff to implement PA
Weaknesses	- tended to not interact with staff - little documented training - operations and development group physically apart by 25 miles - collected metrics, but did not always analyze them	- did not provide training and documentation to help desk group - support for PA process weakened after pilot program - no plans to integrate with other processes	- did not involve the infrastructure - moved the control of PA into development out of operations - little or no training and documentation for help desk and operations	- rush to meet deadlines undermined the following of the PA process - high priority projects allowed to bypass process - process not streamlined due to cutbacks - turf wars	- rapid growth hindered use of processes - entrepreneurial culture clashed with disciplined processes - influential gurus unwilling to support new processes	- saw little need to use metric - no recognition of need to analyze metrics - frequent re-orgs undermined improvements - unwilling to nominate a pilot PA project	- more emphasis on audits than on results - lack of experienced team leads - rapid growth caused frequent priority changes - PA analysis overly detailed

	Company A	Company B	Company C	Company D	Company E	Company F	Company G
AS	50%	45%	48%	83%	40%	68%	60%
Lessons Learned	- development and operations need to work together from the start - infrastructure support groups need to support the PA process and operations	- ensure the long-range commitments of IT - consider a change management process prior to a PA process	- IT executives must ensure that operations control the PA process and that development is involved in the process design from the start	- there are significant benefits from standardizing across all divisions and remote sites; this helps merger integration	- one must be aware of changing and conflicting cultures due to the unstructured and entrepreneurial nature of startups	- important to implement key processes in proper sequence, such as a change management process prior to production services	- use simple, widely agreed upon processes, strategies, and tools to ensure the buy-in of all required support groups

AS = Assessment score for company's production acceptance process

Summary

Production acceptance is the first systems management process we have looked at that significantly involves other departments and for which we offer a structured methodology to develop its procedures. I began with a formal definition of production acceptance followed by a summary of the 14 steps necessary to implement this process successfully.

We then discussed each of the 14 steps in detail and included recommended attributes for a production acceptance process owner, examples of prioritized requirements and policy statements, and a sample of a production acceptance process form. Next I explained the differences between production acceptance of new applications and that of new versions of existing applications and the change management process. The chapter concluded with a case study comparing the production acceptance processes of seven different companies.

Test Your Understanding

1. The production acceptance methodology is consistent and identical across all platforms. (True or False)
2. Service providers typically need just a small number of key representative customers to serve as a barometer of good customer service. (True or False)
3. Which of the following is not a high priority characteristic of a production acceptance process owner?
    a. knowledge of applications
    b. knowledge of operating systems
    c. ability to evaluate documentation
    d. ability to communicate effectively with software developers
4. Production acceptance requires much cooperation and support between the _____ and infrastructure departments.
5. Why are policy statements necessary for a robust production acceptance process?

Suggested Further Readings

1. *Managing the IT Service Process*; Computer Weekly Professional Services; Bruton, Noel; 2004
2. *Effective Computer User Support: How to Manage the IT Help Desk*; Bruton, Noel, 2002; Butterworth-Heinemann
3. *Customer Liaison*, IT Infrastructure Library Services, Greenhalgh, Nevelle, Smaridge, Melanie, CCTA, 2001

CHAPTER 10

Change Management

Introduction

Change management is one of the most critical of systems management processes. In Chapter 21, "Integrating Systems Management Processes," Table 21-2 lists the 12 processes in order of the most interaction with other disciplines. The process of change management easily tops the chart as having the most interactions with other disciplines.

We begin with the definition of change management and point out the subtle but important difference between change control and change coordination. We next present some of the common drawbacks of most change management processes taken from recent surveys of leading infrastructure managers.

The heart of the chapter comes next as we identify the 13 steps required to design and implement an effective change management process. We describe each step in detail and include figures, charts, and tables where appropriate to illustrate salient points. The chapter concludes with an example of how to assess a change management environment.

Definition of Change Management

> ### Change Management
>
> Change management is a process to control and coordinate all changes to an IT production environment. Control involves requesting, prioritizing, and approving changes; coordination involves collaborating, scheduling, communicating, and implementing changes.

Later in this chapter, we define a whole set of terms associated with change management. Let me say at the outset that a change is defined as any modification that could impact the stability or responsiveness of an IT production environment. Some shops interchange the terms change management and change control, but there is an important distinction between the two expressions. Change management is the overall umbrella under which control and change coordination reside. Unfortunately, to many people, the term change control has a negative connotation. Let's talk about it further.

To many IT technicians, change control implies restricting, delaying, or preventing change. But to system, network, and database administrators, change is an essential part of their daily work. They view any impediments to change as something that will hinder them as they try to accomplish their everyday tasks. Their focus is on implementing a large number of widely varying changes as quickly and as simply as possible. Since many of these are routine, low-impact changes, technicians see rigid approval cycles as unnecessary, non-value-added steps. This is a challenge to infrastructure managers initiating a formal change management process. They need the buy-in of the individuals who will be most impacted by the process and are the most suspect of it.

One way to address this dilemma is to break change management into two components—change control and change coordination—and to focus on the latter at the outset. As the process becomes more refined, the emphasis should expand to include more formal requesting, prioritizing, and approvals. Table 10–1 illustrates the scope and components of change management schematically.

Table 10–1 Scope and Components of Change Management

Change Management						
Change Control			**Change Coordination**			
Request	Prioritize	Approve	Collaborate	Schedule	Communicate	Implement

The following list describes each component.

- **Request.** Submit to a reviewing board a hard copy or electronic request for a change to be made. For example, suppose tax tables need to be changed for the new year in a payroll application. The software maintenance programmer for this application would submit the change request to the change advisory board.

- **Prioritize.** Specify the priority of the change request based on criteria that have been agreed upon. In the previous tax/payroll change example, the change would likely be given a high priority.

- **Approve.** Recommend by a duly authorized review board that the change request be scheduled for implementation or that it be deferred for pending action. In the tax/payroll example, the change would likely be approved by the change advisory board pending successful testing of the change.

- **Collaborate.** Facilitate effective interaction between appropriate members of support groups to ensure successful implementation; log and track the change. For the tax/payroll example, this may include database administrators who maintain specific tables and end-users who participate in user-acceptance testing.

- **Schedule.** Agree upon the date and time of the change, which systems and customers will be impacted and to what degree, and who will implement the change. In the previous example, the change would need to occur at the time the new tax tables would go into effect.

- **Communicate.** Inform all appropriate individuals about the change via agreed-upon means. For the tax/payroll example, the communication would go out to all users, service-desk personnel (in the event users call in about the change), and support analysts.

- **Implement.** Enact the change; log final disposition; and collect and analyze metrics. In the previous example, the change would go in and be verified jointly by the implementers and the payroll users.

Drawbacks of Most Change Management Processes

Change management is one of the oldest and most important of the 13 systems management disciplines. You might think that, with so many years to refine this process and grow aware of its importance, change management would be widely used, well designed, properly implemented, effectively executed, and have little room for improvement. Surprisingly, in the eyes of many executives, the opposite is true.

In a recent survey, more than 40 leading infrastructure managers were asked to identify major drawbacks with their current change management processes. Table 10-2 lists the 14 drawbacks they offered, in their own words, and the percentage of managers responding to each one shown as a percent of occurrences. One of the reasons for so many opportunities for improvement is this—it is much easier and more common for shops to implement only parts of change management in a less-than-robust manner than it is to formally institute all the elements of the process.

Table 10-2   Major Drawbacks of Most Current Change Management Processes and Their Rates of Occurrence

Percent of Occurrence	Description of Drawback
95	Not all changes are logged.
90	Changes not thoroughly tested.
80	Lack of enforcement.
75	Lack of effective method of communicating within IT.
65	Coordination within the groups is poor—only the person attending the change meetings is aware of the events; on many occasions, the information is not disseminated throughout the organization.
60	Lack of centralized ownership.
60	Change management is not effective. In some instances, changes are made on the production servers without coordination or communication.
50	Lack of approval policy.
50	Hard copies of "changes" kept in file cabinets.
40	On many occasions, notification is made to all after the fact.
25	Managers and directors required to sign a hard copy of every change.
20	Current process is only form for notification.
20	The process is bureaucratic and not user-friendly.
20	There are several different flavors of change management.

Key Steps Required in Developing a Change Management Process

There are 13 steps required to implement an effective change management process. Each step will be discussed in detail and augmented where appropriate with examples and forms:

1. Identify an executive sponsor.
2. Assign a process owner.
3. Select a cross-functional process design team.
4. Arrange for meetings of the cross-functional process design team.
5. Establish roles and responsibilities for members supporting the design team.
6. Identify the benefits of a change management process.
7. If change metrics exist, collect and analyze them; if not, set up a process to do so.
8. Identify and prioritize requirements.
9. Develop definitions of key terms.
10. Design the initial change management process.
11. Develop policy statements.
12. Develop a charter for a Change Advisory Board (CAB).
13. Use the CAB to continually refine and improve the change management process.

Step 1: Identify an Executive Sponsor

An effective change management process requires the support and compliance of every department in a company that could affect change to an IT production environment. This includes groups within the infrastructure, such as technical services, database administration, network services, and computer operations; groups outside of the infrastructure, such as the applications development departments; and even areas outside of IT, such as facilities.

An executive sponsor must garner support from, and serve as a liaison to, other departments; assign a process owner; and provide guidance, direction, and resources to the process owner. In many instances, the executive sponsor is the manager of the infrastructure, but he or she could also be the manager of the department in which change management resides or he or she could be the manager of the process owner.

Step 2: Assign a Process Owner

As previously mentioned, one of the responsibilities of the executive sponsor is to assign a process owner. The ideal process owner possesses a variety of skills and attributes to accomplish a variety of tasks. These tasks include assembling and leading teams, facilitating brainstorming sessions, conducting change review meetings, analyzing and distributing process metrics, and maintaining documentation.

High on the list of desirable attributes are the abilities to promote teamwork and cooperation and to effectively manage highly diverse groups. Table 10-3 shows a number of other preferred characteristics in priority order. This list should be tailored to individual shops because priority attributes likely vary from one infrastructure to another.

Table 10-3   Prioritized Characteristics of a Change Management Process Owner

Characteristic	Priority
1. Ability to promote teamwork and cooperation	High
2. Ability to manages diversity	High
3. Ability to evaluate documentation	Medium
4. Ability to communicate effectively with developers	Medium
5. Ability to think and plan strategically	Medium
6. Ability to think and act tactically	Medium
7. Knowledge of power and air conditioning systems	Medium
8. Knowledge of applications	Low
9. Knowledge of company's business model	Low
10. Ability to communicate effectively with IT executives	Low
11. Ability to analyze metrics	Low
12. Knowledge of database systems	Low
13. Knowledge of desktop hardware and software	Low
14. Knowledge of software configurations	Low
15. Knowledge of systems software and components	Low
16. Knowledge of network software and components	Low
17. Knowledge of hardware configurations	Low

Step 3: Select a Cross-Functional Process Design Team

The success of a change management process is directly proportional to the degree of buy-in from the various groups that will be expected to comply with it. One of the best ways to ensure this buy-in is to assemble a process design team consisting of representatives from key functional areas. The process owner, with support from the executive sponsor, will select and lead this team. It will be responsible for completing several preparatory steps leading to the design of the initial change management process.

Step 4: Arrange for Meetings of the Cross-Functional Process Design Team

This sounds routine but actually is not. The diversity of a well-chosen team can cause scheduling conflicts, absentee members, or misrepresentation at times of critical decision making. It is best to have consensus from the entire team at the outset as to the time, place, duration, and frequency of meetings. The process owner can then make the necessary meeting arrangements to enact these agreements.

Step 5: Establish Roles and Responsibilities for Members Supporting the Process Design Team

Each individual who has a key role in the support of the process design team should have clearly stated responsibilities. The process owner and the cross-functional design team should propose these roles and responsibilities and obtain concurrence from the individuals identified. Table 10-4 shows examples of what these roles and responsibilities could look like.

Table 10–4   Roles and Responsibilities of Change Management Participants

Role	Responsibility
Executive Sponsor	Provide executive guidance, direction, and support for the design and implementation of a change management process. Serve as primary liaison between the infrastructure organization and other IT organizations.
Project Manager	Serve as primary infrastructure representative on the process design team. Act as a liaison between the team and executive management. May be the manager of the process owner.

Table 10–4 Roles and Responsibilities of Change Management Participants Continued

Role	Responsibility
Process Owner	Serve as the overall lead of the effort to develop, design, and implement the change management process. Conduct weekly meetings of the CAB. Maintain and document future enhancements to the process. Compile and distribute weekly metrics about the process.
Management Owner	Manage and support the process owner. Assist in the development, design, and implementation of the change management process.
Process Contributors	Subject-matter experts and members of the cross-functional team who contribute to the development, design, and implementation of the change management process, particularly as it relates to their particular areas of expertise. Could also be outside suppliers whose changes will be managed by this process.
Management Support	Provide management support to the team members representing departments outside of the infrastructure or remote sites.
Process Facilitator	Used primarily when outside consulting is used to assist in this effort. Facilitate efforts to design and implement the change coordination process. Ensure the establishment of process definition, policy statements, procedures, forms, service metrics, process metrics, and reporting. Schedule, conduct, and report on planning sessions and weekly progress.

Step 6: Identify the Benefits of a Change Management Process

One of the challenges for the process owner and the cross-functional team will be to market the use of a change management process. If an infrastructure is not experienced with marketing a new initiative, this effort will likely not be a trivial task. Identifying and promoting the practical benefits of this type of process can help greatly in fostering its support. The following list offers some examples of common benefits of a change management process:

- **Visibility**. The number and types of all changes logged will be reviewed at each week's CAB meeting for each department or major function. This shows the degree of change activity being performed in each unit.

- **Communication**. The weekly CAB meeting is attended by representatives from each major area. Communication is effectively exchanged among board members about various aspects of key changes, including scheduling and impacts.

- **Analysis**. Changes that are logged into the access database can be analyzed for trends, patterns, and relationships.

- **Productivity**. Based on the analysis of logged changes, some productivity gains may be realized by identifying root causes of repeat changes and eliminating duplicate work. The reduction of database administration change is a good example of this.

- **Proactivity**. Change analysis can lead to a more proactive approach toward change activity.

- **Stability**. All of the previous benefits can lead to an overall improvement in the stability of the production environment. Increased stability benefits customers and support staff alike.

Step 7: If Change Metrics Exist, Collect and Analyze them; If Not, Set Up a Process to Do So

An initial collection of metrics about the types, frequencies, and percentages of change activity can be helpful in developing process parameters such as priorities, approvals, and lead times. If no metrics are being collected, then some initial set of metrics needs to be gathered, even if it must be collected manually. One of the most meaningful of change metrics is the percentage of emergency changes to total changes. This metric is covered in more detail in the next section.

Step 8: Identify and Prioritize Requirements

One of the key preparatory tasks of the cross-functional design team is to identify and prioritize requirements of the change management process. Prioritizing is especially important because budget, time, or resource constraints may prevent all requirements from being met initially. Techniques for effectively brainstorming and prioritizing requirements are presented in Chapter 19, "Developing Robust Processes." Table 10-5 shows some examples of prioritized requirements from a composite of prior clients.

Table 10–5 Prioritized Requirements

Priority	Requirement
High	1. Need to define workflows.
	2. Need to develop a notification process.
	3. Need to establish roles and responsibilities for the communication process.
	4. Need to determine when to communicate what to whom.
	5. Include IT planning group in initial change implementation review.
	6. Include IT planning group in final change implementation review.
Medium High	7. Need to establish initial base metrics; should include count of total changes made and how many were emergency changes.
	8. Must be enforceable.
	9. Should be reportable.
	10. Leverage existing tools (no requirements for new tools initially).
	11. Ensure management buy-in; communicate process to staffs.
	12. Include service metrics.
	13. Include process metrics.
	14. Develop management reporting and trending reports.
Medium	15. Initially concentrate only on infrastructure changes.
	16. Process should be scalable.
	17. Include resolution process; for example, conflicts with scheduling or priorities.
	18. Include escalation process.
	19. Empower staffs to enforce policy statements.
	20. Start small—with just infrastructure and operations initially.
Medium Low	21. Establish a systems management department.
	22. Make process easy to comply with and difficult to circumvent; consider rewards for compliance and penalties for avoidance or circumvention.
	23. Agree on a change coordination process definition.
	24. Establish change coordination process policy statements.
	25. Include a priority scheme for scheduling and implementing.

Priority	Requirement
Low	26. Keep the process simple.
	27. Establish a marketing strategy—what's in it for me (WII-FM).
	28. Eventually extend out to enterprise architecture and planning group.
	29. Present the process in a very positive manner.
	30. Eventually integrate with problem management.

Step 9: Develop Definitions of Key Terms

Change management involves several key terms that should be clearly defined by the design team at the beginning to avoid confusion and misunderstandings later on. Because there are nine terms to define, they all have been placed in Table 10–6 rather than the standard Terms and Definitions box. Planned and emergency changes are especially noteworthy.

Table 10–6   Definition of Change Management Terms

Term	Definition
Change management	The process to *control* and *coordinate* all changes to an IT production environment.
Change control	The requesting, prioritizing, and approving of any requested *production change* prior to the *change coordination* required for its implementation.
Change coordination	The collaboration, scheduling, communication, and implementation of any requested *production change* to the operations environment to ensure that there is no adverse impact to any production systems and there is minimal impact to customers. The initial scope of the change coordination process does not include any changes implemented by personnel outside of the infrastructure department.
Production change	Any activity, of either a *planned* or *emergency* nature, that could potentially impact the stability or responsiveness of a company's IT *production environment*.

Table 10–6   Definition of Change Management Terms Continued

Term	Definition
Planned change	A mandatory change to the *production environment* which is scheduled at least 24 hours in advance.
Emergency change	An urgent, mandatory change requiring manual intervention in less than 24 hours (often 2-4 hours) to restore or prevent interruption of accessibility, functionality, or acceptable performance to a *production application* or to a support service.
Production environment	Any hardware, software, or documentation (electronic or hard copy) component that directly supports a *production application*.
Production application	Any IT application software system designated as necessary for a company to conduct normal business. This includes all nondevelopment applications and all *critical production applications*.
Critical production application	Any IT application software system designated as critical for a company to conduct essential business functions. These functions include generating revenue; acquiring, retaining, and delivering services to customers; providing employees' benefits and wages; and paying suppliers.

Step 10: Design the Initial Change Management Process

This is one of the key activities of the cross-functional team because this is where the team proposes and develops the initial draft of the change management process. The major deliverables produced in this step are:

- A priority scheme
- A change request form
- A review methodology
- Metrics

The priority scheme should apply to both planned changes and emergency changes (these two categories should have been clearly defined in Step 9). A variety of criteria should be identified to distinguish different levels of planned changes. Typical criteria includes quantitative items such as the number of internal and external customers impacted as well as the number of hours to implement and back out the change. The criteria could also include qualitative items such as the degree of complexity and the level of risk.

Some shops employ four levels of planned changes to offer a broader variety of options. Many shops just starting out with formalized change management begin with a simpler scheme comprised of only two levels. Table 10–7 lists some quantitative and qualitative criteria for four levels of planned changes. Table 10–8 does the same for two levels.

Table 10–7   Criteria for Four Levels of Planned Changes

Criteria	Priority Level			
	1	**2**	**3**	**4**
Narrative descriptors	Very High Substantial Significant Critical "A"	High Major Important Principal "B"	Medium Moderate Standard Nominal "C"	Low Minor Optional Time-Permitting "D"
Percent of total external customers impacted	> 90 %	50–90 %	10–49 %	< 10 %
Type of total external customers impacted	Customers of critical applications	Customers of high-priority applications	Customers of medium-priority applications	Customers of low-priority applications
Percent of internal users impacted	> 90 %	50–90 %	10–49 %	< 10 %
Type of internal users impacted	Customers of critical applications	Customers of high-priority applications	Customers of medium-priority applications	Customers of low-priority applications
Critical applications impacted	Yes	No	No	No
Noncritical application downtime required	Yes	Yes	No	No
Amount of additional budget required	> $10,000	< $10,000	0	0
Hours to implement	> 8	5–8	1–4	< 1
Backout plan required	Yes	Yes	No	No

Table 10–7   Criteria for Four Levels of Planned Changes Continued

Criteria	Priority Level			
	1	**2**	**3**	**4**
Hours to back out	> 4	< 4	n/a	n/a
Broadness of scope	Very high	High	Medium	Low
Extent of impact	Very high	High	Medium	Low
Degree of complexity	Very high	High	Medium	Low
Level of risk	Very high	High	Medium	Low
Strategic value	Very high	High	Medium	Low

Table 10–8   Criteria for Two Levels of Planned Changes

Criteria	Impact Level of Planned Changes	
	High	**Low**
Any impact to subscribers	Yes	No
Percent of total external customers impacted	> 25 %	< 25 %
Type of total external customers impacted	Customers of critical applications, and high- and medium-priority applications	Customers of low-priority applications
Percent of internal users impacted	> 50 %	< 50 %
Type of internal users impacted	Customers of critical apps, and high- and med-priority apps	Customers of low-priority apps
Critical applications impacted	Yes	No
Noncritical application downtime required	Yes	No
Amount of additional budget required	> $1,000	< $1,000
Hours to implement	> 4	< 4
Backout plan required	Yes	No
Broadness of scope	High	Low
Extent of impact	High	Low
Degree of complexity	High	Low
Level of risk	High	Low
Strategic value	High	Low

After the team determines priority levels, it must develop lists of actions to be taken depending on the level of planned or emergency change. Table 10–9 shows some sample actions for planned changes by impact level and time frame.

Table 10–9   Action Matrix for Planned Changes

| Actions | Impact Level/Time Frame | | |
	Low/ Anytime	High/Prior to Review Meeting	High/After Review Meeting
Types of approvals required	Supervisor of implementer	Supervisor plus 2 board members or representatives, preferably one familiar with the change and one familiar with the impact	CRB
Advance approval time	1 hour	1 day	At CRB meeting
Advance notification time	N/A	1 day	1 day
Groups to be notified	N/A	Customers impacted	Customers impacted
Preferred time of change	Anytime	Not prime shift	Not prime shift
Backout plan required	No	Yes	Yes

The following list describes sample actions for emergency changes:

1. If not an emergency change, then follow the actions in the action matrix for planned changes.
2. Implementer or recovery team rep notifies all appropriate parties, including the support center of the emergency change.
3. Recovery team should initiate recovery action within 2 hours.
4. Recovery team should determine problem status update interval for support center.
5. If status interval is exceeded, recovery team rep updates support center.
6. Support center to notify all appropriate parties of the update.
7. Repeat steps #5 and #6 until problem is resolved.
8. Support center issues final resolution to all appropriate parties.
9. Implementer logs activity as an emergency change.

10. CAB issues final disposition of the emergency change at the next CAB meeting.

11. Change manager records the board's final disposition of the change into the emergency change request record.

The team next develops a change request form. Two characteristics are always present in such a form: simplicity and accessibility. The form needs to be simple enough to use that minimum explanation is required, yet thorough enough that all pertinent information is provided. The form also needs to be easily accessible to users, preferably through a company's intranet or in a public email folder on a shared drive. Change requests should be stored in a database—preferably a relational database—for subsequent tracking and analysis. Figure 10–1 shows a sample change request form.

Information Technology Change Request Form

Requester_____ Request Date_____ Priority_____

Summary Description of Change _____

_____

Customers Impacted _____

Systems Impacted _____

Expected Start Date/Time of Change _____ Estimated Duration_____

Actual Date/Time of Change _____   Actual Duration _____

Detailed Description of Change_____

_____

_____

_____

_____

For Low-Priority Changes, Requester's Manager's Approval_____

Disposition of Change _____

For High-Priority Changes, CAB Approval _____

Backout Plan in Place?_____   Downtime Required?_____

Estimated Time to Back Out?_____ Downtime Notices Sent Out?_____

Final Disposition of Change_____

Figure 10–1   Sample Change Request Form

The next task for the cross-functional team is to devise a methodology for reviewing all changes. Most shops constitute a CAB that meets weekly to review the prior week's changes and to discuss upcoming changes. The final part of this step involves the establishment of metrics for tracking, analyzing, and trending the number and types of planned and emergency changes occurring every week.

Step 11: Develop Policy Statements

Regardless of how well the cross-functional team designs a change management process, it will not be effective unless there is support, compliance, enforcement, and accountability. These are the objectives of policy statements. They are what give a process visibility and credibility. These statements should reflect the philosophy of executive management, the process design team, and the users at large. The following list illustrates a set of sample policy statements for change management:

1. All hardware and software changes that could potentially impact the stability or the performance of company X's IT production environment are to go through the change management process.
2. The senior director of the infrastructure department is the executive sponsor of the change management process.
3. Employee Y is the IT change manager. In employee Y's absence, employee Z will serve as the IT change manager.
4. The IT change manager is responsible for chairing a weekly meeting of the CAB at which upcoming major changes are discussed, approved, and scheduled; also, the prior week's changes are reviewed and dispositioned by the board.
5. The IT change manager will have sole responsibility of entering the final disposition of each change based on the recommendation of the board.
6. All CAB areas serving in either a voting or advisory role are expected to send a primary or alternate representative to each weekly meeting.
7. All IT staff members and designated vendors implementing production changes are expected to log every change into the current IT tracking database.
8. Board members are required to discuss any unlogged changes they know about at the weekly CAB meeting. These unlogged changes will then be published in the following week's agenda.

9. All planned changes are to be categorized as either high-impact or low-impact based on the criteria established by the CAB. Implementers and their supervisors should determine the appropriate impact level of each change in which they are involved. Any unplanned change must comply with the criteria for an emergency change described in the document mentioned in this item.

10. The IT change manager, in concert with all board members, is expected to identify and resolve any discrepancies in impact levels of changes.

11. Approvals for all types of changes must follow the procedures developed and published by the CAB.

12. The change manager is responsible for compiling and distributing a weekly report on change activity including the trending and analysis of service metrics and process metrics.

Step 12: Develop a Charter for a Change Advisory Board (CAB)

The cornerstone of any change management process is the mechanism provided for the review, approval, and scheduling of changes. In almost all instances this takes the form of a Change Advisory Board (CAB). The charter for the CAB contains the governing rules of this critical forum and specifies items such as primary membership, alternates, approving or delaying of a change, meeting logistics, enforcement, and accountability. During the initial meeting of the CAB, a number of proposals should be agreed on, including roles and responsibilities, terms and definitions, priority schemes and associated actions, policy statements, and the CAB charter itself. The following statements comprise a sample CAB charter:

1. Review all upcoming high-impact change requests submitted to the CAB by the change coordinator as follows:
   Approve if appropriate.
   Modify on the spot (if possible) and approve (if appropriate).
   Send back to requester for additional information.
   Cancel at the discretion of the board.

2. Review a summary of the prior week's changes as follows:
   Validate that all emergency changes from the prior week were legitimate.
   Review all planned change requests from the prior week as to impact level and lead time.
   Bring to the attention of the board any unlogged changes.
   Bring to the attention of the board any adverse impact an implemented change may have caused and recommend a final disposition for these.
   Analyze total number and types of changes from the prior week to evaluate trends, patterns, and relationships.
3. CAB will meet every Wednesday from 3 p.m. to 4 p.m. in room 1375.
4. CAB meeting will eventually become part of a systems management meeting at which the status of problems, service requests, and projects are also discussed.
5. Changes will be approved, modified, or cancelled by a simple majority of the voting members present.
6. Disputes will be escalated to the senior director of the infrastructure department.

Step 13: Use the CAB to Continually Refine and Improve the Change Management Process

Some time should be set aside at every meeting of the CAB to discuss possible improvements to any aspect of the change management process. Improvements voted on by the CAB should then be assigned, scheduled for implementation, and followed up at subsequent meetings.

Emergency Changes Metric

One of the most significant metrics for change management is the number of emergency changes occurring each week, especially when compared to the weekly number of high-impact changes and total weekly changes. There is a direct relationship between the number of emergency changes required and the degree to which a shop is proactive. The higher the number of emergency changes, the more reactive the environment. Numbers vary from shop to shop, but if more than 15 to 20 percent of the total changes are classified as emergency, the shop is considered more reactive than proactive. Just as important as the raw percentages is the trending over time. As improvements to the change process are put in place, there should be a corresponding reduction in the percentage of emergency changes. A low number of emergency changes indicate a highly proactive environment where most changes are thoroughly planned and properly coordinated well in advance. Table 10-10 shows some desirable levels of percentages of emergency changes.

Table 10-10   Desirable Levels of Emergency Changes

Percentages of Emergency Changes	Relative Proactive Level	Relative Reactive Level	Overall Desirability
0-5%	Highly proactive	Barely reactive at all	Highly desirable
6-10%	Proactive	Not very reactive	Desirable
11-15%	Somewhat proactive	Somewhat reactive	Somewhat desirable
16-25%	Barely proactive	Reactive	Not very desirable
> 25%	Not proactive at all	Highly reactive	Highly undesirable

Real Life Experience—One Shop's Rendezvous With Robustness

A police department in a major American city developed, and is using, one of the best change management processes I have ever seen. The department's IT organization assembled a cross-functional team of knowledgeable, internal professionals to design their robust process. Change management became so effective with its online reviews, electronic signatures, and software-induced enforcements that participants eliminated their weekly face-to-face meetings and now perform all necessary activities via their intranet. The group's rendezvous with robustness required almost a year of hard work, but the results proved that their efforts were very worthwhile.

Assessing an Infrastructure's Change Management Process

The worksheets shown in Figures 10-2 and 10-3 present a quick-and-simple method for assessing the overall quality, efficiency, and effectiveness of a change management process. The first worksheet is used without weighting factors, meaning that all 10 categories are weighted evenly for the assessment of a change management process. Sample ratings are inserted to illustrate the use of the worksheet. In this case, the change management process scored a total of 29 points for an overall non-weighted assessment score of 73 percent. Our second sample worksheet compiled an almost identical weighted assessment score of 74 percent.

One of the most valuable characteristics of these worksheets is that they are customized to evaluate each of the 12 processes individually. The worksheets in this chapter apply only to the change management process. However, the fundamental concepts applied in using these evaluation worksheets are the same for all 12 disciplines. As a result, the detailed explanation on the general use of these worksheets presented near the end of Chapter 7, "Availability," also applies to the other worksheets in the book. Please refer to that discussion if you need more information.

Real Life Experience—Mile-High Bliss Needs Changing

A few years ago a satellite broadcasting company asked me to assess, consolidate, and revamp its IT change management process. The company's headquarters was in Southern California with another major division in Denver, Colorado. The IT staff at headquarters welcomed me with open arms, realizing that their change management process was poorly designed, barely followed, and in dire need of improvement.

The Denver site was quite another story. The IT staff there felt they had an excellent change management process already in place as evidenced by how all appropriate personnel were notified immediately of any production change. I could not argue with the effectiveness of their communication system. The problem was that their process did nothing more than provide notification. It was essentially an email system with dozens of distributions used to advise different groups depending on the type of change implemented.

There was no archiving of changes, no reviews or pre-approvals, no prioritizing or categorizing of changes, no change review board, and no analysis or trending of change history. It did not take long to convince them of their shortcomings and to persuade them of the benefits of a more robust and comprehensive change management process.

Change Management Process—Assessment Worksheet						
Process Owner_____ Owner's Manager_____ Date _____						
Category	Questions for Change Management	None 1	Small 2	Medium 3	Large 4	
Executive Support	To what degree does the executive sponsor show support for the change management process with actions such as attending CAB meetings, analyzing trending reports, and ensuring that applications, facilities, and outside vendors use the CAB for all changes?	-	-	3	-	
Process Owner	To what degree does the process owner exhibit desirable traits and effectively conduct the CAB and review a wide variety of changes?	-	-	-	4	
Customer Involvement	To what degree are key customers involved in the design of the process, particularly priority schemes, escalation plans, and the CAB charter?	-	-	3	-	
Supplier Involvement	To what degree are key suppliers, such as technical writers and those maintaining the database, involved in the design of the process?	-	-	-	4	
Service Metrics	To what degree are service metrics analyzed for trends such as availability, the type and number of changes logged, and the number of changes causing problems?	-	2	-	-	
Process Metrics	To what degree are process metrics analyzed for trends such as changes logged after the fact, changes with a wrong priority, absences at CAB meetings, and late metrics reports?	-	-	3	-	
Process Integration	To what degree does the change management process integrate with other processes and tools such as problem management and network management?	1	-	-	-	
Streamlining/ Automation	To what degree is the change management process streamlined by automating actions such as online submittals, documentation, metrics, and training; electronic signatures; and robust databases?	-	2	-	-	
Training of Staff	To what degree is the staff cross-trained on the change management process, and how well is the effectiveness of the training verified?	-	-	3	-	
Process Documentation	To what degree is the quality and value of change management documentation measured and maintained?	-	-	-	4	
	Totals	1	4	12	12	
	Grand Total = 1 + 4 + 12 + 12 = 29 Nonweighted Assessment Score = 29 / 40 = 73%					

Figure 10–2   Sample Assessment Worksheet for Change Management Process

Change Management Process—Assessment Worksheet				
Process Owner_____ Owner's Manager_____ Date _____				
Category	Questions for Change Management	Weight	Rating	Score
Executive Support	To what degree does the executive sponsor show support for the change management process with actions such as attending CAB meetings, analyzing trending reports, and ensuring that applications, facilities, and outside vendors use the CAB for all changes?	5	3	15
Process Owner	To what degree does the process owner exhibit desirable traits and effectively conduct the CAB and review a wide variety of changes?	5	4	20
Customer Involvement	To what degree are key customers involved in the design of the process, particularly priority schemes, escalation plans, and the CAB charter?	3	3	9
Supplier Involvement	To what degree are key suppliers, such as technical writers and those maintaining the database, involved in the design of the process?	1	4	4
Service Metrics	To what degree are service metrics analyzed for trends such as availability, the type and number of changes logged, and the number of changes causing problems?	3	2	6
Process Metrics	To what degree are process metrics analyzed for trends such as changes logged after the fact, changes with a wrong priority, absences at CAB meetings, and late metrics reports?	3	3	9
Process Integration	To what degree does the change management process integrate with other processes and tools such as problem management and network management?	3	1	3
Streamlining/ Automation	To what degree is the change management process streamlined by automating actions such as online submittals, documentation, metrics, and training; electronic signatures; and robust databases?	1	2	2
Training of Staff	To what degree is the staff cross-trained on the change management process, and how well is the effectiveness of the training verified?	5	3	15
Process Documentation	To what degree is the quality and value of change management documentation measured and maintained?	3	4	12
Totals		32	29	95
Weighted Assessment Score = 95 / (32 x 4) = 74%				

Figure 10–3   Sample Assessment Worksheet for Change Management Process with Weighting Factors

Measuring and Streamlining the Change Management Process

We can measure and streamline the change management process with the help of the assessment worksheet shown in Figure 10-2. We can measure the effectiveness of a change management process by analyzing service metrics such as availability, the type and number of changes logged, and the number of changes causing problems. Process metrics—changes logged after the fact, changes with a wrong priority, absences at CAB meetings, and late metrics reports, for example—help us gauge the efficiency of this process. And we can streamline the change management process by automating certain actions—changes logged after the fact, changes with wrong priorities, absences at CAB meetings, and late metrics reports, just to name some.

Summary

Change management is one of the oldest and possibly the most important of the systems management processes, but it often causes infrastructure managers major process challenges. After defining the differences between change management and change control, we presented the results of an executive survey that prioritized these challenges and drawbacks.

We then discussed each of the 13 steps involved with designing and implementing a robust change management process. These steps included assembling a cross-functional team, prioritizing requirements, and establishing priority schemes, policy statements, and metrics. The cornerstone to the entire process is a Change Advisory Board (CAB), and the chartering of this forum is covered in detail. We then provided the customized assessment sheets that can be used to evaluate an infrastructure's change management process.

Test Your Understanding

1. Change management is relatively new among of the 12 systems management disciplines. (True or False)
2. In a robust change management process, the priority scheme applies only to emergency changes. (True or False)
3. Which of the following is an important aspect of a change review board's charter?
   a. validating that all planned changes from the prior week were legitimate
   b. reviewing all emergency changes as to impact level and lead time
   c. analyzing the total number and types of changes from the prior week to evaluate trends, patterns, and relationships
   d. bringing to the attention of the board any logged changes
4. The percentage of _____ _____ to all changes can indicate the relative degree to which an organization is reactive or proactive.
5. Explain why you think a priority scheme for changes is, or is not, worth the overhead cost of administering and enforcing?

Suggested Further Readings

1. http://en.wikipedia.org/wiki/Change_Management_(ITIL)
2. www.microsoft.com/technet/solutionaccelerators/cits/mo/smf/smfchgmg.mspx
3. *Breakthrough IT Change Management*: How to Get Enduring Change Results; 2003; Lientz, Bennet P., Rea, Kathryn P.; Butterworth-Heinemann

CHAPTER 11

Problem Management

Introduction

Problems are a fact of life in all data centers. The sheer complexity of systems and diversity of services offered today all but guarantee that problems will occur. One of the many factors that separate world-class infrastructures from mediocre ones is how well they manage the variety and volume of problems they encounter.

This chapter discusses the entire scope of problem management. It begins as usual with a commonly accepted definition of this process followed by its interpretation and implications. Then we discuss the scope of problem management and show how it differs from change management and request management.

Next we look at the length the key steps required to develop a robust problem management process. Also included is a recent survey of infrastructure managers prioritizing their major issues with problem management in their own shops. The chapter concludes with a discussion on how to develop meaningful metrics for problem management. Just as important are some examples showing how one can easily perform trending analysis on these metrics.

Definition of Problem Management

Regardless of how well-designed its processes or how smooth-running its operations, even a world-class infrastructure will occasionally miss its targeted levels of service. The branch of systems management that deals with the handling of these occurrences is called problem management.

Problem Management

Problem management is a process used to identify, log, track, resolve, and analyze problems impacting IT services.

The identification of problems typically comes in the form of a trouble call from an end-user to a service desk, but problems may also be identified by programmers, analysts, or systems administrators. Problems are normally logged into a database for subsequent tracking, resolution, and analysis. The sophistication of the database and the depth of the analysis vary widely from shop to shop and are two key indicators of the relative robustness of a problem management process. We will discuss these two characteristics in more detail later in this chapter.

Scope of Problem Management

Several of my clients have struggled with distinguishing the three closely related processes of problem management, change management, and request management. While the initial input to these three processes may be similar, the methods for managing a problem, a change, or a request for service typically varies significantly from each other. As a result, the scope of what actually constitutes problem management also varies significantly from shop to shop. Many infrastructures do agree that first-level problem handling, commonly referred to as tier 1, is the minimum basis for problem management. Table 11-1 shows some of the more common variations to this scheme.

Table 11-1   Variations of Problem Management Schemes

Variation Number	Description
1	Tier 1 reporting only; sometimes called incident management
2	Tier 2 reporting only; sometimes called traditional problem management

Variation Number	Description
3	Tier 3 reporting only; sometimes called escalation management
4	Major service disruption; sometimes called crisis management
5	Tier 1 reporting and request management
6	All tiers reporting and request management
7	All tiers reporting and both request and change management

The most integrated approach is the last variation in the table, in which all three tiers of problem management are tightly coupled with change management and request management. Among other things, this means that all calls concerning problems, changes, and service requests go through a centralized help desk and are logged into the same type of database.

Distinguishing Between Problem, Change, and Request Management

Problem, change, and request management are three infrastructure processes that are closely related but distinct. Changes sometimes cause problems or can be the result of a problem. Expanding a database that is running out of storage space may be a good, proactive change, but it may cause backup windows to extend into production time, resulting in a scheduling problem for operations.

The same is true of problems causing or being the result of changes. Request management is usually treated as a subset of problem management, but it applies to individuals requesting services or enhancements, such as a specialized keyboard, a file restore, an advanced-function mouse, extra copies of a report, or a larger monitor. Table 11-2 shows a general delineation of problem, change, and service requests.

Table 11-2 General Delineation of Problem, Change, and Service Requests

Problem Ticket	Change Ticket	Service Request
Problems with a desktop component used by a single customer. Any kind of production service interruption such as: - inability to access the network, an application, or a database - extremely slow response to online production applications - malfunctioning routines within applications Problems of an urgent nature impacting customers generate an associated change ticket. Essentially a "fix when broke" approach to request management.	Adding, deleting, or modifying any production hardware, software, facilities, or documentation impacting more than one customer. All changes are designated as either *emergency changes* or *planned changes*. An emergency change is an urgent, mandatory change impacting customers that must be implemented in less than 24 hours to restore accessibility, functionality, or acceptable performance to a production application or to a support service. All nonemergency changes are designated as planned changes and are assigned one of four priority levels.	Responding to an operational service request. Adding, deleting, or modifying any production hardware, software, facilities, or documentation impacting an individual customer.

To further delineate the differences between problem, change, and service requests, Table 11-3 provides examples of the three types of requests taken from actual infrastructure environments.

Table 11-3 Examples of Problem, Change, and Service Requests

Problem Ticket	Change Ticket	Service Request
Desktop problems that are handled and resolved over the phone. Network accessibility from a desktop. Urgent problems generate a change ticket if problem is not resolvable over the phone. Resolve a functionality problem within a new or existing application.	Add a backup server. Priority Level 4 (P/L-4) Add more disk volumes. (P/L-3) Upgrade server operating systems. (P/L-2) Migrate to a new database architecture. (P/L-1) Respond to an urgent problem. (emergency) Add a new function that has never before existed in the production environment.	Rerun a job. Reprint a report. Restore a file. Upgrade desktop components. File permissions. Delete an unused login, account, password, etc. Assign more disk space without adding more disk volumes. Install a new occurrence of an existing function into a production environment.

Distinguishing Between Problem Management and Incident Management

Some IT shops draw a distinction between the notion of an incident and that of a problem, and by extension, they draw a distinction between incident management and problem management. In these cases, the delineation usually follows the guidelines offered by the IT Infrastructure Library (ITIL), which was discussed in more detail in Chapter 6 "Comparison to ITIL Processes."

In accordance with ITIL best practices, service desk operators initially treat all calls as incidents. After a brief assessment, the operator may determine that the incident does not reflect any kind of failure in the infrastructure but instead is a request of some kind by the user calling in. In this case, the incident falls into the category of a service request, similar to the criteria described in the previous section.

Service desk operators analyze and attempt to resolve those incidents that are not classified as service requests. If the operator is successful in resolving such an incident, it is considered resolved and is designated as closed. If the service desk operator is not able to resolve the incident, it is turned over to a second level, or tier 2, support group for resolution and is then designated as a problem. In short, some IT shops designate tier 1 issues as incidents and their tier 2 issues as problems. The process described in this chapter can apply to both categories of incidents and problems.

Real Life Experience—What You See Not Always What You Get

A relatively large IT organization in a financial services company was determined to staff its service desk with very courteous and knowledgeable personnel. Much money was invested in technical training and telephone etiquette.

Part of the telephone etiquette training included an effective technique to ensure that service desk staff would answer their telephone with a calm, soothing voice. Each call taker had a mirror directly in front of them with the inscription, "What you see is what they hear."

The mirrors were very popular and helped remind the service desk staff that the expressions on their faces often translate into the quality of their voices. A few months after the mirrors were introduced, a new service-desk person joined the staff. His demeanor and technical training qualified him perfectly for the job.

This new recruit invited a fair amount of teasing from his co-workers, however, due to his outrageously long, curled hair and beard. Several of his colleagues joked that he had a face for radio, while others chimed in that he had the perfect look for a service-desk agent. Many claimed he looked scary to them. He didn't really believe that most of his co-workers found his look all that scary until one day he came to work and noticed someone had changed the inscription on his mirror to read, "What you see is what we all fear!"

The Role of the Service Desk

Most all IT organizations have some type of service desk to offer assistance to end-users. In the past, IT managers used various names to designate this function, including help desk, call center, trouble desk, or technical support. As IT evolved to become more customer-oriented, the name of this area changed to that of customer support or the customer service center. With the emphasis today on IT service management, many organizations have renamed their help desks to that of service desk.

The service desk is a function, not a process. A function is defined within a department on an organization chart, has strict organizational boundaries, and is associated with numerous personnel management issues. For example, the implementation of a service desk involves hiring staff, training them, evaluating their performance, offering them career paths and promotions, and rectifying unacceptable behavior. A process has none of these characteristics. Table 11-4 summarizes some of these generic differences between a function and a process.

Table 11-4 Differences Between a Function and a Process

Function	Process
Has strict organizational boundaries	Goes across boundaries
Involves personnel management	Involves process management
Uses performance metrics	Uses process metrics
Example: Service desk	Example: Problem management

Because a service desk is a function and not a process, it is not designated as one of the 12 systems management processes. But the service desk does play a very crucial role in problem management. It serves as the single point of contact into IT for all users and customers; also, it is responsible for accurately logging all calls that come into the service desk, classifying them, handling them as best as possible, and tracking them to completion. The relative effectiveness of a problem management process is directly related to the caliber of the individuals who staff the service desk. It is hard to overstate the significant role the service desk plays in the success of a problem management process.

Segregating and Integrating Service Desks

As IT services grow in many companies, the number of service desks frequently grows. When PCs first came onto the scene, they were usually managed by a support group that was totally separate from the mainframe data center, including a separate service desk for PC-related problems. This pattern of multiple service desks was often repeated as networks grew in size, number, and complexity; the pattern was also prevalent when the Internet blossomed.

As IT organizations began recentralizing in the early and mid-1990s, infrastructure managers were faced with the decision of whether to segregate their service desks or integrate them. By this time, many IT shops had grown out of control because they used multiple call centers—companies with 10 or 15 IT service desks were not uncommon. If non-IT services were included in the mix, employees sometimes had as many as 40 or 50 service numbers to choose from for an inquiry. In one extreme example, a bank provided nearly 100 separate service desks for IT alone, having grown a new one each time an application was put into production.

Over time the benefits of integrating service desks gradually prevailed in most instances. This is not to say that segregated service desks are always worse than integrated ones. Highly diverse user populations, remote locations, and a wide range of services are some reasons why segregated service desks can sometimes be a better solution.

Table 11-5 summarizes the advantages and disadvantages of integrating services desks. Since the advantages and disadvantages of segregating service desks are almost the exact reverse of those for integrating them, the table is not repeated for segregated service desks.

Table 11–5   Advantages and Disadvantages of Integrated Service Desks

Advantages	Disadvantages
1. Simplifies process for customers by reducing numbers to call	1. Lack of specialized support
2. Remote locations may sometimes feel abandoned	2. Enables cross-training of staff
3. Reduces number and variety of tools	3. Diverse user population more difficult to service
4. Integration with other systems management disciplines easier	4. Diversity of services offered very difficult to manage
5. Less expensive to operate	

Real Life Experience—One-Stop Shopping, Eventually

A major motion picture studio had an IT department with seven different help desks that were slated for consolidation. An extensive marketing campaign was used to inform customers of the new single help-desk number with a catchy slogan that said, "One call does it all." The slogan was posted all over the studio.

In order to enact a single service desk number that would provide all of the diverse services previously offered, automated menus were used. So many menus were provided initially that users often became confused and frustrated. Many posters throughout the studio were written over to read, "One call does not do it all!" or "These multiple menus will jerk and bend you!"

The frustrations eventually subsided as the menus were reduced and simplified and as more help-desk agents were added to the staff.

An integrated service desk is not only easier for customers to use, it lends itself to the cross-training of staff. Furthermore, there is a cost savings because companies can standardize the call-tracking tool by collecting all call records on a single, centralized database. Even more is saved by utilizing staff more efficiently. Also, since there are fewer and more standardized help desks, management is easier and less complex. Finally, it is easier to integrate other system management disciplines into it, particularly change management.

The primary advantage of a segregated service desk is the ability to customize specialized support for diverse applications, customers, and services. For example, some consolidated service desks have attempted to offer fax, telephone, facilities, office moves, and other IT-related services only to find they were attempting to do too much with too few resources; they were providing too little service to too many users. In this case, multiple service desks tend to work better, although communication among all of them is critical to their combined success.

A compromise hybrid solution is sometimes used in which all IT customers call a single service desk number that activates a menu system. The customer is then routed to the appropriate section of a centralized service desk depending on the specific service requested.

Key Steps to Developing a Problem Management Process

The following 11 key steps are required to develop a robust problem management process. We then discuss each step in detail.

1. Select an executive sponsor.
2. Assign a process owner.
3. Assemble a cross-functional team.
4. Identify and prioritize requirements.
5. Establish a priority and escalation scheme.
6. Identify alternative call-tracking tools.
7. Negotiate service levels.
8. Develop service and process metrics.
9. Design the call-handling process.
10. Evaluate, select, and implement the call-tracking tool.
11. Review metrics to continually improve the process.

Step 1: Select an Executive Sponsor

A comprehensive problem management process is comprised of individuals from an assortment of IT departments and of suppliers that are external to IT. An executive sponsor is needed to bring these various factions together and to ensure their support. The executive sponsor must also select the problem management process owner, address conflicts that the process owner cannot resolve, and provide executive leadership, direction, and support for the project.

Step 2: Assign a Process Owner

One of the most important duties of the executive sponsor is to assign the appropriate process owner. The process owner will be responsible for assembling and leading a cross-functional process design team, for implementing the final process design and for the ongoing maintenance of the process. The selection of this individual is very key to the success of this project as this person must lead, organize, communicate, team-build, troubleshoot, and delegate effectively.

Table 11–6 shows the priority order of several characteristics I recommend for a problem management process owner to use when choosing this individual. The ability to promote teamwork and cooperation is extremely important due to the large number of level 2 support groups that become involved with problem resolution. This is also why the ability to work with diverse groups is necessary though not at as high in priority. Knowledge of desktops is key due to the overwhelming number of desktop calls. The ability to analyze metrics and trending reports ensures continual improvements to the quality of the process. Effectively communicating and meeting with users is essential to good customer feedback. Other lower-priority characteristics involve a rudimentary working knowledge of areas of likely problems, including database systems, system and network components, facilities issues, and backup systems.

Table 11–6 Problem Management Process Owner Characteristics

Characteristic	Priority
1. Ability to promote teamwork and cooperation	High
2. Knowledge of desktop hardware and software	High
3. Ability to analyze metrics and trending reports	High
4. Ability to meet effectively with users	Medium
5. Ability to work with diverse groups of people	Medium
6. Knowledge of database systems	Low
7. Ability to communicate effectively with developers	Low
8. Knowledge of power and air conditioning systems	Low
9. Knowledge of systems software and components	Low
10. Knowledge of network software and components	Low

Characteristic	Priority
11. Knowledge of applications	Low
12. Knowledge of backup systems	Low

Step 3: Assemble a Cross-Functional Team

A well-designed problem management process involves the participation of several key groups. Mature, highly developed processes may have as many as a dozen areas serving as second-level, tier 2 support. A representative from each of these areas, along with key user reps and tier 1 support, normally comprise such a team.

This team is responsible for identifying and prioritizing requirements, establishing the priority scheme, negotiating internal SLAs, proposing internal process metrics and external service metrics, and finalizing the overall design of the call-handling process. The specific areas participating in this cross-functional process design team vary from shop to shop but there are some common groups that are usually involved in this type of project. The following list includes typical areas represented by such a team:

1. Service desk
2. Desktop hardware support
3. Desktop software support
4. Network support
5. Operations support
6. Applications support
7. Server support (includes mainframe and midrange)
8. Database administration
9. Development groups
10. Key user departments
11. External suppliers

Step 4: Identify and Prioritize Requirements

Once the cross-functional team members have been identified and assembled, one of the team's first orders of business is to identify and prioritize requirements. Specific requirements and their relative priorities depend on an organization's current focus and direction, but several common attributes are usually designed into a robust problem management process. It should be noted that this step does not yet involve the actual implementation of requirements; it focuses on acquiring the team's consensus as to a requirement's inclusion and priority.

A variety of brainstorming and prioritizing techniques are available to do this effectively. In Chapter 19, "Developing Robust Processes," I discuss brainstorming in more detail and list several helpful brainstorming ground rules. A sample of prioritized requirements from former clients is shown in Table 11-7.

Table 11–7   Typical Problem Management Requirements with Priorities

Requirement	Priority
1. Contains closed-loop feedback mechanism	High
2. Distinguishes problems resolved from those closed	High
3. Includes an online tracking tool	High
4. Generates management reports	High
5. Enables accessibility from PCs and Macs	High
6. Analyzes data by problem type	High
7. Includes automated call dispatcher	High
8. Contains a knowledge database for root-cause analysis	Medium
9. Writes records into a relational database	Medium
10. Ties into an asset database	Medium
11. Ties into a personnel database	Medium
12. Generates trend reports from a tracking tool	Medium
13. Enables accessibility from remote locations	Medium
14. Includes an automatic escalation system	Medium
15. Includes an automatic problem-aging system	Medium
16. Leverages existing tools to maximum extent possible	Medium
17. Incorporates online documentation into the tracking tool	Low
18. Provides an online help facility for tracking tool	Low
19. Provides an automated paging system	Low
20. Analyzes data by device type	Low
21. Analyzes data by customer	Low
22. Analyzes data by department	Low
23. Tracks frequency of rerouted problems	Low
24. Integrates with change management	Low

Step 5: Establish a Priority and Escalation Scheme

A well-designed priority scheme is one of the most important aspects of an effective problem management process. Priority schemes vary from shop to shop as to specific criteria, but most all of them attempt to prioritize problems based on severity, impact urgency, and aging. Closely related to the priority scheme is an escalation plan that prescribes how to handle high-priority but difficult-to-resolve problems. Using an even number of levels prevents a tendency to average toward the central, and employing descriptive names rather than numbers is more user-friendly. Table 11–8 is an example of a combined priority scheme and escalation plan from one of my former clients.

Step 6: Identify Alternative Call-Tracking Tools

The call-tracking tool is the cornerstone of an effective problem management process. Requirements for the tools will have already been identified and prioritized in Step 4. Companies usually lean toward either having their tools custom developed or purchasing a commercially available application. I have seen several instances of both types of call-tracking tools, and each kind offers unique advantages and disadvantages. Commercial packages generally offer more flexibility and integration possibilities while custom-developed solutions normally cost less and can be more tailored to a particular environment. In either event, alternative solutions should be identified for later evaluation.

Step 7: Negotiate Service Levels

External service levels should be negotiated with key customer representatives. These agreements should be reasonable, enforceable, and mutually agreed upon by both the customer service department and IT. Internal service levels should be negotiated with internal level 2 support groups and external suppliers. A more detailed discussion of key customers and key suppliers is provided in Chapter 4 "Customer Service."

Table 11–8   Sample Priority and Escalation Scheme

Priority Level	Description	Examples	Expected Response Times	Status Interval to Mgmt
Critical	Total system or application failure or loss of availability to the mission-critical site(s), network(s), system(s), or application(s)	Total system or application is down A remote site is completely unavailable All communication lines between remote sites are down A critical database is corrupted	Immediate	30 minutes
Urgent	Major subset of system or application functionality is unavailable or inoperable	Portions of memory or disk array not functioning Network at risk of failing Severe impact to accounting period close Severe impact to adding customers or services	30 minutes	1 hour
Serious	Significant impact to system or application functionality	Data integrity concerns Reconciliation issues More than 10 customers not receiving service Billing center is down Sales interface is not functioning	1 hour	Daily
High	Some impact to system or application functionality	Training system is down Unable to activate a customer Billing non-pay cutoff is not running or is delayed	4 hours	Daily
Moderate	Minimal impact to system or application functionality	Backups running too long Individual desktop problems Network printer down	Daily	Weekly
Low	Minimal impact to business operations	Inability to set a period-end flag Carriage control/line feed errors on report prints Report format problems	As able	Weekly

Step 8: Develop Service and Process Metrics

Service metrics should be established to support the SLAs that will be in place with key customers. The following are some common problem management service metrics:

1. Wait time when calling help desk
2. Average time to resolve a problem at level 1
3. Average time for level 2 to respond to a customer
4. Average time to resolve problems of each priority type
5. Percentage of time problem is not resolved satisfactorily
6. Percentage of time problem is resolved at level 1
7. Trending analysis of various service metrics

Process metrics should be established to support internal SLAs that will be in place with various level 2 support groups and with key external suppliers. The following list shows some common problem management process metrics:

1. Abandon rate of calls
2. Percentage of calls dispatched to wrong level 2 group
3. Total number of calls per day, week, month
4. Number of calls per level 1 analyst
5. Percentage of calls by problem type, customer, or device
6. Trending analysis of various process metrics

Step 9: Design the Call-Handling Process

This is the central process of problem management and requires the participation of the entire cross-functional team. It dictates how problems are first handled, logged, and analyzed and later how they might be handed off to level 2 for resolution, closing, and customer feedback.

Step 10: Evaluate, Select, and Implement the Call-Tracking Tool

In this step, the alternative call-tracking tools are evaluated by the cross-functional team to determine the final selection. Work should then proceed on implementing the tool of choice. A small subset of calls is sometimes used as a pilot program during the initial phases of implementation.

Step 11: Review Metrics to Continually Improve the Process

All service and process metrics should be reviewed regularly to spot trends and opportunities for improvement. This usually becomes the ongoing responsibility of the process owner.

Opening and Closing Problems

The opening and closing of problems are two of the most critical activities of problem management. Properly opened tickets can lead to quick closing of problems or to appropriately dispatched level 2 support groups for timely resolution. Infrastructures with especially robust problem management processes tie in their call-tracking tool with both an asset management database and a personnel database. The asset database allows call agents to view information about the exact configuration of a desktop and its problem history. The personnel database allows agents to learn the caller's logistics and their recent call history.

Closing a problem should be separate and distinct from resolving it. A problem is normally said to be resolved when an IT service has been restored that had been interrupted. A problem is said to be closed when the customer sends confirmation in one form or another that the resolution activity was satisfactory and that the problem has not reoccurred. In general, a level 2 problem will be resolved by a level 2 support analyst, but it should be closed by the service-desk analyst who opened it.

Analyzing a variety of trending data can help to continually improve the problem management process. This data may concern the types of problems resolved, the average time it took to resolve, devices involved, customers involved, and root causes. Table 11–9 provides a sense of the variety and distribution of problems handled by a typical service desk. This data shows a recent representative month of IT problem calls to a service desk at a major motion picture studio.

Table 11–9   Monthly Distribution of Typical Service Desk Problem Types

Problem Type	Call Volume	Incremental Percent	Accumulative Percent
1. PC software	1,803	36.7	36.7
2. Macintosh software	782	15.9	52.6
3. PC hardware	568	11.6	64.2

Problem Type	Call Volume	Incremental Percent	Accumulative Percent
4. Email	564	11.5	75.7
5. Network operations	395	8.0	83.7
6. Desktop printer hardware	257	5.2	88.9
7. Macintosh hardware	169	3.4	92.3
8. Fax services	107	2.2	94.5
9. Mainframe applications	106	2.2	96.7
10. Mainframe security	44	0.9	97.6
11. Mainframe networks	41	0.9	98.5
12. Mainframe hardware	38	0.8	99.3
13. All others, including voice services, report delivery, and network applications	33	0.7	100.0

Three items are noteworthy:

1. The inclusion of the accumulative percent field gives an immediate snapshot of the distribution of calls. One-third of the calls are the result of problems with PC software; over half the calls are a result of desktop software problems in general (comprised of both PC and Macintosh software).
2. The overwhelming majority of calls—92.3%—are desktop-related.
3. The recent inclusion of fax service requests is showing a healthy start—over 100 requests a month.

Summary snapshot data such as this can be fed into weekly and monthly trend reports to analyze trends, patterns, and relationships. This analysis can then be used to formulate appropriate action plans to address issues for continual improvement.

Client Issues with Problem Management

I conclude this chapter with the results from a recent survey of infrastructure mangers and senior analysts on what they believed were the greatest exposures with their current problem management processes.

The respondents represented more than 40 client companies. They identified, in their own words, 27 separate issues. Table 11–10 lists these issues and their percentage of occurrences.

Table 11–10   Issues with Problem Management Processes

Issue	Percentage of Occurrence
1. Customer satisfaction is not measured after the problem is resolved. (None of the companies surveyed had a postresolution customer-survey process.)	100
2. Multiple levels of support are not clearly defined for client/server and Web-enabled environments.	100
3. Support personnel have very little exposure to newly deployed systems.	95
4. Tier 2 analysts not providing detailed written description of problem resolution.	90
5. Lack of documentation on existing and new systems/applications.	90
6. Roles and responsibilities not clearly defined for problem resolution.	90
7. Service levels of the companies studied not defined for problem resolution.	90
8. Lack of root-cause analysis.	85
9. Help desk staff not properly trained on new releases of applications.	80
10. Lack of centralized ownership.	70
11. Lack of closed-loop feedback.	70
12. Lack of performance or quality incentive metrics.	65
13. Problems not followed through to closure.	60
14. Perception is that help desk is not responsive.	50
15. Problem tracking is poor, leaving the user without a clear understanding of who owns the problem and how to follow up on the resolution process.	50
16. Most of the UNIX or NT problems bypass the service desk and go directly to senior technical staff instead.	50
17. Not one common, enterprise-wide problem management process.	40
18. Service desk staff has very little authority.	40

Issue	Percentage of Occurrence
19. Many calls bypass the service desk.	35
20. Lack of clear demarcation for problem resolution between desktop and LAN group.	30
21. Help desk acts more like a dispatch center than a problem resolution center, leaving users frustrated and feeling like they simply get the runaround while no one is willing to solve problems.	30
22. After-hours support not clearly defined in the client/server environment.	25
23. Escalation not clearly understood.	20
24. Problems are not documented by the service desk personnel.	20
25. The process is extremely bureaucratic. A high number of notification and escalation procedures.	15
26. Sometimes problems just sit around for up to weeks at a time.	15
27. On-call list is on the mainframe but not everyone has mainframe access.	10

Assessing an Infrastructure's Problem Management Process

The worksheets shown in Figures 11-1 and 11-2 present a quick-and-simple method for assessing the overall quality, efficiency, and effectiveness of a problem management process. The worksheet shown in Figure 11-1 is used without weighting factors, meaning that all 10 categories are weighted evenly for the assessment of a problem management process. Sample ratings are inserted to illustrate the use of the worksheet. In this case, the problem management process scored a total of 26 points for an overall nonweighted assessment score of 65 percent, as compared to the second sample worksheet, which compiled a weighted assessment score of 69 percent.

Problem Management Process—Assessment Worksheet						
Process Owner_____ Owner's Manager_____ Date _____						
Category	Questions for Problem Management	None 1	Small 2	Medium 3	Large 4
Executive Support	To what degree does the executive sponsor show support for the problem management process with actions such as holding level 2 support accountable, analyzing trending reports, and setting improvement goals?	-	-	-	4
Process Owner	To what degree does the process owner exhibit desirable traits, improve metrics over time, and maintain and adhere to current service level agreements?	-	2	-	-
Customer Involvement	To what degree are key customers, particularly representatives of critical executives and high-volume desktop users, involved in the design of the process?	-	-	3	-
Supplier Involvement	To what degree are key suppliers, especially level 2 and 3 support staff and desktop suppliers, involved in the design of the process, in terms of their committed response times to calls and availability of spare parts?	-	-	-	4
Service Metrics	To what degree are service metrics analyzed for trends such as calls answered by second ring, calls answered by a person, calls solved at level 1, response times of level 2, and feedback surveys?	-	-	3	-
Process Metrics	To what degree are process metrics analyzed for trends such as calls dispatched to wrong groups, calls requiring repeat follow-up, amount of overtime spent by level 2 and third-party vendors?	-	2	-	-
Process Integration	To what degree does the problem management process integrate with other processes and tools such as change management?	1	-	-	-
Stream-lining/ Automation	To what degree is the problem management process streamlined by automating actions such as paging, exception reporting, and the use of a knowledge database?	-	2	-	-
Training of Staff	To what degree is the staff cross-trained on the problem management process, and how well is the effectiveness of the training verified?	-	-	3	-
Process Documen-tation	To what degree is the quality and value of problem management documentation measured and maintained?	-	2	-	-
Totals		1	8	9	8
Grand Total = 1 + 8 + 9 + 8 = 26						
Nonweighted Assessment Score = 26 / 40 = 65%						

Figure 11-1   Sample Assessment Worksheet for Problem Management Process

Problem Management Process—Assessment Worksheet					
Process Owner_____ Owner's Manager_____ Date _____					
Category	Questions for Problem Management	Weight	Rating	Score	
Executive Support	To what degree does the executive sponsor show support for the problem management process with actions such as holding level 2 support accountable, analyzing trending reports, and setting improvement goals?	5	4	20	
Process Owner	To what degree does the process owner exhibit desirable traits, improve metrics over time, and maintain and adhere to current service level agreements?	5	2	10	
Customer Involvement	To what degree are key customers, particularly representatives of critical executives and high volume desktop users, involved in the design of the process?	1	3	3	
Supplier Involvement	To what degree are key suppliers, especially level 2 and 3 support staff and desktop suppliers, involved in the design of the process, in terms of their committed response times to calls and availability of spare parts?	5	4	20	
Service Metrics	To what degree are service metrics analyzed for trends such as calls answered by second ring, calls answered by a person, calls solved at level 1, response times of level 2, and feedback surveys?	3	3	9	
Process Metrics	To what degree are process metrics analyzed for trends such as calls dispatched to wrong groups, calls requiring repeat follow-up, amount of overtime spent by level 2 and 3 rd party vendors?	3	2	6	
Process Integration	To what degree does the problem management process integrate with other processes and tools such as change management?	3	1	3	
Stream-lining/ Automation	To what degree is the problem management process streamlined by automating actions such as paging, exception reporting, and the use of a knowledge database?	3	2	6	
Training of Staff	To what degree is the staff cross-trained on the problem management process, and how well is the effectiveness of the training verified?	5	3	15	
Process Documen-tation	To what degree is the quality and value of problem management documentation measured and maintained?	1	2	2	
	Totals	34	26	94	
	Weighted Assessment Score = 94 / (34 % 4) = 69%				

Figure 11-2 Sample Assessment Worksheet for Problem Management Process with Weighting Factors

One of the most valuable characteristics of these worksheets is that they are customized to evaluate each of the 12 processes individually. The worksheets in these figures apply only to the problem management process. However, the fundamental concepts applied in using these evaluation worksheets are the same for all 12 disciplines. As a result, the detailed explanation on the general use of these worksheets presented near the end of Chapter 7, "Availability," also applies to the other worksheets in the book. Please refer to that discussion if you need more information.

Measuring and Streamlining the Problem Management Process

We can measure and streamline the problem management process with the help of the assessment worksheet shown in Figure 11–1. We can measure the effectiveness of a problem management process with service metrics such as calls answered by the second ring, calls answered by a person, calls solved at level 1, response times of level 2, and feedback surveys. Process metrics—such as calls dispatched to wrong groups, calls requiring repeat follow-up, and the amount of overtime spent by level 2 and third-party vendors—help us gauge the efficiency of this process. And we can streamline the problem management process by automating actions such as escalation, paging, exception reporting, and the use of a knowledge database.

Summary

This chapter began in the usual manner with a formal definition of problem management, followed by a discussion of the differences between problem management, change management, and request management. Following this we showed how problem management differs from incident management and we described the important role that the service desk plays in the problem and incident management processes.

Next was the core of the chapter, in which we looked at the 11 key steps to developing a robust problem management process. These included preferred characteristics of a process owner, areas that should be represented on a cross-functional team, a sample of prioritized requirements, a representation of a problem priority scheme, and examples of service and process metrics.

We concluded by discussing proper methods to open and close problem tickets; advantages and disadvantages of integrated help desks; and candid results of a survey from over 40 infrastructure managers and analysts on what they believed were their major concerns with their own problem management processes.

Test Your Understanding

1. Problems are normally logged into a database for subsequent tracking, resolution, and analysis. (True or False)
2. One reason so many groups are involved with designing a problem management process is that many of them serve as second level, tier 2 support. (True or False)
3. A customer provides key participation during the time a problem is:
   a. logged
   b. tracked
   c. resolved
   d. closed
4. What types of analyses can be used to reduce the number and duration of problem calls?
5. Describe the advantages and disadvantages of consolidating help desks.

Suggested Further Readings

1. *IT Problem Management*; 2001; Walker, Gary; Prentice Hall
2. www.helpdeskinst.com/
3. http://en.wikipedia.org/wiki/ITIL
4. *Effective Computer User Support: How to Manage the IT Help Desk*; 2002; Bruton, Noel; Butterworth-Heinemann

CHAPTER 12

Storage Management

Introduction

More than most other systems management processes, storage management involves a certain degree of trust. Users entrust us with the safekeeping of their data. They trust that they will be able to access their data reliably in acceptable periods of time. They trust that, when they retrieve it, it will be in the same state and condition as it was when they last stored it. Infrastructure managers trust that the devices they purchase from storage-equipment suppliers will perform reliably and responsively; suppliers, in turn, trust that their clients will operate and maintain their equipment properly.

We will interweave this idea of trust into our discussion on the process of managing data storage. The focus will be on four major areas:

- Capacity
- Performance
- Reliability
- Recoverability

Recoverability plays a fundamental role in disaster recovery. Many an infrastructure has felt the impact of not being able to recover yesterday's data. How thoroughly we plan and manage storage in anticipation of tomorrow's disaster may well determine our success in recovery.

We begin with a formal definition of the storage management process and a discussion of desirable traits in a process owner. We then examine each of the four storage management areas in greater detail and reinforce our discussion with examples where appropriate. We conclude this chapter with assessment worksheets for evaluating an infrastructure's storage management process.

Definition of Storage Management

Storage Management

Storage management is a process used to optimize the use of storage devices and to protect the integrity of data for any media on which it resides.

Optimizing the use of storage devices translates into making sure the maximum amount of usable data is written to and read from these units at an acceptable rate of response. Optimizing these resources also means ensuring that there is an adequate amount of storage space available while guarding against having expensive excess amounts. This notion of optimal use ties in to two of the main areas of storage management: capacity and performance.

Protecting the integrity of data means that the data will always be accessible to those authorized to it and that it will not be changed unless the authorized owner specifically intends for it to be changed. Data integrity also implies that, should the data inadvertently become inaccessible or destroyed, reliable backup copies will enable its complete recovery. These explanations of data integrity tie into the other two main areas of storage management: reliability and recoverability. Each of these four areas warrants a section of its own, but first we need to discuss the issue of process ownership.

Desired Traits of a Storage Management Process Owner

The individual who is assigned as the owner of the storage management process should have a broad basis of knowledge in several areas related to disk space resources. These areas include applications, backup systems, hardware configurations, and database systems. Due to the dynamic nature of disk-space management, the process owner should also be able to think and act in a tactical manner. Table 12–1 lists, in priority order, these and other desirable characteristics to look for when selecting this individual.

Table 12–1   Prioritized Characteristics of a Storage Management Process Owner

Characteristic	Priority
1. Knowledge of applications	High
2. Knowledge of backup systems	High
3. Knowledge of hardware configurations	High
4. Ability to think and act tactically	High
5. Knowledge of database systems	High
6. Ability to work with IT developers	Medium
7. Knowledge of systems software and components	Medium
8. Knowledge of software configurations	Medium
9. Ability to think and plan strategically	Medium
10. Ability to manage diversity	Low
11. Knowledge of network software and components	Low
12. Knowledge of desktop hardware and software	Low
13. Knowledge of power and air conditioning systems	Low

Another issue to keep in mind when considering candidates for storage management process owner is that the individual's traits may also make him or her a candidate to own other related processes—the person may already be a process owner of another process. The following four primary areas of storage management are directly related to other systems management processes:

- Capacity planning
- Performance and tuning
- Change management
- Disaster recovery

The storage management process owner may be qualified to own one or more of these other processes, just as an existing owner of any of these other processes might be suitable to own storage management. In most instances, these process owners report to the manager of technical services, if they are not currently serving in that position themselves.

Storage Management Capacity

Storage management capacity consists of providing sufficient data storage to authorized users at a reasonable cost. Storage capacity is often thought of as large quantities of disk farms accessible to servers or mainframes. In fact, data storage capacity includes main memory and magnetic disk storage for mainframe processors, midrange computers, workstations, servers, and desktop computers in all their various flavors. Data storage capacity also includes alternative storage devices such as optical disks, magnetic drums, open reel magnetic tape, magnetic tape cartridges and cassettes, digital audio tape, and digital linear tape. When it comes to maximizing the efficient use of data storage, most efforts are centered around large-capacity storage devices such as high-volume disk arrays. This is because the large capacities of these devices, when left unchecked, can result in poorly used or wasted space.

There are a number of methods to increase the utilization of large-capacity storage devices. One is to institute a robust capacity planning process across all of IT that will identify far in advance major disk space requirements. This enables planners to propose and budget the most cost-effective storage resources to meet forecast demand. Another more tactical initiative is to monitor disk space usage to proactively spot unplanned data growth, data fragmentation, increased use of extents, and data that has not been accessed for long periods of time. There are a number of tools on the market that can streamline much of this monitoring. The important element here is the process, rather than the tool, that needs to be enforced to heighten awareness about responsible disk space management.

The advent of the personal computer in the 1970s brought with it the refinement of portable disk storage (see Table 12-2) beginning with the diskette or so-called floppy disk. Early versions were 8 inches wide, stored 80 kilobytes of data, and recorded only on one side. Refinements eventually reduced its size to 3.5 inches (see Figure 12-1) and increased its capacity to 1.44 megabytes. By 2001, both Sony Corporation and Phillips Electronics had refined and offered to consumers the universal serial bus (USB) flash drive. These devices were non-volatile (they retained data in absence of power), solid state, and used flash memory. More importantly, they consumed only 5 percent of the power of a small disk drive, were tiny in size, and were very portable. Users have come to know these devices by various names, including:

- Flash drives
- Key drives
- Pen drives
- Thumb drives
- USB keys
- USB memory keys
- USB sticks
- Vault drives

Regardless of what they are called, they have proven to be very reliable and very popular.

Table 12-2 Developments in Portable Disk Storage

Year of Introduction	Common Name	Maximum Capacity
1971	8-inch floppy disk	80 kilobytes (KB)
1976	5.25-inch floppy disk	360KB
1981	3.5-inch floppy disk	720KB
1987	3.5-inch high-density floppy disk	1.44 megabytes (MB)
2001	USB flash drive	2 gigabytes (GB)

Figure 12-1 3.5-Inch Floppy Disk "Reprint courtesy of International Business Machines Corporation, copyright International Business Machines Corporation"

While magnetic disks are the most common type of storage device within an infrastructure, magnetic tape is still an important part of this environment. Huge databases and data warehouses now command much of the attention of storage managers, but all this data is still primarily backed-up to tape. Just as disk technology has advanced, the increased data capacities of tape have also evolved significantly over the past few decades (see Table 12-3).

Table 12-3 Developments in Tape Storage

Year of Introduction	Common Name	Maximum Capacity
1956	10.5-inch open-reel 0.5-inch tape at 800 bytes per inch (bpi)	100MB
1971	10.5-inch open-reel 0.5-inch tape at 1600 bpi	200MB
1978	5-inch cartridge 0.5-inch tape at 6250 bpi	980MB
1993	Digital Linear Tape (DLT)	40GB
1996	Advanced Intelligent Tape (AIT)	50GB

During the 1970s, nine-track magnetic tape density on a 10 1/2-inch open-reel increased from 800 bytes per inch (bpi) to 1,600 bpi, which was a capacity increase from 100 megabytes (MB) to 200MB. Toward the end of that decade, the number of tracks per tape and bytes per track both doubled, increasing the density to 6,250 bpi and the capacity to nearly a gigabyte. Subsequent advances into high density tapes doubled and tripled those capacities during the 1980s. The next technology to be developed in this arena was Digital Linear Tape (DLT), which has a unique helixical bit-pattern striping that results in 30 to 40 gigabytes (GB) per tape (see Figure 12-2). A few years later Sony pioneered Advanced Intelligent Tape (AIT). AIT can store over 50GBper tape and transfer data at six MB per second. Knowledge of these high-density tapes and their cost is important for storage management process owners who have to plan for backup windows, estimated restore times, and onsite and offsite floor space for housing these tapes.

Figure 12-2   Digital Linear Tape (DLT)

Storage Management Performance

There are a variety of considerations that come into play when configuring infrastructure storage for optimal performance. The following list shows some of the most common of these. We will start with performance considerations at the processor side and work our way out to the storage devices.

1. Size and type of processor main memory
2. Number and size of buffers
3. Size of swap space
4. Number and type of channels
5. Device controller configuration
6. Logical volume groups
7. Amount of disk array cache memory
8. Storage area networks (SANs)
9. Network-attached storage (NAS)

The first performance consideration is the size and type of main memory. Processors of all kinds—from desktops up to mainframes—have their performance impacted by the amount of main storage installed in them. The amount can vary from just a few megabytes for desktops to up to tens of gigabytes for mainframes. Computer chip configurations, particularly for servers, also vary from 128MB to 256MB to forthcoming 1GB memory chips. The density can influence the total amount of memory that can be installed in a server due to the limitation of physical memory slots.

In smaller shops, systems administrators responsible for server software may also configure and manage main storage. In larger shops, disk storage analysts likely interact with systems administrators to configure the entire storage environment, including main memory, for optimal performance. These two groups of analysts also normally confer about buffers, swap space, and channels. The number and size of buffers are calculated to maximize data-transfer rates between host processors and external disk units without wasting valuable storage and cycles within the processor. Similarly, swap space is sized to minimize processing time by providing the proper ratio of real memory space to disk space. A good rule of thumb for this ratio used to be to size the swap space to be equal to that of main memory, but today this will vary depending on applications and platforms.

Channels connecting host processors to disk and tape storage devices vary as to their transfer speed, their technology, and the maximum number able to be attached to different platforms. The number and speed of the channels influence performance, response, throughput, and costs. All of these factors should be considered by storage management specialists when designing an infrastructure's channel configurations.

Tape and disk controllers have variable numbers of input channels attaching them to their host processors, as well as variable numbers of devices attaching to their output ports. Analysis needs to be done to determine the correct number of input channels and output devices per controller to maximize performance while still staying within reasonable costs. There are several software analysis tools available to assist in this; often the hardware suppliers can offer the greatest assistance.

A software methodology called a *logical volume group* assembles together two or more physical disk volumes into one logical grouping for performance reasons. This is most commonly done on huge disk-array units housing large databases or data warehouses. The mapping of physical units into logical groupings is an important task that almost always warrants the assistance of performance specialists from the hardware supplier or other sources.

To improve performance of disk transactions, huge disk arrays also have varying sizes of cache memory. Large database applications benefit most from utilizing a very fast—and very expensive—high-speed cache. Because of the expense of the cache, disk-storage specialists endeavor to tune the databases and the applications to make maximum use of the cache. Their goal is to have the most frequently accessed parts of the database residing in the cache. Sophisticated pre-fetch algorithms determine which data is likely to be requested next and then initiate the preloading of it into the cache. The effectiveness of these algorithms greatly influences the speed and performance of the cache. Since the cache is read first for all disk transactions, finding the desired piece of data in the cache—for example, a hit—greatly improves response times by eliminating the relatively slow data transfer from physical disks. Hit ratios (hits versus misses) between 85 percent and 95 percent are not uncommon for well-tuned databases and applications; this high hit ratio helps justify the cost of the cache.

Two more recent developments in configuring storage systems for optimal performance are storage area networks (SANs) and network attached storage (NAS). SAN is a configuration enhancement that places a high-speed fiber-optic switch between servers and disk arrays. The two primary advantages are speed and flexibility. NAS is similar in concept to SAN except that the switch in NAS is replaced by a network. This enables data to be shared between storage devices and processors across a network. There is a more detailed discussion on the performance aspects of these two storage configurations described in Chapter 8, "Performance and Tuning."

Storage Management Reliability

Robust storage management implies that adequate amounts of disk storage are available to users whenever they need it and wherever they are. However, the reliability of disk equipment has always been a major concern of hardware suppliers and customers alike. This emphasis on reliability can be illustrated with a highly publicized anecdote involving IBM that occurred almost 30 years ago.

IBM had always been proud that it had never missed a first customer ship date for any major product in the company's history. In late 1980, it announced an advanced new disk drive (the model 3380) with a first customer ship date of October 1981. Anticipation was high because this model would have tightly packed tracks with densely packed data, providing record storage capacity at an affordable price.

While performing final lab testing in the summer of 1981, engineers discovered that, under extremely rare conditions, the redundant power supply in the new model drive could intermittently malfunction. If another set of conditions occurred at the same time, a possible write error could result. A team of engineering specialists studied the problem for weeks but could not consistently duplicate the problem, which was necessary to enable a permanent fix. A hotly contested debate ensued within IBM about whether the should delay shipment until the problem could be satisfactorily resolved, with each side believing that the opposing position would do irreparable damage to the corporation.

The decision went to the highest levels of IBM management, who decided they could not undermine the quality of their product or jeopardize the reputation of their company by adhering to an artificial schedule with a suspect offering. In August, IBM announced it was delaying general availability of its model 3380 disk drive system for at least three months, perhaps even longer if necessary. Wall Street, industry analysts, and interested observers held their collective breath, expecting major fallout from the announcement. It never came. Customers were more impressed than disappointed by IBM's acknowledgment of the criticality of disk drive reliability. Within a few months the problem was traced to a power supply filter that was unable to handle rare voltage fluctuations. It was estimated at the time that the typical shop using clean, or conditioned, power had less than a one-in-a-million chance of ever experiencing the set of conditions required to trigger the malfunction.

The episode served to strengthen the notion of just how important reliable disk equipment was becoming. With companies beginning to run huge corporate databases on which the success of their business often depended, data storage reliability was of prime concern. Manufacturers began designing into their disk storage systems redundant components such as backup power systems, dual channel ports to disk controllers, and dual pathing between drives and controllers. These improvements significantly increased the reliability of disk and tape storage equipment, in some instances more than doubling the usual one-year mean time between failures (MTBF) for a disk drive. Even with this improved reliability, the drives were far from fault tolerant. If a shop had 100 disk drives—not uncommon at that time—it could expect an average failure rate of one disk drive per week.

Fault-tolerant systems began appearing in the 1980s, a decade in which entire processing environments were duplicated in a hot standby mode. These systems essentially never went down, making their high cost justifiable for many manufacturing companies with large, 24-hour workforces, who needed processing capability but not much in the way of databases. Most of the cost was in the processing part since databases were relatively small and disk storage requirements were low. However, there were other types of companies that had large corporate databases requiring large amounts of disk storage. The expense of duplicating huge disk farms all but put most of them out of the running for fault-tolerant systems.

During this time, technological advances in design and manufacturing drove down the expense of storing data on magnetic devices. By the mid-1980s, the cost per megabyte of disk storage had plummeted to a fraction of what it had been a decade earlier. Smaller, less reliable disks such as those on PCs were less expensive still. But building fault-tolerant disk drives was still an expensive proposition due to the complex software needed to run high-capacity disks in a hot standby mode in concert with the operating system. Manufacturers then started looking at connecting huge arrays of small, slightly less reliable and far less expensive disk drives and operating them in a fault-tolerant mode that was basically independent of the operating systems on which they ran. This was accomplished by running a separate drive in the array for parity bits.

This type of disk configuration was called a redundant array of inexpensive disks (RAID). By the early 1990s, most disk drives were considered inexpensive, moving the RAID Advisory Board to officially change the *I* in RAID to *independent* rather than *inexpensive*. Advances and refinements led to improvements in affordability, performance, and especially reliability. Performance was improved by disk striping, which writes data across multiple drives, increasing data paths and transfer rates and allowing simultaneous reading and writing to multiple disks. This implementation of RAID is referred to as level 0. Reliability was improved through mirroring (level 1) or use of parity drives (level 3 or 5). The result is that RAID has become the de facto standard for providing highly reliable disk-storage systems to mainframe, midrange, and client/server platforms. Table 12–4 lists the five most common levels of RAID.

Table 12–4 RAID Level Descriptions

RAID Level	Explanation
0	Disk striping for performance reasons
1	Mirroring for total redundancy
0 + 1	Combination of striping and mirroring
3	Striping and fault tolerance with parity on totally dedicated parity drives
5	Striping and fault tolerance with parity on nonassociated data drives

Mirroring at RAID level 1 means that all data is duplicated on separate drives so that if one drive malfunctions, its mirrored drive maintains uninterrupted operation of all read and write transactions. Software and microcode in the RAID controller take the failing drive offline and issue messages to appropriate personnel to replace the drive while the array is up and running. More sophisticated arrays notify a remote repair center and arrange replacement of the drive with the supplier with little or no involvement of infrastructure personnel. This level offers virtually continuous operation of all disks.

The combination of striping and mirroring goes by several nomenclatures, including:

- 0,1
- 0 plus 1
- 0+1

As its various names suggest, this level of RAID duplicates all data for high reliability and stripes the data for high performance.

RAID level 3 stripes the data for performance reasons similar to RAID level 0 and, for high reliability, assigns a dedicated parity drive on which parity bits are written to recover and rebuild data in the event of a data drive malfunction. There are usually two to four data drives supported by a single parity drive.

RAID level 5 is similar to level 3 except that parity bits are shared on nonassociated data drives. For example, for three data drives labeled A, B, and C, the parity bits for data striped across drives B and C would reside on drive A; the parity bits for data striped across drives A and C would reside on drive B; the parity bits for data striped across drives A and B would reside on drive C.

A general knowledge about how an application accesses data can help in determining which level of RAID to employ. For example, the relatively random access into the indexes and data files of a relational database make them ideal candidates for RAID 0+1. The sequential nature of log files would make them better candidates for just RAID 1 alone. By understanding the different RAID levels, storage management process owners can better evaluate which scheme is best suited for their business goals, their budgetary targets, their expected service levels, and their technical requirements.

Storage Management Recoverability

There are several methods available for recovering data that has been altered, deleted, damaged, or otherwise made inaccessible. Determining the correct recovery technique depends on the manner in which the data was backed up. Table 12–5 lists four common types of data backups. The first three are referred to as physical backups because operating system software or specialized program products copy the data as it physically resides on the disk without regard to database structures or logical organization—it is purely a physical backup. The fourth is called a logical backup because database management software reads—or backs up—logical parts of the database, such as tables, schemas, data dictionaries, or indexes; the software then writes the output to binary files. This may be done for the full database, for individual users, or for specific tables.

Table 12–5   Types of Data Backups

Type of Backup	Alternate Names
1. Physical full backup	Cold backup
	Full volume backup
	Full offline backup
2. Physical incremental backup	Incremental backup
	Incremental offline backup
3. Physical online backup	Online backup
	Hot backup
	Archive backup
4. Logical backup	Exporting files
	Exporting files into binary files

Physical offline backups require shut down of all online systems, applications, and databases residing on the volume being backed up prior to starting the backup process. Performing several full volume backups of high-capacity disk drives may take many hours to complete and are normally done on weekends when systems can be shut down for long periods of time. Incremental backups also require systems and databases to be shut down, but for much shorter periods of time. Since only the data that has changed since the last backup is what is copied, incremental backups can usually be completed within a few hours if done on a nightly basis.

A physical online backup is a powerful backup technique that offers two very valuable and distinct benefits:

- Databases can remain open to users during the backup process.
- Recovery can be accomplished back to the last transaction processed.

The database environment must be running in an archive mode for online backups to occur properly. This means that fully filled log files, prior to being written over, are first written to an archive file. During online backups, table files are put into a backup state one at a time to enable the operating system to back up the data associated with it. Any changes made during the backup process are temporarily stored in log files and then brought back to their normal state after that particular table file has been backed up.

Full recovery is accomplished by restoring the last full backup and the incremental backups taken since the last full backup and then doing a forward recovery utilizing the archive and log tapes. For Oracle databases, the logging is referred to as redo files; when these files are full, they are copied to archive files before being written over for continuous logging. Sybase, IBM's Database 2 (DB2), and Microsoft's SQL Server have similar logging mechanisms using checkpoints and transaction logs.

Logical backups are less complicated and more time consuming to perform. There are three advantages to performing logical backups in concert with physical backups:

1. Exports can be made online, enabling 24/7 applications and databases to remain operational during the copying process.
2. Small portions of a database can be exported and imported, efficiently enabling maintenance to be performed on only the data required.
3. Exported data can be imported into databases or schemas at a higher version level than the original database, allowing for testing at new software levels.

Another approach to safeguarding data becoming more prevalent today is the disk-to-disk backup. As the size of critical databases continues to grow, and as allowable backup windows continue to shrink, there are a number of advantages to this approach that help to justify its obvious costs. Among these advantages are:

- **Significant reduction in backup and recovery time.** Copying directly to disk is orders of magnitude faster than copying to tape. This benefit also applies to online backups, which, while allowing databases to be open and accessible during backup processing, still incur a performance hit that is noticeably reduced by this method.

- **The stored copy can be used for other purposes.** These can include testing or report generation which, if done with the original data, could impact database performance.

- **Data replication can be employed.** This is a specialized version of a disk backup in which the data is mirrored on one of two drives in real time. At short specified intervals, such as every 30 minutes, the data is copied to an offsite recovery center. Data replication is covered in more detail in Chapter 17, "Business Continuity."

- **Help to cost justify tape backups.** Copying the second stored disk files to tape can be scheduled at any time, provided it ends prior to the beginning of the next disk backup. It may even reduce investment in tape equipment, which can offset the costs of additional disks.

A thorough understanding of the requirements and the capabilities of data backups, restores, and recovery is necessary for implementing a robust storage management process. Several other backup considerations need to be kept in mind when designing such a process. They are as follows:

1. Backup window
2. Restore times
3. Expiration dates
4. Retention periods
5. Recycle periods
6. Generation data groups
7. Offsite retrieval times

8. Tape density
9. Tape format
10. Tape packaging
11. Shelf life
12. Automation techniques

There are three key questions that need to be answered at the outset:

1. How much nightly backup window is available?
2. How long will it take to perform nightly backups?
3. Back to what point in time should recovery be made?

If the time needed to back up all the required data on a nightly basis exceeds the offline backup window, then some form of online backup will be necessary. The method of recovery used depends on whether data will be restored back to the last incremental backup or back to the last transaction completed.

Expiration dates, retention periods, and recycling periods are related issues pertaining to the length of time data is intended to stay in existence. Weekly and monthly application jobs may create temporary data files that are designed to expire one week or one month, respectively, after the data was generated. Other files may need to be retained for several years for auditing purposes or for government regulations. Backup files on tape also fall into these categories. Expiration dates and retention periods are specified in the job-control language that describes how these various files will be created. Recycle periods relate to the elapsed time before backup tapes are reused.

A generation data group (GDG) is a mainframe mechanism for creating new versions of a data file that would be similar to that created with backup jobs. The advantage of this is the ability to restore back to a specific day with simple parameter changes to the job-control language. Offsite retrieval time is the maximum contracted time that the offsite tape storage provider is allowed to physically bring tapes to the data center from the time of notification.

Tape density, format, and packaging relate to characteristics that may change over time and consequently change recovery procedures. Density refers to the compression of bits as they are stored on the tape; it will increase as technology advances and equipment is upgraded. Format refers to the number and configuration of tracks on the tape. Packaging refers to the size and shape of the enclosures used to house the tapes.

The shelf life of magnetic tape is sometimes overlooked and can become problematic for tapes with retention periods exceeding five or six years. Temperature, humidity, handling, frequent changes in the environment, the quality of the tape, and other factors can influence the actual shelf life of any given tape, but five years is a good rule of thumb to use for recopying long-retained tapes.

Mechanical tape loaders, automated tape library systems, and movable tape rack systems can all add a degree of labor-saving automation to the storage management process. As with any process automation, thorough planning and process streamlining must precede the implementation of the automation.

Real Life Experience—Locking Up Approval for a Purchase Request

A primary defense contractor in Southern California maintained a huge tape library with over 50,000 open reel tape volumes hanging on overhead racks. The IT operations manager requested new racks that would lock the tape reels in place. His request was delayed by a lengthy approval process.

During this period, a major earthquake struck that shook the defense company's facility to its core, damaging some of the data center, including the tape library. IT personnel were stunned to see more than 12,000 tape volumes scattered all over the floor, having come dislodged from their tape racks.

The IT operations manager had little difficulty getting his request for new, locking-type tape racks approved a few days later.

Assessing an Infrastructure's Storage Management Process

The worksheets shown in Figures 12-3 and 12-4 present a quick-and-simple method for assessing the overall quality, efficiency, and effectiveness of a storage management process. The first worksheet is used without weighting factors, meaning that all 10 categories are weighted evenly for the assessment of a storage management process. Sample ratings are inserted to illustrate the use of the worksheet. In this case, the storage management process scored a total of 22 points for an overall nonweighted assessment score of 55 percent. The second sample (weighted) worksheet compiled a weighted assessment score of 50 percent.

Storage Management Process—Assessment Worksheet						
Process Owner_____ **Owner's Manager**_____ **Date**_____						
Category	Questions for Storage Management	None 1	Small 2	Medium 3	Large 4
Executive Support	To what degree does the executive sponsor show support for the storage management process with actions such as enforcing disk cleanup policies and questioning needs for more space?	-	2	-	-
Process Owner	To what degree does the process owner exhibit desirable traits, develop and analyze meaningful metrics, and bring them to data owners' attention?	-	2	-	-
Customer Involvement	To what degree are key customers involved in the design and use of the process, particularly the analysis and enforcement of metric thresholds?	-	2	-	-
Supplier Involvement	To what degree are key suppliers, such as hardware manufactures and software utility providers, involved in the design of the process?	1	-	-	-
Service Metrics	To what degree are service metrics analyzed for trends such as outages caused by lack of disk space or disk hardware problems and poor response due to fragmentation or lack of reorgs?	-	2	-	-
Process Metrics	To what degree are process metrics analyzed for trends such as elapsed time for backups, errors during backups, and time to restore?	-	-	3	-
Process Integration	To what degree does the storage management process integrate with other processes and tools such as performance and tuning and capacity planning?	-	-	3	-
Streamlining/ Automation	To what degree is the storage management process streamlined by automating actions such as the initiation of backups, restoring of files, or the changing of sizes or the number of buffers or cache storage?	-	-	-	4
Training of Staff	To what degree is the staff cross-trained on the storage management process, and how well is the effectiveness of the training verified?	-	2	-	-
Process Documentation	To what degree is the quality and value of storage management documentation measured and maintained?	1	-	-	-
	Totals	2	10	6	4
Grand Total = 2 + 10 + 6 + 4 = 22 Non-Weighted Assessment Score = 22 / 40 = 55%						

Figure 12-3   Sample Assessment Worksheet for Storage Management Process

Storage Management Process—Assessment Worksheet				
Process Owner_____ Owner's Manager_____ Date _____				
Category	**Questions for Storage Management**	**Weight**	**Rating**	**Score**
Executive Support	To what degree does the executive sponsor show support for the storage management process with actions such as enforcing disk cleanup policies and questioning needs for more space?	3	2	6
Process Owner	To what degree does the process owner exhibit desirable traits, develop and analyze meaningful metrics, and bring them to data owners' attention?	3	2	6
Customer Involvement	To what degree are key customers involved in the design and use of the process, particularly the analysis and enforcement of metric thresholds?	5	2	10
Supplier Involvement	To what degree are key suppliers, such as hardware manufactures and software utility providers, involved in the design of the process?	3	1	3
Service Metrics	To what degree are service metrics analyzed for trends such as outages caused by either lack of disk space or disk hardware problems and poor response due to fragmentation or lack of reorgs?	5	2	10
Process Metrics	To what degree are process metrics analyzed for trends such as elapsed time for backups, errors during backups, and time to restore?	3	3	9
Process Integration	To what degree does the storage management process integrate with other processes and tools such as performance and tuning and capacity planning?	1	3	3
Streamlining/ Automation	To what degree is the storage management process streamlined by automating actions such as the initiation of backups, restoring of files, or the changing of sizes or the number of buffers or cache storage?	1	4	4
Training of Staff	To what degree is the staff cross-trained on the storage management process, and how well is the effectiveness of the training verified?	3	2	6
Process Documentation	To what degree is the quality and value of storage management documentation measured and maintained?	3	1	3
	Totals	30	22	60
Weighted Assessment Score = 60 / (30 × 4) = 50%				

Figure 12-4 Assessment Worksheet for Storage Management Process with Weighting Factors

One of the most valuable characteristics of these worksheets is that they are customized to evaluate each of the 12 processes individually. The worksheets in this chapter apply only to the storage management process. However, the fundamental concepts applied in using these evaluation worksheets are the same for all 12 disciplines. As a result, the detailed explanation on the general use of these worksheets presented near the end of Chapter 7, "Availability," also applies to the other worksheets in the book. Please refer to that discussion if you need more information.

Measuring and Streamlining the Storage Management Process

We can measure and streamline the storage management process with the help of the assessment worksheet shown in Figure 12-3. We can measure the effectiveness of a storage management process with service metrics such as outages caused by either lack of disk space or disk hardware problems and poor response due to fragmentation or lack of reorganizations. Process metrics—such as elapsed time for backups, errors during backups, and time to restore—help us gauge the efficiency of this process. And we can streamline the storage management process by automating actions such as the initiation of backups, restoring of files, or the changing of sizes or the number of buffers or cache storage.

Summary

This chapter discussed the four major areas of the storage management process: capacity, performance, reliability, and recoverability. We began in our usual manner with a definition for this process and desirable characteristics in a process owner. We then presented key information about each of the four major areas.

We looked at techniques to manage storage capacity from both a strategic and tactical standpoint. A number of performance considerations were offered to optimize overall data-transfer rates in large-capacity storage arrays. We next discussed reliability and recoverability. These are companion topics relating to data integrity, which is the most significant issue in the process of storage management.

The discussion on reliability included an industry example of its importance and how RAID evolved into a very effective reliability feature. A number of considerations for managing backups were included in the discussion on recoverability. The customized assessment sheets were provided to evaluate an infrastructure's storage management process.

Test Your Understanding

1. For disk controllers with cache memory, the lower the hit ratio, the better the performance. (True or False)
2. A physical backup takes into account the structures and logical organization of a database. (True or False)
3. Which of the following is not an advantage of a disk-to-disk backup?
   a. significantly reduces backup and recovery time
   b. is less expensive than a disk-to-tape backup
   c. helps facilitate data replication
   d. the stored copy can be used for other purposes
4. The type of backup that uses database management software to read and copy parts of a database is called a _____ _____ .
5. Describe some of the advantages and disadvantages of storage capacities becoming larger and denser.

Suggested Further Readings

1. http://cs-exhibitions.uni-klu.ac.at/index.php?id=310
2. *Storage Area Networks for Dummies*; 2003; Poelker, Christopher and Nikitin, Alex; For Dummies Publishing
3. www.bitpipe.com/tlist/Data-Replication.html
4. *Using SANs and NAS*; 2002; Preston, Curtis; O'Reilly Media
5. www.emc.com/products/systems/DMX_series.jsp

CHAPTER 13

Network Management

Introduction

This chapter will present the decisions an infrastructure organization must make to manage IT networks, a nontrivial challenge in light of the diversity of current IT environments. Today's networks come in a variety of sizes, scopes, and architectures, from a simple dual-node local network in your house to a sophisticated, encrypted network connecting tens of thousands of nodes worldwide.

There obviously is no single, detailed network management process that applies to all of the various network environments, but there are common elements of the process that apply to almost all network scenarios, and the decisions that shape this process is what we will concentrate on in this chapter. We begin, as usual, with a definition of network management followed by the prioritized traits of the process owner. We next discuss six key decisions that must be made correctly in order to manage a robust network environment. These decisions apply to all network environments, regardless of platforms, protocols, or peripherals. We conclude with the standard assessment sheets customized for the network management process.

Definition of Network Management

Network Management

Network management is a process to maximize the reliability and utilization of network components in order to optimize network availability and responsiveness.

We see that our definition includes elements of two other processes:

- Availability
- Performance and tuning

Maximizing reliability is another way of emphasizing high availability by ensuring network lines and the various components such as routers, switches, and hubs maintain high levels of uptime. Maximizing utilization implies that performance and tuning activities involving these components are optimizing network response.

While availability and performance and tuning are the two processes most closely related to, and affected by, this process, network management actually interacts with six other systems management processes, making it one of the most interrelated of all 12 disciplines. The relationships of each process to all of the others are covered at length in Chapter 21, "Integrating Systems Management Processes."

Key Decisions about Network Management

Before an effective, high-level network management process can be designed, much less implemented, six key decisions need to be made that influence the strategy, direction, and cost of the process. The following questions must be answered. These decisions define the scope of responsibilities and, more important, the functional areas that are charged with employing the process on a daily basis.

1. What will be managed by this process?
2. Who will manage it?
3. How much authority will this person be given?
4. What types of tools and support will be provided?
5. To what extent will other processes be integrated with this process?
6. What levels of service and quality will be expected?

What Will Be Managed by This Process?

This may seem like an obvious question with an obvious answer: we will manage the network. But what exactly does this mean? One of the problems infrastructures experience in this regard is being too vague as to who is responsible for which aspects of the network. This is especially true in large, complex environments where worldwide networks may vary in terms of topology, platform, protocols, security, and suppliers.

For example, some infrastructures may be responsible for both classified and unclassified networks with widely varying security requirements, supplier involvement, and government regulations. This was the case when I managed the network department at a nationwide defense contractor. We decided early on exactly which elements of network management would be managed by our department and which ones would be managed by others. For instance, we all mutually decided that government agencies would manage encryption, the in-house security department would manage network security, and computer operations along with its help desk would administer network passwords.

Was this the only arrangement we could have decided on? Obviously, it was not. Was it the best solution for anyone in a similar situation? That would depend on the situation, since each environment varies as to priorities, directions, costs, and schedule. It was the best solution for our environment at the time. Did we ever need to modify it? Certainly we did. Major defense programs rarely remain static as to importance, popularity, or funding. As external forces exerted their influences on the program, we made appropriate changes to what was included in our network management process. The key point here is to reach consensus as early as possible and to communicate with all appropriate parties as to what will be managed by this process.

Emerging and converging technologies such as wireless connectivity and voice over the Internet protocol (VoIP) are becoming more commonplace. Decisions about which of these network technologies will be included in the overall network management process need to be agreed upon and bought into by all appropriate stakeholders.

Who Will Manage It?

Once we decide on *what* we will manage, we need to decide on *who* will manage it. Initially, this decision should determine which department within the infrastructure will be assigned the responsibility for heading up the design, implementation, and ongoing management of this process. Within that department, a person will be assigned to have overall responsibility for the network-management process.

The ideal candidate to serve as network management process owner should have strong people skills, knowledge of network resources, and a sense of urgency. Table 13–1 offers a more comprehensive list, in priority order, of the traits desired in such an individual. The people skills involve working with developers on application profiles, the mix and arrival pattern of transactions, and planned increases in workloads, as well as working effectively with users on desktop requirements, connectivity, and security.

Table 13–1   Prioritized Characteristics of a Network Management Process Owner

Characteristic	Priority
1. Ability to work with IT developers	High
2. Ability to work effectively with users	High
3. Knowledge of network software and components	High
4. Ability to think and act tactically	High
5. Knowledge of systems software and components	Medium
6. Knowledge of software configurations	Medium
7. Knowledge of hardware configurations	Medium
8. Knowledge of desktop hardware and software	Medium
9. Ability to analyze metrics	Medium
10. Ability to evaluate documentation	Medium
11. Knowledge of applications	Low
12. Knowledge of company's business model	Low
13. Ability to manage diversity	Low
14. Knowledge of backup systems	Low
15. Ability to think and plan strategically	Low

A network-management process owner should be knowledgeable about network operating systems, utility programs, support software, and key hardware components such as routers, switchers, hubs, and repeaters. One of the most valuable traits for the owner of this process is a sense of urgency in tactically responding to, and resolving, a variety of network problems. Other desirable traits include knowledge of infrastructure software and hardware and the ability to analyze metrics.

How Much Authority Will This Person Be Given?

This is probably the most significant question of all because, without adequate authority, the necessary enforcement and resulting effectiveness of the process rapidly diminishes. Few practices accelerate failure more quickly than giving an individual responsibility for an activity without also providing that person with the appropriate authority. Executive support plays a key role here from several perspectives. First, managers must be willing to surrender some of their authority over the network to the individual now responsible for overseeing its management. Second, managers must be willing to support their process owner in situations of conflict that will surely arise. Conflicts involving network management can originate from several sources.

One source of conflict can come from enforcing network security policies such as if, when, and how data over the network will be encrypted or under what instances a single sign-on scheme will be employed for network and application logons. Another common source of network conflict involves user expectations about the infrastructure backing up desktop data instead of the more practical method of saving it to the server. The degree of authority a network management process owner has over network suppliers can also instigate conflict, particularly if managers have not communicated clearly to supplier management about the delegation of authority that is in effect.

The enforcement of network connectivity standards is one of the greatest sources of conflict for network administrators. This is because most users feel that they have adequate justification to warrant an exception, and very few administrators effectively convey the legitimate business reasons for having a connectivity standard. More than once I have heard IT users in highly creative industries such as motion picture and television production companies present their arguments. Their claim is usually that their specialized artistic requirements should allow them to connect suspect devices with unproven interfaces to the network, even though alternate devices with standard interfaces could be used.

On the other hand, I have had opportunity of working with network administrators and process owners who both helped or hurt their cause of enforcing network connectivity standards. The group that undermined their own efforts at enforcement failed for two reasons:

1. They failed to offer compelling arguments to users as to why it was in their own best interest to comply with connectivity standards.

2. The network group did not have adequate tools in place to enforce compliance with the standards.

The group who helped their cause of enforcing network connectivity standards did so by presenting several persuasive reasons why adhering to these standards would benefit users and suppliers alike. Table 13–2 lists the seven categories, with explanations, into which these reasons fall.

Table 13–2   Reasons for Network Connectivity Standards

Category	Explanation
1. Availability	Nonstandard devices can lock up networks, causing online system outages.
2. Performance	Nonstandard hardware can cause nonstop transmissions (so-called network storms), which can significantly slow down online transactions.
3. Deployment	The deployment of a new application often requires installing additional desktop computers. Adhering to standard configurations simplifies the staging and deploying of large numbers of desktop computers.
4. Capacity	Some devices that deviate from standards are improperly configured for the network on which they are connected. This can cause countless retransmissions, unanticipated network traffic, and problems for capacity planners.
5. Security	Most users want to feel assured that their data and applications are secured from external hackers and internal saboteurs. Standard interfaces help to ensure this.
6. Maintenance	Network connectivity standards reduce maintenance time and material costs by requiring less training, fewer spare parts inventory, and less supplier involvement.
7. Troubleshooting	The smaller the variety of devices on the network, the smaller the need for specialized skills and diagnostic equipment necessary to troubleshoot problems.

There is a third perspective concerning an executive who delegates security enforcement authority to a network administrator. This involves the executive's reaction to mistakes the administrator may make. Factors such as experience, training, fatigue, judgment, negligence, oversight, attitude, and abuse should all be considered in determining the appropriate response to a potential misuse of authority.

What Types of Tools and Support Will Be Provided?

Decisions about the type of tools and the amount of vendor support that will be provided directly influence the costs of managing networks. In general, the costs of these two entities are inversely proportional. As more money is spent on vendor support, the need for expensive, sophisticated diagnostic tools should lessen. As more advanced tools are acquired and effectively used by in-house personnel, the need for costly, premium vendor support should correspondingly go down. One exception is classified networks where the granting of security clearances may reduce the number of vendor personnel cleared to a program. In this instance, the costs of vendor overtime and the expenses for sophisticated tools to troubleshoot encrypted lines could both increase.

A variety of network tools are available to monitor and manage a network. Some are incorporated in hardware components, but most are software-based. Costs can range from just a few thousand dollars to literally millions of dollars for multi-year contracts with full onsite maintenance. The expense for tools can sometimes be mitigated by leveraging what other sites may be using, by negotiating aggressive terms with reluctant suppliers, and by inventorying your in-house tools. Several of my clients have discovered they were paying for software licenses for products they were unaware they owned.

One tool often overlooked for network management is one that will facilitate network documentation. The criticality and complexity of today's networks require clear, concise, and accurate documentation for support, repair, and maintenance. Effective network management requires documentation that is both simple to understand yet thorough enough to be meaningful. Useful pieces of this type of documentation is seldom produced because of a lack of emphasis on this important aspect of network management. Couple this with senior network designers' general reluctance to document their diagrams in a manner meaningful to less experienced designers and the challenge of providing this information becomes clear.

There are a number of standard network-diagramming tools available to assist in generating this documentation. The major obstacle is more often the lack of accountability than it is the lack of tools. The executive sponsor and the process both need to enforce documentation policy as it pertains to network management. One of the best tools I have seen offered to network designers is the use of a skilled technical writer who can assist designers over the hurdles of network documentation.

To What Extent Will Other Processes Be Integrated With This Process?

A well-designed network management process will have strong relationships to six other systems management processes (we will discuss this further in Chapter 21). These processes are availability, performance and tuning, change management, problem management, capacity planning, and security. The extent to which network management integrates with these other processes by sharing tools, databases, procedures, or cross-trained personnel will influence the effectiveness of the process.

For example, capacity planning and network management could both share a tool that simulates network workloads to make resource forecasts more accurate. Similarly, a tool that controls network access may have database access controls that the security process could use.

What Levels of Service and Quality Will Be Expected?

The levels of service and quality that network groups negotiate with their customers directly affect the cost of hardware, software, training, and support. This is a key decision that should be thoroughly understood and committed to by the groups responsible for budgeting its costs and delivering on its agreements.

Suppliers of network components (such as routers, switches, hubs, and repeaters) should also be part of these negotiations since their equipment has a direct impact on availability and performance. Long-distance carriers are another group to include in the development of SLAs. Many carriers will not stipulate a guaranteed percentage of uptime in their service contracts because of situations beyond their control, such as natural disasters or manmade accidents (for example, construction mishaps). In these instances, companies can specify certain conditions in the service contract for which carriers will assume responsibility, including spare parts, time to repair, and on-call response times.

Real Life Experience—Locking Up Approval for a Purchase Request

A critical, 30-mile, classified network link for a major American defense contractor began failing intermittently. Numerous network monitoring tools were employed unsuccessfully in attempts to isolate the cause and permanently resolve the problem.

Software suppliers, hardware suppliers, and multiple telephone carriers all tried—to no avail—to get to the root cause of the outages.

Eventually, all eight suppliers were brought in to the same room to meet, confer, and brainstorm a solution. After analyzing volumes of data and eliminating one theory after another, the root cause was identified and resolved. It turned out that one of the three telephone carriers involved with this particular link was doing weekly maintenance on their line every Thursday afternoon for about 30 minutes. This caused just enough interference on the line to take it down. Carrier maintenance schedules were closely scrutinized and coordinated in the future.

SLAs for the network should be revisited whenever major upgrades to hardware or bandwidth are put in place. The SLAs should also be adjusted whenever significant workloads are added to the network to account for increased line traffic, contention on resources, or extended hours of service.

Assessing an Infrastructure's Network Management Process

The worksheets shown in Figures 13-1 and 13-2 present a quick and simple method for assessing the overall quality, efficiency, and effectiveness of a network management process. The first worksheet is used without weighting factors, meaning all 10 categories are weighted evenly for the assessment of a network-management process. Sample ratings are inserted to illustrate the use of the worksheet. In this case, the-network management process scored a total of 23 points for an overall nonweighted assessment score of 58 percent, as compared to the second sample worksheet, which compiled a weighted assessment score of 61 percent.

One of the most valuable characteristics of these worksheets is that they are customized to evaluate each of the 12 processes individually. The worksheets in this chapter apply only to the network management process. However, the fundamental concepts applied in using these evaluation worksheets are the same for all 12 disciplines. As a result, the detailed explanation on the general use of these worksheets presented near the end of Chapter 7, "Availability," also applies to the other worksheets in the book. Please refer to that discussion if you need more information.

Network Management Process—Assessment Worksheet					
Process Owner_____ Owner's Manager_____ Date_____					
Category	Questions for Network Management	None 1	Small 2	Medium 3	Large 4
Executive Support	To what degree does the executive sponsor show support for the network management process with actions such as budgeting for reasonable network tools and training and taking time to get educated on complex networking topics?	1	-	-	-
Process Owner	To what degree does the process owner exhibit desirable traits and ensure that on-call and supplier lists are current and that cross-training is in effect?	-	-	3	-
Customer Involvement	To what degree are key customers involved in the design and the use of the process, especially 24/7 operations personnel?	-	2	-	-
Supplier Involvement	To what degree are key suppliers, such as carriers and network trainers, involved in the design of the process?	-	2	-	-
Service Metrics	To what degree are service metrics analyzed for trends such as network availability, network response times, and elapsed time to logon?	-	2	-	-
Process Metrics	To what degree are process metrics analyzed for trends such as outages caused by network design, maintenance, carriers testing, nonstandard devices, lack of training, or negligence?	-	-	3	-
Process Integration	To what degree does the network management process integrate with other processes and tools such as availability and security?	1	-	-	-
Streamlining/ Automation	To what degree is the network management process streamlined by automating actions such as the notification of network analysts when nodes go offline or when other network triggers are activated?	-	2	-	-
Training of Staff	To what degree is the staff cross-trained on the network management process, and how well is the effectiveness of the training verified?	-	-	-	4
Process Documentation	To what degree is the quality and value of network management documentation measured and maintained?	-	-	3	-
	Totals	2	8	9	4
	Grand Total = 2 + 8 + 9 + 4 = 23 Nonweighted Assessment Score = 23 / 40 = 58%				

Figure 13-1 Sample Assessment Worksheet for Network Management Process

Network Management Process—Assessment Worksheet				
Process Owner_____ Owner's Manager_____ Date _____				
Category	Questions for Network Management	Weight	Rating	Score
Executive Support	To what degree does the executive sponsor show support for the network management process with actions such as budgeting for reasonable network tools and training and taking time to get educated on complex networking topics?	3	1	3
Process Owner	To what degree does the process owner exhibit desirable traits and ensure that on-call and supplier lists are current and that cross-training is in effect?	3	3	9
Customer Involvement	To what degree are key customers involved in the design and the use of the process, especially 24/7 operations personnel?	1	2	2
Supplier Involvement	To what degree are key suppliers, such as carriers and network trainers, involved in the design of the process?	5	2	10
Service Metrics	To what degree are service metrics analyzed for trends such as network availability, network response times, and elapsed time to logon?	3	2	6
Process Metrics	To what degree are process metrics analyzed for trends such as outages caused by network design, maintenance, carriers testing, nonstandard devices, lack of training, or negligence?	5	3	15
Process Integration	To what degree does the network management process integrate with other processes and tools such as availability and security?	1	1	1
Streamlining / Automation	To what degree is the network management process streamlined by automating actions such as the notification of network analysts when nodes go offline or when other network triggers are activated?	3	2	6
Training of Staff	To what degree is the staff cross-trained on the network management process, and how well is the effectiveness of the training verified?	3	4	12
Process Documentation	To what degree is the quality and value of network management documentation measured and maintained?	3	3	9
Totals		30	23	73
Weighted Assessment Score = 73 / (30 × 4) = 61%				

Figure 13-2   Sample Assessment Worksheet for Network Management Process with Weighting Factors

Measuring and Streamlining the Network Management Process

We can measure and streamline the network management process with the help of the assessment worksheet shown in Figure 13.1. We can measure the effectiveness of a network management process with service metrics such as network availability, network response times, and elapsed time to logon. Process metrics—such as outages caused by network design, maintenance, carriers testing, nonstandard devices, lack of training, or negligence—help us gauge the efficiency of this process. And we can streamline a network-management process by automating actions such as the notification of network analysts when nodes go offline or when other network triggers are activated.

Summary

This chapter discussed six key decisions that infrastructure management needs to make to implement a robust network management process. As you might expect with management decisions, they involve little with network technology and much with network processes. Defining the boundaries of the *what*, the *who*, and the *how* of network management are key ingredients for building a strong process foundation.

We offered suggestions on what to look for in a good candidate who will own the network management process and emphasized the need for management to delegate supportive authority, not just accountable responsibility. We also discussed the important task of integrating network management with other related processes and referenced a detailed treatment we will undertake of this topic in Chapter 21. As with previous chapters, we provided customized assessment worksheets for evaluating any infrastructure's network management process.

Test Your Understanding

1. Connecting nonstandard devices to a network can cause it to lock up, causing online system outages. (True or False)
2. Most tools used to monitor and manage networks are hardware-based rather than software-based. (True or False)
3. One of the greatest sources of conflict for a network administrator is the:
    a. enforcement of network connectivity standards
    b. evaluation of desirable characteristics for a network management process owner
    c. identification of exactly what will be managed
    d. determination of how much authority the network management process owner will be given
4. The definition of network management includes elements of the processes of _____ and _____ .
5. Explain why and how the use of advanced network tools reduces the need for more costly premium vendor support.

Suggested Further Readings

1. *Network Management Fundamentals*; 2006; Clemm, Alexander, Pearson Education
2. *Automated Network Management Systems*; 2006; Comer, Douglas E., Prentice Hall

CHAPTER 14

Configuration Management

Introduction

This chapter discusses an activity that is one of the least appealing to those installing infrastructure systems, while at the same time being one of the most necessary to those maintaining those systems. That activity is the documentation of hardware and software configurations. Technically brilliant personnel historically lack the talent or the desire, or both, to clearly document the complexities of their work in a simple, succinct manner. These analysts can often speak in volumes about the significance and application of their efforts but are reluctant to document them in any form. Ironically, their failure to document world-class technical accomplishments can lead to preventing their infrastructures from becoming world-class.

We begin, as usual, with a formal definition of configuration management and describe how it differs from application configuration management and what is called versioning control (defined in the next section). We then describe eight practical ways to improve the configuration management process, including what qualities to look for in a process owner. We conclude with assessment worksheets for evaluating the configuration management process of any infrastructure.

Definition of Configuration Management

> ### Configuration Management
>
> Configuration management is a process to ensure that the interrelationships of varying versions of infrastructure hardware and software are documented accurately and efficiently.

As it pertains to the infrastructure, configuration management refers to coordinating and documenting the different levels of hardware, firmware, and software that comprise mainframes, servers, desktops, databases, and various network devices such as routers, hubs, and switches. It does *not* refer to application software systems or to the verification of various levels of application software in different stages of development, testing, and deployment—these activities are commonly referred to as *versioning control* and are normally managed by the applications development group or by a software quality assurance group within applications development.

Infrastructure hardware such as UNIX servers come in different models requiring different levels of operating system software. As models are upgraded, the operating system may also need to be upgraded. Similarly, upgraded operating systems may require upgraded versions of database management systems software and, eventually, upgraded applications software. Keeping all these various versions of hardware and software accurately updated is the primary responsibility of the owner of the configuration management process. In addition to the hardware and software of the data center, network equipment also needs to be documented in the form of circuit diagrams, network configurations, and backbone schematics.

It is not an easy task to motivate technically oriented individuals to document configurations of what they have worked hard to implement when they would much rather be planning and working on their next implementations. These individuals must be carefully selected if they are to be involved effectively in this activity; they must also be given tools and tips to help improve and streamline the process. In support of this notion, the next section offers eight practical tips for improving configuration management.

Practical Tips for Improving Configuration Management

Many of the best tips I have seen over the years to improve configuration management involve common sense about matching the documentation skill levels of technicians to the task at hand. Utilizing this knowledge, I have listed eight practical tips here for improving configuration management, each of which is followed by a brief explanation:

1. Select a qualified process owner.
2. Acquire the assistance of a technical writer or a documentation analyst.
3. Match the backgrounds of writers to technicians.
4. Evaluate the quality and value of existing configuration documentation.
5. Involve appropriate hardware suppliers.
6. Involve appropriate software suppliers.
7. Coordinate documentation efforts in advance of major hardware and software upgrades.
8. Involve the asset-management group for desktop equipment inventories.

1. Select a Qualified Process Owner

In most instances, a single individual should be selected to own the configuration process. The desired characteristics of this process owner are listed and prioritized in Table 14–1. The process owner should have strong working knowledge of system and network software and their components as well as strong knowledge of software and hardware components. Other preferred attributes include knowledge of applications and desktop systems and the ability to think and act tactically. In some extremely large infrastructure organizations, there may be subprocess owners each for networks, systems, and databases. Even in this case there should be a higher-level manager, such as the technical services manager or even the manager of the infrastructure, to whom each subprocess owner reports.

Table 14–1   Prioritized Characteristics of a Configuration Management Process Owner

Characteristic	Priority
1. Ability to evaluate documentation	High
2. Knowledge of systems software and components	High
3. Knowledge of network software and components	High
4. Knowledge of software configurations	High
5. Knowledge of hardware configuations	High
6. Knowledge of applications	Medium
7. Knowlege of desktop systems	Medium
8. Ability to analyze metrics	Medium
9. Ability to think and act tactically	Medium
10. Ability to work effectively with IT developers	Low
11. Ability to inspire teamwork and coordination	Low
12. Ability to manage diversity	Low

2. Acquire the Assistance of a Technical Writer or a Documentation Analyst

Most shops have access to a technical writer who can generate narratives, verbiage, or procedures; or they have access to a documentation analyst who can produce diagrams, flowcharts, or schematics. Offering the services of one of these individuals, even if only for short periods of time, can reap major benefits in terms of technicians producing clear, accurate documentation in a fairly quick manner.

Another benefit of this approach is that it removes some of the stigma that many technical specialists have about documentation. Most technicians derive their satisfaction from designing, implementing, or repairing sophisticated systems and networks, not from writing about them. Having an assistant to do much of the nuts-and-bolts writing can ease both the strain and the effort technicians feel when required to do documentation.

One of the concerns raised about the use of technical writers or documentation analysts is their expense. In reality, the cost of extended recovery times that are the result of outdated documentation on critical systems and networks—particularly when localized disasters are looming—far exceeds the salary of one full-time-equivalent scribe. Documentation costs can further be reduced by contracting out for these services on a part-time basis, by sharing the resource with other divisions, and by using documentation tools to limit labor expense. Such tools include online configurators and network diagram generators.

3. Match the Backgrounds of Writers to Technicians

This suggestion builds on the prior improvement recommendation of having a technical writer or documentation analyst work directly with the originator of the system being written about. Infrastructure documentation comes in a variety of flavors but generally falls into five broad configuration categories:

- Servers
- Disk volumes
- Databases
- Networks
- Desktops

There are obvious subcategories such as networks breaking out into LANs, wide-area networks (WANs), backbones, and voice.

The point here is that the more you can match the background of the technical writer to the specifications of the documentation, the better the finished product. This will also produce a better fit between the technician providing the requirements and the technical writer who is meeting them.

4. Evaluate the Quality and Value of Existing Configuration Documentation

Evaluating existing documentation can reveal a great deal about the quality and value of prior efforts at recording current configurations. Identifying which pieces of documentation are most valuable to an organization, and then rating the relative quality of the content, is an excellent method to quickly determine which areas need improvements the most.

In Chapter 20, "Using Technology to Automate and Evaluate Robust Processes," we present a straightforward technique to conduct such an evaluation. It has proven to be very helpful at several companies, especially those struggling to assess their current levels of documentation.

5. Involve Appropriate Hardware Suppliers

Different models of server hardware may support only limited versions of operating system software. Similarly, different sizes of disk arrays will support differing quantities and types of channels, cache, disk volumes, and densities. The same is true for tape drive equipment. Network components (such as routers and switches) and desktop computers all come with a variety of features, interconnections, and enhancements.

Hardware suppliers, while often the most qualified, are least involved in assisting with a client's documentation. This is not to say the supplier will generate free detailed diagrams about all aspects of a layout, although I have experienced server and disk suppliers who did just that. But most suppliers will be glad to help keep documentation about their equipment current and understandable. It is very much in their best interest to do so, both from a serviceability standpoint and from a marketing one. Sometimes all it takes is asking.

6. Involve Appropriate Software Suppliers

Similar to their hardware counterparts, infrastructure software suppliers can be an excellent source of assistance in documenting which levels of software are running on which models of hardware. In the case of servers and operating systems, the hardware and software suppliers are almost always the same. This reduces the number of suppliers with whom you may need to work, but not necessarily the complexity of the configurations.

For example, one of my clients had hundreds of servers almost evenly divided among the operating systems HP/UNIX, Sun/Solaris, and Microsoft/NT with three or four variations of versions, releases, and patch levels associated with each supplier. Changes to the software levels were made almost weekly to one or more servers, requiring almost continual updates to the software and hardware configurations. Assistance from the suppliers as to anticipated release levels and the use of an online tool greatly simplified the process.

Software for database management, performance monitoring, and data backups also comes in a variety of levels and for specific platforms. Suppliers can be helpful in setting up initial configurations such for complex disk to tape backup schemes and may also offer online tools to assist in the upkeep of the documentation.

7. Coordinate Documentation Efforts in Advance of Major Hardware and Software Upgrades

The upgrading of major hardware components such as multiple servers or large disk arrays can render volumes of configuration documentation obsolete. The introduction of a huge corporate database or an enterprise-wide data warehouse could significantly alter documentation about disk configurations, software levels, and backup servers. Coordinating in advance and simultaneously the many different documentation updates with the appropriate individuals can save time, reduce errors, and improve cooperation among disparate groups.

8. Involve the Asset-Management Group for Desktop Equipment Inventories

One of the most challenging of configuration management tasks involves the number, types, and features of desktop equipment. As mentioned previously, we do not include asset management in these discussions of infrastructure processes because many shops turn this function over to a procurement or purchasing department.

Regardless of where asset management is located in the reporting hierarchy, it can serve as a tremendous resource for keeping track of the myriad paperwork tasks associated with desktops, including the names, departments, and location of users; desktop features; software licenses and copies; hardware and software maintenance agreements; and network addresses. Providing asset managers with an online asset management system can make them even more productive both to themselves and to the infrastructure. The configuration management process owner still needs to coordinate all these activities and updates, but he or she can utilize asset management to simplify an otherwise enormously tedious task.

Real Life Experience—A Surprising Version of Hide-and-Go-Seek

Years ago I supervised three around-the-clock shifts of computer operators in a relatively large data center. On a regular basis we would upgrade processors and install additional disk drives and controllers. As a result, the hardware configurations seemed to be constantly changing and we would periodically verify cabling and hardware connections to ensure the hardcopy configuration diagrams matched the physical configurations.

Verifying cabling and hardware connections consisted of lifting tiled segments that covered the raised flooring. While visiting the evening shift operators one night, I decided to verify a hardware connection that had been questioned earlier in the day. I reached for a floor plunger to lift the appropriate tile segment off the raised floor. I looked down expecting to see a mass of computer cables.

Much to my shock and surprise, instead of cables I was looking down at one of my computer operators who was staring back up at me. He quickly put his finger to his lips and requested my silence. It seemed that on this rather slow night, part the crew had wagered for a free lunch by playing an impromptu game of hide-and-go-seek.

Shaking my head and rolling my eyes, I quietly replaced the floor tile as the operator nodded and smiled in gratitude. He eventually won the game, and lunch, but only after giving me assurances that this was the last time he would go underground.

Assessing an Infrastructure's Configuration Management Process

The worksheets shown in Figures 14-1 and 14-2 present a quick and simple method for assessing the overall quality, efficiency, and effectiveness of a configuration management process. The first worksheet is used without weighting factors, meaning that all 10 categories are weighted evenly for the assessment of a configuration management process. Sample ratings are inserted to illustrate the use of the worksheet. In this case, the configuration management process scored a total of 22 points for an overall nonweighted assessment score of 55 percent, as compared to the second sample worksheet, which compiled a weighted assessment score of 62 percent.

One of the most valuable characteristics of these worksheets is that they are customized to evaluate each of the 12 processes individually. The worksheets in the figures apply only to the configuration management process. However, the fundamental concepts applied in using these evaluation worksheets are the same for all 12 disciplines. As a result, the detailed explanation on the general use of these worksheets presented near the end of Chapter 7, "Availability," also applies to the other worksheets in the book. Please refer to that discussion if you need more information.

Configuration Management Process—Assessment Worksheet					
Process Owner_____ Owner's Manager_____ Date _____					
Category	Questions for Configuration Management	None 1	Small 2	Medium 3	Large 4
Executive Support	To what degree does the executive sponsor show support for the configuration management process with actions such as reviewing migration strategies and holding documentation owners accountable for accuracy and timeliness?	-	-	3	-
Process Owner	To what degree does the process owner exhibit desirable traits, enforce migration strategies, and understand configuration documentation?	-	-	3	-
Customer Involvement	To what degree are key customers, such as repair technicians and facilities and operations personnel, involved in the design and use of the process?	1	-	-	-
Supplier Involvement	To what degree are key suppliers, such as those documenting and updating configuration diagrams, involved in the design of the process?	1	-	-	-
Service Metrics	To what degree are service metrics analyzed for trends such as the number of times analysts, auditors, or repair technicians find out-of-date configuration documentation?	-	2	-	-
Process Metrics	To what degree are process metrics analyzed for trends such as the elapsed time between altering the physical or logical configuration and having it reflected on configuration diagrams?	1	-	-	-
Process Integration	To what degree does the configuration management process integrate with the change management process and its associated tools?	-	2	-	-
Streamlining/ Automation	To what degree is the configuration management process streamlined by automating actions such as updating multiple pieces of documentation requiring the same update?	-	-	-	4
Training of Staff	To what degree is the staff cross-trained on the configuration management process, and how well is the effectiveness of the training verified?	-	-	3	-
Process Documentation	To what degree is the quality and value of configuration management documentation measured and maintained?	-	2	-	-
Totals		3	6	9	4
Grand Total = 3 + 6 + 9 + 4 = 22 Nonweighted Assessment Score = 22 / 40 = 55%					

Figure 14-1   Sample Assessment Worksheet for Configuration Management Process

Configuration Management Process—Assessment Worksheet				
Process Owner_____ Owner's Manager_____ Date _____				
Category	Questions for Configuration Management	Weight	Rating	Score
Executive Support	To what degree does the executive sponsor show support for the configuration management process with actions such as reviewing migration strategies and holding documentation owners accountable for accuracy and timeliness?	1	3	3
Process Owner	To what degree does the process owner exhibit desirable traits, enforce migration strategies, and understand configuration documentation?	5	3	15
Customer Involvement	To what degree are key customers, such as repair technicians and facilities and operations personnel, involved in the design and use of the process?	3	1	3
Supplier Involvement	To what degree are key suppliers, such as those documenting and updating configuration diagrams, involved in the design of the process?	1	1	1
Service Metrics	To what degree are service metrics analyzed for trends such as the number of times analysts, auditors, or repair technicians find out-of-date configuration documentation?	3	2	6
Process Metrics	To what degree are process metrics analyzed for trends such as the elapsed time between altering the physical or logical configuration and having it reflected on configuration diagrams?	1	1	1
Process Integration	To what degree does the configuration management process integrate with the change management process and its associated tools?	3	2	6
Streamlining/ Automation	To what degree is the configuration management process streamlined by automating actions such as updating multiple pieces of documentation requiring the same update?	5	4	20
Training of Staff	To what degree is the staff cross-trained on the configuration management process, and how well is the effectiveness of the training verified?	3	3	9
Process Documentation	To what degree is the quality and value of configuration management documentation measured and maintained?	5	2	10
Totals		30	22	74
Weighted Assessment Score = 74 / (30 x 4) = 62%				

Figure 14-2 Sample Assessment Worksheet for Configuration Management Process with Weighting Factors

Measuring and Streamlining the Configuration Management Process

We can measure and streamline the configuration management process with the help of the assessment worksheet shown in Figure 14-1. We can measure the effectiveness of a configuration management process with service metrics such as the number of times analysts, auditors, or repair technicians find out-of-date configuration documentation. Process metrics, such as the elapsed time between altering the physical or logical configuration and noting it on configuration diagrams, help us gauge the efficiency of this process. And we can streamline the configuration management process by automating certain actions—the updating of multiple pieces of documentation requiring the same update, for example.

Summary

This chapter discussed what configuration management is, how it relates to the infrastructure, and how if differs from the notion of versioning control more commonly found in applications development. We began with a formal definition of this process to help highlight these aspects of configuration management. We then offered eight practical tips on how to improve the configuration management process.

A common theme running among these tips is the partnering of configuration management personnel with other individuals—technical writers, documentation analysts, hardware and software suppliers, and the asset management group, for example—so that designers and analysts do not have to perform the tedious task of documenting complex configurations when, in all likelihood, they would much rather be implementing sophisticated systems. These partnerships were all discussed as part of the improvement proposals. We concluded with our usual assessment worksheets, which we can use to evaluate the configuration management process of an infrastructure.

Test Your Understanding

1. Network equipment is usually not included as part of configuration management because there is little need to document network hardware. (True or False)
2. One of the most challenging of configuration management tasks involves the number, types, and features of desktop equipment. (True or False)
3. Which of the following is not a practical tip for improving configuration management?
   a. involve appropriate hardware suppliers
   b. involve appropriate business users
   c. involve appropriate software suppliers
   d. involve the asset management group for desktop equipment inventories
4. One of the concerns raised about the use of technical writers or documentation analysts is their _____ .
5. What role could hardware or software suppliers play in providing meaningful configuration documentation?

Suggested Further Readings

1. www.icmhq.com/index.html
2. www.ecora.com/ecora/
3. *Practical CM: Best Configuration Management Practices* (2000); Lyon, David D., Butterworth Heinemann

CHAPTER 15

Capacity Planning

Introduction

The focus of this chapter is how to plan for the adequate capacity of computer resources within an infrastructure. Just as your perception of whether a cup is either half full or half empty may indicate whether you are an optimist or a pessimist, so also may a person's view of resource capacity indicate his or her business perception of IT. For example, a server operating at 60-percent capacity may be great news to a performance specialist who is trying to optimally tune response times. But, to an IT financial analyst trying to optimize resources from a cost standpoint, this may be disturbing news of unused resources and wasted costs. This chapter explains and bridges these two perspectives.

We start as usual with a formal definition of the process. This is followed by some of the reasons that capacity planning is seldom done very well in most infrastructures. Next is a list of the key steps necessary for developing and implementing an effective capacity planning process. Included within this discussion is the identification of the resources most commonly involved with capacity planning, itemized in approximate priority order. Additional benefits, helpful hints, and hidden costs of upgrades round out the remainder of this chapter.

Definition of Capacity Planning

As its name implies, the systems management discipline of capacity planning involves the planning of various kinds of resource capacities for an infrastructure.

> **Capacity Planning**
>
> Capacity planning is a process to predict the types, quantities, and timing of critical resource capacities that are needed within an infrastructure to meet accurately forecasted workloads.

As we will see, ensuring adequate capacity involves four key elements that are underscored in this definition:

- The type of resource capacities required, such as servers, disk space, or bandwidth
- The size or quantities of the resource in question
- The exact timing of when the additional capacity is needed
- Decisions about capacity that are based on sound, thorough forecasts of anticipated workload demands

Later in this chapter we will look at the steps necessary to design an effective capacity planning program. These four elements are an integral part of such a process. But first we will discuss why capacity planning is seldom done well in most infrastructure organizations.

Why Capacity Planning Is Seldom Done Well

There are two activities in the management of infrastructures that historically are not done well, if at all. These are documentation and capacity planning. The reason for poor, little, or no documentation is straightforward. Few individuals have the desire or the ability to produce quality technical writing. Managers do not always help the situation—many of them do not emphasize the importance of documentation, so the writing of procedures drops to a low priority and is often overlooked and forgotten until the time when it is needed in a critical situation.

But what about capacity planning? Almost every infrastructure manager and most analysts will acknowledge the importance of ensuring that adequate capacity is planned for and provided. There is nothing inherently difficult or complex about developing a sound capacity planning program. So why is it so seldom done well?

In my experience, there are seven primary reasons why many infra-structures fail at implementing an effective capacity planning program (as detailed in the following list). We will discuss each of these reasons and suggest corrective actions.

1. Analysts are too busy with day-to-day activities.
2. Users are not interested in predicting future workloads.
3. Users who are interested cannot forecast accurately.
4. Capacity planners may be reluctant to use effective measuring tools.
5. Corporate or IT directions may change from year to year.
6. Planning is typically not part of an infrastructure culture.
7. Managers sometimes confuse capacity management with capacity planning.

1. Analysts Are Too Busy with Day-To-Day Activities

The two groups of people who need to be most involved with an effective capacity planning process are systems analysts from the infrastructure area and programmer analysts from the application development area. But these two groups of analysts are typically the ones most involved with the day-to-day activities of maintenance, troubleshooting, tuning, and new installations. Little time is set aside for planning activities.

The best way to combat this focus on the tactical is to assign a group within the infrastructure to be responsible for capacity planning. It may start out with only one person designated as the process owner. This individual should be empowered to negotiate with developers and users on capacity planning issues, always being assured of executive support from the development side.

2. Users Are Not Interested in Predicting Future Workloads

Predicting accurate future workloads is one of the cornerstones of a worthwhile capacity plan. But just as many IT professionals tend to focus on tactical issues, so also do end-users. Their emphasis is usually on the here and now, not on future growth in workloads.

Developers can help capacity planners mitigate this tendency in two ways:

1. Explaining to end-users how accurate workload forecasts assist in justifying additional computer capacity to ensure acceptable system performance in the future.
2. Working with capacity planners to simplify the future workload worksheet to make it easier for users to understand it and to fill it out.

3. Users Who Are Interested Cannot Forecast Accurately

Some end-users clearly understand the need to forecast workload increases to ensure acceptable future performance, but they do not have the skills, experience, or tools to do so. Joint consultations with both developers and capacity planners who can show users how to do this can help alleviate this drawback.

4. Capacity Planners May Be Reluctant to Use Effective Measuring Tools

Newly appointed capacity planners are sometimes reluctant to use new or complex measurement tools that they may have just inherited. Cross-training, documentation, consultation with the vendor, and turnover from prior users of the tool can help overcome this reluctance.

5. Corporate or IT Directions May Change From Year to Year

One of the most frequent reasons I hear for the lack of comprehensive capacity plans is that strategic directions within a corporation and even an IT organization change so rapidly that any attempt at strategic capacity planning becomes futile. While it is true that corporate mergers, acquisitions, and redirections may dramatically alter a capacity plan, the fact is that the actual process of developing the plan has inherent benefits. I will discuss some of these benefits later in this chapter.

6. Planning Is Typically Not Part of an Infrastructure Culture

My many years of experience with infrastructures bear this out. Most infrastructures I worked with were created to manage the day-to-day tactical operations of an IT production environment. What little planning was done was usually at a low priority and often focused mainly on budget planning.

Many infrastructures today still have no formal planning activities chartered within their groups, leaving all technical planning to other areas inside IT. This is slowly changing with world-class infrastructures realizing the necessity and benefits of sound capacity planning. A dedicated planning group for infrastructures is suggested.

7. Managers Sometimes Confuse Capacity Management with Capacity Planning

Capacity management involves optimizing the utilization or performance of infrastructure resources. Managing disk space to ensure that maximum use is occurring is a common example, but this is not capacity planning. Capacity management is a tactical activity that focuses on the present. Capacity planning is a strategic activity that focuses on the future. Understanding this difference should help minimize confusion between the two.

How to Develop an Effective Capacity Planning Process

The following list details the nine major steps associated with implementing a sound capacity planning process. A thorough discussion of each of them follows.

1. Select an appropriate capacity planning process owner.
2. Identify the key resources to be measured.
3. Measure the utilizations or performance of the resources.
4. Compare utilizations to maximum capacities.
5. Collect workload forecasts from developers and users.
6. Transform workload forecasts into IT resource requirements.
7. Map requirements onto existing utilizations.
8. Predict when the shop will be out of capacity.
9. Update forecasts and utilizations.

Step 1: Select an Appropriate Capacity Planning Process Owner

The first step in developing a robust capacity planning process is to select an appropriately qualified individual to serve as the process owner. This person is responsible for designing, implementing, and maintaining the process and is empowered to negotiate and delegate with developers and other support groups.

First and foremost, this individual must be able to communicate effectively with developers because much of the success and credibility of a capacity plan depends on accurate input and constructive feedback from developers to infrastructure planners. This person also must be knowledgeable on systems and network software and components, as well as with software and hardware configurations.

Several other medium- and lower-priority characteristics are recommended in selecting the capacity planning process owner (see Table 15-1). These traits and their priorities obviously vary from shop to shop, depending on the types of applications provided and services offered.

Table 15–1 Prioritized Characteristics for a Capacity Planning Process Owner

Characteristic	Priority
1. Ability to work effectively with developers	High
2. Knowledge of systems software and components	High
3. Knowledge of network software and components	High
4. Ability to think and plan strategically	High
5. Knowledge of software configurations	Medium
6. Knowledge of hardware configurations	Medium
7. Ability to meet effectively with customers	Medium
8. Knowledge of applications	Medium
9. Ability to talk effectively with IT executives	Medium
10. Ability to promote teamwork and cooperation	Medium
11. Knowledge of database systems	Low
12. Ability to analyze metrics and trending reports	Low
13. Knowledge of power and air conditioning systems	Low
14. Knowledge of desktop hardware and software	Low

Step 2: Identify the Key Resources to be Measured

Once the process owner is selected, one of his or her first tasks is to identify the infrastructure resources that must have their utilizations or performance measured. This determination is made based on current knowledge about which resources are most critical to meeting future capacity needs. In many shops, these resources revolve around network bandwidth, the number and speed of server processors, or the number, size, or density of disk volumes comprising centralized secondary storage. A more complete list of possible resources follows:

1. Network bandwidth
2. Centralized disk space
3. Centralized processors in servers
4. Channels
5. Tape drives
6. Centralized memory in servers
7. Centralized printers
8. Desktop processors
9. Desktop disk space
10. Desktop memory

Step 3: Measure the Utilizations or Performance of the Resources

The resources identified in Step 2 should now be measured as to their utilizations or performance. These measurements provide two key pieces of information.

1. A utilization baseline from which future trends can be predicted and analyzed.
2. The quantity of excess capacity available for each component.

For example, a critical server may be running at an average of 60 percent utilization during peak periods on a daily basis. These daily figures can be averaged and plotted on a weekly and monthly basis to enable trending analysis.

Resource utilizations are normally measured using several different tools. Each tool contributes a different component to the overall utilization matrix. One tool may provide processor and disk channel utilizations. Another may supply information on disk-space utilization; still another may provide insight into how much of that space is actually being used within databases.

This last tool can be very valuable. Databases are often pre-allocated by database administrators to a size that they feel supports growth over a reasonable period of time. Knowing how full those databases actually are, and how quickly they are filling up, provides a more accurate picture of disk space utilization. In environments where machines are used as database servers, this information is often known only to the database administrators. In these cases, it is important to establish an open dialog between capacity planners and database administrators and to obtain access to a tool that provides this crucial information.

Step 4: Compare Utilizations to Maximum Capacities

The intent here is to determine how much excess capacity is available for selected components. The utilization or performance of each component measured should be compared to the maximum usable capacity. Note that the maximum usable is almost always less than the maximum possible. The maximum usable server capacity, for example, is usually only 80 to 90 percent. Similar limitations apply for network bandwidth and cache storage hit ratios. By extrapolating the utilization trending reports and comparing them to the maximum usable capacity, the process owner should now be able to estimate at what point a given resource is likely to exhaust its excess capacity.

Step 5: Collect Workload Forecasts from Developers and Users

This is one of the most critical steps in the entire capacity planning process, and it is the one over which you have the least control. Developers are usually asked to help users complete IT workload forecasts. As in many instances of this type, the output is only as good as the input. Working with developers and some selected pilot users in designing a simple yet effective worksheet can go a long way to easing this step. Figure 15-1 shows a sample user workload forecast worksheet. This should be customized as much as possible to meet the unique requirements of your particular environment.

User Workload Forecast Worksheet

User Name   User Department   Extension   Date

Application Full System Name   Acronym

Brief Functional Description of the Application: _____

Developer Name   Developer Department   Date

	Currently	6 Mos	1 Year	2 Years
1. Number of total users				
2. Number of concurrent users	___	___	___	___
3. Number of processing-oriented transactions/day (type-1)	___	___	___	___
4. Number of input/output-oriented transactions/day (type-2)	___	___	___	___
5. Amount of disk space in Gigabytes (GB)	___	___	___	___
6. Expected response time in seconds (type-1)	___	___	___	___
7. Expected response time in seconds (type-2)	___	___	___	___
8. Centralized print requirements (pages/day)	___	___	___	___
9. Backup requirements	___	___	___	___
10. Desktop processing requirements	___	___	___	___
11. Desktop disk requirements	___	___	___	___
12. Desktop print requirements	___	___	___	___
13. Remote network requirements	___	___	___	___
14. Other requirements	___	___	___	___
	___	___	___	___
	___	___	___	___

Signature Block

Application User   Developer   Capacity Planner

Application User's Manager   Developer's Manager   Capacity Planner's Manager

Figure 15-1   Sample User Workload Forecast Worksheet

Step 6: Transform Workload Forecasts into IT Resource Requirements

After the workload forecasts are collected, the projected changes must be transformed into IT resource requirements. Sophisticated measurement tools or a senior analyst's expertise can help in changing projected transaction loads, for example, into increased capacity of server processors. The worksheets also allow you to project the estimated time frames during which workload increases will occur. For major application workloads, it is wise to utilize the performance centers that key suppliers of the servers, database software, and enterprise applications now offer.

Step 7: Map Requirements onto Existing Utilizations

The projected resource requirements derived from the workload projections of the users in Step 6 are now mapped onto the charts of excess utilization from Step 4. This mapping shows the quantity of new capacity that will be needed by each component to meet expected demand.

Step 8: Predict When the Shop Will Be Out of Capacity

The mapping of the quantity of additional capacity needed to meet projected workload demands also pinpoints the time frame during which these upgraded resources will be required.

Step 9: Update Forecasts and Utilizations

The process of capacity planning is not a one-shot event but rather an ongoing activity. Its maximum benefit is derived from continually updating the plan and keeping it current. The plan should be updated at least once per year. Shops that use this methodology best are the shops that update their plans every quarter. Note that the production acceptance process also uses a form of capacity planning when determining resource requirements for new applications.

Additional Benefits of Capacity Planning

Along with enabling analysts to assess when, how much, and what type of additional hardware resources will be needed, a comprehensive capacity planning program offers other benefits as well. Four of these advantages are as follows:

1. Strengthens relationships with developers and end-users
2. Improves communications with suppliers
3. Encourages collaboration with other infrastructure groups
4. Promotes a culture of strategic planning as opposed to tactical firefighting

1. Strengthens Relationships with Developers and End-Users

The process of identifying and meeting with key users to discuss anticipated workloads usually strengthens the relationships between IT infrastructure staff and end-using customers. Communication, negotiation, and a sense of joint ownership can all combine to nurture a healthy, professional relationship between IT and its customers.

2. Improves Communications with Suppliers

Suppliers are generally not unlike any other support group in that they do not enjoy last-minute surprises. Involving key suppliers and support staffs with your capacity plans can promote effective communications among these groups. It can also make their jobs easier in meeting deadlines, reducing costs, and offering additional alternatives for capacity upgrades.

3. Encourages Collaboration with Other Infrastructure Groups

A comprehensive capacity plan by necessity involves multiple support groups. Network services, technical support, database administration, operations, desktop support, and even facilities may all play a role in capacity planning. In order for the plan to be thorough and effective, all these various groups must support and collaborate with each other.

Real Life Experience—Two Sides to Every Story

An executive at a marketing company knew each of his 12 departments would be generating enough reports and memos to justify at least two printers for each group.

To reduce costs, he encouraged his staff to print everything on both sides of the paper and ordered only half as many printers as originally planned.

> The idea had merit in theory, but it failed miserably in execution. Few users were willing or able to use two-sided reports, and eventually more printers had to be purchased at costs greater than if the original larger order had been placed.

4. Promotes a Culture of Strategic Planning as Opposed to Tactical Firefighting

By definition, capacity planning is a strategic activity. To do it properly, one must look forward and focus on the plans of the future instead of the problems of the present. One of the most significant benefits of developing an overall and ongoing capacity planning program is the institutionalizing of a strategic planning culture.

Helpful Hints for Effective Capacity Planning

Developing a comprehensive capacity plan can be a daunting challenge at the outset; it requires dedication and commitment to maintain it on an ongoing basis. The following hints can help minimize this challenge:

1. Start small.
2. Speak the language of your customers.
3. Consider future platforms.
4. Share plans with your suppliers.
5. Anticipate nonlinear cost ratios.
6. Plan for occasional workload reductions.
7. Prepare for the turnover of personnel.
8. Strive to continually improve the process.
9. Evaluate the hidden costs of upgrades.

1. Start Small

Many a capacity planning effort fails after a few months because it encompassed too broad a scope too early on. This is especially true for shops that have had no previous experience in this area. In these instances, it is wise to start with just a few of the most critical resources—say, processors or bandwidth—and gradually expand the program as more experience is gained.

2. Speak the Language of Your Customers

When requesting workload forecasts from your developers, and especially your end-using customers, discuss these in terms that the developers and customers understand. For example, rather than asking for estimated increases in processor utilization, inquire as to how many additional concurrent users are expected to use the application or how many of a specific type of transaction is likely to be executed during peak periods.

3. Consider Future Platforms

When evaluating tools to be used for capacity planning, keep in mind new architectures that your shop may be considering and select packages that can be used on both current and future platforms. Some tools that appear well-suited for your existing platforms may have little or no applicability to planned architectures.

4. Share Plans with Suppliers

If you plan to use your capacity planning products across multiple platforms, it is important to inform your software suppliers of your plans. During these discussions, make sure that add-on expenses—the costs for drivers, agents, installation time and labor, copies of licenses, updated maintenance agreements, and the like—are identified and agreed upon up-front. Reductions in the costs for license renewals and maintenance agreements can often be negotiated based on all of the other additional expenses.

5. Anticipate Nonlinear Cost Ratios

One of my esteemed college professors was fond of saying that indeed we live in a nonlinear world. This is certainly the case when it comes to capacity upgrades. Some upgrades will be linear in the sense that doubling the amount of a planned increase in processors, memory, channels, or disk volumes will double the cost of the upgrade. But if the upgrade approaches the maximum number of cards, chips, or slots that a device can hold, a relatively modest increase in capacity may end up costing an immodest amount for additional hardware.

6. Plan for Occasional Workload Reductions

A forecasted change in workload may not always cause an increase in the capacity required. Departmental mergers, staff reductions, and productivity gains may result in the reduction of some production workloads. Similarly, development workloads may decrease as major projects become deployed. While increases in needed capacity are clearly more likely, reductions are possible. A good guideline to use when questioning users about future workloads is to emphasize changes, not just increases.

7. Prepare for the Turnover of Personnel

Over time, all organizations experience some degree of personnel turnover. To minimize the effects of this on capacity planning efforts, ensure that at least two people are familiar with the methodology and that the process is fully documented.

8. Strive to Continually Improve the Process

One of the best ways to continually improve the capacity planning process is to set a goal to expand and improve at least one part of it with each new version of the plan. Possible enhancements could include the addition of new platforms, centralized printers, or remote locations. A new version of the plan should be created at least once a year and preferably every six months.

9. Evaluate the Hidden Costs of Upgrades

Most upgrades to infrastructure hardware resources have many hidden costs associated with them. We'll look at these additional expenses more thoroughly in the next section.

Uncovering the Hidden Costs of Upgrades

Even the most thorough technical and business analysts occasionally overlook an expense associated with a capacity upgrade. Identifying, understanding, and quantifying these hidden costs is critical to the success and credibility of a capacity planning program. The following list details many of these unseen expenses:

1. Hardware maintenance
2. Technical support
3. Software maintenance
4. Memory upgrades
5. Channel upgrades
6. Cache upgrades
7. Data backup time
8. Operations support
9. Offsite storage
10. Network hardware
11. Network support
12. Floor space
13. Power and air conditioning

1. Hardware Maintenance

Some hardware maintenance agreements allow for minimal upgrades at the same annual rate as the original contract. These tend to be the exception. Most agreements have escalation clauses that drive up annual hardware maintenance costs.

2. Technical Support

Multiprocessors, larger cache memories, and additional units of disk volumes usually require operating-system modifications from technical support.

3. Software Maintenance

Modified or upgraded operating systems can result in increased license fees and maintenance costs.

4. Memory Upgrades

Additional processors can eventually saturate main memory and actually slow down online response rather than improve it, especially if memory utilization was high to start with and high-powered processors are added. Memory upgrades may be needed to balance this out.

5. Channel Upgrades

Additional disks can sometimes saturate channel utilization, causing memory or processor requests to wait on busy channels. Upgrades to channels may be needed to correct this.

6. Cache Upgrades

Additional disks can also undermine the benefits of cache storage by decreasing hit ratios due to increased requests for disks. Expanded cache may be required to address this.

7. Data Backup Time

Increasing the amount of data in use by adding more disk space may substantially increase data backup time, putting backup windows at risk. Faster channels or more tape drives may be needed to resolve this.

8. Operations Support

Increasing backup windows and generally adding more data center equipment may require more operations support.

9. Offsite Storage

Additional tapes that have to be stored offsite due to increased amounts of data to back up may result in additional expense for offsite storage.

10. Network Hardware

Increasing the amount of tape equipment for more efficient data backup processing may require additional network hardware.

11. Network Support

Additional network hardware to support more efficient tape backup processing may require additional network support.

12. Floor Space

Additional boxes (such as servers, tape drives, or disk controllers) require data center floor space, which eventually translates into added costs.

13. Power and Air Conditioning

Additional data-center equipment requires air conditioning and electrical power; this eventually can translate into increased facilities costs.

Assessing an Infrastructure's Capacity Planning Process

The worksheets shown in Figures 15-2 and 15-3 present a quick-and-simple method for assessing the overall quality, efficiency, and effectiveness of a capacity planning process. The first worksheet is used without weighting factors, meaning that all 10 categories are weighted evenly for the assessment of a capacity planning process. Sample ratings are inserted to illustrate the use of the worksheet. In this case, the capacity planning process scored a total of 20 points for an overall nonweighted assessment score of 50 percent. The second sample worksheet compiled a weighted assessment score of 47 percent.

One of the most valuable characteristics of these worksheets is that they are customized to evaluate each of the 12 processes individually. The worksheets in this chapter apply only to the capacity planning process. However, the fundamental concepts applied in using these evaluation worksheets are the same for all 12 disciplines. As a result, the detailed explanation on the general use of these worksheets presented near the end of Chapter 7, "Availability," also applies to the other worksheets in the book. Please refer to that discussion if you need more information.

Capacity Planning Process—Assessment Worksheet						
Process Owner_____ Owner's Manager_____ Date_____						
Category	Questions for Capacity Planning	None 1	Small 2	Medium 3	Large 4	
Executive Support	To what degree does the executive sponsor show support for the capacity planning process with actions such as analyzing resource utilization trends and ensuring that managers of users return accurate workload forecasts?	1	-	-	-	
Process Owner	To what degree does the process owner exhibit desirable traits and the ability to translate user workload forecasts into capacity requirements?	-	2	-	-	
Customer Involvement	To what degree are key customers, such as high-volume users and major developers, involved in the design and use of the process?	1	-	-	-	
Supplier Involvement	To what degree are key suppliers, such as bandwidth and disk storage providers, involved in the design of the process?	-	2	-	-	
Service Metrics	To what degree are service metrics analyzed for trends such as the number of instances of poor response due to inadequate capacity on servers, disk devices, or the network?	-	-	3	-	
Process Metrics	To what degree are process metrics analyzed for trends such as lead time for users to fill out workload forecasts and the success rate of translating workload forecasts into capacity requirements?	-	-	-	4	
Process Integration	To what degree does the capacity planning process integrate with other processes and tools such as performance and tuning and network management?	-	-	3	-	
Streamlining/ Automation	To what degree is the capacity planning process streamlined by automating actions such as the notification of analysts when utilization thresholds are exceeded, the submittal of user forecasts, and the conversion of user workload forecasts into capacity requirements?	1	-	-	-	
Training of Staff	To what degree is the staff cross-trained on the capacity planning process, and how well is the effectiveness of the training verified?	-	2	-	-	
Process Documentation	To what degree is the quality and value of capacity planning documentation measured and maintained?	1	-	-	-	
	Totals	**4**	**6**	**6**	**4**	
Grand Total = 4 + 6 + 6 + 4 = 20 Nonweighted Assessment Score = 20/40 = 50%						

Figure 15-2 Sample Assessment Worksheet for Capacity Management Process

Category	Questions for Capacity Planning	Weight	Rating	Score
Capacity Planning Process—Assessment Worksheet				
Process Owner_____ Owner's Manager_____ Date _____				
Executive Support	To what degree does the executive sponsor show support for the capacity planning process with actions such as analyzing resource utilization trends and ensuring that managers of users return accurate workload forecasts?	5	1	5
Process Owner	To what degree does the process owner exhibit desirable traits and the ability to translate user workload forecasts into capacity requirements?	5	2	10
Customer Involvement	To what degree are key customers, such as high-volume users and major developers, involved in the design and use of the process?	5	1	5
Supplier Involvement	To what degree are key suppliers, such as bandwidth and disk storage providers, involved in the design of the process?	3	2	6
Service Metrics	To what degree are service metrics analyzed for trends such as the number of instances of poor response due to inadequate capacity on servers, disk devices, or the network?	3	3	9
Process Metrics	To what degree are process metrics analyzed for trends such as lead time for users to fill out workload forecasts and the success rate of translating workload forecasts into capacity requirements?	3	4	12
Process Integration	To what degree does the capacity planning process integrate with other processes and tools such as performance and tuning and network management?	1	3	3
Streamlining/ Automation	To what degree is the capacity planning process streamlined by automating actions such as the notification of analysts when utilization thresholds are exceeded, the submittal of user forecasts, and the conversion of user workload forecasts into capacity requirements?	1	1	1
Training of Staff	To what degree is the staff cross-trained on the capacity planning process, and how well is the effectiveness of the training verified?	3	2	6
Process Documentation	To what degree is the quality and value of capacity planning documentation measured and maintained?	3	1	3
Totals		32	20	60
Weighted Assessment Score = 60/(32 × 4) = 47%				

Figure 15-3   Assessment Worksheet for Capacity Management Process with Weighting Factors

Measuring and Streamlining the Capacity Planning Process

We can measure and streamline the capacity planning process with the help of the assessment worksheet shown in Figure 15-2. We can measure the effectiveness of a capacity planning process with service metrics such as the number of instances of poor response due to inadequate capacity on servers, disk devices, or the network. Process metrics—such as the number of instances of poor response due to inadequate capacity on servers, disk devices, or the network—help us gauge the efficiency of this process. We can be streamline the capacity planning process by automating certain actions—the notification to analysts when utilization thresholds are exceeded, the submittal of user forecasts, and the conversion of user-workload forecasts into capacity requirements, for example.

Summary

Capacity planning is a strategic activity that focuses on planning for the future. It is sometimes confused with capacity management, which is a tactical activity that focuses on issues in the present. This chapter discussed these differences, starting with a formal definition of capacity planning followed by some of more common reasons this process is typically done poorly in many infrastructures.

The major part of this chapter presented the nine key steps required to develop a robust capacity planning process. Included within this discussion were recommended characteristics for a process owner, resources to consider for inclusion, a sample user worksheet for workload forecasts, and an example of utilization mapping.

A short section describing several additional benefits of a sound capacity planning process followed next, along with numerous helpful hints I have accumulated over the years implementing these processes. Next came a description of various hidden costs of upgrades that are frequently overlooked. Similar to previous chapters, this one concluded with explanations and worksheets on how to assess, measure, and streamline the capacity planning process.

Test Your Understanding

1. The ratio of upgrade costs to upgrade capacities is almost always a linear, or constant, relationship. (True or False)
2. In order to quickly establish a new capacity planning effort, one should start with as broad a scope as possible. (True or False)
3. Which of the following is not a primary reason for infrastructures failing at implementing an effective capacity planning program?
   a. analysts are too busy with day-to-day activities
   b. users are not interested in predicting future workloads
   c. capacity planners may be reluctant to use effective measuring tools
   d. corporate or IT directions may remain static from year to year
4. Two activities in the management of infrastructures that historically are not done well are _____ and _____.
5. Why do workload forecasts need to be translated from a business perspective into an IT perspective?

Suggested Further Readings

1. www.itworld.com/Net/3215/swol-1195-unix/
2. http://searchdatacenter.techtarget.com/sDefinition/0,,sid80_gci1082579,00.html
3. http://en.wikipedia.org/wiki/Capacity_management
4. *Capacity Planning for Web Services: Metrics, Models and Methods*; 2001; Menasce, D.A., Almeida, V.A.F.; Prentice Hall PTR
5. *Guerrilla Capacity Planning: A Tactical Approach to Planning for Highly Scalable Applications and Services*; 2006; Gunther, Neil J.; Springer
6. Association for Computer Operations Managers (AFCOM); www.afcom.com

CHAPTER 16

Strategic Security

Introduction

Just as IT infrastructures have evolved from mainframes to the Internet, so also have security systems. The process that began primarily as a means to protect mainframe operating systems now must protect applications, databases, networks, and desktops—not to mention the Internet and its companions, extranets, and intranets. While there are dedicated security processes that pertain to each of these entities, there needs to be a strategic security process governing the integration and compatibility of these specialized systems.

This chapter presents an overall process for developing a strategic security program. It begins with our formal definition of strategic security and then presents the 12 steps necessary to design such a process. The initial steps discuss executive support and selecting a process owner. As with our other processes, we identify and prioritize characteristics of this individual. One of the next steps involves taking an inventory of the current security environment to identify tools and procedures that may have become dormant over the years.

Then we look at the cornerstone of any robust security program: the establishment and enforcement of enterprise-wide security policies. We provide examples of policies and procedures currently in use at selected client sites to help illustrate these points. We conclude the chapter with methods on how to evaluate, measure, and streamline a strategic security process.

Definition of Strategic Security

Strategic Security

Strategic security is designed to safeguard the availability, integrity, and confidentiality of designated data and programs against unauthorized access, modification, or destruction.

Availability implies that appropriate individuals can access data and programs from whatever means necessary for them to conduct their company's business. Integrity implies that data and programs have the same content and format as what was originally intended. Confidentiality implies that sensitive data is accessed only by individuals properly authorized. The data and programs referred to in this definition are considered to be corporate assets to be protected just as critically as patents, trademarks, and competitive advantages. In support of this, the focus will be on designing a process from which strategic security policies are developed, approved, implemented, and enforced.

Developing a Strategic Security Process

The following list details the 12 steps involved with developing a strategic security process. We will discuss each one in this section.

1. Identify an executive sponsor.
2. Select a process owner.
3. Define goals of strategic security.
4. Establish review boards.
5. Identify, categorize, and prioritize requirements.
6. Inventory current state of security.
7. Establish security organization.
8. Develop security policies.
9. Assemble planning teams.
10. Review and approve plans.
11. Evaluate technical feasibility of plans.
12. Assign and schedule the implementation of plans.

Step 1: Identify an Executive Sponsor

There must be an executive sponsor to champion and support the strategic security program. This individual provides management direction, serves on the executive security review board, and selects the security process owner.

Step 2: Select a Security Process Owner

The executive sponsor must select a security process owner who will manage the day-to-day activities of the process. The process owner assembles and facilitates the cross-functional team that will brainstorm requirements; the process owner also participates on the technical security review board that, among other things, develops standards and implementation plans for various security policies. A strong candidate for this position will demonstrate a strategic outlook; a good working knowledge of system, network, and application software; and a keen insight into the analysis of security metrics. Table 16-1 offers a comprehensive list, in priority order, of desirable characteristics of a security process owner.

Table 16-1   Prioritized Characteristics of a Security Process Owner

Characteristic	Priority
1. Knowledge of applications	High
2. Knowledge of system software and components	High
3. Knowledge of network software and components	High
4. Ability to analyze metrics	High
5. Ability to think and plan strategically	High
6. Ability to work effectively with IT developers	Medium
7. Knowledge of company's business model	Medium
8. Ability to talk effectively with IT executives	Medium
9. Knowledge of backup systems	Medium
10. Knowledge of desktop hardware and software	Medium
11. Knowledge of software configurations	Medium
12. Knowledge of hardware configurations	Low
13. Ability to meet effectively with IT customers	Low
14. Ability to think and act tactically	Low

Step 3: Define Goals of Strategic Security

Executives should define and prioritize the specific goals of strategic security. Three characteristics that executives should consider in this regard are the availability, integrity, and confidentiality of data. The scope of strategic security should also be defined to clarify which, if any, business units and remote sites will be included in the plan, as well as to what extent it will be enterprise-wide.

Step 4: Establish Review Boards

The assessment and approval of security initiatives work best through a process of two separately chartered review boards. The first is an executive-level review board chartered with providing direction, goals, and policies concerning enterprise-wide security issues. Its membership should represent all key areas of IT and selected business units.

The second board comprises senior analysts and specialists who are qualified to evaluate the technical feasibility of security policies and initiatives proposed by the executive board; this board also sets enforceable security standards and procedures. Figure 16-1 shows password management, an example of a security procedure. Depending on this board's charter, it may also be responsible for assisting in the implementation of initiatives.

Step 5: Identify, Categorize, and Prioritize Requirements

Representatives from each of the two review boards, along with other appropriate subject-matter experts, should meet to identify security requirements, categorize them according to key areas for security issues (see Table 16-2), and then prioritize them.

Procedures for Selecting Secure Passwords

Passwords are used to safeguard the access to information to which you have been entrusted. Unfortunately, one of the simplest and most common means of violating this safeguard is to inadvertently allow another individual to learn your password. This could give an unauthorized person capability to access and alter company information that you are responsible for protecting.

The following procedures are intended as guidelines for selecting passwords that greatly reduce the likelihood of a password being accidentally divulged or intentionally detected. If you have questions about the use of these procedures, please contact your security administrator.

I. General Guidelines

1. Never show, give, tell, or send your password to anyone. This includes close friends, coworkers, repair technicians, and supervisors.
2. Never write your password down or leave it out on your desk or in a desk drawer, or on your desktop or laptop terminal.
3. Change your password at least every 90 days, or whenever you have logged on remotely, or whenever you suspect someone may have accidentally or intentionally detected your password.
4. Log off your desktop or laptop terminal whenever you leave it unattended for more than a few minutes.
5. Consider basing the complexity of your password, as well as the frequency with which you change it, on the level of access authority you have. For example, update capability may warrant a password more complex and frequently changed than simple inquiry only access.

II. What NOT to use in Selecting a Secure Password

1. Do not use any word, or any concatenation of a word, that can be found in any dictionary, including foreign and technical dictionaries.
2. Do not use any proper noun such as a city, a landmark, or bodies of water.
3. Do not use any proper names, be they from real life, literature, or the arts.
4. Do not use any words spelled backwards.
5. Do not use any common keyboard patterns such as "yuiop."
6. Do not include the @ or # characters in your password since some machines interpret these as delimiter or eraser characters.
7. Do not use all uppercase alphabetic characters.
8. Do not use all lowercase alphabetic characters.
9. Do not use all numeric characters.
10. Do not use less than 6 characters in your password.
11. Do not use common number schemes such as birthdays, phone numbers, or license plates, even if you try to disguise them with slashes, hyphens, or blanks.

Figure 16-1   Password Management Procedure (1 of 2)

III. What Your Password SHOULD Contain

1. Your password should contain at least 6 characters.
2. Your password should contain at least one uppercase alphabetic character.
3. Your password should contain at least one lowercase alphabetic character.
4. Your password should contain at least one numeric character.
5. Consider including one special or non-alphanumeric character in your password.
6. A single occurrence of an uppercase, lowercase, or special character should not be at the beginning or end of your password.
7. Consider using a personal acronym to help you remember highly unique passwords, such as:

   we Bought his/her towels 4 us. (wBh/ht4u)
   or
   good Passwords are Not 2 hard 2 find. (gPaN2h2f)

Figure 16-1   Password Management Procedure (2 of 2)

Table 16-2   Key Areas for Categorizing Security Issues

Key Area	Security Issues
Client/server	Antivirus
	Desktop software
	Email
Network/Internet	Firewalls
	Intrusion detection
	Remote access
	Encryption
Data center	Physical access
	Databases
	Application software
	Operating systems
Security policies	Executive proposals
	Technical evaluation
	Approval and implementation
	Communication and enforcement

Step 6: Inventory Current State of Security

This step involves taking a thorough inventory of all current security-related items to determine what you already have in-house and what may need to be developed or purchased. These items should include:

- Security policies approved, adhered to, and enforced
- Security policies approved but not adhered to or enforced
- Security policies drafted but not yet approved
- Existing software security tools with the ability to be used for enforcement
- Existing hardware security tools with the ability to be used for enforcement
- Current security metrics available to analyze:
  Virus attacks
  Password resets
  Multiple sign-ons
  Trouble tickets

Step 7: Establish Security Organization

Establish a centralized security organization, to be headed by a security manager, based on the following:

- Input from the two review boards
- The list of requirements
- The inventory of current security policies, tools, and metrics

The location of the security organization and the responsibilities and authorities of the security manager will be jointly determined by the two security review boards and other appropriate areas of management.

Step 8: Develop Security Policies

Based on the inventory of existing security policies, eliminate obsolete or ineffective policies, modify those policies requiring changes, and develop necessary new policies. Figure 16-2 shows a sample corporate security policy and Figure 16-3 shows a sample security policy on the use of the Internet.

M E M O R A N D U M

To: All Employees of Company XYZ

From: Mr. KnowItAll, Chief Executive Officer

Subject: Corporate Security Policy–Electronic Media

Date: July 1, 2007

The purpose of this memorandum is to establish a Corporate-wide Security Policy covering any and all electronic information and data at Company XYZ.   It is further intended that these policies and procedures be conveyed to, and understood by, every employee of XYZ.

Many companies today conduct a substantial portion of their business electronically.   This electronic business comes in a variety of forms including, but not limited to, mail, files, reports, commerce, and weather information. It is important that as an employee of XYZ you understand:

- This information and data is considered a corporate asset of XYZ.

- Your rights and responsibilities as they pertain to electronic information and data.

The following policies should aid in this understanding.

1. All data, programs, and documentation created, stored, or maintained on any electronic equipment owned or leased by XYZ is the property of XYZ.

2. The ownership by XYZ of the above mentioned material extends to any copies of this material, regardless of whether the copies are in hard document form, electronic form, or on any kind of storage media such as magnetic tape, hard drive disks, or floppy diskettes.

3. All electronic mail messages sent or received by an employee of XYZ is the property of XYZ.

4. Use of the Internet is intended primarily to assist employees in the performance of their job duties and responsibilities, such as researching inforamation or to communicate with outside individuals on business related matters. Any improper use of the Internet such as for sending, downloading, viewing, copying, or printing of any inappropriate material will be grounds for disciplinary action.

5. Employees are prohibited from using any XYZ computers to illegally use or copy any licensed or copyrighted software.

Figure 16-2   Sample Corporate Security Policy (1 of 2)

6. All data, programs, documentation, electronic mail messages, and Internet screens and printouts shall be used only for, and in the conduct of, XYZ business.

7. To ensure an employee's right to privacy, sensitive information, such as personnel records or salary data, will be accessed only by those whose job requires such access.

8. Employees will be given access to the data they require to perform their duties. All employees will be held personally accountable for the information entrusted to them to ensure there is no unauthorized disclosure, misuse, modification, or destruction.

9. Authorizing documents and passwords will be used to manage and control access to data, programs, and networks.

10. All data, programs, and documentation deemed to be of a production nature are under the custodianship of the Chief Information Officer. This custodianship requires that all reasonable measures be taken to safeguard the use and integrity of this material, including a documented disaster recovery plan.

11. All XYZ managers are responsible for ensuring that every new employee and contractor reporting to them who has access to electronic programs and data understand these policies and procedures.

12. All XYZ managers are responsible for ensuring that any terminating employee reporting to them have all passwords and electronic accesses removed at the time of termination.

13. These policies constitute the majority, but not necessarily all, of the key security issues involving electronic media. The rapidly changing nature of information technology may periodically obsolete some policies and require the inclusion of new ones. In any event, all XYZ employees are expected to conduct themselves at all times in a professional, ethical, and legal manner regarding their use of XYZ information resources.

14. Any violation by an employee of these policies constitutes grounds for disciplinary action, up to and including termination.

15. A copy of these policies and procedures will be kept on file by the XYZ for review by any regulating agency.

Figure 16-2   Sample Corporate Security Policy (2 of 2)

M E M O R A N D U M

To: All Employees of Company XYZ
From: Mr. CareerIsOver, Chief Information Officer
Subject: Corporate Security Policy–Use of the Internet

Date: July 1, 2007

The purpose of this memorandum is to describe in greater detail the corporate security policies regarding the use of the Internet. The overall intent of these policies is to ensure that the Internet is used as a productivity tool by employees of company XYZ, is utilized in a professional and ethical manner, and does not in any way put company XYZ at risk for fraudulent or illegal use.

1. INTENDED USE—The use of Internet access equipment at XYZ is intended primarily for conducting business of XYZ. Internet communications, transactions, and discussions may be viewed by personnel authorized by XYZ. Distribution of proprietary data or any confidential information about employees, contractors, consultants, and customers of XYZ is strictly prohibited.

2. PERSONAL USE—Personal use of the Internet should be limited to use during employees' personal time, and goods or services ordered through the Internet must be billed to your home phone or credit card. Internet access equipment at XYZ should not be used for chain letters, personal or group communications of causes or opinions, communications in furtherance of any illegal activity, personal mass mailings, gaining access to information inappropriate to the business environment or otherwise prohibited by local, state, or federal law. XYZ reserves the right to view information that is accessed by employees through the Internet to ensure that nonbusiness-related use of XYZ equipment does not impact business need.

3. CERTIFICATION—Programs (including screen savers, compilers, browsers, etc.) obtained from the Internet shall not be installed and used on XYZ computers, or relevant electronic devices, without first being certified by XYZ IT Department and placed on XYZ common network sever for company access and usage. All documents (stored either on electronic media or diskette) received from Internet sources or any source outside XYZ must be passed through a virus-scanning program before they are used or copied. Instructions on how to do this are available from XYZ IT Department.

4. RESTRICTIONS—XYZ reserves the right to restrict access to inappropriate or nonbusiness-related Internet sites and may do so at any time.

5. VIOLATIONS—Any violation of these policies by an employee of XYZ constitutes grounds for disciplinary action, up to and including termination.

Figure 16-3   Sample Internet Security Policy

Step 9: Assemble Planning Teams

Cross-functional teams should be assembled to develop implementation plans for new policies, procedures, initiatives, and tools proposed by the either of the two security review boards.

Step 10: Review and Approve Plans

The executive security review board should review the implementation plans from a standpoint of policy, budget, schedule, and priority.

Step 11: Evaluate Technical Feasibility of Plans

The technical security review board should evaluate the implementation plans from a standpoint of technical feasibility and adherence to standards.

Step 12: Assign and Schedule the Implementation of Plans

Individuals or teams should be assigned responsibilities and schedules for executing the implementation plans.

Real Life Experience—In This Case, One Out of Three Is Bad

I was employed at a mortgage company in 2005 which instituted new security policies involving laptop computers and their associated 'smart cards'. The smart cards, which looked like credit cards, contained security information and a personalized password to protect laptops from unauthorized use.

Security policies advised employees to never write their smart card password down, to never store their smart card in the same case as the laptop, and to always lock their laptops in the trunks of their cars when traveling. Unfortunately for one new employee, he heeded only one of these three guidelines.

The employee worked at a branch office in the Northeastern United States that was experiencing a particularly severe winter. While driving to work in sub-zero temperatures, the worker stopped at a convenience store ("...for just a second," he reported) to grab a cup of hot coffee. Per policy, his laptop was dutifully locked in his trunk.

Unfortunately, his car was stolen within seconds. Even more unfortunately, he had stored his smart card in the laptop case which held his laptop. His final misfortune was that he had written his password down on a Post-it® note and attached it to his smart card. His luck finally changed a day later when the car was recovered with the laptop apparently untouched. Software tests verified that the laptop had not been tampered with, much to the relief of the suddenly more security-conscious employee.

Assessing an Infrastructure's Strategic Security Process

The worksheets shown in Figures 16-4 and 16-5 present a quick-and-simple method for assessing the overall quality, efficiency, and effectiveness of a strategic security process. The first worksheet is used without weighting factors, meaning that all 10 categories are weighted evenly for the assessment of a strategic security process. Sample ratings are inserted to illustrate the use of the worksheet. In this case, the strategic security process scored a total of 27 points for an overall nonweighted assessment score of 68 percent. The second sample worksheet compiled a weighted assessment score of 71 percent.

One of the most valuable characteristics of these worksheets is that they are customized to evaluate each of the 12 processes individually. The worksheets in this chapter apply only to the strategic security process. However, the fundamental concepts applied in using these evaluation worksheets are the same for all 12 disciplines. As a result, the detailed explanation on the general use of these worksheets presented near the end of Chapter 7, "Availability," also applies to the other worksheets in the book. Please refer to that discussion if you need more information.

Security Process—Assessment Worksheet					
Process Owner_____ Owner's Manager_____ Date _____					
Category	Questions About Security	None 1	Small 2	Medium 3	Large 4
Executive Support	To what degree does the executive sponsor show support for the security process with actions such as enforcing a security policy or authorizing the process owner to do so?	-	-	-	4
Process Owner	To what degree does the process owner exhibit desirable traits and the ability to develop and execute a strategic security plan?	-	-	3	-
Customer Involvement	To what degree are key customers, such as owners of critical data or auditors, involved in the design and use of the process?	-	2	-	-
Supplier Involvement	To what degree are key suppliers, such as those for software security tools or encryption devices, involved in the design of the process?	1	-	-	-
Service Metrics	To what degree are service metrics analyzed for trends such as the number of outages caused by security breaches and the amount of data altered, damaged, or deleted due to security violations?	-	-	3	-
Process Metrics	To what degree are process metrics analyzed for trends such as the number of password resets requested and granted and the number of multiple sign-ons processed over time?	-	2	-	-
Process Integration	To what degree does the security process integrate with other processes and tools such as change management and network management?	-	2	-	-
Streamlining/ Automation	To what degree is the security process streamlined by automating actions such as the analysis of password resets, network violations, or virus protection invocations?	-	-	3	-
Training of Staff	To what degree is the staff cross-trained on the security process, and how well is the effectiveness of the training verified?	-	-	3	-
Process Documentation	To what degree is the quality and value of security documentation measured and maintained?	-	-	-	4
Totals		1	6	12	8
Grand Total = 1 + 6 + 12 + 8 = 27 Nonweighted Assessment Score = 27/40 = 68%					

Figure 16-4   Sample Assessment Worksheet for Security Process

Security Process—Assessment Worksheet				
Process Owner_____ Owner's Manager_____ Date _____				
Category	**Questions About Security**	**Weight**	**Rating**	**Score**
Executive Support	To what degree does the executive sponsor show support for the security process with actions such as enforcing a security policy or authorizing the process owner to do so?	5	4	20
Process Owner	To what degree does the process owner exhibit desirable traits and the ability to develop and execute a strategic security plan?	3	3	9
Customer Involvement	To what degree are key customers, such as owners of critical data or auditors, involved in the design and use of the process?	3	2	6
Supplier Involvement	To what degree are key suppliers, such as those for software security tools or encryption devices, involved in the design of the process?	3	1	3
Service Metrics	To what degree are service metrics analyzed for trends such as the number of outages caused by security breaches and the amount of data altered, damaged, or deleted due to security violations?	5	3	15
Process Metrics	To what degree are process metrics analyzed for trends such as the number of password resets requested and granted and the number of multiple sign-ons processed over time?	3	2	6
Process Integration	To what degree does the security process integrate with other processes and tools such as change management and network management?	1	2	2
Streamlining/ Automation	To what degree is the security process streamlined by automating actions such as the analysis of password resets, network violations, or virus protection invocations?	1	3	3
Training of Staff	To what degree is the staff cross-trained on the security process, and how well is the effectiveness of the training verified?	3	3	9
Process Documentation	To what degree is the quality and value of security documentation measured and maintained?	3	4	12
Totals		30	27	85
Weighted Assessment Score = 85/(30 × 4) = 71%				

Figure 16-5 Sample Assessment Worksheet for Security Process with Weighting Factors

Measuring and Streamlining the Security Process

We can measure and streamline the security process with the help of the assessment worksheet shown in Figure 16-4. We can measure the effectiveness of a security process with service metrics such as the number of outages caused by security breaches and the amount of data altered, damaged, or deleted due to security violations. Process metrics, such as the number of password resets requested and granted and the number of multiple sign-ons processed over time, help us gauge the efficiency of this process. Finally, we can streamline the security process by automating certain actions—for example, the analysis of password resets, network violations, or virus protection invocations.

Summary

This chapter presented the 12 steps involved with establishing a strategic security process. Key among these steps is developing, approving, implementing, and enforcing strategic security policies.

Our recommendation in this regard is to utilize a two-level review process. One level is for executive review to ensure corporate business goals and directions are supported by these policies. The other level is for technical review to ensure policies, along with their enforcement, are technically feasible and compatible with existing security standards. The chapter included several examples of security policies and procedures. We concluded this chapter with customized assessment worksheets to evaluate an infrastructure's strategic security process.

Test Your Understanding

1. The cornerstone of any robust security program is the establishment and enforcement of enterprise-wide security policies. (True or False)
2. The location of a security organization within a company should be determined solely by the security manager. (True or False)
3. Which of the following is an acceptable guideline for selecting a password?
    a. use of a word spelled backwards
    b. use of a personal acronym
    c. use of a keyboard pattern such as 'qwerty'
    d. use of a common name from arts or literature
4. The primary goal of strategic security is to safeguard the _____, _____, and _____ of designated data and programs.
5. How do corporate assets that are protected by IT security systems differ from other types of corporate assets?

Suggested Further Readings

1. http://en.wikipedia.org/wiki/Information_security
2. http://csrc.nist.gov/publications/nistpubs/
3. *Designing a Safe House for Data.(data centers)*; Security Management; 2005; Reese, Lloyd F.
4. *Risk Management for Computer Security: Protecting Your Network & Information Assets*; 2005; Jones, A, Ashenden, D.; Butterworth-Heinemann

CHAPTER 17

Business Continuity

Introduction

The better prepared we are for an IT infrastructure disaster, the less likely it seems to occur. This would not appear to make much sense in the case of natural disasters such as earthquakes, floods, or tornados. We have probably all met a few IT specialists who believe they can command the physical elements, but I have yet to see it demonstrated. When it comes to more localized events, such as broken water pipes, fires, or gas leaks, being fully prepared to deal with their consequences can minimize the adverse impact they can have on your computer systems.

This chapter discusses how to plan for the continuity of critical business processes during and immediately after a major disruption of service resulting from either a localized or a wide-spread disaster. We begin with a definition of business continuity, which leads us into the steps required to design and test a business continuity plan. An actual case study is used to highlight these points. We explain the important distinctions between disaster recovery, contingency planning, and business continuity. Some of the more nightmarish events that can be associated with poorly tested recovery plans are presented as well as some tips on how to make testing more effective. We conclude the chapter with worksheets for evaluating your own business continuity plan.

Definition of Business Continuity

> **Business Continuity**
>
> Business continuity is a methodology to ensure the continuous operation of critical business systems in the event of widespread or localized disasters to an infrastructure environment.

There are several key phrases in this definition. The *continuous operation of critical business systems* is another way of saying *the act of staying in business*, meaning that a disaster of any kind will not substantially interrupt the processes necessary for a company to maintain its services. Widespread disasters are normally major natural disasters, such as floods, earthquakes, or tornadoes—events that are sometimes legally referred to as acts of God.

It's interesting to note that most all major telephone companies and line carriers will not enter into formal SLAs about the availability of their services because they say they cannot control either acts of God or acts of human negligence (such as backhoes digging up telephone lines). The key point of the definition is that business continuity is a methodology involving planning, preparation, testing, and continual updating.

Case Study: Disaster at the Movie Studio

A number of years ago, I managed the main IT infrastructure for a major motion picture studio in Beverly Hills, California. An event just prior to my hiring drastically changed the corporation's thinking about disaster recovery, which led the company to ask me to develop a disaster recovery program of major proportions.

Two of this studio's most critical applications were just coming online and were being run on IBM AS/400 midrange processors. One of the applications involved the scheduling of broadcast times for programs and commercials for the company's new premier cable television channel. The other application managed the production, distribution, and accounting of domestic entertainment videos, laser discs, and interactive games. The company had recently migrated the development and production versions of these applications onto two more advanced models of the IBM AS/400—9406-level machines utilizing reduced instruction set computing (RISC) technology.

During the development of these applications, initial discussions began about developing a business continuity plan for these AS/400s and their critical applications. Shortly after the deployment of these applications, the effort was given a major jump-start from an unlikely source. A distribution transformer that powered the AS/400 computer room from outside the building short-circuited and exploded. The damage was so extensive that repairs were estimated to take up to five days. With no formal recovery plan yet in place, IT personnel, suppliers, and customers all scurried to minimize the impact of the outage.

A makeshift disaster-recovery site located 40 miles away was quickly identified and activated with the help of one of the company's key vendors. Within 24 hours, the studio's AS/400 operating systems, application software, and databases were all restored and operational. Most of the critical needs of the AS/400 customers were met during the six days that it eventually took to replace the failed transformer.

Three Important Lessons Learned from the Case Study

This incident accelerated the development of a formal business continuity plan and underscored the following three important points about recovering from a disaster:

- There are noteworthy differences between the concept of disaster recovery and that of business resumption.
- The majority of disasters are relatively small, localized incidents, such as broken water mains, fires, smoke damage, or electrical equipment failures.
- You need firm commitment from executive management to proceed with a formal business continuity plan.

Concerning the first point, there are noteworthy differences between the concept of disaster recovery and that of business resumption. Business resumption is defined here to mean that critical department processes can be performed as soon as possible after the initial outage. The full recovery from the disaster usually occurs many days after the business resumption process has been activated.

In this case, the majority of company operations impacted by the outage were restored in less than a day after the transformer exploded. It took nearly four days to replace all the damaged electrical equipment and another two days to restore operations to their normal state. Distinguishing between these two concepts helped during the planning process for the formal business continuity program—it enabled a focus on business resumption in meetings with key customers, while the focus with key suppliers could be on disaster recovery.

It is worth noting how the Information Technology Infrastructure Library (ITIL), discussed in Chapter 6, "Comparison to ITIL Processes," distinguishes between these two concepts. ITIL version 2 and version 3 each introduced the notion of IT Service Continuity Management. This is essentially a combination of business continuity and disaster recovery. ITIL stresses that that IT technical recovery are closely aligned to an organization's business continuity plan. ITIL refers to these resulting plans as service continuity plans.

The second important point that this event underscored was that the majority of disasters most likely to cause lengthy outages to computer centers are relatively small, localized incidents, such as broken water mains, fires, smoke damage, or electrical equipment failures. They typically are not the flash floods, powerful hurricanes, or devastating earthquakes frequently highlighted in the media.

This is not to say that we should not be prepared for these major disasters. Infrastructures that plan and test recovery strategies for smaller incidents are usually well on their way to having a program to handle any size of calamity. While major calamities do occur, they are far less likely and are often overshadowed by the more widespread effects of the disaster on the community. What usually makes a localized computer center disaster so challenging is that the rest of the company is normally operational and desperately in need of the computer center services that have been disrupted.

The third point was that this extended unplanned outage resulted in a firm commitment from executive management to proceed with a formal business continuity plan. In many ways, business continuity is like an insurance policy. You do not really need it until you really need it. This commitment became the first important step toward developing an effective business continuity process. A comprehensive program requires hardware, software, budget, and the time and efforts of knowledgeable personnel. The support of executive management is necessary to make these resources available.

Steps to Developing an Effective Business Continuity Process

The following list details the 13 steps required to develop an effective business continuity process. For the purposes of our discussion, business continuity is a process within a process in that we are including steps that involve contracting for outside services. We realize that, depending on the size and scope of a shop, not every business continuity process requires this type of service provider. We include it here in the interest in being thorough and because a sizable percentage of shops do utilize this kind of service.

1. Acquire executive support.
2. Select a process owner.
3. Assemble a cross-functional team.
4. Conduct a business impact analysis.
5. Identify and prioritize requirements.
6. Assess possible business continuity recovery strategies.
7. Develop a request for proposal (RFP) for outside services.
8. Evaluate proposals and select the best offering.
9. Choose participants and clarify their roles on the recovery team.
10. Document the business continuity plan.
11. Plan and execute regularly scheduled tests of the plan.
12. Conduct a lessons-learned postmortem after each test.
13. Continually maintain, update, and improve the plan.

Step 1: Acquire Executive Support

The acquisition of executive support, particularly in the form of an executive sponsor, is the first step necessary for developing a truly robust business continuity process. As mentioned earlier, there are many resources required to design and maintain an effective program. These all need funding approval from senior management to initiate the effort and to see it through to completion.

Another reason this support is important is that managers are typically the first to be notified when a disaster actually occurs. This sets off a chain of events involving management decisions about deploying the IT recovery team, declaring an emergency to the disaster recovery service provider, notifying facilities and physical security, and taking whatever emergency preparedness actions may be necessary. By involving management early in the design process, and by securing their emotional and financial buy-in, you increase the likelihood of management understanding and flawlessly executing its roles when a calamity does happen.

There are several other responsibilities of a business continuity executive sponsor. One is selecting a process owner. Another is acquiring support from the managers of the participants of the cross-functional team to ensure that participants are properly chosen and committed to the program. These other managers may be direct reports, peers within IT, or, in the case of facilities, outside of IT. Finally, the executive sponsor needs to demonstrate ongoing support by requesting and reviewing frequent progress reports, offering suggestions for improvement, questioning unclear elements of the plan, and resolving issues of conflict.

Step 2: Select a Process Owner

The process owner for business continuity is the most important individual involved with this process because of the many key roles this person plays. The process owner must assemble and lead the cross-functional team in such diverse activities as preparing the business impact analysis, identifying and prioritizing requirements, developing business continuity strategies, selecting an outside service provider, and conducting realistic tests of the process. This person should exhibit several key attributes and be selected very carefully. Potential candidates include an operations supervisor, the data center manager, or even the infrastructure manager.

The executive sponsor needs to identify as many of these key attributes in an individual and choose the individual accordingly. Table 17–1 lists these characteristics in priority order. The finished plan needs to be well-documented and kept current, making the ability to evaluate documentation highly desirable. So, too, is the ability to talk effectively with executives, particularly when prioritizing their critical processes and applications. A strong working knowledge of network software and components is recommended because any recovery process taking place today relies heavily on the connectivity and compatibility of backup networks to those at the customer site.

Table 17–1   Prioritized Characteristics of a Business Continuity Process Owner

Characteristic	Priority
1. Ability to evaluate documentation	High
2. Ability to talk effectively with IT executives	High
3. Knowledge of network software and components	High
4. Knowledge of backup systems	High
5. Ability to think and plan strategically	High

Characteristic	Priority
6. Knowledge of applications	Medium
7. Ability to meet effectively with IT customers	Medium
8. Knowledge of systems software and components	Medium
9. Knowledge of software configurations	Medium
10. Knowledge of hardware configurations	Medium
11. Ability to work effectively with IT developers	Low
12. Knowledge of database systems	Low
13. Knowledge of desktop hardware and software	Low
14. Ability to think and act tactically	Low

Knowledge of backup systems is also very key since the restore process—with its numerous variables that can hamper recovery—is so critical to this activity. The last high-priority characteristic is the ability to think and act strategically. This means designing a process that keeps the strategic business priorities of the company in mind when deciding which processes need to be recovered first.

Step 3: Assemble a Cross-Functional Team

Representatives of appropriate departments from several areas inside and outside of IT should be assembled into a cross-functional design team. The specific departments involved vary from shop to shop, but the following list shows a representation of typical groups normally participating in a cross-functional design team. This team works on requirements, conducts a business impact analysis, selects an outside service provider, designs the final overall recovery process, identifies members of the recovery team, conducts tests of the recovery process, and documents the plan.

1. Computer operations
2. Applications development
3. Key customer departments
4. Facilities
5. Data security
6. Physical security
7. Network operations
8. Server and systems administration
9. Database administration

Step 4: Conduct a Business Impact Analysis

Even the most thorough of business continuity plans will not be able to cost-justify the expense of including every business process and application in the recovery. An inventory and prioritization of critical business processes should be taken representing the entire company. Key IT customers should help coordinate this effort to ensure that all critical processes are included. Processes that must be resumed within 24 hours to prevent serious business impact, such as loss of revenue or major impact to customers, are rated as an A priority. Processes that must be resumed within 72 hours are rated as a B, and processes greater than 72 hours are rated C. These identifications and prioritizations will be used to propose business continuity strategies.

BIA

BIA stands for business impact analysis. It involves prioritizing critical business processes based on the financial and operational impact of a process being idled.

Step 5: Identify and Prioritize Requirements

One of the first activities of the cross-functional team is to brainstorm the identity of requirements for the process, such as business, technical, and logistical requirements. Business requirements include defining the specific criteria for declaring a disaster and determining which processes are to be recovered and in what time frames. Technical requirements include what type of platforms will be eligible as recovery devices for servers, disk, and desktops and how much bandwidth will be needed. Logistical requirements include the amount of time allowed to declare a disaster as well as transportation arrangements at both the disaster site and the recovery site.

Step 6: Assess Possible Business Continuity Recovery Strategies

Based on the business impact analysis and the list of prioritized requirements, the cross-functional team should propose and assess several alternative business continuity recovery strategies. These will likely include alternative remote sites within the company and geographic hot sites supplied by an outside provider.

Step 7: Develop a Request for Proposal (RFP) for Outside Services

Presuming that the size and scope of the shop is sufficiently large and that the requirements involving business continuity warrant outside services, the cross-functional team develops request for proposal (RFP), which is a proposal for an outside provider to supply disaster recovery services. Options should include multiple-year pricing, guaranteed minimum amount of time to become operational, costs of testing, provisions for local networking, and types of onsite support provided. Criteria should be weighted to facilitate the evaluation process.

Step 8: Evaluate Proposals and Select the Best Offering

The weighted criteria previously established by the cross-functional team are now used by them to evaluate the responses to the RFP. Visits to the bidder's facilities and testimonials from customers should be part of the evaluation process. The winning proposal should go to the bidder who provides the greatest overall benefit to the company, not simply to the bidder who is the lowest cost provider.

Step 9: Choose Participants and Clarify Their Roles on the Recovery Team

The cross-functional team chooses the individuals who will participate in the recovery activities after any declared disaster. The recovery team may be similar to the cross-functional team as suggested in Step 5, but should not be identical. Additional members should include representatives from the outside service provider, key customer representatives based on the prioritized business impact analysis, and the executive sponsor. Once the recovery team is selected, it is imperative that each individual's role and responsibility is clearly defined, documented, and communicated.

Step 10: Document the Business Continuity Plan

The last official activity of the cross-functional team is to document the business continuity plan for use by the recovery team, which then has the responsibility for maintaining the accuracy, accessibility, and distribution of the plan. Documentation of the plan must also include up-to-date configuration diagrams of the hardware, software, and network components involved in the recovery.

Step 11: Plan and Execute Regularly Scheduled Tests of the Plan

Business continuity plans should be tested a minimum of once per year. During the test, a checklist should be maintained to record the disposition and duration of every task that was performed for later comparison to those of the planned tasks. Infrastructures with world-class disaster recovery programs test at least twice per year. When first starting out, particularly for complex environments, consider developing a test plan that spans up to three years—every six months the tests can become progressively more involved, starting with program and data restores, followed by processing loads and print tests, then initial network connectivity tests, and eventually full network and desktop load and functionality tests.

Dry-run tests are normally thoroughly planned well in advance, widely communicated, and generally given high visibility. Shops with very robust business continuity plans realize that maintaining an effective plan requires testing that is as close to simulating an actual disaster as possible. One way to do this is to conduct a full-scale test in which only two or three key people are aware that it is not an actual disaster. These types of drills often flush out minor snags and communication gaps that could prevent an otherwise flawless recovery. Thoroughly debrief the entire team afterward, making sure to explain the necessity of the secrecy.

Step 12: Conduct a Lessons-Learned Postmortem after Each Test

The intent of the lessons-learned postmortem is to review exactly how the test was executed as well as to identify what went well, what needs to be improved, and what enhancements or efficiencies could be added to improve future tests.

Step 13: Continually Maintain, Update, and Improve the Plan

An infrastructure environment is ever-changing. New applications, expanded databases, additional network links, and upgraded server platforms are just some of the events that render the most thorough of disaster recovery plans inaccurate, incomplete, or obsolete. A constant vigil must be maintained to keep the plan current and effective. When maintaining a business continuity plan, additional concerns to keep in mind include changes in personnel affecting training, documentation, and even budgeting for tests.

Real Life Experience—Emergency Contacts for a Real Emergency

Hurricane Katrina ravaged New Orleans in August 2005 and provided numerous lessons about what constitutes effective response to a massive disaster. But one of the lessons from Katrina involving emergency contacts surprised many of us. I was speaking at a conference in New Orleans a year after Katrina and later attended a session sponsored by the retail office supply company Office Depot.

Office Depot had dozens of stores impacted by Katrina and the speaker explained the difficulty his company had in getting in touch with the hundreds of employees who had evacuated the surrounding area. Most employees had listed their spouses or significant others as their emergency contacts, and because most employees had evacuated with these same emergency contacts, it was difficult to reach many of them.

The company came up with a rather novel but creative solution for future situations like this. It recommended that, if possible, employees list their grandmothers as emergency contacts. The reasoning is that most grandmothers, regardless of the age of their grandchildren, tend to keep track of them. While it seems unusual and unorthodox, it is proving to be quite effective and is being adopted by other companies as well.

Nightmare Incidents with Disaster Recovery Plans

During my 25 years of managing and consulting on IT infrastructures, I have experienced directly, or indirectly through individuals with whom I have worked, a number of nightmarish incidents involving disaster recovery. Some are humorous, some are worthy of head-scratching, and some are just plain bizarre. In all cases, they totally undermined what would have been a successful recovery from either a real or simulated disaster. Fortunately, no single client or employer with whom I was associated ever experienced more than any two of these, but in their eyes, even one was too many. The following incidents illustrate how critical the planning, preparation, and performance of the disaster recovery plan really is:

1. Backup tapes have no data on them.
2. Restore process has never been tested and found to not work.
3. Restore tapes are mislabeled.
4. Restore tapes cannot be found.
5. Offsite tape supplier has not been paid and cannot retrieve tapes.
6. Graveyard-shift operator does not know how to contact recovery service.
7. Recovery service to a classified defense program is not cleared.
8. Recovery service to a classified defense program is cleared, but individual personnel are not cleared.
9. Operator cannot fit tape canister onto the plane.
10. Tape canisters are mislabeled.

The first four incidents all involve the handling of the backup tapes required to restore copies of data rendered inaccessible or damaged by a disaster. Verifying that the backup and—more important—the restore process is completing successfully should be one of the first requirements of any disaster recovery program. While most shops verify the backup portion of the process, more than a handful do not test that the restore process also works. Labels and locations can also cause problems when tapes are marked or stored improperly.

Although rare, I did know of a client who was denied retrieval of a tape because the offsite tape storage supplier had not been paid in months. Fortunately, it was not during a critical recovery. Communication to, documentation of, and training of all shifts on the proper recovery procedures are a necessity. Third-shift graveyard operators often receive the least of these due to their off hours and higher-than-normal turnover. These operators especially need to know who to call and how to contact offsite recovery services.

Classified environments can present their own brand of recovery nightmares. One of my classified clients had applied for a security clearance for its offsite tape storage supplier and had begun using the service prior to receiving clearance. When the client's military customer found out, the tapes were confiscated. In a related issue, a separate defense contractor cleared its offsite vendor for a secured program but failed to clear the one individual who worked nights, which is when a tape was requested for retrieval. The unclassified worker could not retrieve the classified tape that night, delaying the retrieval of the tape and the restoration of the data for at least a day.

The last two incidents involve tape canisters used during a full dry-run test of restoring and running critical applications at a remote hot site 3,000 miles away. The airline in question had just changed its policy for carry-on baggage, preventing the canisters from staying in the presence of the recovery team. Making matters worse was the fact that they were mislabeled, causing over six hours of restore time to be lost. Participants at the lesson-learned debriefing had much to talk about during its marathon postmortem session.

Assessing an Infrastructure's Disaster Recovery Process

The worksheets shown in Figures 17-1 and 17-2 present a quick-and-simple method for assessing the overall quality, efficiency, and effectiveness of a business continuity process. The first worksheet is used without weighting factors, meaning that all 10 categories are weighted evenly for the assessment of a disaster recovery process. Sample ratings are inserted to illustrate the use of the worksheet. In this case, the disaster recovery process scored a total of 26 points for an overall nonweighted assessment score of 65 percent. The second sample worksheet compiled a nearly identical weighted assessment score of 66 percent.

One of the most valuable characteristics of these worksheets is that they are customized to evaluate each of the 12 processes individually. The worksheets in this chapter apply only to the business continuity process. However, the fundamental concepts applied in using these evaluation worksheets are the same for all 12 disciplines. As a result, the detailed explanation on the general use of these worksheets presented near the end of Chapter 7, "Availability," also applies to the other worksheets in the book. Please refer to that discussion if you need more information.

Business Continuity Process—Assessment Worksheet					
Process Owner_____ Owner's Manager_____ Date _____					
Category	Questions About Business Continuity	None 1	Small 2	Medium 3	Large 4
Executive Support	To what degree does the executive sponsor show support for the business continuity process with actions such as ensuring business units prioritize critical processes and applications and budgeting for periodic testing of recovery plans?	-	-	3	-
Process Owner	To what degree does the process owner exhibit desirable traits and the ability to execute and evaluate dry runs of business continuity plans?	-	2	-	-
Customer Involvement	To what degree are key customers, particularly owners of critical business processes, involved in the design and use of the process?	-	2	-	-
Supplier Involvement	To what degree are disaster recovery service providers or staffs at hot backup sites involved in the design and testing of the process?	-	-	-	4
Service Metrics	To what degree are service metrics analyzed for trends such as the number of critical applications able to be run at backup sites and the number of users that can be accommodated at the backup site?	1	-	-	-
Process Metrics	To what degree are process metrics analyzed for trends such as the frequency and authenticity of dry-run tests and the improvements suggested from postmortem sessions after dry-run tests?	-	2	-	-
Process Integration	To what degree does the business continuity process integrate with the facilities management process and its associated tools?	1	-	-	-
Streamlining/ Automation	To what degree is the business continuity process streamlined by automating actions such as the scheduling of tapes for offsite storage and the retrieval of tapes for disaster recovery restoring?	-	-	-	4
Training of Staff	To what degree is the staff cross-trained on the business continuity process, and how well is the effectiveness of the training verified?	-	-	3	-
Process Documentation	To what degree is the quality and value of business continuity documentation measured and maintained?	-	-	-	4
Totals		2	6	6	12
Grand Total = 2 + 6 + 6 + 12 = 26 Nonweighted Assessment Score = 26 / 40 = 65%					

Figure 17-1   Sample Assessment Worksheet for Business Continuity Process

Business Continuity Process—Assessment Worksheet					
Process Owner_____	Owner's Manager_____			Date _____	
Category	Questions About Business Continuity	Weight	Rating	Score	
Executive Support	To what degree does the executive sponsor show support for the business continuity process with actions such as ensuring business units prioritize critical processes and applications and budgeting for periodic testing of recovery plans?	5	3	15	
Process Owner	To what degree does the process owner exhibit desirable traits and the ability to execute and evaluate dry runs of business continuity plans?	3	2	6	
Customer Involvement	To what degree are key customers, particularly owners of critical business processes, involved in the design and use of the process?	5	2	10	
Supplier Involvement	To what degree are disaster recovery service providers or staffs at hot backup sites involved in the design and testing of the process?	3	4	12	
Service Metrics	To what degree are service metrics analyzed for trends such as the number of critical applications able to be run at backup sites and the number of users that can be accommodated at the backup site?	3	1	3	
Process Metrics	To what degree are process metrics analyzed for trends such as the frequency and authenticity of dry-run tests and the improvements suggested from postmortem sessions after dry-run tests?	3	2	6	
Process Integration	To what degree does the business continuity process integrate with the facilities management process and its associated tools?	1	1	1	
Streamlining/ Automation	To what degree is the business continuity process streamlined by automating actions such as the scheduling of tapes for offsite storage and the retrieval of tapes for disaster recovery restoring?	1	4	4	
Training of Staff	To what degree is the staff cross-trained on the business continuity process, and how well is the effectiveness of the training verified?	5	3	15	
Process Documentation	To what degree is the quality and value of business continuity documentation measured and maintained?	3	4	12	
	Totals	32	26	84	
	Weighted Assessment Score = 84/ (32 × 4) = 66%				

Figure 17-2 Sample Assessment Worksheet for Business Continuity Process with Weighting Factors

Measuring and Streamlining the Disaster Recovery Process

We can measure and streamline a business continuity process with the help of the assessment worksheet shown in Figure 17–1. We can measure the effectiveness of a business continuity process with service metrics such as the number of critical applications that can be run at backup sites and the number of users that can be accommodated at the backup site. Process metrics—such as the frequency and authenticity of dry-run tests and the improvements suggested from postmortem sessions after dry-run tests—help us gauge the efficiency of this process. And we can streamline the disaster recovery process by automating actions such as the scheduling of tapes for offsite storage and the retrieval of tapes for disaster recovery restorations.

Summary

We began this chapter with the definition of disaster recovery and then we discussed a case study of an actual disaster, the aftermath of which I was directly involved. This led to the explanation of the 13 steps used to develop a robust disaster recovery program. Some of the more salient steps include requirements, a business impact analysis, and the selection of the appropriate outside recovery services provider. Over the years I have experienced or been aware of numerous nightmare incidents involving disaster recovery and I presented many of those. The final section offers customized assessment sheets used to evaluate an infrastructure's disaster recovery process.

Test Your Understanding

1. The terms *disaster recovery*, *contingency planning*, and *business continuity* all have the same meaning. (True or False)
2. Business continuity plans should be tested a minimum of once every two years. (True or False)
3. A business impact analysis results in a prioritization of:
    a. critical business processes
    b. vital corporate assets
    c. important departmental databases
    d. essential application systems
4. Several business continuity _____ _____ should be proposed based on the results of the business impact analysis.
5. Describe why a firm commitment from executive management is so important in the development of a formal business continuity program.

Suggested Further Readings

1. www.business-continuity-world.com/
2. http://en.wikipedia.org/wiki/Business_continuity_planning
3. www.disaster-recovery-guide.com/
4. www.disasterrecoveryworld.com/
5. *Business Continuity: Best Practices—World-Class Business Continuity Management, Second Edition*; 2003; Hiles, Andrew; Rothstein Associates, Inc.

CHAPTER 18

Facilities Management

Introduction

This chapter discusses the major elements associated with managing the physical environment of an infrastructure. We begin by offering a formal definition of facilities management and discussing some of the implications this definition represents. Next we list the many entities involved with facilities management, including a few that are normally overlooked. This leads to a key topic of designating a process owner and the traits most desirable in such an individual.

One of the most critical responsibilities of the process owner is to proactively ensure the stability of the physical infrastructure environment. In support of this, we list the major risks that many infrastructures are exposed to along with methods to proactively address them. We conclude with a quick and simple method to assess the overall quality of an infrastructure's facilities management process.

Definition of Facilities Management

Facilities Management

Facilities management is a process to ensure that an appropriate physical environment is consistently supplied to enable the continuous operation of all critical infrastructure equipment.

The words for this definition have been chosen carefully. An *appropriate physical environment* implies that all environmental factors (such as air conditioning, humidity, electrical power, static electricity, and controlled physical access) are accounted for at the proper levels on a continuous basis. The term *all critical infrastructure equipment* refers not only to hardware in the data center, but to key infrastructure devices located outside of the centralized facility, including switch rooms, vaults, wiring closets, and encryption enclosures.

Major Elements of Facilities Management

If we were to ask typical infrastructure managers to name the major elements of facilities management, they would likely mention common items such as air conditioning, electrical power, and perhaps fire suppression. Some may also mention smoke detection, uninterruptible power supplies (UPS), and controlled physical access. Few of them would likely include less common entities such as electrical grounding, vault protection, and static electricity.

UPS

UPS stands for uninterruptible power supply and is a temporary battery backup in the event of commercial power loss. UPS units are normally used to power data centers for 15-20 minutes until such time that commercial power is restored or until longer term backup generators come online. Portable UPS units are now available for servers, workstations, and desktops outside of a data center.

A comprehensive list of the major elements of facilities management is as follows:

1. Air conditioning
2. Humidity
3. Electrical power
4. Static electricity
5. Electrical grounding
6. Uninterruptible power supply (UPS)

 7. Backup UPS batteries
 8. Backup generator
 9. Water detection
10. Smoke detection
11. Fire suppression
12. Facility monitoring with alarms
13. Earthquake safeguards
14. Safety training
15. Supplier management
16. Controlled physical access
17. Protected vaults
18. Physical location
19. Classified environment

Temperature and humidity levels should be monitored constantly, either electronically or with recording charts, and reviewed once each shift to detect any unusual trends. The advent of high-density devices such as blade servers can result in hot spots within a data center. These concentrations of heat need to be addressed with proper cooling design. The use of virtualization, in which servers are partitioned with multiple applications, is another way to address this. Electrical power includes continuous supply at the proper voltage, current, and phasing as well as the conditioning of the power. Conditioning purifies the quality of the electricity for greater reliability. It involves filtering out stray magnetic fields that can induce unwanted inductance, doing the same to stray electric fields that can generate unwanted capacitance, and providing surge suppression to prevent voltage spikes. Static electricity, which affects the operation of sensitive equipment, can build up in conductive materials such as carpeting, clothing, draperies, and other non-insulating fibers. Antistatic devices can be installed to minimize this condition. Proper grounding is required to eliminate outages and potential human injury due to short circuits. Another element sometimes overlooked is whether UPS batteries are kept fully charged.

Water and smoke detection are common environmental guards in today's data centers as are firesuppression mechanisms. Facility-monitoring systems and their alarms should be visible and audible enough to be seen and heard from almost any area in the computer room, even when noisy equipment such as printers are running at their loudest. Equipment should be anchored and secured to withstand moderate earthquakes. The large mainframes of yesteryear used to be safely anchored, in part, by the massive plumbing for water-cooled processors and by the huge bus and tag cables that interconnected the various units. In today's era of fiber-optic cables, air-cooled processors, and smaller boxes designed for non-raised flooring, this built-in anchoring of equipment is no longer as prevalent.

Emergency preparedness for earthquakes and other natural or man-made disasters should be a basic part of general safety training for all personnel working inside a data center. They should be knowledgeable about emergency powering off, evacuation procedures, first-aid assistance, and emergency telephone numbers. Training data-center suppliers in these matters is also recommended.

Most data centers have acceptable methods of controlling physical access to their machine rooms, but not always for vaults or rooms that store sensitive documents, check stock, or tapes. The physical location of a data center can also be problematic. A basement level may be safe and secure from the outside, but it might also be exposed to water leaks and evacuation obstacles, particularly in older buildings. Locating a data center along outside walls of a building can sometimes contribute to sabotage from the outside. Classified environments almost always require data centers to be located as far away from outside walls as possible to safeguard them from outside physical forces such as bombs or projectiles as well as from electronic-sensing devices.

In fairness to infrastructure managers and operations personnel, several of these elements may be under the management of the facilities department for which no one in IT would have direct responsibility. But even in this case, infrastructure personnel and operations managers would normally want and need to know who to go to in the facilities department for specific types of environmental issues.

The Facilities Management Process Owner

This brings us to the important issue of designating a facilities management process owner. There are two key activities associated with this designation:

- Determining the scope of this person's responsibilities
- Identifying desirable traits, or skill sets, of such an individual

Determining the Scope of Responsibilities of a Facilities Management Process Owner

The previous discussion about the major elements of facilities management demonstrates that a company's facilities department plays a significant role in managing the physical environment of a company's data center. Determining the exact boundary of responsibilities between the facilities department and IT's facilities management is critical. Clearly scoping out the areas of responsibility and, more important, the degree of authority between these two groups usually spells the difference between resolving a facilities problem in a data center quickly and efficiently versus dragging out the resolution amid chaos, miscommunication, and strained relationships.

For example, suppose a power distribution unit feeding a critical server fails. A computer operations supervisor would likely call in electricians from the facilities department to investigate the problem. Their analysis may find that the unit needs to be replaced and that a new unit will take days to procure, install, and make operational. Alternative solutions need to be brainstormed and evaluated between facilities and IT to determine each option's costs, time, resources, practicality, and long-term impact, and all this activity needs to occur in a short amount of time—usually less than an hour. This is no time to debate who has responsibility and authority for the final decisions. That needs to have been determined well in advance. Working with clearly defined roles and responsibilities shortens the time of the outage to the clients, lessens the chaos, and reduces the effort toward a satisfactory resolution.

The lines of authority between an IT infrastructure and its facilities department will vary from shop to shop depending on size, platforms, degree of outsourcing, and other factors. The key point here is to ensure that the two departments clearly agree upon, communicate to their staffs, and ensure compliance with these boundaries.

Desired Traits of a Facilities Management Process Owner

The owner of the facilities management process almost always resides in the computer operations department. There are rare exceptions—small shops or those with unique outsourcing arrangements—in which the facilities management process owner is part of the facilities department and matrixed back to IT or is part of the IT executive staff. In any event, the selection of the person assigned the responsibility for a stable physical operating environment is an important decision. An understanding of at least some of the basic components of facilities management, such as power and air conditioning, is a high-priority characteristic of an ideal candidate.

Table 18–1 lists, in priority order, a variety of desirable traits that an infrastructure manager might look for in such an individual. Knowledge of hardware configurations is a high priority because understanding how devices are logically connected and physically wired and how they can be impacted environmentally helps in their operation, maintenance, and recoverability. The high priority for backup systems refers both to physical backups such as UPS, electrical generators, and air conditioning as well as to data backup that may need to be restored after physical interruptions. The restore activity drives the need to be familiar with database systems. The ability to think and plan strategically comes into play when laying out computer rooms, planning for expansion, and anticipating advances in logical and physical technologies.

Table 18–1   Prioritized Characteristics of a Facilities Management Process Owner

Characteristic	Priority
1. Knowledge of hardware configurations	High
2. Knowledge of backup systems	High
3. Knowledge of database systems	High
4. Knowledge of power and air conditioning systems	High
5. Ability to think and plan strategically	High
6. Ability to evaluate documentation	Medium
7. Ability to meet effectively with IT executives	Medium
8. Ability to promote teamwork and cooperation	Medium
9. Ability to manage diversity	Medium
10. Knowledge of company's business model	Low
11. Ability to work effectively with developers	Low
12. Knowledge of software configurations	Low
13. Knowledge of network software and components	Low
14. Ability to think and act tactically	Low

Evaluating the Physical Environment

As we read from our definition, the facilities management process ensures the continuous operation of critical equipment. The overriding implication is that the physical environment in which these devices operate is sound, stable, and likely to stay that way. But how does one determine the current state of their physical environment and what the likely trend of its state will become?

There are a number of sources of information that can assist data center managers in evaluating the current state of their physical environment. The following list details some of the more common of these sources. Outages logs normally associated with availability reports should point to the frequency and duration of service interruptions caused by facilities. If the problem-management system includes a robust database, it should be easy to analyze trouble tickets caused by facilities issues and highlight trends, repeat incidents, and root causes.

1. Outage logs
2. Problem tickets
3. Facilities department staff
4. Hardware repair technicians
5. Computer operators
6. Support staff
7. Auditors

The remaining sources are of a more human nature. Facilities department staff can sometimes speak to unusual conditions they observed as part of normal walk-throughs, inspections, or routine maintenance. Similarly, hardware supplier repair technicians can typically spot when elements of the physical environment appear out of the ordinary. Some of the best observers of their physical surroundings are computer operators, especially off-shift staff who are not as distracted by visitors, telephone calls, and the more hectic pace of prime shift. Support staff who frequent the data center (such as network, systems or database administrators) are also good sources of input as to possible glitches in the physical environment. Finally, there are facilities-type auditors whose job is to identify irregularities in the physical operation of the data center and recommend actions to correct them.

Major Physical Exposures Common to a Data Center

Most operations managers do a reasonable job at keeping their data centers up and running. Many shops go for years without experiencing a major outage specifically caused by the physical environment. But the infrequent nature of these types of outages can often lull managers into a false sense of security and lead them to overlook the risks to which they may be exposed. The following list details the most common of these. The older the data center, the greater these exposures. I have clients who collectively have experienced at least half of these exposures during the past three years. Many of their data centers were less than 10 years old.

1. Physical wiring diagrams out of date
2. Logical equipment configuration diagrams and schematics out of date
3. Infrequent testing of UPS
4. Failure to recharge UPS batteries
5. Failure to test generator and fuel levels
6. Lack of preventive maintenance on air conditioning equipment
7. Annunciator system not tested
8. Fire-suppression system not recharged
9. Emergency power-off system not tested
10. Emergency power-off system not documented
11. Hot spots due to blade servers
12. Infrequent testing of backup generator system
13. Equipment not properly anchored
14. Evacuation procedures not clearly documented
15. Circumvention of physical security procedures
16. Lack of effective training to appropriate personnel

Keeping Physical Layouts Efficient and Effective

In addition to ensuring a stable physical environment, the facilities management process owner has another responsibility that is sometimes overlooked. The process owner must ensure efficiencies are designed into the physical layout of the computer facility. A stable and reliable operating environment will result in an effective data center. Well-planned physical layouts will result in an efficient one. Analyzing the physical steps that operators take to load and unload printers, to relocate tapes, to monitor consoles, and to perform other routine physical tasks can result in a well-designed floor plan that minimizes time, minimizes motion, and maximizes efficiency.

One other point to consider in this regard is the likelihood of expansion. Physical computer centers, not unlike IT itself, are an ever-changing entity. Factoring in future expansion due to capacity upgrades, possible mergers, or departmental reorganizations can assist in keeping current floor plans efficient in the future.

Tips to Improve the Facilities Management Process

There are a number of simple actions that can be taken to improve the facilities management process (as shown in the following list). Establishing good relationships with key support departments such as the facilities department and local government inspecting agencies can help keep maintenance and expansion plans on schedule. This can also lead to a greater understanding of what the infrastructure group can do to enable both of these agencies to better serve the IT department.

1. Nurture relationships with facilities department.
2. Establish relationships with local government inspecting agencies, especially if you are considering major physical upgrades to the data center.
3. Consider using video cameras to enhance physical security.
4. Analyze environmental monitoring reports to identify trends, patterns, and relationships.
5. Design adequate cooling for hot spots due to concentrated equipment.
6. Check on effectiveness of water and fire detection and suppression systems.
7. Remove all tripping hazards in the computer center.
8. Check on earthquake preparedness of data center (devices anchored down, training of personnel, and tie-in to disaster recovery).

Video cameras have been around for a long time to enhance and streamline physical security, but their condition is occasionally overlooked. Cameras must be checked periodically to make sure that the recording and playback mechanism is in good shape and that the tape is of sufficient quality to ensure reasonably good playback.

Environmental recording devices also must be checked periodically. Many of these devices are quite sophisticated; they collect a wealth of data about temperature, humidity, purity of air, hazardous vapors, and other environmental measurements. The data is only as valuable as the effort expended to analyze it for trends, patterns, and relationships. A reasonably thorough analysis should be done on this type of data quarterly. Anticipating hot spots due to concentrated servers and providing adequate cooling in such instances can prevent serious outages to critical systems.

In my experience, most shops do a good job of periodically testing their backup electrical systems such as UPS, batteries, generators, and power distribution units (PDUs), but not such a good job of testing their fire detection and suppression systems. This is partly due to the huge capital investment companies make into their electrical backup systems—managers want to ensure a good return on such a sizable outlay of cash. Maintenance contracts for these systems frequently include inspection and testing, at least at the outset. However, this is seldom the case with fire detection and suppression systems. Infrastructure personnel need to be proactive in this regard by insisting on regularly scheduled inspection and maintenance of these systems as well as up-to-date evacuation plans.

Real Life Experience—Operators Devise Shocking Solution

A municipality data center once decided to improve the comfort levels of its computer operators by replacing the raised floor vinyl covers in its data center with carpeted floor panels. The operators were very appreciative of the softer flooring, but noticed static electricity would often build up in them and discharge when they touched the command consoles, often causing a disruption to service.

The facilities department and console vendors devised a solution involving the simple grounding of the consoles, but the work could not be done until the weekend, which was four days away. In the meantime, operators devised their own temporary solution by discharging the built-up charges prior to any console actions by touching, and lightly shocking, unsuspecting co-workers.

One of the simplest actions to take to improve a computer center's physical environment is to remove all tripping hazards. While this sounds simple and straightforward, it is often neglected in favor of equipment moves, hardware upgrades, network expansions, general construction, and—one of the most common of all—temporary cabling that ends up being semi-permanent. This is not only unsightly and inefficient; it can be outright dangerous as physical injuries become a real possibility. Operators and other occupants of the computer center should be trained and authorized to keep the environment efficient, orderly, and safe.

The final tip is to make sure the staff is trained and practiced on earthquake preparedness, particularly in geographic areas most prone to this type of disaster.

Common practices such as anchoring equipment, latching cabinets, and properly storing materials should be verified by qualified individuals several times per year.

Facilities Management at Outsourcing Centers

Shops that outsource portions of their infrastructure services—co-location of servers is an example—often feel that the responsibility for the facilities management process is also outsourced and no longer of their concern. While outsourcers have direct responsibilities for providing stable physical environments, the client has an indirect responsibility to ensure this will occur. During the evaluation of bids and in contract negotiations, appropriate infrastructure personnel should ask the same types of questions about the outsourcer's physical environment that they would ask if it were their own computer center.

Assessing an Infrastructure's Facilities Management Process

The worksheets shown in Figures 18-1 and 18-2 present quick and simple methods for assessing the overall quality, efficiency, and effectiveness of a facilities management process. The first worksheet is used without weighting factors, meaning that all 10 categories are weighted evenly for the assessment of a facilities management process. Sample ratings are inserted to illustrate the use of the worksheet. In this case, the facilities management process scored a total of 25 points for an overall nonweighted assessment score of 63 percent. The weighted assessment score is coincidentally an identical 63 percent based on the sample weights used on our worksheet.

One of the most valuable characteristics of these worksheets is that they are customized to evaluate each of the 12 processes individually. The worksheets in this chapter apply only to the facilities management process. However, the fundamental concepts applied in using these evaluation worksheets are the same for all 12 disciplines. As a result, the detailed explanation on the general use of these worksheets presented near the end of Chapter 7, "Availability," also applies to the other worksheets in the book. Please refer to that discussion if you need more information.

Facilities Management Process—Assessment Worksheet						
Process Owner_____ Owner's Manager_____ Date _____						
Category	Questions About Facilities Management	None 1	Small 2	Medium 3	Large 4
Executive Support	To what degree does the executive sponsor show support for the facilities management process with actions such as budgeting for the monitoring and redundancy of environmental systems?	-	2	-	-
Process Owner	To what degree does the process owner exhibit desirable traits and familiarity with environmental monitoring systems?	-	-	3	-
Customer Involvement	To what degree are key customers, such as the operations and network groups, involved in the design and use of the process?	-	-	3	-
Supplier Involvement	To what degree are facilities personnel, and their suppliers, involved in the design of the process?	-	2	-	-
Service Metrics	To what degree are service metrics analyzed for trends such as the number of outages due to facilities management issues and the number of employee safety issues measured over time?	-	2	-	-
Process Metrics	To what degree are process metrics analyzed for trends such as the frequency of preventative maintenance and inspections of air conditioning, smoke detection, and fire suppression systems and the testing of uninterruptible power supplies and backup generators?	1	-	-	-
Process Integration	To what degree does the facilities management process integrate with the disaster recovery process and its associated tools?	-	2-	-	-
Streamlining/ Automation	To what degree is the facilities management process streamlined by automating actions such as notifying facilities personnel when environmental monitoring thresholds are exceeded for air conditioning, smoke detection, and fire suppression?	-	-	3	-
Training of Staff	To what degree is the staff cross trained on the facilities management process, and how well is the effectiveness of the training verified?	-	-	-	4
Process Documentation	To what degree is the quality and value of facilities management documentation measured and maintained?	-	-	3	-
	Totals	1	8	12	4
	Grand Total = 1 + 8 + 12 + 4 = 25 Nonweighted Assessment Score = 25 / 40 = 63%				

Figure 18-1   Sample Assessment Worksheet for Facilities Management Process

Facilities Management Process—Assessment Worksheet				
Process Owner_____ Owner's Manager_____ Date _____				
Category	**Questions About Facilities Management**	**Weight**	**Rating**	**Score**
Executive Support	To what degree does the executive sponsor show support for the facilities management process with actions such as budgeting for the monitoring and redundancy of environmental systems?	1	2	2
Process Owner	To what degree does the process owner exhibit desirable traits and familiarity with environmental monitoring systems?	3	3	9
Customer Involvement	To what degree are key customers, such as the operations and network groups, involved in the design and use of the process?	3	3	9
Supplier Involvement	To what degree are facilities personnel, and their suppliers, involved in the design of the process?	5	2	10
Service Metrics	To what degree are service metrics analyzed for trends such as the number of outages due to facilities management issues and the number of employee safety issues measured over time?	3	2	6
Process Metrics	To what degree are process metrics analyzed for trends such as the frequency of preventative maintenance and inspections of air conditioning, smoke detection, and fire suppression systems and the testing of uninterruptible power supplies and backup generators?	5	1	5
Process Integration	To what degree does the facilities management process integrate with the disaster recovery process and its associated tools?	1	2	2
Streamlining/ Automation	To what degree is the facilities management process streamlined by automating actions such as notifying facilities personnel when environmental monitoring thresholds are exceeded for air conditioning, smoke detection, and fire suppression?	1	3	3
Training of Staff	To what degree is the staff cross trained on the facilities management process, and how well is the effectiveness of the training verified?	5	4	20
Process Documentation	To what degree is the quality and value of facilities management documentation measured and maintained?	3	3	9
Totals		30	25	75
Weighted Assessment Score = 75 / (30 x 4) = 63%				

Figure 18-2 Sample Assessment Worksheet for Facilities Management Process with Weighting Factors

Measuring and Streamlining the Facilities Management Process

We can measure and streamline a facilities management process with the help of the assessment worksheet shown in Figure 18–1. We can measure the effectiveness of a facilities management process with service metrics such as the number of outages due to facilities management issues and the number of employee safety issues measured over time. Process metrics—for example, the frequency of preventative maintenance and inspections of air conditioning, smoke detection, and fire suppression systems and the testing of uninterruptible power supplies and backup generators—help us gauge the efficiency of this process. And we can streamline the facilities management process by automating actions such as notifying facilities personnel when environmental monitoring thresholds are exceeded for air conditioning, smoke detection, and fire suppression.

Summary

A world-class infrastructure requires stable and reliable facilities to ensure the continuous operation of critical equipment to process critical applications. We began this chapter with a definition of facilities management built around these concepts. Maintaining a high-quality production environment requires familiarity with numerous physical elements of facilities management. We listed and discussed the most common of these. The diversity of these elements shows the scope of knowledge desired in a facilities management process owner.

Next we discussed the topic of selecting a process owner, including alternatives that some shops use in the placement of this key individual. One of the prime responsibilities of a process owner is to identify and correct major physical exposures. We offered several sources of information to assist in evaluating an infrastructure's physical environment and identified several of the risks common to data centers. The final part of this chapter presented customized assessment sheets used to evaluate an infrastructure's facilities management process.

Test Your Understanding

1. The lines of authority between IT and its facilities department will vary from shop to shop depending on size, platforms, and degrees of outsourcing. (True or False)
2. The only way to eliminate static electricity is to remove conducting materials such as carpeting, clothing, draperies, and other noninsulating fibers. (True or False)
3. All of the following are major elements of facilities management except for:
   a. backup generator
   b. backup tape library
   c. fire-suppression system
   d. backup UPS batteries
4. Most shops do a good job of periodically testing their backup electrical systems, but do less than a good job testing _____ and _____ systems.
5. What factors would you consider in locating a data center within a large building?

Suggested Further Readings

1. www.nemertes.com/articles/facilities_management_and_the_ data_center_mind_the_gap_where_physical_meets_virtual_
2. *Build the Best Data Center Facility for Your Business (Networking Technology*; 2005; Alger, Douglas; Cisco Press
3. Association for Computer Operations Managers (AFCOM); http://www.afcom.com
4. *Designing a Safe House for Data.(data centers)*; Security Management; 2005; Reese, Lloyd F.

CHAPTER 19

Developing Robust Processes

Introduction

One of the distinctions that separate world-class infrastructures from those that are just marginal is the robustness of their processes. In this chapter we examine how to develop robust processes for maximum effectiveness. We also show how this prepares them for the appropriate use of technology.

We begin by reviewing several of the other factors that are usually evident in any world-class infrastructure. Next we discuss in detail the 24 characteristics common to any well-designed robust process, with examples to clarify some of the salient points. The last of these 24 characteristics involves the application of technology to automate selected steps. It is this use, and occasional misuse, of technology and automation that often separates the well-managed infrastructure from the poorly operated one. We conclude the chapter by discussing the differences between formal and informal processes, effective brainstorming ground rules, and methods to prioritize requirements.

What Contributes to a World-Class Infrastructure

There are many criteria that distinguish a world-class infrastructure from that of a mediocre one. Table 19–1 summarizes 11 of the most common of these factors. We will look at each of these criteria more closely.

Table 19–1   Common Criteria of World-Class Infrastructures

World-Class Infrastructures	Mediocre Infrastructures
1. Totally supported by executive management	1. Little or no support from executive management
2. Meaningful metrics analyzed, not just collected	2. Convenient metrics, not necessarily meaningful, collected, or analyzed
3. Proactive approach to problem solving, change management, availability, performance and tuning, and capacity planning	3. Reactive approach to problem solving, change management, availability, performance and tuning, and capacity planning
4. Service desk focus on call management, not just call tracking	4. Service desk focus on call tracking, not call management
5. Employees empowered to make decisions and improvements	5. Employees empowered very little, or not at all
6. Standards well developed and adhered to	6. Standards poorly developed with little or no enforcement
7. Employees well trained	7. Employees poorly trained
8. Employees well equipped	8. Employees poorly equipped
9. Processes designed with robustness throughout them	9. Processes designed with little or no robustness in them
10. Technology effectively used to automate streamlined processes	10. Technology applied, if at all, inappropriately
11. Functions of systems management integrated	11. Little or no integration of systems management functions

1. Executive Support

As we discussed in Chapter 1, "Acquiring Executive Support," executive support is one of the primary prerequisites for implementing a world-class infrastructure. Executive support does not mean the mere approval of budgets for hardware, software, and human resources—executives in many firms with mediocre infrastructures readily approve budgets. Executive support begins with an IT executive who actively participates in the planning, development, and decision-making processes of systems management, but there must also be support from executives of other areas as well.

Active participation by executives can take on many forms. It may involve executives taking the time to understand the challenges and obstacles of providing sound infrastructures. It may consist of managers helping to prioritize which functions of systems management are most important to their firms. It may result in executives backing up their staffs when negotiating reasonable—rather than unrealistic (more frequently the case)—service levels with customers. Finally, it may be the CIO or his or her representative ensuring that other departments within IT, notably applications development, actively support and comply with established infrastructure policies, procedures, and standards.

2. Meaningful Metrics Analyzed

Over the years I have observed that one of the most common characteristics that differentiate well-managed infrastructures from those poorly managed is the use of metrics. One of the first distinctions in this regard is the difference between merely collecting data and establishing truly meaningful metrics as derived from this data.

For example, most companies today collect some type of data about outages to their online systems, regardless of whether the systems are hosted on mainframes, client-servers, or the Internet. A typical metric may be to measure a particular system's percentage of uptime over a given period of time and to establish a target goal—for instance, 99 percent uptime. The data collected in this example may include the start and end times of the outage, the systems impacted, and the corrective actions taken to restore service. The metric itself is the computation of the uptime percentage on a daily, weekly, or monthly basis for each online system measured. Compiling the outage data into a more meaningful metric may involve segregating the uptime percentage between prime shift and off shift. Or it could be reporting on actual system downtime in minutes or hours, as opposed to the percentage of availability. A meaningful availability metric may also be a measure of output as defined by the customer. For example, we had a purchasing officer customer who requested that we measure availability based on the number of purchase orders his staff was able to process on a weekly basis.

Real Life Experience—A New Technology by Any Other Name

An aerospace firm was running highly classified data over expensively encrypted network lines. High network availability was of paramount importance to ensure the economic use of the costly lines as well as the productive use of the highly paid specialists using them. Intermittent network outages began occurring at some point but proved elusive to troubleshoot. Finally, we trended the data and noticed a pattern that seemed to center around the afternoon of the third Thursday of every month.

This monthly pattern eventually led us and our suppliers to uncover the fact that our telephone carrier was performing routine line maintenance for disaster recovery the third Thursday of every month. The switching involved with this maintenance was producing just enough line interference to affect the sensitivity of our encrypted lines. The maintenance was consequently modified for less interference and the problem never reoccurred. Analyzing and trending the metrics data led us directly to the root cause and eventual resolution of the problem.

Instituting meaningful metrics helps improve the overall management of an infrastructure, but the ultimate use of them involves their analysis to reveal trends, patterns, and relationships. This in-depth analysis can often lead to the root cause of problems and a more proactive approach to meeting service levels.

3. Proactive Approach

World-class infrastructures employ a proactive approach to identify and prevent potential problems impacting performance and availability. Marginal infrastructures are forced to take a more reactive approach toward problem solving. For example, a proactive strategy may use the analysis of meaningful utilization metrics to predict when an out-of-capacity condition is likely to occur. Armed with this information, technicians can then decide whether to add more capacity or to reschedule or reduce workloads to prevent outages or performance problems. A reactive approach allows no time to identify these conditions and to make proactive decisions. Other performance and capacity indicators such as memory swaps and bandwidths can similarly be analyzed to proactively identify and prevent bottlenecks and outages.

4. Call Management

Well-managed infrastructures do far more than simply log problems in their call centers. Technicians in these environments track, age, and escalate calls; they pinpoint root causes and solicit customer feedback; and they analyze trends, patterns, and relationships between problems, changes, and other factors. Call management is really the cornerstone of a sound problem management philosophy. Marginal infrastructure organizations often do not see or understand the integrated relationships between problem management and other management areas such as change, availability, networks, and performance and tuning.

5. Employee Empowerment

Many firms are reluctant to empower their employees. Some managers believe only supervisory-level staff are capable of making technical decisions or personnel judgments. Others may feel employees are not capable or well trained enough to be decisive. Still others fear that that granting employees more authority results in them requesting more compensation. Progressive infrastructure organizations tend to mitigate these empowerment issues with communication, training, empathy, and support.

The issue of management support can be key in determining an employee-empowerment program's success or failure. Employees are bound to make incorrect judgments on occasion when empowered with new decision-making authorities. Supportive managers who show the interest and time to understand and correct the faulty decision-making seldom see poor judgments repeated.

6. Well-Developed Standards

Standards can apply to virtually every aspect of IT, from versions of desktop software to mainframe operating systems; from dataset naming conventions to password construction; and from email systems to network protocols. When properly applied, standards can simplify maintenance, shorten deployment times, and ultimately reduce costs. But proper application requires that standards be thoroughly developed and effectively enforced.

Many shops develop only those standards that are simple to deploy or easy to enforce. In this sense these companies are similar to those that collect only the metrics that are simple to implement or easy to measure. In both cases, the real value of these activities is compromised.

A world-class infrastructure, on the other hand, usually identify all stakeholders of a particular standard prior to its development and invite them to participate in its design, implementation, and enforcement. These stakeholders typically consist of representatives of user groups most impacted by the standard, including internal and external customers and suppliers. Their participation goes a long way to ensuring buy-in, support, and compliance.

7. Well-Trained Employees

World-class infrastructures invest heavily in training their staffs. This training may take the form of on-the-job training, onsite classroom instruction, offsite courses at local facilities, out-of town classes, or customized training conducted by vendors. Top-rated infrastructures often employ a buddy system, or a one-on-one mentoring program in which experienced senior-level technicians share both the content and the application of their knowledge with junior-level staff. Cross-training between infrastructure departments—such as between operations and networks or between system administration and database administration—is another effective method used by well-managed organizations to optimize employee training.

8. Well-Equipped Employees

World-class infrastructures not only have well-trained employees, they have well-equipped employees. Less-sophisticated shops sometimes sacrifice hardware and software tools in the name of cost savings. This is often a false economy that can drag out problem resolution times, extend the length of outages, occasionally duplicate work efforts, and eventually frustrate key staff members to the point that they seek employment elsewhere.

While budget items need to be justified and managed, top-rated infrastructures usually find the means to provide the tools their technicians need. These tools may include pagers, cell phones, personal assistant palmtops, laptops, at-home high-speed network connections, and specialized software for desktops.

9. Robust Processes

World-class infrastructures know how to develop, design, and maintain robust processes. This topic will be described at length in the next section.

10. Effective Use of Technology

Managers of highly regarded infrastructures understand that the best application of technology—especially automation—comes only after processes have been designed with robustness and then streamlined. Mediocre shops often rush to automate prior to streamlining. This almost inevitably leads to chaos brought about by processes that are highly automated but poorly designed. The next chapter will cover this in detail.

11. Integrated Systems Management Functions

World-class infrastructures go beyond just having well-designed systems management functions. The leaders of these organizations know how to select and integrate several of these processes. Chapter 21, "Integrating Systems Management Processes," explains the importance of combining some of these functions and describes in detail how both tactical and strategic functions should be integrated.

Characteristics of a Robust Process

The ninth criterion of a world-class infrastructure, as we just saw, is the use of robust processes. What exactly is meant by a process being truly robust and what characteristics are inherent in such a process? This section addresses those questions. The following lists 24 of the most common attributes of a robust process. We will discuss each of them in detail.

1. Process objective is identified.
2. Executive sponsor is identified and involved.
3. Process owner is identified and given responsibility for and authority over the process.
4. Key customers are identified and involved.
5. Secondary customers are identified and consulted.
6. Process suppliers are identified and involved.
7. Process inputs are identified.
8. Process outputs are identified.
9. Process is described by a sound business model.
10. Process hierarchy is understood.
11. Execution is enforceable.

12. Process is designed to provide service metrics.
13. Service metrics are recorded and analyzed, not just collected.
14. Process is designed to provide process metrics.
15. Process metrics are recorded and analyzed, not just collected.
16. Documentation is thorough, accurate, and easily understood.
17. Process contains all required value-added steps.
18. Process eliminates all non-value-added steps.
19. Process guarantees accountability.
20. Process provides incentives for compliance and penalties for avoidance or circumvention.
21. Process is standardized across all appropriate departments and remote sites.
22. Process is streamlined as much as possible and practical.
23. Process is automated wherever practical, but only after streamlining.
24. Process integrates with all other appropriate processes.

1. Process Objective Is Identified

The overall objective of the process needs to be stated, written down, shared with all appropriate parties, and agreed to and clearly understood by all process design participants. The objective should answer the questions of what problem the process will solve, which issues it will address, and how the process will add value and quality to the environment.

2. Executive Sponsor Is Identified and Involved

Each process needs to have an executive sponsor who is passionate about the successful design and ongoing execution of the process. This person provides support, resources, insight, and executive leadership. Any required participation or communication with other groups, either inside or outside of the infrastructure, is typically arranged by the executive sponsor. This individual is often the manager of the process owner.

3. Process Owner Is Identified and Given Responsibility for and Authority Over the Process

This person leads the team that designs the process, identifies the key customers and suppliers of it, and documents its use. The process owner executes, communicates, and measures the effectiveness of the process on an ongoing basis.

4. Key Customers Are Identified and Involved

Key customers are those individuals who are the immediate users and direct beneficiaries of the process. For example, suppose you are designing processes to request the reprint of a report or the restoration of a file. Key customers for these processes may be users who are most likely to request these services on a regular basis. Their involvement in developing the process is important to ensure practical design and ease of use.

5. Secondary Customers Are Identified and Consulted

Secondary customers are those that may use a process less frequently than primary customers or who may be the eventual rather than immediate beneficiaries of the process. Using the example in #4, if administrative assistants are making the original requests for reprints or restorations, then their managers are likely to be the secondary customers of the process. Their consultation can be helpful since they may be the ultimate users of the process.

6. Process Suppliers Are Identified and Involved

Process suppliers are the individuals who provide the specific inputs to a process. These suppliers may be

- Internal to an IT infrastructure (for example, data-entry departments)
- External to an IT infrastructure but internal to IT (a development group inputting change requests)
- External to IT but internal to a company (an outside user group supplying report modification information)
- External to a company (hardware and software vendors who may provide details about how an upgrade is to be performed)

7. Process Outputs Are Identified

These are the specific deliverables or services being provided to the primary and secondary customers. The quality of the delivery and content of these outputs is usually measured with service metrics.

8. Process Inputs Are Identified

These are the specific input entities required by the process. They may take the form of soft inputs such as data, information, or requests; or they may be hard inputs such as diskettes, tapes, or other physical entities.

9. Process Is Described by a Sound Business Model

In simple terms, a robust process should make common business sense. The benefits of using the process should exceed the cost and efforts expended to design, execute, and maintain the process. The business side of a robust process sometimes involves leasing agreements, maintenance agreements, and service level agreements.

10. Process Hierarchy Is Understood

Some processes have secondary processes, or sub-processes, underneath them. Individuals who are developing well-designed robust processes know and understand the relationships between the primary and secondary processes.

11. Execution Is Enforceable

Almost any process, regardless of design, must be enforced to be effective. Whenever possible and practical, software techniques such as passwords, authorizations, audit trails, or locks should be used to enforce compliance with a process. When technical enforcement is not practical, management support, review boards, metrics, or other procedural techniques should be used to ensure enforcement.

12. Process Is Designed to Provide Service Metrics

Most processes measure something associated with their output. Often this involves a quantitative measure such as transaction processes per second or jobs completed per hour.

In addition to these, a robust process also focuses on qualitative measures that are oriented toward the end-user. These metrics show the relative quality of the service being provided. For example, service metrics involving a report-delivery process may include not only how often the report is delivered on time but whether it was delivered to the right individual, in the correct format, with accurate content, and on the proper media. Service metrics should measure the benefits of the process to the end-users in their own terms. The metrics should be customer oriented and focused on measuring the right thing; that is, these metrics should exhibit effectiveness.

13. Service Metrics Are Compiled and Analyzed, Not Just Collected

Mediocre infrastructures often invest a fair amount of time, money, and energy to collect and compile metrics; then they do little to analyze them. The real value of meaningful measurements comes from thoroughly and consistently examining these metrics for trends, patterns, and relationships and then applying the results of the analysis to improve the effectiveness of the particular service being measured.

14. Process Is Designed to Provide Process Metrics

Robust processes have not only service metrics associated with them but process metrics as well. The key difference between a service metric and a process metric is that a service metric focuses on how effective a process is in regards to a customer, while a process metric focuses on how efficient a process is in regards to a supplier.

A process metric indicates the productivity of a procedure by measuring such things as resources consumed or cycle times. The frequency of on-time delivery of reports is a service metric because it measures the end result of the process (which is what the customer gets). The number of times the report had to be reprinted to obtain acceptable quality is a process metric because it measures the amount of effort required to produce the end product. Common examples of process metrics include abnormally ending job processing, rerouting problems, rerunning jobs, reprinting reports, and restoring files.

In Chapter 4, "Customer Service," we discussed an enhanced version of the customer/supplier matrix that incorporated both service metrics and process metrics. This characteristic reinforces the notion that process metrics should be supplier-oriented and focused on *measuring the entity right* rather than *measuring the right entity*. In other words, these metrics determine efficiency. Table 19-2 summarizes the differences between service metrics and process metrics.

Table 19–2   Differences Between Service Metrics and Process Metrics

Service Metric	Process Metric
Focuses on the customer	Focuses on the supplier
Measures levels of effectiveness	Measures levels of efficiency
Deals with the quality of output	Deals with the quality of input
Examples include:	Examples include:
–system availability	–job and transaction throughput
–response times	–elapsed cycle times
–accuracy of content	–quantity of resources consumed
–ontime delivery	–abnormal job terminations
–network access	–rerouting of problems
–database integrity	–reruns, reprints, restores

15. Process Metrics Are Compiled and Analyzed, Not Just Collected

Just as service metrics need to be compiled and analyzed, so do process metrics. The importance of analyzing missed process metrics is often overlooked when the associated service metrics are met. This could be the case in terms of a service metric involving output delivery being met even though the job and its output had to be reprocessed numerous times. As with service metrics, the real value of meaningful process metrics comes from thoroughly and consistently examining them for trends, patterns, and relationships and then applying the results of the analysis to improve the efficiency of the particular service being measured.

16. Documentation Is Thorough, Accurate, and Easily Understood

Documentation is one of the fundamentals that clearly separate mediocre infrastructures from those that are truly world-class. Well-written documentation facilitates the training, maintenance, and marketing of key processes. Progressive shops hold appropriate staffs accountable for reading and understanding key documentation by making it part of their performance reviews. These shops also have their new employees test the clarity and readability of the writing while ensuring that senior analysts and technical leads have validated the accuracy of the material. Thorough documentation eases the tasks of verifying that all required value-added steps are present and that all non-value-added steps have been eliminated.

Effective documentation can come in various forms and can be evaluated in various ways. Some of these forms include online and hard-copy narrative procedures, diagramed illustrations (such as flowcharts or bubble charts), and Web-enabled help menus. Later in this chapter we offer a proven method for effectively evaluating all the various forms of process documentation.

17. Process Contains All Required Value-Added Steps

To use a legal analogy, value-added steps are to a robust process what the truth is to a credible witness's testimony. The process should contain the value-added steps, all of the value-added steps, and nothing but the value-added steps. Two key attributes of a robust process are those of effectiveness and efficiency. Process effectiveness means that all existing steps are adding value to the end result. Key customers, suppliers, and process owners should meet prior to and after development of the documentation to identify all the value-added steps and to ensure that all are appropriately inserted into the final process.

18. Process Eliminates All Non-Value-Added Steps

If a step is not directly contributing value to the overall objective of the process, it should be eliminated. This attribute is critical to eventually automating the process. Two activities are required to completely eliminate all non-value-added steps:

1. All steps in a process, regardless of how small, even if previously undocumented, need to be identified. This comprehensive list of the exact steps of a procedure is commonly referred to as the informal process. (The next section discusses the differences between and significance of formal and informal processes.)
2. An extremely critical evaluation of each of these steps needs to be conducted with an eye toward eliminating any steps that do not directly contribute to the desired output of a process.

19. Process Guarantees Accountability

Process metrics, performance charts, and trending reports should be used to quickly identify when a department or an individual is not following the prescribed procedure, with direct feedback to and consequences from management. In order for this to work, the process designers and owners must give management sufficient tools to carry out their enforcement. Management, in turn, must follow up with fair, timely, and appropriate actions to ensure process compliance in the future.

20. Process Provides Incentives for Compliance and Penalties for Avoidance or Circumvention

One of the most effective incentives for compliance is efficiency. If it takes more time and effort to go *around* a process than to go *through* it, most employees will choose to go through it (use the process). The challenge is to remove the obstacles normally associated with using a process and to insert roadblocks for circumvention. Properly streamlining and then automating a process can encourage its use. Security measures such as passwords and locks, as well as management measures such as exception reports and accountability, can discourage circumvention.

21. Process Is Standardized Across all Appropriate Departments and Remote Sites

Some processes may have been developed at different remote sites at different times and consequently have slightly different standards of implementation. For example, one of my clients had an older change management process at a remote site based on an email system and a newer version at the central site based on an Access database system. Before either process could be optimized, an agreed standard needed to be reached, which it was. Nonstandard processes often come into play as a result of acquisitions, mergers, or takeovers. The technical challenge of implementing an agreed-upon standard is often much easier than actually reaching that consensus in the first place, which often involves politics.

22. Process Is Streamlined as Much as Possible and Practical

Streamlining a process involves removing all non-value-added steps, eliminating redundant steps, placing the steps in the most efficient sequence possible, and streamlining individual steps as much as possible. For long established processes, this may be difficult to accomplish due to users being deeply entrenched in inefficient practices. Here are three of the most common responses we get when we ask why a particular process cannot or should not be changed:

- We've always done it that way.
- It seems to work most of the time, so why bother changing it?
- Analyst X designed this process, and only he can change it.

(We hear this last response even after analyst X has left the department.) These explanations are not adequate justifications for keeping a process the same when improvements through streamlining are clearly warranted. Once non-value-added steps are removed, streamlining should proceed: eliminate redundant steps, place the steps in the most efficient sequence possible, and streamline individual steps as much as possible.

23. Process Is Automated Wherever Practical, but Only after Streamlining

Automation can end up being either beneficial or detrimental depending on how the automation is designed and implemented. Due to the importance and complexity of this attribute, we will discuss it more in the next section.

24. Process Integrates with all Other Appropriate Processes

Several processes within systems management naturally complement each other. For example, problem and change management are separate processes, but they often rely on each other for optimum effectiveness. Similarly, performance/tuning and capacity planning are almost always closely related to each other. The degree to which processes complement and integrate with each other is a valuable characteristic and is the topic of Chapter 21, "Integrating Systems Management Processes."

Understanding the Differences Between a Formal Process and an Informal Process

Most IT professionals are familiar with the concept of a formal process. By this we mean a procedure or methodology in which all of the major steps are explained and documented. The write-up is normally signed off on by a manager in authority, disseminated to appropriate members of the staff, and made accessible for future reference in either electronic or hard-copy form. Written procedures on how to reboot servers, initiate online systems, or back up or restore data are common examples of formal processes.

An informal process is a far more detailed account of its corresponding formal process. An analogy from the culinary arts illustrates this difference. Suppose you decide to duplicate a specialty of a gourmet cook by following his published recipe. You adhere precisely to each of the prescribed steps and create a dish that looks exactly like the original. But after the first bite, you know immediately that something just doesn't seem right. It's close but just a bit off the mark. Soon afterward you have the opportunity to watch this chef prepare the exact same dish in person. With her recipe in your hand, you note how she follows the exact steps in the exact order as you did. But occasionally she swirls the pan briefly and adds a pinch of this and a dash of that—steps so seemingly insignificant as to almost be ignored. In this case, the recipe listing the steps is the formal process, but if the small, innocuous steps that make the dish taste just right are included in the directions, you have the informal process— the sum of all the actual detailed steps involved.

The reason this is important is that knowledge of the small, critical steps of a process—little known and almost always undocumented—is a prerequisite to effective process improvement, streamlining, and eventual automation. Shops unaware of the complete informal procedure associated with a systems management process often fail in their attempts to redesign it into a robust process; they fail because tiny but significant steps are left out.

Helpful Ground Rules for Brainstorming

The development of a robust process requires several activities that are best facilitated with brainstorming sessions. These sessions can prove to be invaluable in gathering optimal designs, consensus of opinion, and all-important buy-in from diverse groups. But if they aren't managed properly, they can also be time-consuming, expensive, and lacking in results. Over the years I have accumulated a list of helpful ground rules to make brainstorming sessions efficient, worthwhile, and effective:

1. Agree on the clear objective(s) of the brainstorming.
2. Stay focused on the objectives(s).
3. Treat everyone as equals.
4. Listen respectfully to each person's input.
5. Participate honestly and candidly.
6. Maintain confidentiality when appropriate.
7. Keep an open mind; suspend personal agendas.
8. Ask anything—there are no dumb questions.
9. Question anything you don't understand.
10. Speak only one voice at a time; no side conversations.
11. Ensure everything relevant gets written down.
12. If prioritizing, agree upon specific technique.
13. If attempting consensus, agree upon voting method.
14. Start and end on time—session, breaks, lunch.
15. Critique the brainstorming session for improvements.
16. Treat these as guidelines, not rules; customize as needed.

Methods for Prioritizing Requirements

A common use of brainstorming is to identify the requirements for a particular discipline. Once members of a cross-functional team have identified a large list of requirements, they often struggle with ways to gain consensus on prioritizing them. Getting 10-15 members of a team to agree on the rankings of as many as 50 items can be a laborious, frustrating, time-consuming challenge. There are several effective methods that teams can use to develop an agreed-upon list of requirements by order of importance.

Three administrative tasks need to occur before establishing priorities:

1. Display all requirements in plain view of all members of the cross-functional team. Flip charts, whiteboards, smart-boards, or laptop projection systems are ideal for this.

2. The team needs to closely scrutinize the list to merge any similar requirements and to reword requirements needing additional clarity. Revisions to the list must be done with the consent of the entire team.

3. Finally, the new list of requirements should be renumbered.

The most straightforward team approach for prioritizing a list of requirements is to ask each team member to assign a high, medium, or low designation to each requirement. These designations can be converted to numerical values (for example, high = 3, medium = 2, low = 1) to develop a quantification matrix like the sample shown in Table 19-3. The requirements can then be ranked according to their total values.

Table 19–3   Sample Quantification Matrix to Prioritize n-Requirements

	Team Member #1	Team Member #2	Team Member #3	Team Member #4	Team Member #5	Totals
Requirement #1	2	3	1	2	2	10
Requirement #2	1	3	2	3	2	11
Requirement #3	1	2	1	2	3	9
Requirement #4	2	3	2	3	2	12
Requirement #n	1	2	1	2	2	8

In the example shown in the table, the cross-functional team consists of five members who are evaluating n requirements. One drawback of this approach, particularly for small teams, is that it limits the range of priority values. With five members voting, the maximum value of a requirement is $5 * 3 = 15$ and the minimum is $5 * 1 = 5$. This means only 11 unique values (5 through 15) could be assigned. If 30 or 40 requirements are being evaluated, many will have duplicate values assigned to them. One way to address this is to add two more designations for each requirement and to adjust the values accordingly. One designation would be a combination of high/medium and the other a combination of medium/low. The new values now become high = 5, high/medium = 4, medium = 3, medium/low = 2, and low = 1. The new range of values now becomes 5 through 25, resulting in 21 unique values. This obviously does not guarantee the elimination of requirements with identical priorities, but it does greatly reduce their likelihood.

Another method—and one that yields the greatest range of priorities—is to have each member of the team numerically rank all requirements from the most important to the least important, with the most important given a value of 1, the second most important given a value of 2, and so on. The values of each requirement are then totaled. The requirement with the lowest total value is ranked first in the list of priorities (highest priority), the requirement with the next lowest total value is ranked second, and so on. This method is known as the nominal group technique (NGT) and is best used when precise delineations of priorities are needed. The drawback to it is the additional administrative work needed to generate and compile all of the necessary values.

A popular variation to the NGT is to limit the number of items ranked to only the top half or top quarter, depending on the number of requirements and team members. This works particularly well when there is a large number of requirements to prioritize and a relatively small group of individuals to rank them. For example, if there are 20 requirements to be ranked by a team of 10 members, then having each member ranking half or 10 of the items is a good approach. On the other hand, if there are 30 requirements to be prioritized by a team of 5 members, then asking each member to rank one-quarter, or 7, of the items is the approach to take.

Summary

This chapter began by presenting 11 criteria that distinguish a world-class infrastructure from that of a mediocre one. Then we looked at each of these in detail. Since one of the key criteria is that the processes used by an infrastructure be robust in nature, we went on to describe 24 characteristics of a robust process, including the automation of processes, the evaluation of documentation, and the integration of systems management processes. The next Chapter covers the automation and documentation of processes, and Chapter 21 covers process integration.

Test Your Understanding

1. A robust process eliminates all non-value-added steps. (True or False)
2. Most any process, regardless of design, must be enforced to be effective. (True or False)
3. Which one of the following is more of a service metric rather than a process metric?
   a. reruns of jobs
   b. reprints of reports
   c. response times of transactions
   d. restores of files
4. The key difference between a service metric and a process metric is that a service metric focuses on how effective a process is in regards to a _____ while a process metric focuses on how efficient a process is in regards to a _____.
5. What types of training would you recommend for service-desk personnel to enable them to improve the quality of their services to users?

Suggested Further Readings

1. *Process Mapping, Process Improvement and Process Management*; 2005; Madison, Dan; Paton Press
2. *More for Less: The Power of Process Management*; 2008; Spanyi, Andrew; Meghan-Kiffer Press
3. *Operations Management: Processes and Value Chains, 8th Edition*; 2006; Krajewski, Lee J., Ritzman, Larry P., Malhotra, Manoj K.; Prentice Hall
4. *A Handbook of Techniques for Formative Evaluation*; 1999; George, Judith, Cowan, John; FALMER/KP

CHAPTER 20

Using Technology to Automate and Evaluate Robust Processes

Introduction

One of the distinctions that separate world-class infrastructures from marginal ones is the degree to which their processes are automated. In the first part of this chapter we present three important preparatory steps necessary for automating a process successfully and discuss how to use technology properly in this activity.

We then show how to evaluate the robustness of any process, using both weighted and nonweighted methods, based on 24 characteristics of the process. We conclude with a thorough discussion on how to evaluate the quality and value of any type of infrastructure process documentation.

Automating Robust Processes

How well a process is automated with technology often distinguishes whether an infrastructure is world-class, merely average, or even mediocre. The reason for this is that automation can frequently be a double-edged sword for IT shops. When properly applied, automation can greatly streamline processes, reduce cycle times, increase efficiency, minimize errors, and generally improve the overall service levels of an infrastructure.

When improperly applied, automation can do more harm than if never attempted in the first place. This can be due to the fact that applying automation to a poorly designed process merely results in a highly automated poor process. The output may be arrived at more quickly, but in all likelihood it will be unacceptable in quality and content. Applying the wrong type of technology to automate a process can also cause more problems than not automating at all. For example, one company attempted to automate part of their output processing with mechanical feeders that virtually eliminated the expensive and highly repetitive manual loading of paper into laser printers. Later, managers realized that only a limited type of specially bonded paper worked properly, causing them to eventually go back to the manual process.

Processes should not be automated until three key conditions have been met:

1. **The process should be well-designed and standardized to the maximum extent achievable.** Say, for example, the process you are automating is used in multiple instances or at multiple sites. If the process has been well-designed and standardized at the outset, the eventual automation techniques can be migrated to the other occurrences of the process. This helps to cost-justify the expense of the automation.

2. **The process must be streamlined as much as possible.** This is accomplished by eliminating all non-value-added steps and by ensuring all the necessary value-added steps are included. This should apply to all instances of a standardized process. This ensures that, no matter which parts of the process are selected as candidates for automation, they are, in fact, vital elements of the procedure.

3. **Discretion should be exercised**. Select only those parts of a process for which automation solidly applies and then apply the proper type of technology. In other words, this is no time to be a proving ground for new technology. Many well-intentioned attempts at automating an entire process have failed miserably due to managers rushing to be the first to use their environments as a test bed for advanced but unproven techniques. This same automation may work in small parts of a process but not the process in its entirety.

Managers should fully understand the type and scope of automation being planned. Automation types usually come in the form of hardware, software, or some combination of the two. For example, some large-volume, high-speed laser printers use both hardware and software to automate the functions of loading, stacking, separating, bursting, and decollating output. Similarly, tape library systems can be automated to load, mount, dismount, and store tape cartridges.

In each example, both the type and scope of automation come into play. Automation of one centralized, high-speed laser printer may be appropriate for an output process that is well-designed, homegrown, and highly controlled. It may not be appropriate for smaller, diverse departmental printing due to cost, complexity, and maintainability. Similarly, an automated tape library system may not be appropriate in environments of low-volume, high-diversity, low-centralization, and multiple platforms. The message here is to thoroughly evaluate the type and scope of technology of the automation tools you might choose to use for each particular part of a process.

Understanding the need to standardize, streamline, and evaluate before one automates is only part of the puzzle. The sequence of these four activities is extremely critical to the success of any automation initiative. Many shops I have worked with want to automate first, thinking it will be bring about immediate efficiencies, cost savings, and improved quality of services. In most instances, the result is just the reverse. Instead of having a poorly designed manual process, you now end up with a poorly designed automated process. Greater inefficiencies, lower levels of quality, and eventually higher costs normally follow.

The only correct sequence of activities is as follows:

1. Standardize a well-designed process.
2. Streamline that process.
3. Evaluate thoroughly the relative fit of the automation technology to the process parts.
4. Automate the appropriate pieces with proper technology.

One of my more literature-oriented clients put this guideline to rhyme to help his staff remember it:

> First standardize, streamline, and evaluate,
> Before you decide to automate.

Table 20–1 summarizes the best and the worst possible sequence scenarios for preparing for the automation of infrastructure processes.

Table 20–1   Sequence Scenarios for Process Automation

Best Possible Sequence	Worst Possible Sequence
1. Standardize the process	1. Automate the entire process
2. Streamline the process	2. Attempt to streamline the process
3. Evaluate automation technology	3. Attempt to standardize the process
4. Automate appropriate parts with proper technology	

Evaluating an Infrastructure Process

Once you are familiar with the attributes that characterize a robust process, you can evaluate almost any process within your infrastructure. There are a variety of methods for doing this, and I will describe two common methods that I have used with prior clients.

1. A straightforward nonweighted technique.
2. A customized variation of the first that employs weighted values for each of the attributes.

In the first method, each of the 24 attributes is rated as to the level of its importance. In many cases, the attribute is either clearly in existence or it is not. If the attribute is present, it is given a rating of 2; if it is not present, it is given a rating of 0. In those cases where it may be difficult to ascertain whether a characteristic is fully realized but is, in some degree, present, it is rated as 1. Table 20–2 shows the results of an evaluation I conducted at three separate companies involving a process to install and migrate new levels of operating system software. Company X represents a prime defense contractor; company Y depicts a major motion picture studio; and company Z signifies a start-up dotcom e-tailor. The advantage of this method is that it is quick, simple, and easy to understand. Manager and analysts can use technology in the form of spreadsheets and databases to automate parts of this evaluation process by setting up templates and directories to sort and categorize these evaluations.

Table 20–2 Process Evaluation Ratings of Three Selected Companies

Criteria	Company Ratings		
	X	Y	Z
1. Process objective is identified.	2	2	2
2. Executive sponsor is identified and involved.	2	0	1
3. Process owner is identified and given responsibility for and authority over the process.	2	1	1
4. Process inputs are identified.	1	1	1
5. Process suppliers are identified and involved.	1	0	0
6. Key customers are identified and involved.	2	2	1
7. Secondary customers are identified and consulted.	2	1	0
8. Process outputs are identified.	2	2	2
9. Process is described by sound business model.	1	0	2
10. Process hierarchy is understood.	2	1	1
11. Execution is enforceable.	2	1	2
12. Process is designed to provide service metrics.	2	2	2
13. Service metrics are recorded and analyzed, not just collected.	1	1	2
14. Process is designed to provide process metrics.	2	1	0
15. Process metrics are recorded and analyzed, not just collected.	1	1	0
16. Documentation is thorough, accurate, and easily understood.	2	0	1
17. Process contains required value-added steps.	2	2	2
18. Process eliminates all non-value-added steps.	2	1	1
19. Process guarantees accountability.	1	0	0
20. Process provides incentives for compliance and penalties for avoidance or circumvention.	1	0	1
21. Process is standardized across all appropriate departments and remote sites.	2	1	1
22. Process is streamlined as much as possible and practical.	2	1	0
23. Process is automated wherever practical but only after streamlining.	2	1	1
24. Process integrates with all other appropriate processes.	1	0	1
Totals	**40**	**22**	**25**

An alternative method of evaluating a process involves using weighted attributes. While all 24 attributes of a robust process are considered important, some characteristics may be more relevant or less significant than others, depending on an infrastructure's particular environment. In this case, a numerical weighted value is assigned to each attribute. A common practice is to assign a weight of 3 for high importance, 2 for medium, and 1 for low importance. Each attribute is then evaluated for a 0, 1, or 2 rating similar to the nonweighted method. The weight and rating is then multiplied to give a final value for each characteristic.

The advantage of this method over the nonweighted one is that this technique allows you to customize the weightings to suit your particular environment and thus give a more accurate appraisal of your process. This method is especially useful when evaluating multiple processes in the same infrastructure so that comparisons and inferences against a standard can be drawn. Table 20-3 shows the weightings, ratings, and values from an evaluation I recently performed for a change management process. Managers and analysts can again use technology similar to that proposed for the nonweighted method to help automate parts of this technique.

Table 20-3 Characteristics of a Robust Process

Characteristic	Weight	Rating	Value
1. Process objective is identified.	3	2	6
2. Executive sponsor is identified and involved.	2	2	4
3. Process owner is identified and given responsibility for and authority over the process	3	2	6
4. Process inputs are identified.	2	1	2
5. Process suppliers are identified and involved.	2	1	2
6. Key customers are identified and involved.	3	2	6
7. Secondary customers are identified and consulted.	1	2	2
8. Process outputs are identified.	2	2	4
9. Process is described by sound business model.	1	1	2
10. Process hierarchy is understood.	1	2	2
11. Execution is enforceable.	1	2	2
12. Process is designed to provide service metrics.	3	2	6
13. Service metrics are recorded and analyzed, not just collected.	3	1	3

Characteristic	Weight	Rating	Value
14. Process is designed to provide process metrics.	1	2	2
15. Process metrics are recorded and analyzed, not just collected.	1	1	1
16. Documentation is thorough, accurate, and easily understood.	2	2	4
17. Process contains required value-added steps.	3	2	6
18. Process eliminates all non-value-added steps.	2	2	4
19. Process guarantees accountability.	2	1	2
20. Process provides incentives for compliance and penalties for avoidance or circumvention.	1	1	1
21. Process is standardized across all appropriate departments and remote sites.	2	2	4
22. Process is streamlined as much as possible and practical.	3	2	6
23. Process is automated wherever practical but only after streamlining.	1	2	2
24. Process integrates with all other appropriate processes.	2	1	2

Evaluating Process Documentation

An important aspect of any process is the documentation that accompanies it. Many shops develop excellent processes but fail to document them adequately. After an initially successful implementation of the process, many of these procedures become unused due to lack of documentation, particularly as new staff members who are unfamiliar with the process attempt to use it.

Some documentation is usually better than none at all, but adding value and quality to it increases the likelihood of the proper use of the process it describes. Evaluating the quality of documentation can easily become a very subjective activity. Few techniques exist to objectively quantify the quality and value of process documentation. That is why the following methodology is so unique and beneficial. I developed this approach over several years while working with many clients who were struggling with ways to determine both the quality and the value of their process documentation.

The purpose of evaluating the *quality* of content is to show to what degree the material is suitable for use. The purpose of evaluating its *value* is to show how important the documentation is to the support of the process and how important the process is to the support of the business. The quality of the content of documentation is evaluated with 10 common characteristics of usability. Table 20-4 lists these characteristics of quality of content and gives a definition of each.

Table 20-4   Documentation Quality Characteristics and Definitions

No.	Quality Characteristic	Definition
1.	Ownership	This characteristic rates the degree to which the three key ownership roles—process owner, documentation custodian, and technical writer—are clearly identified, understood, and supported. For some processes, the same individual may have all three roles. In most cases, the documentation custodian maintains the process documentation and reports to the process owner.
2.	Readability	This characteristic rates the clarity and simplicity of the written documentation. Items evaluated include the use of common words, terms, and phrases; correct spelling; proper use of grammar; and minimal use of acronyms, along with explanations of those that are used but not widely known. This characteristic especially looks at how well the level of the material matches the skill and experience level of the audience.
3.	Accuracy	This characteristic rates the technical accuracy of the material.
4.	Thoroughness	This characteristic rates how well the documentation has succeeded in including all relevant information.
5.	Format	This characteristic rates the overall organization of the material; how easy it is to follow; how well it keeps a consistent level of technical depth; and to what degree it is documenting and describing an actual process rather than merely duplicating tables, spreadsheets, and metrics.
6.	Accessibility	This characteristic rates the ease or difficulty of accessibility.
7.	Currency	This characteristic rates the degree to which the current version of the documentation is up to date and the frequency with which it is kept current.
8.	Ease of updates	This characteristic rates the relative ease or difficulty with which the documentation can be updated, including revision dates and distribution of new versions.

No.	Quality Characteristic	Definition
9.	Effectiveness	This characteristic rates the overall usability of the documentation, including the use of appropriate examples, graphics, color coding, use on multiple platforms, and compliance with existing standards if available.
10.	Accountability	This characteristic rates the degree to which the documentation is being read, understood, and effectively used; all appropriate users are identified and held accountable for proper use of the documentation.

Table 20-5 Documentation Value Characteristics and Definitions

No.	Value Characteristic	Definition
1.	Criticality of the process	This characteristic describes how critical the process detailed by this documentation is to the successful business of the company.
2.	Frequency of use	This characteristic describes how frequently the documentation is used or referenced.
3.	Number of users	This characteristic describes the approximate number of personnel who will likely want or need to use this documentation.
4.	Variety of users	This characteristic describes the variety of different functional areas or skill levels of personnel who will likely use this documentation.
5.	Impact of Nonuse	This characteristic describes the level of adverse impact that is likely to occur if the documentation is not used properly.

The characteristic in both the quality and value figures were rated on a 0 to 3 scale based on the degree to which elements of each characteristic were met. Table 20-6 describes these ratings and their meanings.

Table 20-6 Rating Quality and Value Characteristics of Documentation

Rating	Description
0	None or an insignificant amount of the characteristic has been met.
1	A small portion of the characteristic has been met.

Table 20-6   Rating Quality and Value Characteristics of Documentation Continued

Rating	Description
2	A significant, though not entire, portion of the characteristic has been met or is present.
3	All aspects of the characteristic have been met or are present.

Benefits of the Methodology to Evaluate Process Documentation

There are three major benefits to this method of documentation evaluation:

1. It gives a snapshot of the quality of existing documentation. It supplies this at a particular point in time, particularly documentation of high value. If improvements are made to the material which result in new ratings, they can be compared to the current rating.
2. This method provides the ability to customize the criteria for measuring the quality and value of documentation. This allows for an evaluator to reflect changes in priority, strategy, or direction. In this way, the methodology remains applicable regardless of the specific criteria used.
3. It allows for comparisons. The third benefit of this method is that it allows for comparisons of documentation between different types of processes within an infrastructure using the same standard of measure.

A client at a satellite broadcasting company recently asked me to evaluate a variety of their infrastructure process documentation. Table 20-7 lists the 32 pieces of documentation that I assessed and shows the wide diversity of material involved in the review.

Table 20-7   Types of Infrastructure Documentation Evaluated for Quality and Value

Number	Description of Documentation
1.	Procedure for logging all calls
2.	Method for prioritizing calls
3.	Determining ownership of problems
4.	How to escalate problems

Number	Description of Documentation
5.	Resolution status of problems
6.	Trending analysis from clarify viewer
7.	Problem management performance reports
8.	Responsibilities of help desk staff
9.	User feedback procedures
10.	Use of training plans
11.	Analysis of cell phone invoices
12.	Analysis of monthly cost trending
13.	VMS/UNIX initiation procedures
14.	New equipment planning request
15.	Use of site scan tool
16.	Monthly review of vendor performance
17.	Change management procedures
18.	Charter of domain architecture teams
19.	Monthly IT business review
20.	Submitting request for service form
21.	Administration of service-level agreements
22.	Disaster-recovery plan
23.	Application support
24.	Work initiation process
25.	Systems development life cycle
26.	Project management procedures
27.	Production acceptance process
28.	Data-center administration
29.	Backup and restore procedures
30.	Production scheduling process
31.	Network and server operations
32.	File transfer procedures

Table 20-8 lists the results of assessing the *quality* characteristics of each piece of documentation and shows the variety of numerical totals that resulted. Table 20-9 lists the results of assessing the *value* characteristics for each of the same pieces of documentation. Next we'll discuss how these two pieces of information can be used together to indicate which pieces of documentation should be improved upon first.

Table 20-8   Ratings of Quality Characteristics for Various Types of Infrastructure Process Documentation

Documentation	Ownership	Readability	Accuracy	Thoroughness	Format
17. Change Management	3	3	3	2	3
1. Logging Calls	3	3	3	3	2
2. Prioritizing Calls	3	3	3	3	2
24. Work Initiation	3	3	2	3	3
4. Escalation	3	3	3	3	2
8. Resp. Service Desk Staff	2	3	3	3	3
14. New Equip. Planning	3	2	3	3	2
20. Request for Service	3	3	3	3	3
29. Backups/Restores	2	2	3	3	3
3. Ownership of Problems	2	3	2	3	2
12. Monthly Cost Trending	3	2	3	3	2
25. Sys. Dev. Life Cycle	2	3	2	2	3
26. Project Management	2	3	2	2	3
9. User Feedback	3	3	2	2	2
13. VMS/UNIX Procedures	2	3	3	3	2
15. Site Scan Tool	2	3	3	3	2
23. Application Support	3	3	3	2	2
32. File Transfers	2	3	2	3	3
7. Prob.Mgmt.Perf. Report	2	2	3	2	2
16. Monthly Vendor Review	2	2	3	2	2
19. Monthly IT Bus. Review	3	3	3	2	1
28. Data Ctr Adminstrative	2	3	2	3	3
11. Cell Phone Invoices	3	2	3	3	1
5. Resolution of Problems	2	3	2	2	2
18. Domain Arch. Teams	2	3	3	1	2
27. Production Acceptance	2	3	2	2	2
30. Prod Sched/Processing	2	3	1	2	3
31. Network/Server Ops	2	3	1	2	3
6. Trending Analysis	2	2	2	2	1
10. Training plans	1	3	2	1	2
21. SLA Administration	1	3	2	2	2
22. Disaster Recovery	3	3	2	1	1

Accessability	Currency	Updatability	Effectiveness	Accountability	Total
2	3	3	3	3	28
3	3	2	3	2	27
3	3	2	3	2	27
2	3	3	3	2	27
2	2	3	3	2	26
2	3	2	3	2	26
3	3	2	2	3	26
2	3	2	2	2	26
3	3	2	3	2	26
3	3	2	3	2	25
2	3	3	3	1	25
2	3	3	2	2	25
2	3	3	2	2	25
3	2	2	2	3	24
2	2	3	2	2	24
2	3	2	2	2	24
2	2	3	2	2	24
3	2	2	2	2	24
2	3	3	2	2	23
2	3	3	2	2	23
1	3	3	2	2	23
3	1	2	2	2	23
1	3	2	2	2	22
3	3	3	2	1	21
2	2	1	2	2	21
2	2	2	2	2	21
3	1	2	2	2	21
3	1	2	2	2	21
2	3	2	2	2	20
2	2	2	2	1	18
1	2	2	2	1	18
1	1	2	2	2	18

Table 20-9 Ratings of Value Characteristics for Various Types of Infrastructure Process Documentation

Documentation	Criticality	Frequency	User Number	User Variety	Impact	Totals
17. Change Management	3	3	3	3	3	15
4. Escalation	3	3	2	3	3	14
22. Disaster Recovery	3	2	3	3	3	14
27. Production Acceptance	3	2	3	3	3	14
29. Backups/Restores	3	3	3	2	3	14
32. File Transfers	3	3	3	3	2	14
2. Prioritizing Calls	2	3	2	3	3	13
3. Ownership of Problems	2	3	2	3	3	13
9. User Feedback	2	3	3	3	2	13
18. Domain Architecture Teams	2	3	2	3	3	13
19. Monthly IT Business Review	3	2	2	3	3	13
20. Request for Service	2	3	3	3	2	13
21. SLA Administration	2	3	3	3	1	13
30. Production Scheduling/ Processing	3	3	2	2	3	13
31. Network/Server Operations	3	2	2	3	3	13
5. Resolution Status	2	3	2	3	2	12
15. Site Scan Tool	3	2	2	2	3	12
23. Application Support	3	2	2	2	3	12
24. Work Initiation	2	2	3	3	2	12
25. System Development Life Cycle	2	2	3	3	2	12
26. Project Management	2	2	3	3	2	12
1. Logging Calls	2	3	2	2	2	11
6. Trending Analysis (C/V)	2	2	2	3	2	11
7. Problem Mgmt. Perf. Reports	2	2	2	3	2	11
11. Cell Phone Invoices	1	3	3	3	1	11
12. Monthly Cost Trending	2	2	2	3	2	11

Documentation	Criticality	Frequency	User Number	User Variety	Impact	Totals
13. VMS/UNIX Procedures	3	1	2	2	3	11
16. Monthly Vendor Review	2	2	2	3	2	11
10. Training plans	3	1	2	1	3	10
8. Responsibilities of Ser. Desk Staff	2	1	2	1	3	9
14. New Equipment Planning	2	1	2	2	2	9
28. Data Center Administrative	2	2	2	2	1	9

Once both the quality and value characteristics are evaluated, the two sets of attributes can be shown on a quality/value matrix (see Figure 20-1). Quality ratings are shown along the horizontal axis increasing to the right. Value ratings are shown along the vertical axis increasing as it ascends. Each axis is scaled from the lowest quality and value ratings up to the maximum possible. The benefit of this matrix is that it depicts both the value and quality of each piece of documentation on a single chart.

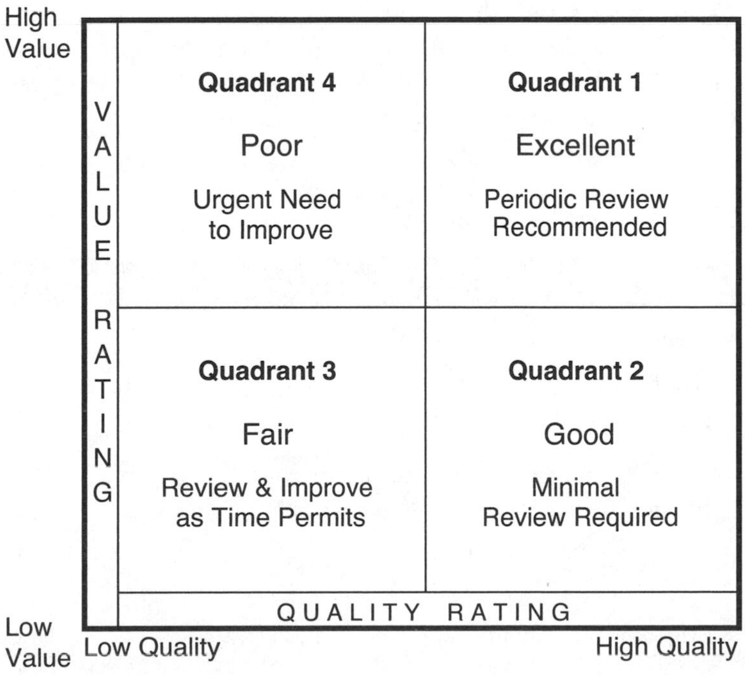

Figure 20-1   Quality/Value Matrix

The matrix is then divided into four quadrants. Points in the upper-right quadrant (1) represent documentation that is both high in value and high in quality. This is the desired place to be and constitutes excellent documentation that requires little or no improvements and only periodic reviews to ensure continued high quality. Points in the lower-right quadrant (2) signify material that is high in quality but of a lower value to a particular infrastructure. Documentation in this area is generally rated as good but could be improved.

The lower-left quadrant (3) represents documentation that is relatively low in both value and quality. Material in this area is designated as only fair and needs to be improved in quality. Since the value is low, improvements are suggested on a time-permitting basis. Points in the upper-left quadrant (4) indicate documentation that is high in value but low in quality. Documentation in this area is considered to be at the greatest risk since it represents material that is of particular importance to this organization but is of poor quality. Documentation in this quarter of the matrix should be improved as soon as possible to prevent adverse impact to processes, procedures, and services.

Table 20-10 shows the combinations of the totals of the quality ratings from Table 20-8 and the totals of the value ratings from Table 20-9. Each entry is again numbered with the identifiers used in Table 20-7. Figure 20-2 shows the quality/value matrix populated with the identifiers of each piece of documentation in their appropriate quadrants. This depiction clearly shows which pieces of documentation need the greatest improvement in the most urgent manner.

Table 20-10 Quality and Value Ratings

Rating	Description	Quality	Value	Quad
17	Change management	28	15	1
4	Escalation	26	14	1
2	Prioritizing calls	27	13	1
24	Work initiation	27	12	1
20	Request for service	26	13	1
3	Ownership of problems	25	13	1
25	Systems development life cycle	25	12	1
26	Project management	25	12	1
9	User feedback	24	13	1

Rating	Description	Quality	Value	Quad
15	Site scan tool	24	12	1
23	Application support	24	12	1
29	Backups/restores	26	14	1
32	File transfers	24	14	1
1	Logging calls	27	11	2
8	Responsibilities of help-desk staff	26	9	2
14	New equipment planning	26	9	2
12	Monthly cost trending	25	11	2
13	VMS/UNIX procedures	24	11	2
7	Problem mgmt. perf reports	23	11	3
16	Monthly vendor review	23	11	3
11	Cell phone invoices	22	11	3
28	Data center administrative	23	9	3
6	Trending analysis (clarify viewer)	20	11	3
10	Training plans	18	10	3
27	Production acceptance	21	14	4
19	Monthly IT business review	23	13	4
18	Domain architecture teams	21	13	4
30	Production scheduling/processing	21	13	4
31	Network/server operations	21	13	4
5	Resolution status	21	12	4
21	SLA administration	18	13	4
22	Disaster recovery	18	14	4

Those identifiers closest to the upper-left corner of quadrant 4 are in the greatest need of quick improvement because they are of the highest value to the organization and yet have the lowest level of quality. In this specific evaluation, it happened to be the documentation for disaster recovery denoted by identifier 22. Once these particular pieces of documentation are identified in the populated quality/value matrix, Table 20-8 can be used to determine which specific characteristics of documentation quality need to be improved most.

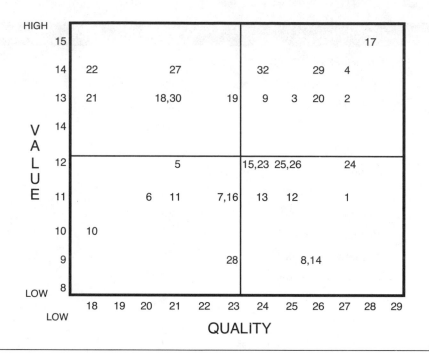

Figure 20–2 Populated Quality/Value Matrix

Software technology in the form of statistical analysis programs that integrate with any number of graphical presentation products provide a means to automate the generation of these displays and reports.

Real Life Experience—No Calm Before this Storm

During the Summer of 2004, I worked with a mortgage client in Southern California which had a large, financial processing center in Tampa, Florida, close to the shore. Reports surfaced that a tropical depression off the coast was fast developing into major Hurricane Charley and was headed directly toward Tampa.

A number of us participated in technical contingency planning to relocate operations to recovery sites in either Chicago or New York. Amidst all these technical discussions came the voice of a business user who meekly asked, "What about the loan documents?"

It turned out that there were thousands of loan documents awaiting final funding that were in cardboard boxes on the first floor of the building. After funding, the documents would be scanned and stored as electronic images.

Forecasters predicted 8- to 10-foot (2.5- to 3.0-meter) wave surges resulting in certain ruin of the documents. There was no documentation on how to recover the documents. Suddenly, all of the recovery efforts focused on moving the documents to safer, higher elevations.

All turned out well in the end. The loan documents were all safely stored at higher ground and the hurricane made a sharp right turn just before landfall and missed Tampa altogether. The company did decide to scan the loan hardcopies earlier in the process and to document the recovery and relocation of the documents.

Summary

First we discussed the fact that processes must be well-designed, standardized, and streamlined before any attempt is made at automation. And then automation should be done only on those parts of a process for which it makes sense. Next we looked at the key activities involved with automating a process and emphasized the importance of following the proper sequence of steps.

Then we talked about ways to evaluate infrastructure processes in terms of robustness. We looked at both weighted and nonweighted rating methods using 24 attributes of a robust process.

An effective methodology for evaluating process documentation concluded this chapter. We looked at the importance of evaluating both the quality and the value of the documentation content, giving 10 quality characteristics and 5 value characteristics. Then we offered 32 types of infrastructure documentation that might be evaluated for quality and value and saw how the resulting ratings can be plotted on a quality/value matrix. Where they fall on the matrix indicates which documentation needs to be improved the quickest to keep infrastructure processes as robust as possible.

Test Your Understanding

1. Automation types usually come in the form of either hardware-only or software-only but not a combination of the two. (True or False)
2. Many shops develop excellent processes but fail to document them adequately. (True or False)
3. When planning for the automation of a process, the correct sequence of activities is:
   a. standardize, streamline, evaluate, automate
   b. streamline, evaluate, standardize, automate
   c. evaluate, automate, streamline, standardize
   d. standardize, evaluate, automate, streamline
4. Two primary characteristics used to evaluate documentation are _____ and _____.
5. Discuss some of the drawbacks of automating a process before it has been streamlined.

Suggested Further Readings

1. *A Handbook of Techniques for Formative Evaluation*; 1999; George, Judith W., Cowan, John; FALMER/KP
2. *Technical Translation: Usability Strategies for Translating Technical Documentation*; 2006; Byrne, Jody; Springer
3. www.mycoted.com/Nominal_Group_Technique

CHAPTER 21

Integrating Systems Management Processes

Introduction

At this point we have thoroughly discussed the 12 processes of systems management and how to develop the procedures that comprise and support them in a robust manner. Now we will look more closely at the various relationships between these 12 processes to learn which ones integrate with which in the best manner. Understanding to what degree a process is tactical or strategic in nature helps us understand the integrating relationships between them.

Distinguishing Strategic Processes from Tactical Processes

Most IT professionals seem capable of distinguishing between strategic and tactical activities. But it has been my experience that infrastructure personnel cannot always apply these differences to system management processes. Table 21-1 lists some of the key differences between strategic and tactical processes of systems management.

Table 21-1 Differences between Strategic Processes and Tactical Processes

Strategic	Tactical
1. Long range in nature	1. Short range in nature
2. Two- to three-year focus	2. Day-to-day focus
3. Supports long-term business goals	3. Supports short-term SLAs
4. May require months to see results	4. Should see results within a few days or weeks
5. May require additional budget approvals to implement	5. Should already be in the existing budget

It is important to understand which systems management processes are strategic and which are tactical because each process integrates with, and depends on, other processes for optimal use. For example, production acceptance, change management, and problem management all interact with each other when implemented properly. Knowing which of these three key processes is tactical versus strategic helps to better understand their relationships to each other. Two processes that are both tactical will interact differently than two processes that are strategic, and each of these pairs will interact differently from a pair that is a mixture of strategic and tactical. Knowledge of a process's orientation can also assist in selecting process owners who are more aligned with that process's orientation. Some prospective owners may have more ability in the strategic area, while others may be better suited for tactical processes.

Identifying Strategic Processes

We have described and given formal definitions for each of the 12 systems management processes in previous chapters. Examining these definitions and combining this analysis with the properties of strategic processes given in Table 21-1 results in five of these processes being designated as strategic:

1. Production acceptance
2. Capacity planning
3. Strategic security
4. Business continuity
5. Facilities management

While all of these strategic processes have tactical aspects associated with them, the significant value of each one lies more in its strategic attributes. For example, the tactical part of production acceptance, capacity planning, and disaster recovery involves the important activities of deploying production software, installing hardware upgrades, and restoring business operations, respectively. But analysts responsible for these critical events could not execute them successfully without a strategic focus involving thorough planning and preparation.

Similarly, strategic security and facilities management tactically monitor the logical and physical environments for unauthorized access or disturbance on a continual basis. But the overriding objective of ensuring the ongoing integrity and use of the logical and physical environments requires significant strategic thinking to plan, enforce, and execute the necessary policies and procedures.

Identifying Tactical Processes

We now turn our attention from strategic processes to tactical ones. Employing a method similar to what we used in the strategic area, we identify seven processes as being tactical in nature (as detailed in the following list). Just as the strategic processes contained tactical elements, some of the tactical processes contain strategic elements. For example, the network and storage management processes involve not only the installation of network and storage equipment but the planning, ordering, and scheduling of such hardware as well—activities that require months of advance preparation. But the majority of activities associated with these two processes are tactical in nature, involving real-time monitoring of network and storage resources to ensure they are available and in sufficient quantity.

1. Availability
2. Performance and tuning
3. Change management
4. Problem management
5. Storage management
6. Network management
7. Configuration management

The Value of Distinguishing Strategic from Tactical Processes

There are four reasons to identifying systems management processes as either strategic or tactical in nature:

1. **Some analysts are strategically oriented while others are tactically oriented.** Understanding which processes are strategically or tactically oriented can facilitate a more suitable match when selecting a process owner for a particular discipline.
2. **The emphasis an infrastructure places on specific processes can indicate its orientation toward systems management processes.** An infrastructure that focuses mostly on tactical processes tends to be more reactive in nature, while those focusing on strategic processes tend to be more proactive in nature.
3. **Managers can identify which of their 12 infrastructure processes need the most refinement by assessing them.** Knowing the orientation of the processes requiring the most improvements indicates whether the necessary improvements are tactical or strategic in nature.
4. **Categorizing processes as either tactical or strategic assists in addressing integration issues.** In a world-class infrastructure, each of the systems management processes integrate with one or more of the other processes for optimal effectiveness. Understanding which processes are tactical and which are strategic helps facilitate this integration.

In brief, they are summarized as follow:

1. Facilitates the selection of process owners
2. Indicates an infrastructure's orientation
3. Quantifies orientation of improvement needs
4. Optimizes the integration of processes

Relationships Between Strategic and Tactical Processes

As previously mentioned, each of the 12 systems management processes integrate with, and depend on, other processes for optimal use. In fact, we are about to see that all of them interact with at least one of the other processes. Several interact with more than half of the remaining total. Some processes have no significant interaction, or relationship, with another specific process. So how do we know which processes form what type of relationships with which others?

Figure 21-1 gives us these answers. Each of the 12 processes is listed across the top and down the left side of the matrix and is designated as either tactical or strategic. If the combination of two tactical processes results in a significant process relationship, then the interaction of the two is designated T for *tactical*. If the combination of two strategic processes results in a significant process relationship, then the interaction of the two is designated S for *strategic*. If a significant relationship is the result of the combination of a tactical and a strategic discipline, then the interaction is designated as M for *mixture*. If the combination of any two processes, either tactical or strategic, results in no significant interaction, then the intersecting box is blank.

	(T) AV	(T) PT	(S) PA	(T) CM	(T) PM	(T) SM	(T) NM	(T) CF	(S) CP	(S) SE	(S) BC	(S) FM
(T)AV				T_1	T_2		T_3					
(T)PT					T_4	T_5	T_6		M_7			
(S)PA				M_8	M_9				S_{10}	S_{11}		
(T)CM	T_1		M_8		T_{12}	T_{13}	T_{14}	T_{15}	M_{16}	M_{17}		
(T)PM	T_2	T_4	M_9	T_{12}			T_{18}					
(T)SM		T_5		T_{13}					M_{19}		M_{20}	
(T)NM	T_3	T_6		T_{14}	T_{18}				M_{21}	M_{22}		
(T)CF				T_{15}								
(S)CP		M_7	S_{10}	M_{16}		M_{19}	M_{21}					S_{23}
(S)SE			S_{11}	M_{17}			M_{22}					
(S)BC						M_{20}						S_{24}
(S)FM									S_{23}		S_{24}	

Legend

AV – Availability management PM – Problem management CP – Capacity planning
PT – Performance and tuning SM – Storage management SE – Strategic security
PA – Production acceptance NM – Network management BC – Business continuity
CM – Change management CF – Configuration management FM – Facilities management

T – Both processes in the relationship are tactical.
S – Both processes in the relationship are strategic.
M – The relationship is a mixture of tactical and strategic processes.
(T) – Process is tactical in nature.
(S) – Process is strategic in nature.

Figure 21-1 Relationships of Strategic and Tactical Processes

Subscripts refer to the explanations of relationships described in the forthcoming section titled "Examining the Integrated Relationships between Strategic and Tactical Processes."

The matrix in Figure 21-1 supplies several pieces of valuable information. It represents which processes are designated as tactical and which are strategic. It shows how each process interacts (or does not interact) with others and whether that interaction is entirely tactical, strategic, or a mixture of the two. Finally, the matrix quantifies which processes have the most interaction and which have the least. Knowledge of these interactions leads to better managed infrastructures, and managers of well-run infrastructures understand and utilize these relationships. We will examine the generic issues of integrating those processes that are solely tactical, solely strategic, and a mixture of the two.

Difficulties with Integrating Solely Tactical Processes

Referring to Figure 21-1, we see there are 11 relationships involving solely tactical processes. We list these 11 relationships in Table 21-2. One of the difficulties of integrating solely tactical processes is the tendency to emphasize only short-term goals and objectives. Tactical processes by their nature have very limited planning horizons, sometimes forcing an hour-to-hour focus of activities. If left unchecked, this tendency could undermine efforts at long-range, strategic planning.

Table 21-2   Relationships of Solely Tactical Processes

Relationship Number	1st Strategic Process	2nd Tactical Process
1	Availability	Change management
2	Availability	Problem management
3	Availability	Network management
4	Performance and tuning	Problem management
5	Performance and tuning	Storage management
6	Performance and tuning	Network management
7	Change management	Problem management
8	Change management	Storage management
9	Change management	Network management
10	Change management	Configuration management
11	Problem management	Network management

Another concern with purely tactical processes is that most of these now involve 24/7 coverage. The emphasis on around-the-clock operation can often infuse an organization with a reactive, firefighting type of mentality rather than a more proactive mentality. A third issue arises out of the focus on reactive, continuous operation, and that is the threat of burnout. Shops that devote most of their systems management efforts on tactical processes run the risk of losing their most precious resource—human talent.

Difficulties with Integrating Solely Strategic Processes

There are four relationships based solely on strategic processes and these are listed in Table 21-3. One of the difficulties with strategic relationships is that a continuing emphasis on long-range planning sometimes results in key initiatives not getting implemented. Thorough planning needs to be followed with effective execution. Another issue that more directly involves the staff is that most infrastructure analysts are more tactical than strategic in their outlooks, actions, and attitudes. These relationships must be managed by individuals with a competent, strategic focus. A final concern with strategic relationships is that budgets for strategic resources, be they software, hardware or human, often get diverted to more urgent needs.

Table 21-3   Relationships of Solely Strategic Processes

Relationship Number	1st Strategic Process	2nd Tactical Process
1	Production acceptance	Capacity planning
2	Production acceptance	Strategic security
3	Capacity planning	Facilities management
4	Business continuity	Facilities management

Difficulties with Integrating Tactical and Strategic Processes

Referring again to Figure 21-1, we see there are nine relationships formed by a combination of tactical and strategic processes. These nine are listed in Table 21-4. The first, and likely most obvious, difficulty is the mixing of tactical and strategic processes, the orientations of which may appear at odds with each other. Conventional thinking would conclude that short-range tactical actions do not mix well with long-range strategic plans. But common goals of reliable, responsive systems, excellent customer service, and the accomplishment of business objectives can help to reconcile these apparent discrepancies.

Table 21-4   Relationships of Tactical and Strategic Processes

No.	Tactical Process	Strategic Process
1	Performance and tuning	Capacity management
2	Change management	Production acceptance
3	Change management	Capacity management
4	Change management	Strategic security
5	Problem management	Production acceptance
6	Storage management	Capacity management
7	Storage management	Business continuity
8	Network management	Strategic security
9	Network management	Capacity management

Another concern with integrating these two dissimilar types of processes is that it throws together process owners whose orientation between short- and long-range focus may conflict. Again, the emphasis on common goals can help to alleviate these divergent views.

A final issue involving relationships of mixed processes is the need to recognize which elements are truly tactical and which are truly strategic. For example, the combination of tactical change management and strategic capacity management is a mixed-process relationship. But some changes may require weeks of advanced planning, resulting in a strategic focus on what is normally a tactical discipline. Similarly, the last step of a major capacity upgrade is the installation of the hardware; this is a tactical activity associated with a normally strategic discipline. Knowing and understanding these differences can help to better facilitate the relationships of mixed processes.

Examining the Integrated Relationships Between Strategic and Tactical Processes

The previous sections discussed generic issues associated with integrating processes. Here we will look at each of the 24 relationships shown in Figure 21-1 in greater detail (in the order of the subscripts in the figure).

1. **AV/CM(T).** Availability and change management are tactical processes. The relationship here centers mostly on scheduled outages which should be handled as scheduled changes. Unscheduled outages should be treated as problems.

2. **AV/PM(T).** Both availability and problem management are tactical processes and involve handling outages and problems on a real-time basis. Any incident that impacts continuous availability is referred to as an *outage* and it is usually handled as a problem. Just as problems can be categorized as to severity, urgency, priority, and impact, outages can be categorized. A scheduled outage that results in a longer-than-planned downtime may be logged as a problem, but in all likelihood, it will be a lower priority than an unscheduled outage. Similarly, outages occurring during prime time are no doubt more severe than those occurring during the off-shifts.

3. **AV/NM(T).** Networks now play a crucial role in ensuring online availability. Outages of entire networks are rare these days because of the use of highly reliable network components and redundant configurations. When network outages do occur, the availability of several systems is usually impacted due to the integrated nature of today's systems.

4. **PT/PM(T).** Performance and tuning and problem management are very closely related (often being thought of as the same issue), but there are important differences. Slow online response times, long-running jobs, excessive loading times, and ever-increasing tape backup times are performance problems since they directly affect end-user services. As such, they should be treated as problems and handled through the problem management process. But just as not all problems should be considered performance issues, not all performance issues should be considered problems. The ongoing maintenance of indices, directories, extents, page space, and swap areas; the number and size of buffers; the amount of local memory; and the allocation

of cache storage are normally regarded as sound, preventative performance and tuning activities rather than problems. When done in a timely and proper manner, they should prevent problems as opposed to causing them.

5. **PT/SM(T).** Lack of sufficient storage space, including main memory, virtual storage, cache buffering, raw physical disk storage, or logical storage groups can often result in poor online or batch performance.

6. **PT/NM(T).** The configuration of various network devices such as routers, repeaters, hubs, and network servers can affect online performance just as various software parameters such as network retries, line speeds, and the number and size of buffers can alter transaction response times.

7. **PT/CP(M).** This is our first relationship that mixes a tactical process (performance and tuning) with a strategic one (capacity planning). Poor performance and slow response times can certainly be attributed to lack of adequate capacity planning. If insufficient resources are available due to larger-than-expected workload growth or due to a greater number of total or concurrent users, then poor performance will no doubt result.

8. **PA/CM(M).** This relationship is another mixture of tactical and strategic processes. New applications and major upgrades to existing applications should be brought to the attention of and discussed at a change review board. But the board should understand that for these types of implementations, a far more comprehensive production acceptance process is needed rather than just the change management process.

9. **PA/PM(M).** This relationship between strategic production acceptance and tactical problem management occurs whenever a new application is being proposed or a major upgrade to an existing application is being planned. (For the purposes of this discussion, I will use the terms *problem management* and *level 1 service-desk staff* synonymously.)

As soon as the new system or upgrade is approved, the various infrastructure support groups, including level 1 service-desk staff, become involved. By the time deployment day arrives, the service-desk staff should have already been trained on the new application and should be able to anticipate the types of calls from users.

During the first week or two of deployment, level 2 support personnel for the application should be on the service desk to assist with call resolution, to aid in cross-training level 1 staff, and to analyze call activity. The analysis should include call volume trends and what types of calls are coming in from what types of users.

10. **PA/CP(S)**. This is the first of three systems management relationships in which both processes are strategic. New applications or major upgrades to existing applications need to go through a capacity planning process to ensure that adequate resources are in place prior to deployment.

    These resources include servers, processors, memory, channels, disk storage, tape drives and cartridges, network bandwidth, and various facilitation items such as floor space, air conditioning, and conditioned and redundant electrical power. Commercial ERP systems such as SAP, Oracle, or PeopleSoft may require upgrades to the hosting operating system or database.

    The capacity planning for a new application may also determine that additional resources are needed for the desktop environment. These may include increased processing power, extensions to memory, or special features such as fonts, scripts, or color capability. One of my clients implemented SAP for global use and required variations of language and currency for international use.

11. **PA/SE(S)**. This is another all-strategic relationship. New applications should have clearly defined security policies in place prior to deployment. An application security administrator should be identified and authorized to manage activities such as password expirations and resets, new-user authorization, retiring userids, and training of the help-desk staff.

12. **CM/PM(T)**. Change management and problem management are directly related to each other in the sense that some changes result in problems and some problems, in attempting resolution, result in changes. The number of changes that eventually cause problems and the number of problems that eventually cause changes are two good metrics to consider using. The collection and analysis of these metrics can be more readily facilitated by implementing the same online database tool to log and track both problems and changes.

13. **CM/SM(T)**. Changes to the type, size, or configuration of disk storage, tape libraries, main memory, or cache buffering should all go through an infrastructure's change management process.

14. **CM/NM(T)**. Changing hubs, routers, switches, components within these devices, or the amounts or allocations of bandwidth should be coordinated through a centralized change management process. Some shops have a separate change management process just for network modifications, but this is not recommended.

15. **CM/CF(T)**. Any changes to hardware or software configurations should be administered through both the change management process (to implement the change) and the configuration management process (to document and maintain the change). The types of configuration changes that apply here include application software, system software and hardware, network software and hardware, microcode, and physical and logical diagrams of network, data center, and facilities hardware.

16. **CM/CP(M)**. The strategic side of this relationship involves long-range capacity planning. Once the type, size, and implementation date of a particular resource is identified, it can then be passed over to the more tactical change management process to be scheduled, communicated, and coordinated.

17. **CM/SE(M)**. This relationship again mixes the tactical with the strategic. The strategic portion of security involves corporate security policies and enforcement. Changes such as security settings on firewalls, new policies on the use of passwords, or upgrades to virus software should all through the change management process.

18. **PM/NM(T)**. The reactive part of network management that impacts individual users is directly tied to problem management. The same set of tools, databases, and call-in numbers used by the help desk for problem management should be used for network problems.

19. **SM/CP(M)**. Capacity planning is sometimes thought of only in terms of servers, processors, or network bandwidth, but most any capacity plan needs to factor in storage in all its various forms, including main memory, cache, disk arrays, server disks, tape drives and cartridges, and even desktop and workstation storage.

20. **SM/BC(M)**. One of the key aspects of business continuity is the ability to restore valid copies of critical data from backup tapes. One of the key responsibilities of storage management is to ensure that restorable copies of critical data are available in the event of a disaster, so there is an obvious relationship between these two processes.

21. **NM/CP(M)**. Just as network management should not have a separate change management process, it also should not have a separate capacity planning process for network resources such as hubs, routers, switches, repeaters, and especially bandwidth. This relationship is often overlooked in shops where the network has grown or changed at a rate much different from that of the data center.

22. **NM/SE(M)**. The expanding connectivity of companies worldwide and the proliferation of the Internet exposes many networks to the risk of unauthorized access to corporate assets, as well as to the intentional or inadvertent altering of corporate data. Managing network security creates a natural relationship between these two processes.

23. **CP/FM(S)**. An element of capacity planning sometimes overlooked is the effect that upgraded equipment has on the physical facilities of a data center. More than once a new piece of equipment has arrived in a computer room only to find there were no circuits or plugs or outlets with the proper adapters on which to connect it. Robust capacity planning processes will always include facilities management as part of its requirements.

24. **BC/FM(S)**. This is the final all-strategic relationship. Statistics indicate that most IT disasters are confined or localized to a small portion of the data center. As a result, proper facilities management can often prevent potential disasters. A comprehensive business continuity plan that includes periodic testing and dry runs can often uncover shortcomings in facilities management that can be corrected to prevent potential future disasters.

Real Life Experience—ITIL Uses a Different Tactic with Processes

The IT Infrastructure Library (ITIL), in my opinion, is one of the best frameworks of best practices for infrastructure processes. But there is one aspect of ITIL terminology that tends to go against common vernacular. This is its description of tactical processes.

Most IT professionals with whom I have worked can easily distinguish between the terms 'strategic' and 'tactical'. But ITIL applies the 'tactical' term to describe processes that are longer term in nature and customer- or management-oriented, which many of us would term as 'strategic' (see Chapter 6, "Comparison to ITIL Processes"). For the shorter-term, end-user-oriented processes, ITIL uses the term 'operational', which many of us would term as 'tactical'.

Confused? You are not alone. I have certified more than 1,000 individuals on the fundamentals of ITIL and this is one of the areas most misunderstood when it comes to ITIL terminology. Clearly, this is one of the few aspects of ITIL where the framers decided to use a different tact.

Significance of Systems Management Process Relationships

As previously mentioned, Figure 21-1 displays a wealth of information about the relationships of systems management processes. One final subject worth discussing is those processes that have the greatest number of relationships with others, as well as the significance of such information.

Table 21-5 is a sorted list of the number of relationships associated with each discipline. This list also represents the relative importance of individual system management functions. We see that change management has the highest number with eight. This should not be surprising. In today's complex infrastructure environments, the quality and robustness of change management has a direct effect on the stability and responsiveness of IT services offered.

Table 21-5   Number of Associated Relationships by Discipline

Processes	Number of Relationships	Related Processes
1. Change management	8	Availability; performance and tuning; production acceptance; configuration management; capacity planning; network management; storage management; strategic security
2. Network management	6	Availability; performance and tuning; problem management; change management; capacity planning; strategic security

Processes	Number of Relationships	Related Processes
3. Capacity planning	6	Performance and tuning; change management; production acceptance; network management; storage management; facilities management
4. Problem management	5	Availability; performance and tuning; change management; production acceptance; network management
5. Production acceptance	4	Problem management; change management; capacity planning; strategic security
6. Storage management	4	Performance and tuning; change management; capacity planning; disaster recovery
7. Performance/tuning	3	Problem management; capacity planning; storage management
8. Availability	2	Problem management; change management
9. Strategic security	2	Change management; production acceptance
10. Business Continuity	2	Storage management; facilities management
11. Facilities management	2	Capacity planning; disaster recovery
12. Configuration management	1	Change management

This tells us that one of the first places to look to improve an IT infrastructure is its change management function. Developing it into a more robust process will also likely improve several of the other processes with which it frequently interacts. Speaking of the frequency of interactions, I have not included the relationships of change management to performance and tuning, disaster recovery, or facilities management due to the low frequency of major changes that occur in these areas.

Problem management is next on the list with five relationships to other processes. This should come as no surprise because we have often mentioned the close relationship between problem management and change management. In fact, each of the five processes that relate to problem management also relates to change management. What may be a bit surprising is that capacity planning is also listed as having five relationships. Many shops underestimate the importance of sound capacity planning and do not realize that doing it properly requires interaction with these other five processes.

Next is production acceptance, with four relationships to other processes. Following this is the trio of performance and tuning, network management, and storage management, each of which has three relationships to other processes. Availability and security are next with two relationships each, followed by configuration management, disaster recovery, and facilities management with one relationship each.

The significance of these relationships is that they point out the relative degree of integration required to properly implement these processes. Shops that implement a highly integrated process like change management in a very segregated manner usually fail in their attempt to have a robust change process. While each process is important in its own right, the list in Table 21-5 is a good guideline as to which processes we should look at first in assessing the overall quality of an infrastructure.

Summary

World-class infrastructures not only employ the 12 processes of systems management, they integrate them appropriately for optimal use. A variety of integration issues arise that are characterized, in part, by whether the processes are strategic or tactical in nature. This chapter began by presenting the differences between strategic and tactical processes of systems management and then identifying which of the 12 fell into each category. We next discussed issues that occur when integrating strategic, tactical, or a mixture of processes.

The key contribution of this chapter was the development of a matrix that shows the 24 key relationships between the 12 processes. The matrix designated each relationship as either strategic, tactical, or a mixture, and each was then discussed in greater detail. Finally, we looked at which processes interact the most with others and discussed the significance of this.

Test Your Understanding

1. Two processes that are both tactical will interact the same way as two processes that are both strategic. (True or False)
2. One of the difficulties with strategic relationships is that a continuing emphasis on long-range planning sometimes results in key initiatives not getting implemented. (True or False)
3. The infrastructure process with the largest number of relationships to other processes is:
   a. problem management
   b. network management
   c. capacity planning
   d. change management
4. Categorizing processes as either tactical or strategic assists in addressing _____ issues.
5. Discuss some of the reasons it is important to understand which systems management processes are strategic and which are tactical.

Suggested Further Readings

1. *IT Infrastructure Library (ITIL) Service Delivery Book*; 2001; The Stationary Office, Government of the United Kingdom
2. *IT Infrastructure Library (ITIL) Service Support Book*; 2001; The Stationary Office, Government of the United Kingdom
3. www.itsmf.com

CHAPTER 22

Special Considerations for Client-Server and Web-Enabled Environments

Introduction

The challenge facing many infrastructure managers today is how to apply the structure of these mainframe-developed processes to the less-structured environment of client/servers and to the relatively unstructured environment of the Internet. In this final chapter we look at some special aspects of systems management that we need to consider for these newer emerging environments.

We begin by examining several issues relating to processes implemented in a client/server environment that differ significantly from those implemented in a mainframe or midrange environment. Some of these topics could have been included in their respective process chapters, but I included them here instead because of the unique nature of the client/server environment to these processes. We conclude with a brief look at some of the cultural differences in a web-enabled environment as they relate to systems management processes.

Client-Server Environment Issues

There are five key issues worth discussing in relation to applying systems management processes to a client/server environment:

1. Vendor relationships
2. Multiplatform support
3. Performance and tuning challenges
4. Disaster-recovery planning
5. Capacity planning

Vendor Relationships

Vendor relationships take on additional importance in a client/server shop. This is due in part to a greater likelihood of multiple platforms being used in such an environment. Traditional mainframe shops limit their platforms to only one or two manufacturers due to the expense and capabilities of these processors. Fewer platforms mean fewer vendors need to be relied upon for marketing services, technical support, and field maintenance.

Multiplatform Support

However, in a client/server environment, multiple platforms are frequently used due to their lower cost and diverse architectures, which allow them to be tailored and tuned to specific enterprise-wide applications. Client/server shops typically employ three or more types of servers from manufacturers such as Sun, HP, IBM, and Compaq. Both hardware and software vendors are greater in number in a client/server environment due to the variety of equipment and support packages required in such a shop. The sheer number of diverse products makes it difficult for companies to afford to use mostly in-house expertise to support these assets. This means it's even more important for infrastructure managers to nurture a sound relationship with vendors to ensure they provide the necessary levels of support.

Another issue that the presence of a variety of server platforms raises is that of technical support. Supporting multiple architectures, such as NT or any number of UNIX variants, requires existing technicians to be trained—and likely spread thin—across multiple platforms or the hiring of additional technicians specializing in each platform. In either case, the total cost of supporting multiple technologies should be considered prior to implementing systems management processes.

Performance and Tuning Challenges

A third topic to consider in a client/server environment involves a number of performance and tuning challenges. The first challenge arises from the large number of different operating system levels typically found in a client/server environment. Diverse architectures such as Linux, NT, and all the various versions of UNIX (for example, IBM/AIX, HP/UNIX, and Sun/Solaris) are based on widely varying operating systems. They require different skill sets and, in some cases, different software tools to effectively tune their host server systems.

The various performance and tuning challenges include:

1. Variations in operating system levels
2. Impact of database structures
3. Integration of disk storage arrays
4. Application system changes
5. Complexities of network components
6. Differing types of desktop upgrades

Even shops that have standardized on a single architecture—for example, Sun/Solaris—face the likelihood of running multiple levels of the operating systems when a large number of servers is involved. Key tuning components, such as memory size, the number and length of buffers, and the quantity of parallel channels, may change from one level of operating system to the next, complicating the tuning process. This occurs less in a mainframe or midrange environment where fewer processors with larger capacities result in fewer varieties of operating system levels.

The dedication of an entire server to a specific application is another issue to consider when discussing the tuning of operating systems in a client/server environment. In a mainframe shop, most applications typically run on a single instance of an operating system as opposed to client/server applications that often run on dedicated platforms. You might think that this would simplify operating system tuning since the application has the entire server to itself. But, in fact, the frequent application updates, the expansion of usable data, the upgrades of hardware, and the continual growth of users can make the tuning of these operating systems more challenging than those of mainframes and midranges.

A second tuning challenge involves the structure of databases. As the use and number of users of the client/server application increase, so does the size of its database. This growth can require ongoing changes to a number of tuning parameters, such as directories, extents, field sizes, keys, and indices. As the number of total users increases, the transaction mix to the database changes, requiring tuning changes. As the number of concurrent users increases, adjustments must be made to reduce contention to the database.

A third tuning issue involves the use of large-capacity storage arrays. Improvements in reliability and cost/performance have made large-capacity storage arrays popular resources in client/server environments. Huge databases and data warehouses can be housed economically in these arrays. Several databases are normally housed in a single array to make the storage devices as cost effective as possible. When the size or profile of a single database changes, tuning parameters of the entire array must be adjusted. These include cache memory, cache buffers, channels to the physical and logical disk volumes, the configuration of logical volumes, and the configuration of the channels to the server.

Application systems in a client/server environment tend to be changed and upgraded more frequently than mainframe applications due to the likely growth of users, databases, and functional features. These changes usually require tuning adjustments to maintain performance levels. Application and database changes also affect network tuning. Most firms use an enterprise-wide network to support multiple applications. Different applications bring different attributes of network traffic. Some messages are large and infrequent while others are short and almost continuous. Networks in these types of environments must be tuned constantly to account for these ongoing variations in network traffic.

Desktop computers share a variety of applications in client/server shops. As more applications are made accessible to a given desktop, it will most likely need to be retuned and upgraded with additional processors, memory, or disk drives. The tuning becomes more complicated as the variety of applications change within a specific department.

Disaster-Recovery Planning

A fourth topic to consider in a client/server environment is that of disaster recovery and business continuity. The following list features five issues that make this systems management function more challenging in such an environment. The first issue involves the variation in types of server platforms in a client/server shop, where critical applications likely reside on servers of differing architectures.

1. Greater variation in types of server platforms
2. Larger number of servers to consider
3. Network connectivity more complex
4. Need to update more frequently
5. Need to test more frequently

Effective disaster-recovery plans are not easy to develop under the best of circumstances. It becomes even more complicated when multiple server architectures are involved. This leaves disaster-recovery planners with three options:

1. **Select a single server architecture**. Ensure this is an architecture on which the majority of mission-critical applications reside and around which one can develop the recovery process at the exclusion of the other critical applications. While this approach simplifies disaster-recovery planning, it can expose the company to financial or operational risk by not providing necessary systems in the event of a long-duration disaster.
2. **Select a standard server architecture.** Run all critical applications on this single architecture. This simplifies the disaster-recovery model to a single architecture but may require such extensive modifications to critical applications as to outweigh the benefits. In any event, thorough testing will have to be conducted to ensure full compatibility in the event of a declared disaster.
3. **Design the recovery process with multiple server platforms**. Ensure that these platforms can accommodate all critical applications. This approach will yield the most comprehensive disaster recovery plan, but it is also the most complex to develop, the most cumbersome to test, and the most expensive to implement. Nevertheless, for applications that are truly mission-critical to a company, this is definitely the strategy to use.

The second disaster-recovery issue to consider is the larger number of servers typically required to support mission-critical applications, even if the servers are all of a similar architecture. Multiple servers imply that there will be more control software, application libraries, and databases involved with the backing up, restoring, and processing of segments of the recovery processes. These segments all need to be thoroughly tested at offsite facilities to ensure that business processing can be properly resumed.

Network connectivity becomes more complicated when restoring accessibility to multiple applications on multiple servers from a new host site. Extensive testing must be done to ensure connectivity, interoperability, security, and performance. Connectivity must be established among desktops, databases, application systems, and server operating systems. There must be interoperability between servers with different architectures. The network that is being used during a disaster recovery must have the same level of security against unauthorized access as when normal processing is occurring. Performance factors such as transaction response times are sometimes degraded during the disaster recovery of client/server applications due to reduced bandwidth, channel saturation, or other performance bottlenecks. Heightened awareness of these network issues and thorough planning can help maintain acceptable performance levels during disaster recoveries.

Many client/server applications start small and grow into highly integrated systems. This natural tendency of applications to grow necessitates changes to the application code, to the databases that feed them, to the server hardware and software that run them, to the network configurations that connect them, and to the desktops that access them. These various changes to the operating environment require disaster-recovery plans and their documentation to be frequently updated to ensure accurate and successful execution of the plans.

These various changes also necessitate more frequent testing to assure that none of the modifications to the previous version of the plan undermines its successful implementation. Some of these changes may result in new requirements for a disaster recovery service provider, when used; these need to be thoroughly tested by this supplier as well.

Capacity Planning

The final systems management issue to consider in a client/server environment is capacity planning. The use of applications in such an environment tends to expand more quickly and more unpredictably than those in a mainframe environment. This rapid and sometimes unexpected growth in the use of client/server applications produces increased demand for the various resources that support these systems. These resources include server processors, memory, disk, channels, network bandwidth, storage arrays, and desktop capacities.

The increasing demand on these resources necessitates accurate workload forecasts for all of these resources to ensure that adequate capacity is provided. Frequent updates to these forecasts are important to assure that an overall capacity plan is executed that results in acceptable performance levels on a continuing basis.

Web-Enabled Environment Issues

This final section presents some topics to consider when implementing systems management processes in a web-enabled environment. One of the benefits of well-designed systems management processes is their applicability to a wide variety of platforms. When properly designed and implemented, systems management processes can provide significant value to infrastructures in mainframe, midrange, client/server, and web-enabled shops.

But just as we saw with client/server environments, there are some special issues to consider when applying systems management processes to those application environments that are web-enabled through the Internet. Most of these issues center on the inherent cultural differences that exist between mature mainframe-oriented infrastructures and the less structured environment of web-enabled applications. Most all companies today are using the Internet for web-enabled applications, but the degree of use, experience, and reliance varies greatly.

With these environmental attributes of use, experience, reliance and other factors, we can divide companies using web-enabled applications into one of three categories. The first consists of traditional mainframe-oriented companies which are just about to start using widespread web-enabled applications. The second category involves moderate-sized but growing enterprises which started using web-enabled applications early on. The third category consists of dotcom companies which rely mostly on the Internet and web-enabled applications to conduct their business. Table 22-1 shows the environmental attributes and cultural differences among these three categories of companies that use web-enabled applications.

Table 22-1   Environmental Attributes and Cultural Differences

Environmental Attribute	Traditional Fortune 500 Company About to Use the Web	Moderate, Growing Company Using the Web Early On	Dotcom Company Relying Solely on the Web from Start-Up
Years in Existence	Greater than 50 years	Less than 15 years	Less than 5 years
IT processing orientation	Mostly mainframe and some midrange	Mostly client/server, some midrange and Web	Mostly web and some client/server
Planning horizon for major IT decisions	2-3 years	1-2 years	Less than 1 year
Average years of IT experience of staff	Greater than 15 years	5-10 years	1-5 years
Ratio of mainframe to web-enabled years of experience of staff	10:1	1:1	Negligible
Relative amount of structure and process within their infrastructures	Extensive	Moderate	Marginal
Planning time for most major changes	2-4 weeks	1-7 days	12-48 hours
Likelihood of a disaster-recovery plan	Large	Medium	Small
Criticality of web-enabled applications to the enterprise	Low	Medium	High
Reliance on meaningful metrics	Great	Some	Little

Real Life Experience—Tap Dancing in Real Time

A CEO at a dotcom start-up was eager to show his staff how he could display their company website in real-time at his staff meetings. Unfortunately for his IT performance team, he picked the one day when a new operating system release went in improperly and slowed response down to a crawl. The technical support manager had to do some quick tap dancing when he was called into the meeting to explain what happened. Ironically, this was the same manager who had set up the displayable website in the first place.

Traditional Companies

Organizations comprising the first of the three categories are traditional Fortune 500 companies that have been in existence for well over 50 years, with many of them over 100 years old. Most of them still rely on mainframe computers for their IT processing of primary applications (such as financials, engineering, and manufacturing), although a sizable amount of midrange processing is also done. Many have already implemented some client/server applications but are just starting to look at web-enabled systems. The conservative and mature nature of these companies results in a planning horizon of two to three years for major IT decisions such as enterprise-wide business applications or large investments in systems management. Many of these firms develop and maintain five-year IT strategic plans.

IT personnel in this first category of companies average greater than 15 years of experience, with many exceeding 20 years. Since most of these companies have well-established mainframe environments in place, their staffs have valuable experience with designing and implementing systems management processes for their mainframe infrastructures. Their ratio of mainframe years of experience to web-enabled years of experience is a relatively high 10 to 1. Their long experience with mainframes and short experience with the Web can hinder their implementation of infrastructure processes in the web-enabled environment if they are unwilling to acknowledge cultural differences between the two environments.

Infrastructure personnel who work in mature mainframe shops understand how well-designed processes can bring extensive structure and discipline to their environments. If the process specialists for web-enabled applications are isolated from the mainframe specialists, as they frequently are in traditional companies, cultural clashes with process design and implementation are likely. The best approach is to have a single process group that applies to all platforms, including mainframes and web-enabled environments.

Major IT changes in traditional infrastructures are scheduled weeks in advance. A culture clash may occur when the more rigid mainframe change standards are applied to the more dynamic nature of the Web environment. Compromises may have to be made, not so much to compromise standards, but to accommodate environmental differences.

Mainframe shops have had decades of experience learning the importance of effective disaster-recovery planning for their mission-critical applications. Much time and expense is spent on testing and refining these procedures. As applications in these companies start to become web-enabled, it becomes a natural progression to include them in the disaster-recovery plan as well. The conservative nature of many of these companies coupled with the relative newness of the Internet often results in them migrating only the less critical applications on to the Web and, thus, into disaster-recovery plans. It is a bit ironic that companies with the most advanced disaster-recovery plans use them for web-enabled applications of low criticality, while firms with less developed disaster-recovery plans use them for web-enabled applications of high criticality.

The maturity of traditional companies affords them the opportunity to develop meaningful metrics. The more meaningful the metrics become to IT managers, to suppliers, and especially to customers, the more these groups come to rely on these measurements. Meaningful metrics help them isolate trouble spots, warn of pending problems, or highlight areas of excellence.

Moderate and Growing Companies

Companies in this category are moderate (less than 5,000 employees or less than $5 billion in annual sales) but growing enterprises which have been in existence for less than 15 years. They run most of their critical processing on client/server platforms and some midrange computers but have also been using web-enabled applications for noncritical systems from early in their development. These firms are now moving some of their critical processing to the Web. The size and diversity of many of these up-and-coming firms are expanding so rapidly that their IT organizations have barely a year to plan major IT strategies.

IT personnel in this type of company typically have five to 10 years of experience and a ratio of mainframe-to-web experience approximating 1 to 1. The IT staffs in these companies have less seniority than those in traditional mainframe shops, unless the company is an acquisition or a subsidiary of a traditional parent company. Because their mainframe-to-web experience is lower, staffs in this category of company are usually more open to new ideas about implementing infrastructure processes but may lack the experience to do it effectively. Creating teams that combine senior- and junior-level process analysts can help mitigate this. Setting up a technical mentoring program between these two groups is an even better way to address this issue.

The structure and discipline of the infrastructures in these moderate but growing companies are less than what we find in traditional companies but greater than that in dotcom firms. This can actually work to the company's advantage if executives use the initiatives of infrastructure processes to define and strengthen the structures they want to strengthen. Major IT changes tend to be scheduled, at most, one week in advance; normally, they are scheduled only a few days in advance. This can present a challenge when implementing change management for important web-enabled changes. Again, executive support can help mitigate this culture clash.

Disaster-recovery plans in this type of company are not as refined as those in traditional IT shops. Because many of the applications run on client/server platforms, disaster recovery is subject to many of the issues described in the client/server section of this chapter. The good news is that some type of disaster-recovery planning is usually in its early stages of development and can be modified relatively easily to accommodate web-enabled applications. These systems are usually of medium criticality to the enterprise and should therefore receive the support of upper management in integrating them into the overall disaster-recovery process. Meaningful management metrics in these companies are not as well developed or as widely used as in traditional companies and should be an integral part of any systems management process design.

Dotcom Companies

Dotcom companies are interesting entities to study. During the late 1990s, the use of the term became widespread, signifying the relative youth and immaturity of many of these enterprises, particularly in the area of their infrastructures. In comparison to the other two categories of companies, dotcoms were new on the scene (with an average age of less than five years). Most of their mission-critical applications are centered on a primary website and are web-enabled. Some of their supporting applications are client/server-based.

The culture of most dotcoms is quick and urgent, with events taking place almost instantaneously. The planning horizon for major IT decisions rarely spans a year and it can be as short as three months. One such company I consulted for actually decided on, planned, and implemented a major migration from SQL Server databases to Oracle databases for its mission-critical application—all within a three-month period. The challenge in these environments is to design systems management processes that were flexible enough to handle such a quick turnaround yet robust enough to be effective and enforceable. Thorough requirements planning helps greatly in this regard.

Dotcom personnel generally have an average of one to five years of IT experience. Typically, there are one or two senior-level IT professionals who help launch the original website and participate in the start-up of the company. The entrepreneurial nature of most dotcom founders results in their hiring of like-minded IT gurus who are long on technical expertise but short on structure and discipline. As a result, there is often a significant culture clash in dotcoms when they attempt to implement infrastructure processes into an environment that may have thrived for years with a lack of structure and discipline. Since there is negligible mainframe experience on staff, systems management processes are often viewed as threats to the dynamic and highly responsive nature of a dotcom—a nature that likely brought the company its initial success. At some point, dotcoms reach a size of critical mass where their survival depends on structured processes and discipline within their infrastructures. Knowing when this point is close to being reached, along with addressing it with robust systems management processes, is what separates sound dotcom infrastructures from those most at risk.

The average planning time for major IT changes in a dotcom is 12 to 48 hours. Implementing a change management process into this type of environment requires a significant shift in culture, extensive executive support, and a flexible, phased-in approach. With few infrastructure processes initially in place at a dotcom, the likelihood is small that disaster-recovery planning exists for any applications, let alone the web-enabled ones. Since most mission-critical applications at a dotcom are web-enabled, this is one of the processes that should be implemented first. Another infrastructure initiative that should be implemented early on, but often is not, is the use of meaningful metrics. The dynamic nature of dotcoms often pushes the development and use of meaningful metrics in these companies to the back burner. As previously mentioned, dotcoms reach a point of critical mass for their infrastructures. This is also the point at which the use of meaningful metrics becomes essential, both to the successful management of the infrastructure and to the proper running of web-enabled applications.

Summary

This chapter identified several special issues to consider when implementing systems management processes in a client/server or a web-enabled environment. The client/server issues involved vendor relationships, multiple platform support, performance and tuning challenges, disaster-recovery planning, and capacity planning. A discussion of each issue then followed, along with methods to address each one.

The web-enabled issues were presented in terms of three categories of companies in which they occur. We looked at environmental attributes and cultural differences for each of these categories and put them into perspective in terms of their impact on web-enabled applications.

Test Your Understanding

1. Performance factors such as transaction response times are sometimes degraded during the disaster recovery of client/server applications due to reduced bandwidth, channel saturation, or other performance bottlenecks. (True or False)
2. The use of applications in a client/server environment tends to expand less quickly and more predictably than those in a mainframe environment. (True or False)
3. Which of the following is not a performance-tuning consideration for a client/server environment:
   a. impact of database structures
   b. standardization of network interfaces
   c. application system changes
   d. differing types of desktop upgrades
4. Huge databases and data warehouses today can be housed economically in _____ .
5. Summarize the cultural differences between a traditional mainframe data center and those of a web-enabled environment.

Suggested Further Readings

1. *Real Web Project Management: Case Studies and Best Practices from the Trenches*; 2002; Shelford, Thomas J., Remillard, Gregory A.; Addison-Wesley Professional
2. www.readwriteweb.com/archives/2006_web_technology_trends.php
3. *Advances in Universal Web Design and Evaluation: Research, Trends and Opportunities*; 2006; Kurniawan, Sri, Zaphiris, Panayiotis; IGI Global

Frequently Asked Questions

Systems Management (SM)

SM-Q1: What criteria was used to determine the 12 disciplines of systems management?

SM-A1: The 12 disciplines of systems are based on my personal experience in managing seven different infrastructures and in consulting with dozens of clients and computer user group representatives.

SM-Q2: Should systems management processes be modified according to platform environment?

SM-A2: In most cases no. Many of the structures and disciplines of system management processes developed for mainframe and midrange environments, when properly designed and implemented, can optimize client/server and web-enabled environments.

SM-Q3: What is the single biggest inhibitor to an effective systems management program?

SM-A3: The single biggest inhibitor to an effective systems management program is lack of executive management support. Many IT executives still view IT primarily as the developer and maintainer of application systems. An infrastructure organization is still viewed by many as a necessary evil. That is, it is utility-like in expectations of reliability but often the cobbler's son in terms of receiving minimal budgets, nominal support, and negligible attention.

Availability (AV)

AV-Q1: What component of availability is best to measure?

AV-A1: This will vary from shop to shop as some measure data center availability, others measure server or network availability. The most common measurement is end-to-end user availability of the application at the desktop.

AV-Q2: What is the difference between an application experiencing an outage and an application experiencing extremely slow response?

AV-A2: Very little to the end user. When transaction response times of 1-2 seconds degrade significantly (for example, to greater than 15 seconds), the perception of the end-user is that the system is down. In theory, the system is down only if the failing component is unrecoverable. In practice, transactions taking more than a few minutes to respond are typically thought of as an outage to availability and should be treated as such.

AV-Q3: Should Service Level Agreements (SLAs) focus more on availability or response times?

AV-A3: SLAs should focus most on whatever is of the greatest importance to end-users. In many instances, this will involve providing both high availability and acceptable response times. In all cases, SLAs should be negotiated based on reasonable and agreed-upon expectations.

AV-Q4: What role does a supplier play in providing high availability IT services?

AV-A4: Simply put, a great deal. Well-managed and well-measured infrastructures can pinpoint which components are contributing the most to poor availability. If these components are owned and managed by external suppliers, then they should be held accountable for the poor availability and for implementing corrective actions.

Performance and Tuning (PT)

PT-Q1: What is one of the best ways to measure response-time performance?

PT-A1: Measure the percent of transactions completing within a specified threshold of time. For example, 95 percent of all transactions will complete in less than two seconds.

PT-Q2: Why not measure average response times?

PT-A2: Average response times can be skewed by rogue transactions that can inflate the elapse time of online transactions. Rogue transactions are frequently caused by aberrational events, such as device lockouts, power spikes, or network interruptions.

PT-Q3: Can improvements to database tuning actually hurt response-time metrics?

PT-A3: Surprisingly, the answer is yes. A technique sometimes used to improve database performance involves chaining together frequently used transactions to reduce keystrokes. While the result normally improves an end-user's efficiency by reducing manual interventions, metrics that measure responses as the time between keystrokes actually increase disproportionately.

Problem Management (PM)

PM-Q1: What percentage of calls should be resolved at level 1?

PM-A1: This will vary by shop and by how integrated a call center is, but generally 60 percent to 80 percent is considered acceptable. The more diversified the help desk, the lower the number. The key is to properly handoff unresolved problems to level 2 as quickly as possible and to appropriate group the first time.

PM-Q2: Should help desks be integrated all into one or should they be kept separate?

PM-A2: Integrating all into one is usually preferable because of the ease of use for customers and the opportunity to cross-train help desk analysts.

PM-Q3: Is there any way to combine the flexibility of an integrated help desk with the specialized focus of a segregated one?

PM-A3: Yes. Use a menu answering system to route calls by call type to separate but centralized help desks.

Change Management (CM)

CM-Q1: What is one of the most critical metrics to measure in change management?

CM-A1: One of the most critical metrics to measure is the percentage of emergency changes made on a weekly and monthly basis.

CM-Q2: Why is measuring the percentage of emergency changes so critical to change management?

CM-A2: The percentage of emergency changes made is usually a good indicator as to the reactiveness or proactiveness of an infrastructure. A higher percentage of emergency changes generally indicates a more reactive infrastructure.

CM-Q3: What is the difference between change management and change control?

CM-A3: Change management focuses on the coordination, scheduling, and communicating of production changes and is generally viewed as a more collaborative approach to handling changes. Change control is a more restrictive method of handling changes, usually focusing on approval or disapproval of changes, but is sometimes required to bring an out-of-control change environment back under control.

Production Acceptance (PA)

PA-Q1: When should an infrastructure organization first get involved with production acceptance?

PA-A1: An infrastructure organization should first get involved with production acceptance as soon as a new application is approved for implementation. This ensures that operations personnel and capacity planners are involved up front.

PA-Q2: Which infrastructure factors usually delay deployment of a new application?

PA-A2: More times than not, a new application is delayed by the infrastructure failing to provide adequate capacity of resources. These may be in the form of processing power of servers, amount of usable disk space, or even desktop capacities such as processor speed, memory size, or printer capability.

PA-Q3: What is the best way for an infrastructure to prevent delays in deploying a new application due to lack of adequate capacities?

PA-A3: Work with developers to create an accurate forecast of the capacity requirements that will be needed by the new application well in advance of the launch date and ensure all requirements are identified and met in time.

PA-Q4: What role, if any, does desktop support play in production acceptance?

PA-A4: Desktop support plays a very key role in production acceptance in that they must ensure the proper quantity of, and upgrades to, appropriate desktops are all in place prior to the initial date of production.

Configuration Management (CF)

CF-Q1: What entities comprise configuration management?

CF-A1: Application software either purchased or developed in-house running on mainframes, servers or desktops; database management software running on mainframes or servers; system software running on mainframes, servers, or desktops; network software; and data center, network, or desktop hardware.

CF-Q2: How is configuration management different from software migration?

CF-A2: Software migration is actually a subset of configuration management in which a new version of an application, an operating system, or a database system is implemented across multiple mainframes, servers, or desktops.

CF-Q3: What role, if any, does asset management play in configuration management?

CF-A3: Asset management normally consists of maintaining an accurate inventory of the exact number and version or model of each piece of software and hardware within an IT environment. It also includes all of the licenses, contracts, and maintenance agreements for each entry in the inventory. Asset management normally does not describe the interrelationships of hardware and software to each other, which is the mainstay of a comprehensive configuration management process.

CF-Q4: What effect, if any, did Y2K have on configuration management?

CF-A4: In many shops in the United States, Y2K actually improved configuration management by forcing application inventories to be updated for accuracy. Duplicate, unused, or retired applications were often discovered as a result of trying to determine which applications in an organization were Y2K compliant and which were not.

Capacity Planning (CP)

CP-Q1: What is the main obstacle to instituting a sound capacity planning process?

CP-A1: Not having accurate workload forecasts from end-users.

CP-Q2: What are some of the reasons users give for lack of accurate forecasts?

CP-A2: Users often say they cannot predict workload expansions, changes in staff size, increases in the demands of their own customers, and an inability to understand the technical aspects of IT resources.

CP-Q3: How can these explanations for inaccurate user forecasts be mitigated?

CP-A3: On the business side, users should be urged to discuss with their own management upcoming budget forecasts, changes in staff size, and anticipated increases in customer demand to better predict future workload increases. On the technical side, IT analysts and developers should ask end-users about workload changes in terms they understand and avoid using complicated technical jargon.

CP-Q4: What type of questions should be asked of users on a workload forecast survey?

CP-A4: Typical questions should include the expected number of total users, the number of concurrent users, number total transaction per time period, types of transactions, amount of disk space required, and data backup requirements.

CP-Q5: Which infrastructure resources are most likely to be capacity constrained?

CP-A5: This will clearly vary from shop to shop but in approximate priority order they are network bandwidth, centralized disk space, centralized processors in servers, channels, tape drives, centralized memory in servers, backup windows, centralized printers, desktop processors, desktop disk space, and desktop memory.

Network Management (NM)

NM-Q1: What were some of the original causes of network outages?

NM-A1: Unreliable hardware, poorly trained staff, and lack of redundancy accounted for many of the original outages to network services.

NM-Q2: What are some of the current causes of network outages?

NM-A2: Hardware is much more reliable, staffs are much better trained, and redundancy of equipment has greatly improved network availability. The complexity of today's networks and the Web make them currently more vulnerable to hackers, non-standard devices, and lack of adequate bandwidth.

NM-Q3: Should network monitoring be performed by the computer operations group or should it be performed by the network service group?

NM-A3: This will depend on the size and scope of network services. In general, for a 24x7 type environment, it usually works best to have computer operations monitoring the network on a 24x7 basis.

Storage Management (SM)

SM-Q1: What is the difference between backing-up data and archiving data?

SM-A1: Backing-up data usually involves copying it to another media, such as disk to tape, or copying it to a different location (such as offsite). Archiving is usually done on the same media in the same location for quick restoring and access. Disk-to-disk or hierarchical storage management systems are examples of this.

SM-Q2: What is the difference between backing up a file, a volume, and a database?

SM-A2: The differences normally lie in the restoring process. File restores are typically quick and simple. Volume restores are straightforward but can be time-consuming. Database restores are much more complicated, may be time-consuming, and they almost always require the expertise of a database administrator.

SM-Q3: What options are available when backing up a database?

SM-A3: Standard recovery to the last successful backup; more recent recovery to the last checkpoint; and most current forward recovery back to the last successful transaction.

SM-Q4: What are the tradeoffs between the various types of backups and recoveries?

SM-A4: In general, the more recent the recovery, the more complex the process. Checkpoints and forward recoveries require logs and other overhead that can impact performance during both the backup and the restore processes.

SM-Q5: Which version of RAID is best?

SM-A5: There are tradeoffs among the various versions of RAID between expense, performance, and redundancy. In general, RAID 0+1 provides the greatest redundancy but costs the most and has the greatest impact on performance.

Security (SE)

SE-Q1: What is one of the greatest external risks to the security of data?
SE-A1: Opening documents of unknown origin that contain destructive viruses.

SE-Q2: What is one of the greatest internal risks to the security of data?

SE-A2: Failing to adequately safeguard and manage passwords to critical or sensitive data.

SE-Q3: What is one of the easiest yet often unused ways to safeguard critical or sensitive data?

SE-A3: Making a secured backup copy of the data and safeguarding its storage.

Business Continuity (BC)

BC-Q1: What is the most common type of data center disaster?

BC-A1: Surprisingly, it is not a major calamity such as an earthquake, a flood, bombs, or terrorism. The most common disaster is a localized incident such as a water main break, small fires, and facilitation breakdowns involving electrical power or air conditioning.

BC-Q2: What type of disaster typically results in the severest impact to a data center?

BC-A2: Small localized disasters such as water breaks, small fires, or air conditioning failures that leave the data center disabled while the rest of the company is operating usually has the severest impact. A natural disaster, such as a major earthquake, normally affects all parts of a company and can actually minimize the urgency of restoring IT operations—particularly if life or limb is at risk.

BC-Q3: What is the difference between business continuity and disaster recovery?

BC-A3: Business continuity focuses on keeping the company's core businesses operating, with or without IT. Disaster recovery focuses on restoring some or all of IT operations and services.

BC-Q4: What is usually one of the biggest challenges with disaster recovery?

BC-A4: Determining the relative priorities of applications as to which are most critical; keeping these priorities up-to-date.

BC-Q5: What is the difference between recovering from a disaster and recovering from lost or damaged data?

BC-A5: Recovering from a disaster normally involves formal arrangements with a disaster-recovery service provider. Recovering from lost or damaged data involves restoring files and databases from backup, archival, or offsite storage.

Facilities Management (FM)

FM-Q1: What types of facilities problems can cause interruptions to a data center?

FM-A1: Voltage spikes, static electricity, and ground shorts can all cause interruptions to a data center.

FM-Q2: What types of cures can prevent these kinds of facilities outages?

FM-A2: Ensuring all equipment is properly grounded and using properly sized power distribution units (PDUs) can help prevent these types of facilities outages.

FM-Q3: For what period of time will a typical bank of Uninterruptible Power Supply (UPS) batteries keep a data center up and running?

FM-A3: While this depends greatly on the number, type, rating, and state-of-charge of the batteries in question, most systems provide 20 to 30 minutes of emergency electrical power.

FM-Q4: Can a data center that is protected by UPS still incur an outage due to a momentary interruption in electrical power?

FM-A4: Yes, if the UPS batteries have not been re-charged from prior use. I have talked to several operations managers who were caught off-guard by not realizing their UPS batteries were less than fully charged.

FM-Q5: What should operations personnel do when a data center goes on UPS batteries?

FM-A5: Several actions should be taken immediately when UPS batteries are activated. First, appropriate managers and facilities personnel should be notified of the condition. If monitoring systems are in place, efforts should be made to determine the cause of the condition. If it appears that normal power cannot be restored within the expected life of the UPS batteries and no backup generators are available, users should be notified of a pending interruption of services. Software systems should then be taken down with a prescribed and orderly method, after which the affected hardware should be powered off in a properly sequenced manner.

FM-Q6: What is one of the greatest data center exposures in facilities management?

FM-A6: An insidious condition can often build in a data center when frequent and continuous upgrades of equipment cause the electrical power and air conditioning loads to exceed the available capacities.

FM-Q7: How can critical systems be further protected against facilities outages?

FM-A7: By placing redundant servers and disk units on separate electrical circuits, on separate power distribution units, and on separate air conditioning units.

FM-Q8: How often should a backup generator be tested?

FM-A8: This will vary depending on the size, type, and rating of the generator, but most generator specialists recommend a full power-on test at least once every six months. Some of my clients schedule and conduct full switch-over tests on a monthly basis.

Summary of Definitions

Availability: the process of optimizing the availability of production systems by accurately measuring, analyzing, and reducing outages.

Business Continuity: a methodology to ensure the continuous operation of critical business systems in the event of wide-spread or localized disasters to an infrastructure environment.

Capacity Planning: a process to predict the types, quantities, and timing of capacities which critical resources within an infrastructure need in order to meet accurately forecasted workloads.

Change Management: a process to categorize, coordinate, approve, and communicate all changes to an IT production environment.

Configuration Management: a process to ensure that records are accurately and efficiently updated as to what version of software currently runs on which hardware.

Facilities Management: a process to ensure an appropriate physical environment is consistently supplied to enable the continuous operation of all critical infrastructure equipment.

Network Management: a process to maximize the reliability and utilization of network components in order to optimize network availability.

Performance and Tuning: a methodology to maximize throughput and minimize response times of batch jobs, online transactions, and internet activities.

Problem Management: a process to identify, log, track, resolve, and analyze problems impacting IT services.

Production Acceptance: a methodology to consistently and successfully deploy application systems into a production environment regardless of the hosting platform.

Strategic Security: a process designed to safeguard the availability, integrity, and confidentiality of designated data and programs against unauthorized access, modification, or destruction.

Storage Management: a process to optimize the use of storage devices and to protect the integrity of data for any media on which they reside.

Systems Management: the activity of identifying and integrating various products and processes in order to provide a stable and responsive IT environment.

Assessment Worksheets Without Weighting Factors

Availability Process—Assessment Worksheet					
Process Owner_____ **Owner's Manager**_____ **Date**_____					
Category	**Questions for Availability**	**None 1**	**Small 2**	**Medium 3**	**Large 4**
Executive Support	To what degree does the executive sponsor show support for the availability process with actions such as analyzing trending reports of outages and holding support groups accountable for outages?				
Process Owner	To what degree does the process owner exhibit desirable traits and ensure timely and accurate analysis and distribution of outage reports?				
Customer Involvement	To what degree are key customers involved in the design and use of the process, including how availability metrics and service level agreements will be managed?				
Supplier Involvement	To what degree are key suppliers, such as hardware firms, software developers, and service providers, involved in the design of the process?				
Service Metrics	To what degree are service metrics analyzed for trends such as percentage of downtime to users and dollar value of time lost due to outages?				
Process Metrics	To what degree are process metrics analyzed for trends such as the ease and quickness with which servers can be re-booted?				
Process Integration	To what degree does the availability process integrate with other processes and tools such as problem management and network management?				
Streamlining/ Automation	To what degree is the availability process streamlined by automating actions such as the generation of outage tickets and the notification of users when outages occur?				
Training of Staff	To what degree is the staff cross-trained on the availability process, and how well is the effectiveness of the training verified?				
Process Documentation	To what degree is the quality and value of availability documentation measured and maintained?				
	Totals				
Grand Total **Nonweighted Assessment Score**					

Performance and Tuning Process—Assessment Worksheet					
Process Owner_____ Owner's Manager_____ Date _____					
Category	Questions for Performance and Tuning	None 1	Small 2	Medium 3	Large 4
Executive Support	To what degree does the executive sponsor show support for the performance and tuning process with actions such as budgeting for reasonable tools and appropriate training?				
Process Owner	To what degree does the process owner exhibit desirable traits and know the basics of tuning system, database, and network software?				
Customer Involvement	To what degree are key customers involved in the design and use of the process, including how response time metrics and SLAs will be managed?				
Supplier Involvement	To what degree are key suppliers such as software performance tools providers and developers involved in the design of the process?				
Service Metrics	To what degree are service metrics analyzed for trends such as response times and the number and complexity of chained transactions?				
Process Metrics	To what degree are process metrics analyzed for trends such as the amount of overhead used to measure online performance, the number of components measured for end-to-end response, and the cost to generate metrics?				
Process Integration	To what degree does the performance and tuning process integrate with other processes such as storage management and capacity planning?				
Streamlining/ Automation	To what degree is the performance and tuning process streamlined by automating actions—such as the load balancing of processors, channels, logical disk volumes, or network lines—and by notifying analysts whenever performance thresholds are exceeded?				
Training of Staff	To what degree is the staff cross-trained on the performance and tuning process, and how well is the effectiveness of the training verified?				
Process Documentation	To what degree is the quality and value of performance and tuning documentation measured and maintained?				
Totals					
Grand Total Nonweighted Assessment Score					

		None 1	Small 2	Medium 3	Large 4
Production Acceptance Process - Assessment Worksheet					
Process Owner_____ Owner's Manager_____ Date _____					
Category	**Questions About Production Acceptance**				
Executive Support	To what degree does the executive sponsor show support for the production acceptance process with actions such as engaging development managers and their staffs in this process?				
Process Owner	To what degree does the process owner exhibit desirable traits and understand application development and deployment?				
Customer Involvement	To what degree are key customers, especially from development, operations and the help desk, involved in the design and use of the process?				
Supplier Involvement	To what degree are key suppliers, such as 3 rd party vendors, trainers, and technical writers, involved in the design of the process?				
Service Metrics	To what degree are service metrics analyzed for trends such as the amount of positive feedback from users, and the number of calls to the help desk, immediately after deployment?				
Process Metrics	To what degree are process metrics analyzed for trends such as the frequency and duration of delays to deployment and the accuracy and timeliness of documentation and training?				
Process Integration	To what degree does the production acceptance process integrate with other processes and tools such as change management and problem management?				
Streamlining/ Automation	To what degree is the production acceptance process streamlined by automating actions such as the documentation of a new application and online training for it by means of the intranet?				
Training of Staff	To what degree is the staff cross-trained on the production acceptance process, and how well is the effectiveness of the training verified?				
Process Documentation	To what degree is the quality and value of production acceptance documentation measured and maintained?				
	Totals				
	Grand Total Assessment Score				

Change Management Process—Assessment Worksheet					
Process Owner_____ Owner's Manager_____ Date _____					
Category	Questions for Change Management	None 1	Small 2	Medium 3	Large 4
Executive Support	To what degree does the executive sponsor show support for the change management process with actions such as attending CAB meetings, analyzing trending reports, and ensuring that applications, facilities, and outside vendors use the CAB for all changes?				
Process Owner	To what degree does the process owner exhibit desirable traits and effectively conduct the CAB and review a wide variety of changes?				
Customer Involvement	To what degree are key customers involved in the design of the process, particularly priority schemes, escalation plans, and the CAB charter?				
Supplier Involvement	To what degree are key suppliers, such as technical writers and those maintaining the database, involved in the design of the process?				
Service Metrics	To what degree are service metrics analyzed for trends such as availability, the type and number of changes logged, and the number of changes causing problems?				
Process Metrics	To what degree are process metrics analyzed for trends such as changes logged after the fact, changes with a wrong priority, absences at CAB meetings, and late metrics reports?				
Process Integration	To what degree does the change management process integrate with other processes and tools such as problem management and network management?				
Streamlining/ Automation	To what degree is the change management process streamlined by automating actions such as online submittals, documentation, metrics, and training; electronic signatures; and robust databases?				
Training of Staff	To what degree is the staff cross-trained on the change management process, and how well is the effectiveness of the training verified?				
Process Documentation	To what degree is the quality and value of change management documentation measured and maintained?				
	Totals				
	Grand Total Nonweighted Assessment Score				

Problem Management Process—Assessment Worksheet						
Process Owner_____ Owner's Manager_____ Date _____						
Category	Questions for Problem Management	None 1	Small 2	Medium 3	Large 4
Executive Support	To what degree does the executive sponsor show support for the problem management process with actions such as holding level 2 support accountable, analyzing trending reports, and setting improvement goals?				
Process Owner	To what degree does the process owner exhibit desirable traits, improve metrics over time, and maintain and adhere to current service level agreements?				
Customer Involvement	To what degree are key customers, particularly representatives of critical executives and high-volume desktop users, involved in the design of the process?				
Supplier Involvement	To what degree are key suppliers, especially level 2 and 3 support staff and desktop suppliers, involved in the design of the process, in terms of their committed response times to calls and availability of spare parts?				
Service Metrics	To what degree are service metrics analyzed for trends such as calls answered by second ring, calls answered by a person, calls solved at level 1, response times of level 2, and feedback surveys?				
Process Metrics	To what degree are process metrics analyzed for trends such as calls dispatched to wrong groups, calls requiring repeat follow-up, amount of overtime spent by level 2 and third-party vendors?				
Process Integration	To what degree does the problem management process integrate with other processes and tools such as change management?				
Stream-lining/ Automation	To what degree is the problem management process streamlined by automating actions such as paging, exception reporting, and the use of a knowledge database?				
Training of Staff	To what degree is the staff cross-trained on the problem management process, and how well is the effectiveness of the training verified?				
Process Documen-tation	To what degree is the quality and value of problem management documentation measured and maintained?				
	Totals				
	Grand Total Nonweighted Assessment Score				

Storage Management Process—Assessment Worksheet					
Process Owner_____ Owner's Manager_____ Date_____					
Category	Questions for Storage Management	None 1	Small 2	Medium 3	Large 4
Executive Support	To what degree does the executive sponsor show support for the storage management process with actions such as enforcing disk cleanup policies and questioning needs for more space?				
Process Owner	To what degree does the process owner exhibit desirable traits, develop and analyze meaningful metrics, and bring them to data owners' attention?				
Customer Involvement	To what degree are key customers involved in the design and use of the process, particularly the analysis and enforcement of metric thresholds?				
Supplier Involvement	To what degree are key suppliers, such as hardware manufactures and software utility providers, involved in the design of the process?				
Service Metrics	To what degree are service metrics analyzed for trends such as outages caused by lack of disk space or disk hardware problems and poor response due to fragmentation or lack of reorgs?				
Process Metrics	To what degree are process metrics analyzed for trends such as elapsed time for backups, errors during backups, and time to restore?				
Process Integration	To what degree does the storage management process integrate with other processes and tools such as performance and tuning and capacity planning?				
Streamlining/ Automation	To what degree is the storage management process streamlined by automating actions such as the initiation of backups, restoring of files, or the changing of sizes or the number of buffers or cache storage?				
Training of Staff	To what degree is the staff cross-trained on the storage management process, and how well is the effectiveness of the training verified?				
Process Documentation	To what degree is the quality and value of storage management documentation measured and maintained?				
Totals					
Grand Total Non-Weighted Assessment Score					

Network Management Process—Assessment Worksheet						
Process Owner_____ Owner's Manager_____ Date _____						
Category	Questions for Network Management	None 1	Small 2	Medium 3	Large 4	
Executive Support	To what degree does the executive sponsor show support for the network management process with actions such as budgeting for reasonable network tools and training and taking time to get educated on complex networking topics?					
Process Owner	To what degree does the process owner exhibit desirable traits and ensure that on-call and supplier lists are current and that cross-training is in effect?					
Customer Involvement	To what degree are key customers involved in the design and the use of the process, especially 24/7 operations personnel?					
Supplier Involvement	To what degree are key suppliers, such as carriers and network trainers, involved in the design of the process?					
Service Metrics	To what degree are service metrics analyzed for trends such as network availability, network response times, and elapsed time to logon?					
Process Metrics	To what degree are process metrics analyzed for trends such as outages caused by network design, maintenance, carriers testing, nonstandard devices, lack of training, or negligence?					
Process Integration	To what degree does the network management process integrate with other processes and tools such as availability and security?					
Streamlining/ Automation	To what degree is the network management process streamlined by automating actions such as the notification of network analysts when nodes go offline or when other network triggers are activated?					
Training of Staff	To what degree is the staff cross-trained on the network management process, and how well is the effectiveness of the training verified?					
Process Documentation	To what degree is the quality and value of network management documentation measured and maintained?					
	Totals					
	Grand Total Nonweighted Assessment Score					

Configuration Management Process—Assessment Worksheet					
Process Owner_____ Owner's Manager_____ Date _____					
Category	Questions for Configuration Management	None 1	Small 2	Medium 3	Large 4
Executive Support	To what degree does the executive sponsor show support for the configuration management process with actions such as reviewing migration strategies and holding documentation owners accountable for accuracy and timeliness?				
Process Owner	To what degree does the process owner exhibit desirable traits, enforce migration strategies, and understand configuration documentation?				
Customer Involvement	To what degree are key customers, such as repair technicians and facilities and operations personnel, involved in the design and use of the process?				
Supplier Involvement	To what degree are key suppliers, such as those documenting and updating configuration diagrams, involved in the design of the process?				
Service Metrics	To what degree are service metrics analyzed for trends such as the number of times analysts, auditors, or repair technicians find out-of-date configuration documentation?				
Process Metrics	To what degree are process metrics analyzed for trends such as the elapsed time between altering the physical or logical configuration and having it reflected on configuration diagrams?				
Process Integration	To what degree does the configuration management process integrate with the change management process and its associated tools?				
Streamlining/ Automation	To what degree is the configuration management process streamlined by automating actions such as updating multiple pieces of documentation requiring the same update?				
Training of Staff	To what degree is the staff cross-trained on the configuration management process, and how well is the effectiveness of the training verified?				
Process Documentation	To what degree is the quality and value of configuration management documentation measured and maintained?				
	Totals				
	Grand Total Nonweighted Assessment Score				

Capacity Planning Process—Assessment Worksheet					
Process Owner_____ Owner's Manager_____ Date _____					
Category	Questions for Capacity Planning	None 1	Small 2	Medium 3	Large 4
Executive Support	To what degree does the executive sponsor show support for the capacity planning process with actions such as analyzing resource utilization trends and ensuring that managers of users return accurate workload forecasts?				
Process Owner	To what degree does the process owner exhibit desirable traits and the ability to translate user workload forecasts into capacity requirements?				
Customer Involvement	To what degree are key customers, such as high-volume users and major developers, involved in the design and use of the process?				
Supplier Involvement	To what degree are key suppliers, such as bandwidth and disk storage providers, involved in the design of the process?				
Service Metrics	To what degree are service metrics analyzed for trends such as the number of instances of poor response due to inadequate capacity on servers, disk devices, or the network?				
Process Metrics	To what degree are process metrics analyzed for trends such as lead time for users to fill out workload forecasts and the success rate of translating workload forecasts into capacity requirements?				
Process Integration	To what degree does the capacity planning process integrate with other processes and tools such as performance and tuning and network management?				
Streamlining/ Automation	To what degree is the capacity planning process streamlined by automating actions such as the notification of analysts when utilization thresholds are exceeded, the submittal of user forecasts, and the conversion of user workload forecasts into capacity requirements?				
Training of Staff	To what degree is the staff cross-trained on the capacity planning process, and how well is the effectiveness of the training verified?				
Process Documentation	To what degree is the quality and value of capacity planning documentation measured and maintained?				
	Totals				
	Grand Total Nonweighted Assessment Score				

Security Process—Assessment Worksheet					
Process Owner_____ Owner's Manager_____ Date _____					
Category	Questions About Security	None 1	Small 2	Medium 3	Large 4
Executive Support	To what degree does the executive sponsor show support for the security process with actions such as enforcing a security policy or authorizing the process owner to do so?				
Process Owner	To what degree does the process owner exhibit desirable traits and the ability to develop and execute a strategic security plan?				
Customer Involvement	To what degree are key customers, such as owners of critical data or auditors, involved in the design and use of the process?				
Supplier Involvement	To what degree are key suppliers, such as those for software security tools or encryption devices, involved in the design of the process?				
Service Metrics	To what degree are service metrics analyzed for trends such as the number of outages caused by security breaches and the amount of data altered, damaged, or deleted due to security violations?				
Process Metrics	To what degree are process metrics analyzed for trends such as the number of password resets requested and granted and the number of multiple sign-ons processed over time?				
Process Integration	To what degree does the security process integrate with other processes and tools such as change management and network management?				
Streamlining/ Automation	To what degree is the security process streamlined by automating actions such as the analysis of password resets, network violations, or virus protection invocations?				
Training of Staff	To what degree is the staff cross-trained on the security process, and how well is the effectiveness of the training verified?				
Process Documentation	To what degree is the quality and value of security documentation measured and maintained?				
	Totals				
Grand Total **Nonweighted Assessment Score**					

Business Continuity Process—Assessment Worksheet						
Process Owner_____ Owner's Manager_____ Date _____						
Category	**Questions About Business Continuity**	**None 1**	**Small 2**	**Medium 3**	**Large 4**	
Executive Support	To what degree does the executive sponsor show support for the business continuity process with actions such as ensuring business units prioritize critical processes and applications and budgeting for periodic testing of recovery plans?					
Process Owner	To what degree does the process owner exhibit desirable traits and the ability to execute and evaluate dry runs of business continuity plans?					
Customer Involvement	To what degree are key customers, particularly owners of critical business processes, involved in the design and use of the process?					
Supplier Involvement	To what degree are disaster recovery service providers or staffs at hot backup sites involved in the design and testing of the process?					
Service Metrics	To what degree are service metrics analyzed for trends such as the number of critical applications able to be run at backup sites and the number of users that can be accommodated at the backup site?					
Process Metrics	To what degree are process metrics analyzed for trends such as the frequency and authenticity of dry-run tests and the improvements suggested from postmortem sessions after dry-run tests?					
Process Integration	To what degree does the business continuity process integrate with the facilities management process and its associated tools?					
Streamlining/ Automation	To what degree is the business continuity process streamlined by automating actions such as the scheduling of tapes for offsite storage and the retrieval of tapes for disaster recovery restoring?					
Training of Staff	To what degree is the staff cross-trained on the business continuity process, and how well is the effectiveness of the training verified?					
Process Documentation	To what degree is the quality and value of business continuity documentation measured and maintained?					
	Totals					
	Grand Total Nonweighted Assessment Score					

Facilities Management Process—Assessment Worksheet					
Process Owner_____ Owner's Manager_____ Date _____					
Category	Questions About Facilities Management	None 1	Small 2	Medium 3	Large 4
Executive Support	To what degree does the executive sponsor show support for the facilities management process with actions such as budgeting for the monitoring and redundancy of environmental systems?				
Process Owner	To what degree does the process owner exhibit desirable traits and familiarity with environmental monitoring systems?				
Customer Involvement	To what degree are key customers, such as the operations and network groups, involved in the design and use of the process?				
Supplier Involvement	To what degree are facilities personnel, and their suppliers, involved in the design of the process?				
Service Metrics	To what degree are service metrics analyzed for trends such as the number of outages due to facilities management issues and the number of employee safety issues measured over time?				
Process Metrics	To what degree are process metrics analyzed for trends such as the frequency of preventative maintenance and inspections of air conditioning, smoke detection, and fire suppression systems and the testing of uninterruptible power supplies and backup generators?				
Process Integration	To what degree does the facilities management process integrate with the disaster recovery process and its associated tools?				
Streamlining/ Automation	To what degree is the facilities management process streamlined by automating actions such as notifying facilities personnel when environmental monitoring thresholds are exceeded for air conditioning, smoke detection, and fire suppression?				
Training of Staff	To what degree is the staff cross-trained on the facilities management process, and how well is the effectiveness of the training verified?				
Process Documentation	To what degree is the quality and value of facilities management documentation measured and maintained?				
	Grand Total Nonweighted Assessment Score				

Assessment Worksheets With Weighting Factors

Availability Process—Assessment Worksheet				
Process Owner_____ Owner's Manager_____ Date _____				
Category	**Questions for Availability**	**Weight**	**Rating**	**Score**
Executive Support	To what degree does the executive sponsor show support for the availability process with actions such as analyzing trending reports of outages and holding support groups accountable for outages?			
Process Owner	To what degree does the process owner exhibit desirable traits and ensure timely and accurate analysis and distribution of outage reports?			
Customer Involvement	To what degree are key customers involved in the design and use of the process, including how availability metrics and service level agreements will be managed?			
Supplier Involvement	To what degree are key suppliers, such as hardware firms, software developers and service providers, involved in the design of the process?			
Service Metrics	To what degree are service metrics analyzed for trends such as percentage of downtime to users and dollar value of time lost due to outages?			
Process Metrics	To what degree are process metrics analyzed for trends such as the ease and quickness with which servers can be re-booted?			
Process Integration	To what degree does the availability process integrate with other processes and tools such as problem management and network management?			
Streamlining/ Automation	To what degree is the availability process streamlined by automating actions such as the generation of outage tickets and the notification of users when outages occur?			
Training of Staff	To what degree is the staff cross-trained on the availability process, and how well is the effectiveness of the training verified?			
Process Documentation	To what degree is the quality and value of availability documentation measured and maintained?			
	Totals			

Performance and Tuning Process—Assessment Worksheet				
Process Owner_____ Owner's Manager_____ Date _____				
Category	Questions for Performance and Tuning	Weight	Rating	Score
Executive Support	To what degree does the executive sponsor show support for the performance and tuning process with actions such as budgeting for reasonable tools and appropriate training?			
Process Owner	To what degree does the process owner exhibit desirable traits and know the basics of tuning system, database, and network software?			
Customer Involvement	To what degree are key customers involved in the design and use of the process, including how response time metrics and service level agreements will be managed?			
Supplier Involvement	To what degree are key suppliers such as software performance tools providers and developers involved in the design of the process?			
Service Metrics	To what degree are service metrics analyzed for trends such as response times and the number and complexity of chained transactions?			
Process Metrics	To what degree are process metrics analyzed for trends such as the amount of overhead used to measure online performance, the number of components measured for end-to-end response, and the cost to generate metrics?			
Process Integration	To what degree does the performance and tuning process integrate with other processes and tools such as storage management and capacity planning?			
Streamlining/ Automation	To what degree is the performance and tuning process streamlined by automating actions—such as the load balancing of processors, channels, logical disk volumes, or network lines—and by notifying analysts whenever performance thresholds are exceeded?			
Training of Staff	To what degree is the staff cross-trained on the performance and tuning process, and how well is the effectiveness of the training verified?			
Process Documentation	To what degree is the quality and value of performance and tuning documentation measured and maintained?			
	Totals			

Production Acceptance Process - Assessment Worksheet				
Process Owner_____	Owner's Manager_____		Date _____	
Category	Questions About Production Acceptance	Weight	Rating	Score
Executive Support	To what degree does the executive sponsor show support for the production acceptance process with actions such as engaging development managers and their staffs in this process?			
Process Owner	To what degree does the process owner exhibit desirable traits and understand application development and deployment?			
Customer Involvement	To what degree are key customers, especially from development, operations, and the help desk, involved in the design and use of the process?			
Supplier Involvement	To what degree are key suppliers, such as 3rd party vendors, trainers and technical writers, involved in the design of the process?			
Service Metrics	To what degree are service metrics analyzed for trends such as the amount of positive feedback from users and the number of calls to the help desk, immediately after deployment?			
Process Metrics	To what degree are process metrics analyzed for trends such as the frequency and duration of delays to deployment and the accuracy and timeliness of documentation and training?			
Process Integration	To what degree does the production acceptance process integrate with other processes and tools such as change management and problem management?			
Streamlining/ Automation	To what degree is the production acceptance process streamlined by automating actions such as the documentation of a new application and online training for it by means of the intranet?			
Training of Staff	To what degree is the staff cross-trained on the production acceptance process, and how well is the effectiveness of the training verified?			
Process Documentation	To what degree is the quality and value of production acceptance documentation measured and maintained?			
	Totals			

Change Management Process—Assessment Worksheet				
Process Owner_____ Owner's Manager_____ Date _____				
Category	Questions for Change Management	Weight	Rating	Score
Executive Support	To what degree does the executive sponsor show support for the change management process with actions such as attending CAB meetings, analyzing trending reports, and ensuring that applications, facilities, and outside vendors use the CAB for all changes?			
Process Owner	To what degree does the process owner exhibit desirable traits and effectively conduct the CAB and review a wide variety of changes?			
Customer Involvement	To what degree are key customers involved in the design of the process, particularly priority schemes, escalation plans, and the CAB charter?			
Supplier Involvement	To what degree are key suppliers, such as technical writers and those maintaining the database, involved in the design of the process?			
Service Metrics	To what degree are service metrics analyzed for trends such as availability, the type and number of changes logged, and the number of changes causing problems?			
Process Metrics	To what degree are process metrics analyzed for trends such as changes logged after the fact, changes with a wrong priority, absences at CAB meetings, and late metrics reports?			
Process Integration	To what degree does the change management process integrate with other processes and tools such as problem management and network management?			
Streamlining/ Automation	To what degree is the change management process streamlined by automating actions such as online submittals, documentation, metrics, and training; electronic signatures; and robust databases?			
Training of Staff	To what degree is the staff cross-trained on the change management process, and how well is the effectiveness of the training verified?			
Process Documentation	To what degree is the quality and value of change management documentation measured and maintained?			
	Totals			

\multicolumn{4}{c}{**Problem Management Process—Assessment Worksheet**}			

Category	Questions for Problem Management	Weight	Rating	Score
Executive Support	To what degree does the executive sponsor show support for the problem management process with actions such as holding level 2 support accountable, analyzing trending reports, and setting improvement goals?			
Process Owner	To what degree does the process owner exhibit desirable traits, improve metrics over time, and maintain and adhere to current service level agreements?			
Customer Involvement	To what degree are key customers, particularly representatives of critical executives and high volume desktop users, involved in the design of the process?			
Supplier Involvement	To what degree are key suppliers, especially level 2 and 3 support staff and desktop suppliers, involved in the design of the process, in terms of their committed response times to calls and availability of spare parts?			
Service Metrics	To what degree are service metrics analyzed for trends such as calls answered by second ring, calls answered by a person, calls solved at level 1, response times of level 2, and feedback surveys?			
Process Metrics	To what degree are process metrics analyzed for trends such as calls dispatched to wrong groups, calls requiring repeat follow-up, amount of overtime spent by level 2 and 3 rd party vendors?			
Process Integration	To what degree does the problem management process integrate with other processes and tools such as change management?			
Stream-lining/ Automation	To what degree is the problem management process streamlined by automating actions such as paging, exception reporting, and the use of a knowledge database?			
Training of Staff	To what degree is the staff cross-trained on the problem management process, and how well is the effectiveness of the training verified?			
Process Documen-tation	To what degree is the quality and value of problem management documentation measured and maintained?			
	Totals			

Process Owner_____ Owner's Manager_____ Date _____

Storage Management Process—Assessment Worksheet				
Process Owner_____ Owner's Manager_____ Date _____				
Category	Questions for Storage Management	Weight	Rating	Score
Executive Support	To what degree does the executive sponsor show support for the storage management process with actions such as enforcing disk cleanup policies and questioning needs for more space?			
Process Owner	To what degree does the process owner exhibit desirable traits, develop and analyze meaningful metrics, and bring them to data owners' attention?			
Customer Involvement	To what degree are key customers involved in the design and use of the process, particularly the analysis and enforcement of metric thresholds?			
Supplier Involvement	To what degree are key suppliers, such as hardware manufactures and software utility providers, involved in the design of the process?			
Service Metrics	To what degree are service metrics analyzed for trends such as outages caused by either lack of disk space or disk hardware problems and poor response due to fragmentation or lack of reorgs?			
Process Metrics	To what degree are process metrics analyzed for trends such as elapsed time for backups, errors during backups, and time to restore?			
Process Integration	To what degree does the storage management process integrate with other processes and tools such as performance and tuning and capacity planning?			
Streamlining/ Automation	To what degree is the storage management process streamlined by automating actions such as the initiation of backups, restoring of files, or the changing of sizes or the number of buffers or cache storage?			
Training of Staff	To what degree is the staff cross-trained on the storage management process, and how well is the effectiveness of the training verified?			
Process Documentation	To what degree is the quality and value of storage management documentation measured and maintained?			
	Totals			

Network Management Process—Assessment Worksheet				
Process Owner_____ Owner's Manager_____ Date _____				
Category	Questions for Network Management	Weight	Rating	Score
Executive Support	To what degree does the executive sponsor show support for the network management process with actions such as budgeting for reasonable network tools and training and taking time to get educated on complex networking topics?			
Process Owner	To what degree does the process owner exhibit desirable traits and ensure that on-call and supplier lists are current and that cross-training is in effect?			
Customer Involvement	To what degree are key customers involved in the design and the use of the process, especially 24/7 operations personnel?			
Supplier Involvement	To what degree are key suppliers, such as carriers and network trainers, involved in the design of the process?			
Service Metrics	To what degree are service metrics analyzed for trends such as network availability, network response times, and elapsed time to logon?			
Process Metrics	To what degree are process metrics analyzed for trends such as outages caused by network design, maintenance, carriers testing, nonstandard devices, lack of training, or negligence?			
Process Integration	To what degree does the network management process integrate with other processes and tools such as availability and security?			
Streamlining / Automation	To what degree is the network management process streamlined by automating actions such as the notification of network analysts when nodes go offline or when other network triggers are activated?			
Training of Staff	To what degree is the staff cross-trained on the network management process, and how well is the effectiveness of the training verified?			
Process Documentation	To what degree is the quality and value of network management documentation measured and maintained?			
	Totals			

Configuration Management Process—Assessment Worksheet				
Process Owner_____ Owner's Manager_____ Date _____				
Category	**Questions for Configuration Management**	**Weight**	**Rating**	**Score**
Executive Support	To what degree does the executive sponsor show support for the configuration management process with actions such as reviewing migration strategies and holding documentation owners accountable for accuracy and timeliness?			
Process Owner	To what degree does the process owner exhibit desirable traits, enforce migration strategies, and understand configuration documentation?			
Customer Involvement	To what degree are key customers, such as repair technicians and facilities and operations personnel, involved in the design and use of the process?			
Supplier Involvement	To what degree are key suppliers, such as those documenting and updating configuration diagrams, involved in the design of the process?			
Service Metrics	To what degree are service metrics analyzed for trends such as the number of times analysts, auditors, or repair technicians find out-of-date configuration documentation?			
Process Metrics	To what degree are process metrics analyzed for trends such as the elapsed time between altering the physical or logical configuration and having it reflected on configuration diagrams?			
Process Integration	To what degree does the configuration management process integrate with the change management process and its associated tools?			
Streamlining/ Automation	To what degree is the configuration management process streamlined by automating actions such as updating multiple pieces of documentation requiring the same update?			
Training of Staff	To what degree is the staff cross-trained on the configuration management process, and how well is the effectiveness of the training verified?			
Process Documentation	To what degree is the quality and value of configuration management documentation measured and maintained?			
	Totals			

Capacity Planning Process—Assessment Worksheet				
Process Owner_____ Owner's Manager_____ Date _____				
Category	Questions for Capacity Planning	Weight	Rating	Score
Executive Support	To what degree does the executive sponsor show support for the capacity planning process with actions such as analyzing resource utilization trends and ensuring that managers of users return accurate workload forecasts?			
Process Owner	To what degree does the process owner exhibit desirable traits and the ability to translate user workload forecasts into capacity requirements?			
Customer Involvement	To what degree are key customers, such as high-volume users and major developers, involved in the design and use of the process?			
Supplier Involvement	To what degree are key suppliers, such as bandwidth and disk storage providers, involved in the design of the process?			
Service Metrics	To what degree are service metrics analyzed for trends such as the number of instances of poor response due to inadequate capacity on servers, disk devices, or the network?			
Process Metrics	To what degree are process metrics analyzed for trends such as lead time for users to fill out workload forecasts and the success rate of translating workload forecasts into capacity requirements?			
Process Integration	To what degree does the capacity planning process integrate with other processes and tools such as performance and tuning and network management?			
Streamlining/ Automation	To what degree is the capacity planning process streamlined by automating actions such as the notification of analysts when utilization thresholds are exceeded, the submittal of user forecasts, and the conversion of user workload forecasts into capacity requirements?			
Training of Staff	To what degree is the staff cross-trained on the capacity planning process, and how well is the effectiveness of the training verified?			
Process Documentation	To what degree is the quality and value of capacity planning documentation measured and maintained?			
	Totals			

Security Process—Assessment Worksheet				
Process Owner_____ Owner's Manager_____ Date _____				
Category	**Questions About Security**	**Weight**	**Rating**	**Score**
Executive Support	To what degree does the executive sponsor show support for the security process with actions such as enforcing a security policy or authorizing the process owner to do so?			
Process Owner	To what degree does the process owner exhibit desirable traits and the ability to develop and execute a strategic security plan?			
Customer Involvement	To what degree are key customers, such as owners of critical data or auditors, involved in the design and use of the process?			
Supplier Involvement	To what degree are key suppliers, such as those for software security tools or encryption devices, involved in the design of the process?			
Service Metrics	To what degree are service metrics analyzed for trends such as the number of outages caused by security breaches and the amount of data altered, damaged, or deleted due to security violations?			
Process Metrics	To what degree are process metrics analyzed for trends such as the number of password resets requested and granted and the number of multiple sign-ons processed over time?			
Process Integration	To what degree does the security process integrate with other processes and tools such as change management and network management?			
Streamlining/ Automation	To what degree is the security process streamlined by automating actions such as the analysis of password resets, network violations, or virus protection invocations?			
Training of Staff	To what degree is the staff cross-trained on the security process, and how well is the effectiveness of the training verified?			
Process Documentation	To what degree is the quality and value of security documentation measured and maintained?			
	Totals			

Business Continuity Process—Assessment Worksheet					
Process Owner_____	Owner's Manager_____			Date _____	
Category	**Questions About Business Continuity**	**Weight**	**Rating**	**Score**	
Executive Support	To what degree does the executive sponsor show support for the business continuity process with actions such as ensuring business units prioritize critical processes and applications and budgeting for periodic testing of recovery plans?				
Process Owner	To what degree does the process owner exhibit desirable traits and the ability to execute and evaluate dry runs of business continuity plans?				
Customer Involvement	To what degree are key customers, particularly owners of critical business processes, involved in the design and use of the process?				
Supplier Involvement	To what degree are disaster recovery service providers or staffs at hot backup sites involved in the design and testing of the process?				
Service Metrics	To what degree are service metrics analyzed for trends such as the number of critical applications able to be run at backup sites and the number of users that can be accommodated at the backup site?				
Process Metrics	To what degree are process metrics analyzed for trends such as the frequency and authenticity of dry-run tests and the improvements suggested from postmortem sessions after dry-run tests?				
Process Integration	To what degree does the business continuity process integrate with the facilities management process and its associated tools?				
Streamlining/ Automation	To what degree is the business continuity process streamlined by automating actions such as the scheduling of tapes for offsite storage and the retrieval of tapes for disaster recovery restoring?				
Training of Staff	To what degree is the staff cross-trained on the business continuity process, and how well is the effectiveness of the training verified?				
Process Documentation	To what degree is the quality and value of business continuity documentation measured and maintained?				
	Totals				

Facilities Management Process—Assessment Worksheet				
Process Owner_____ Owner's Manager_____ Date_____				
Category	**Questions About Facilities Management**	**Weight**	**Rating**	**Score**
Executive Support	To what degree does the executive sponsor show support for the facilities management process with actions such as budgeting for the monitoring and redundancy of environmental systems?			
Process Owner	To what degree does the process owner exhibit desirable traits and familiarity with environmental monitoring systems?			
Customer Involvement	To what degree are key customers, such as the operations and network groups, involved in the design and use of the process?			
Supplier Involvement	To what degree are facilities personnel, and their suppliers, involved in the design of the process?			
Service Metrics	To what degree are service metrics analyzed for trends such as the number of outages due to facilities management issues and the number of employee safety issues measured over time?			
Process Metrics	To what degree are process metrics analyzed for trends such as the frequency of preventative maintenance and inspections of air conditioning, smoke detection, and fire suppression systems and the testing of uninterruptible power supplies and backup generators?			
Process Integration	To what degree does the facilities management process integrate with the disaster recovery process and its associated tools?			
Streamlining/ Automation	To what degree is the facilities management process streamlined by automating actions such as notifying facilities personnel when environmental monitoring thresholds are exceeded for air conditioning, smoke detection, and fire suppression?			
Training of Staff	To what degree is the staff cross-trained on the facilities management process, and how well is the effectiveness of the training verified?			
Process Documentation	To what degree is the quality and value of facilities management documentation measured and maintained?			
	Totals			

Historical Perspective

Winston Churchill once said that the farther backward you can look, the farther forward you are likely to see. This can apply to any field of endeavor and implies that the vision ahead of us is sometimes brought into clearer focus by first looking back over from where we came. This appendix presents an historical perspective of information technology (IT) during its infancy in the middle of the 20th century. My intent here is to present some of the key attributes which characterized IT environments of that time and to show how these attributes contributed to the early development of systems management.

I begin by describing a timeline from the late 1940s through the late 1960s, highlighting key events in the development of IT and its inherent infrastructures of the time.

I then look at some of the key requirements of an ideal IT environment that were lacking during that era. These deficiencies led to the next major breakthrough in IT—the development of the IBM System/360.

Timelining Early Developments of Systems Management

Historians generally disagree as to when the modern IT era began because IT is an evolving entity. Inventors and scientists have experimented with devices for counting and tabulating since before the early use of the abacus.

In 1837, English mathematician Charles Babbage conceived of an Analytical Engine, which could store programs to compute mathematical functions. While lack of funding prevented him from developing it much past an initial prototype, it amazingly contained many of the concepts of early digital computers that would take nearly a century to develop.

George Boole developed Boolean Algebra in 1854. Simply described, it is the mathematics of counting on two fingers which led scientists to consider two-state mathematical machines utilizing devices that were either on or off. A few years later, advances were made in which electrical impulses were first used as a means to count and calculate numbers. A minor breakthrough occurred in the 1870s when mathematician/scientist Eric Von Neuman invented a reliable electrical/mechanical device to perform mathematical operations. His apparatus was simply called the Neuman Counting Machine. In 1889, Herman Hollerith invented punched tape, and later punched cards, to electronically store binary information.

The first half of the 20th century saw an era of refinements, enhancements, and further breakthroughs in the field of electrical/mechanical accounting machines. In 1939, English engineer Alan Turing developed a two-state machine that could perform operations read from a punched tape. His so-called Turing Machine was later used to decipher coded messages for Great Britain during World War II. In 1945, mathematician John von Neumann conceived the notion that electronic memory could be used to store both the data to be processed and the instructions on how to program it.

By 1946, the field of accounting and the emerging electronics industry combined forces to develop the first truly electronic calculating machine. The term *computer* had not yet come into existence. Instead, it was known by its cumbersome acronym, ENIAC, which stood for Electronic Numerical Integrated Accounting Calculator. Dr. John W. Mauchly and J. P. Eckert, Jr. of the University of Pennsylvania headed up a large team of engineers to develop ENIAC for complex ballistics analysis for the U. S. Army Air Corps.

Real Life Experience—Playing Tic-Tac-Toe Against Electrons

When I was in elementary school in the mid-1960s, a classmate and I won our school's annual science fair with an exhibit on how an electric motor works. Our win enabled us to enter a major regional science fair for junior and high school students. While our relatively simple project warranted us an honorable mention at the regional fair, what impressed me most was the electronic Tic-Tac-Toe machine that won 1st place overall.

The machine consisted of dozens of electro-mechanical relays with hundreds of wires going out one side to a large display screen configured with three rows of three squares; out of the other side, wires connected to a keypad with the familiar nine squares from which players could enter their Xs. After a player entered his selection, the relays made loud clicking sounds as they turned on and off for about 10 seconds before showing the machine's response on the display. Of course, the machine never lost. The exhibiter called his project a Computerized Tic-Tac-Toe Game and it drew huge crowds of onlookers. Years later, as I read about IBM' s Deep Blue super computer winning against world chess champions, I think back to those noisy, slow-acting relays and marvel at how far we have come.

By today's standards, ENIAC would clearly be considered primitive. The electronics consisted mostly of large vacuum tubes that generated vast amounts of heat and consumed huge quantities of floor space (see Figure E-1). The first version of ENIAC filled an entire room of 20 square feet (6.1 square meters). Nonetheless, it was a significant advance in the infant industry of electronic computing. Remington Rand helped sponsor major refinements to this prototype computer in 1950. The new version, called ENIAC II, may have started a long standing tradition in IT of distinguishing hardware and software upgrades by incremental numbering.

In 1952, Remington Rand introduced a totally new model of electronic computer. Many of the vacuum tubes were now replaced with a revolutionary new electronic device developed by Bell Laboratories: the transistor. In addition to saving space and reducing heat output, transistors had much faster switching times, which translated into more computing power in terms of cycles per second. This increase in computing power meant that larger programs could process greater quantities of data in shorter amounts of time. The new transistorized model of this computer was named UNIVAC, short for universal accounting calculator.

Figure E-1 U.S. Army Photo of ENIAC

UNIVAC made a splashy debut in November 1952 by becoming the first electronic calculating machine used in a presidential election. Its use was not without controversy. Many were skeptical of the machine's reliability; delays and occasional breakdowns did little to improve its reputation. Understandably, many Democrats questioned the accuracy of the results, which showed Republican candidate Dwight D. Eisenhower defeating Democratic challenger Adlai J. Stevenson.

Out of these humble and sometimes volatile beginnings grew an infant IT industry that, in the span of just a few short decades, would become one of the world's most important business forces. Also out of this came the beginnings of systems management. The experiences of UNIVAC at the 1952 presidential election presented computer manufacturers with some harsh realities and provided them with some important lessons. Marketing groups and technical teams within UNIVAC both realized that, for their product to succeed, it must be perceived by businesses and the public in general as being reliable, accurate, and responsive.

The message was not lost on competing companies. International Business Machines (IBM), Control Data Corporation (CDC), and Digital Equipment Corporation (DEC), among others, also saw the need to augment the engineering breakthroughs of their machines with sound availability design. These manufacturers knew only too well that nothing would undermine their technology more quickly than long and frequent outages, slow performance, and marginal throughput. This emphasis on availability, performance and tuning, and batch throughput planted the seeds of systems management. As a result, suppliers began providing redundant circuits, backup power supplies, and larger quantities of main memory to improve the performance and reliability of their mainframes.

Mainframe

Mainframe originally referred to the primary metal cabinet that housed the central processing unit (CPU), main memory, and I/O channels of early computers. Later, the term referred to any large-scale computer to distinguish it from midrange computers, servers, and workstations.

The term *mainframe* had a practical origin. Most of the circuitry and cabling for early computers were housed in cabinets constructed with metal frames. Control units for peripheral devices (such as card readers, printers, tape drives, and disk storage) were also housed in metal frames. In order to distinguish the various peripheral cabinets from those of the main, or central processing unit (CPU), the frame containing the CPU, main memory, and main input/output (I/O) channels was referred to as the mainframe. The term has since come to refer to any large-scale computing complex in which the CPU has computing power and capabilities far in excess of server and desktop computers.

CPU

CPU is short for Central Processing Unit and is the basic and core portion of any computer. A CPU consists of two primary parts: an arithmetic and logical unit (ALU), which electronically adds (and, through variation, subtracts, multiplies, and divides) and compares numbers; and a control unit (CU), which oversees all of the operational functions of the computer.

I/O Channel

An I/O (Input/Output) channel is the primary physical connection between a CPU and the control units of peripheral devices such as tape drives, disk drives, and printers. The physical cabling of early I/O channels were called bus and tags; modern high-speed I/O cables use fiber-optic technology. Associated with I/O channels is software that runs programs to send, receive, and confirm the successful transfer of data.

By 1960, mainframe computers were becoming more prevalent and more specialized. Demand was slowly increasing in American corporations, in major universities, and within the federal government. Companies employed business-oriented computers in their accounting departments for applications such as accounts receivables and payables. Universities used scientifically oriented computers for a variety of technical applications, such as analyzing or solving complex engineering problems. Numerically intensive programs came to be known as number crunchers.

Business-Oriented Computer

A business-oriented computer is one that runs an operating system, compilers, and application software that is specifically designed to process business applications such as payrolls, accounts receivable/payable, and inventories.

Several departments within the federal government employed both scientific and business-oriented computers. The Census Bureau began using computers for the 1960 national census. These computers initially assisted workers in tabulating and statistically analyzing the vast amounts of data collected from all over the country. With the population booming, there was far more data to acquire and organize than ever before. While these early versions of computers were slow and cumbersome by today's standards, they were well-suited for storing and handling these larger amounts of population demographic information.

Scientifically Oriented Computer

A scientifically oriented computer is one that runs an operating system, compilers, and application software that is specifically designed to process scientific applications such as engineering analysis, mathematical computations, and scientific formulas.

The 1960 presidential election was another event that gave added visibility to the use of computers. By this time, business computers were being used and accepted as a reliable method of counting votes. The Department of Defense was starting to use scientific computers for advanced research projects and high technology applications. The National Aeronautics and Space Administration (NASA), in concert with many of its prime contractors in private industry, was making extensive use of specialized scientific computers to design and launch the first U.S.-manned spacecraft as part of Project Mercury.

The Need for a General-Purpose Computer

This increased use of computers exposed a deficiency of the systems that were available at the time. As the number and types of applications grew, so also did the specialization of the machines on which these programs ran. Computers designed to run primarily business-oriented systems (such as payrolls and account ledgers, for example) typically ran only those kinds of programs. On the other hand, organizations running scientific applications generally used computers specifically designed for these more technical programs. The operating systems, programming languages, and applications associated with business-oriented computers differed greatly from those associated with scientifically oriented machines.

This dichotomy created problems of economics and convenience. Most organizations—whether industrial, governmental, or academic—using computers in this era were large in nature and their business and scientific computing needs began overlapping. Many of these firms found that it became expensive, if not prohibitive, to purchase a variety of different computers to meet their various needs.

A separate dilemma arose for firms that had only one category of programs to run: How to accommodate programs of varying size and resource requirements quickly and simply on the same computer. For example, the operating system (OS) of many computers designed only for business applications would need to be reprogrammed, and in some cases rewired, depending on the processing, memory, I/O, and storage requirements of a particular job.

OS

OS is short for operating system, which is a set of machine-level software routines that controls the various functions of the computer's operating environment. These functions include managing memory space, queuing requests, prioritizing tasks, performing I/O operations, conducting error analysis and corrections, and sending messages to operators and users.

Constant altering of the operating environment to meet the changing needs of applications presented many drawbacks. The work of reprogramming operating systems was highly specialized and contributed to increased labor costs. The changes were manually performed and were therefore prone to human error, which adversely impacted availability. Even when completed flawlessly, the changes were time-consuming and thus reduced batch throughput and turnaround. Systems management would be better served if error-prone, time-consuming, and labor-intensive changes to the operating environment could be minimized.

As the need to manage the entire operating environment as a system became apparent, the requirement for a more general-purpose computer began to emerge. Exactly how this was accomplished is the subject of the next section.

A Look at the Early Development of IBM

While this book does not focus on any one hardware or software supplier, when one particular supplier has played a key role in the development of systems management, it is worth discussing. A book on desktop operating systems would no doubt trace some of the history of Microsoft Corporation. A book on integrated computer chips would likely discuss Intel Corporation. Here we will take a brief look at IBM.

In 1914, a young salesman named Thomas Watson left his secure job at the National Cash Register (NCR) Corporation in Cincinnati, Ohio, to form his own company. Watson called his new company the Calculating, Tabulating, and Recording (CTR) Company, which specialized in calculating devices, time clocks, meat scales, and other measuring equipment.

Within a few years, his company extended its line of products to include mechanical office equipment such as typewriters and more modern adding machines. Watson was a man of vision who saw his company expanding in size and scope around the world with a whole host of advanced office products. In the early 1920s, he renamed his company the International Business Machines (IBM) Corporation. (While IBM was not, strictly speaking, international when it was renamed—it had no facilities outside the United States—Watson envisioned it quickly becoming a global empire and was in the process of opening a small branch office in Toronto, Canada.)

IBM grew consistently and significantly throughout Watson's tenure as chairman and chief executive officer (CEO) during the first half of the 20th century. The growth of IBM came not only in terms of sales and market share but in its reputation for quality products, good customer service, and cooperative relationships between management and labor. In 1956, Thomas Watson, Sr. turned over the reins of his company to his son, Thomas Watson, Jr.

The Junior Watson had been groomed for the top spot at IBM for some time, having worked in key management positions for a number of years. He had the same drive as his father to make IBM a premier worldwide supplier of high-quality office products. Watson Jr. built and expanded on many of his father's principles.

For example, he realized that, for the company to continue gaining market share, customer service needed to be one of its highest priorities. Coupled with, and in support of, that goal was the requirement for effective marketing. As to quality, Watson not only demanded it in his company's products, he insisted it be an integral part of the extensive research into leading-edge technologies as well. Certainly not least among corporate values was Watson's insistence of respect for every individual who worked for IBM. These goals and values served IBM well for many years.

During its halcyon years in the 1970s and early 1980s, IBM's name became synonymous with highly reliable data-processing products and services. Perhaps the clearest example of IBM's reputation around that time was a saying heard often within the IT industry: "No CIO ever got fired for buying IBM products." Of course, things at IBM would change dramatically in the late 1980s, but prior to that it was arguably the industry leader within IT.

By building on his father's foundation, Watson Jr. is properly credited with turning IBM into such an industry leader. However, his vision for the long-range future of IBM did differ from that of his father's. The senior Watson was relatively conservative, manufacturing and marketing products for markets which already existed. Watson Jr., however, was also intent on exploring new avenues and markets. The new frontier of computers fascinated him, and he saw these machines as the next potential breakthrough in office products.

Prior to becoming IBM's CEO, Watson Jr. had already started slowly moving the company in new directions. More budget was provided for research and development into computer technology and new products were introduced in support of this new technology. Keypunch machines, card collators, and card sorters were among IBM's early entries into this emerging world of computers.

During the late 1950s, Watson Jr. accelerated his company's efforts at tapping into the markets of computer technology. He also wanted to advance the technology itself with increased funding for research and development. The research covered a broad range of areas within computer technology, including advanced hardware, operating systems, and programming languages.

One of the most successful efforts at developing a computer-programming language occurred at IBM in 1957. A team led by IBM manager Jim Backus unveiled a new scientific programming language called FORTRAN, for FORmula TRANslator. Specifically designed to run higher-level mathematics programs, it was ideally suited for solving complex analysis problems in engineering, chemistry, physics, and biology.

Over time, FORTRAN became one of the most widely used scientific programming languages in the world.

Two years after FORTRAN became available, a business-oriented programming language was introduced. It was called COBOL for COmmon Business Oriented Language. While IBM did not solely lead the effort to develop COBOL it did support and participate in the COmmittee on DAta SYstems Languages (CODASYL), which sponsored its development. As popular as FORTRAN became for the scientific and engineering communities, COBOL became even more popular for business applications, eventually becoming the de facto business programming language standard for almost three decades.

By the early 1960s, IBM had introduced several successful models of digital computers for use by business, government, and academia. An example of this was the model 1401 business computer, a very popular model used by accounting departments in many major American companies. Despite its popularity and widespread use, the 1401 line, along with most other computers of that era, suffered from specialization. Suppose you had just run an accounts receivable application on your 1401 and now wanted to run an accounts payable program. Since different application software routines would be used by the new program, some of the circuitry of the computer literally would need to be re-wired in order to run the application. Due to the specialized nature of the 1401, only certain types of business applications could run on it, and only one could be run at a time.

The specialized nature of computers in the early 1960s was not confined to applications and programming languages. The types of I/O devices which could be attached to and operated on a computer depended on its specific architecture. Applications which required small amounts of high-speed data typically would not run on computers with devices storing large amounts of data at slow speeds.

To overcome the drawbacks of specialization, a new type of computer would need to be designed from the ground up. As early as 1959, planners at IBM started thinking about building a machine that would be far less cumbersome to operate. Shortly thereafter, Watson Jr. approved funding for a radically new type of IBM computer system to be called the System/360. It would prove to be one of the most significant business decisions in IBM's history.

The Significance of the IBM System/360

The overriding design objective of the System/360 (S/360) was to make it a general-purpose computer: business-oriented, scientific, and everything in between. (The 360 designation was chosen to represent all degrees of a compass.) This objective brought with it a whole host of design challenges, not the least of which was the development of an entirely new operating system.

This new operating system, dubbed OS/360, proved to be one of the costliest and most difficult challenges of the entire project. At one point, more than 2,000 programmers were working day and night on OS/360. Features such as multi-programming, multi-tasking, and independent channel programs were groundbreaking characteristics never before attempted at such a sophisticated level. Some of the more prominent features of the S/360, and a brief explanation of each, are shown in Table E-1.

Table E-1   Features of the IBM System/360

Feature	Description
Multi-tasking	Ability to run multiple programs at the same time
Multi-programming	Ability to run programs coded in different languages at the same time on the same machine
Standard Interface	Ability to connect a variety of I/O devices via a standard channel interface
Scalability	Ability to add memory and channels to the same machine
Upward compatibility	Ability to run the same program on upgraded versions of the operating system
Downward compatibility	Ability to run programs from older versions of operating systems on the new S/360 version
Multiple types of operating systems	Ability to support multiple types of operating systems, including the Primary Control Program (PCP), Multi-programming with a Fixed number of Tasks (MFT), and Multi-programming with a Variable number of Tasks (MVT)
Family of models	Provision of computers in varying sizes and configurations
Integrated circuitry	State-of-the-art integrated circuitry to increase performance
Independent channels	Ability to allow I/O channels to operate separately from, but simultaneously with, the main processor
Error correction code	Combination of self-correcting hardware and software to increase reliability
Redundant components	Duplication of critical circuitry and components such as power supplies

Two other design criteria for OS/360 which complicated its development were upward and downward compatibility. Downward compatibility meant that programs which were originally coded to run on some of IBM's older models (for example, the 1401) would be able to run on the new S/360 computer under OS/360. Upward compatibility meant that programs coded to run on the first models of S/360 and under the first versions of OS/360 would also run on future models of the S/360 hardware and the OS/360 software. In other words, the architecture of the entire system would remain compatible and consistent.

The challenges and difficulties of developing an operating system as mammoth and complex as OS/360 are well documented in IT literature. One of the more interesting works is *The Mythical Man Month* by Frederick Brooks. The thrust of the book is effective project management, but it also discusses some of the many lessons learned from tackling a project as huge as S/360.

By 1963, the S/360 project was grossly over budget and far behind schedule. Watson's accountants and lawyers were understandably concerned about the escalating costs of an effort that had yet to produce a single product or generate a single dollar of revenue. The total cost of developing the S/360 (US $5B—or $30B 2005 dollars) was estimated to exceed the total net worth of the IBM Corporation. Watson was literally betting his entire company on what many felt was a questionable venture.

Moreover, there were many in the industry, both within and outside of IBM, who questioned whether the S/360 would really fly. Even if the many hardware problems and software bugs could be solved, would conservative companies really be willing to pay the large price tag for an unproven and radically different technology?

The answer to these concerns came on April 4, 1964, when IBM announced general availability of the S/360 (see Figure E-2). The system was an immediate and overwhelming success. Orders for the revolutionary new computing system were so intense that the company could barely keep up with demand. In less than a year, IBM had more than made back its original investment in the system and upgrades with even more advanced features were being planned.

Why was the S/360 so successful? What factors contributed to its unprecedented demand? The answers to these questions are as numerous and varied as the features which characterized this system. S/360 was powerful, high-performing, and reliable. Perhaps most significant, it was truly a general-purpose computing system. Accountants could run COBOL-written business programs at the same time engineers were running FORTRAN-written scientific programs.

Figure E-2 Operator Console of IBM System/360 (Reprint Courtesy of International Business Machines Corporation, copyright International Business Machines Corporation)

In addition to its general-purpose design, the S/360's independent channels with standard interfaces allowed a variety of high-speed I/O devices to operate concurrently with data being processed. This design architecture resulted in greatly improved operational productivity with increased throughput and reduced turnaround times.

Some observers even felt there were socio-political elements adding to the popularity of the S/360. During the early 1960s, the United States was well on its way to meeting President John Kennedy's commitment to land a man on the moon and safely return him to earth by the end of the decade. Most of the country rallied behind this national mission to defeat the USSR in the space race. The new technologies required for this endeavor, while perhaps not well understood by the masses, were nonetheless encouraged and certainly not feared. Computers were seen as both necessary and desirable. Technology curricula increased and enrollments in engineering schools reached all-time highs. The IBM S/360 was viewed by many as the epitome of this embracing of technological pursuits.

How S/360 Impacted Systems Management

Two significant criteria for effective systems management were advanced with the introduction of the S/360: managing batch performance and improving availability. Prior to the S/360, most computers required extensive changes in order to run different types of programs. As previously stated, these changes were often error-prone, time-consuming, and labor-intensive. With the S/360, many of these changes became unnecessary and consequently eliminated. Multiple compilers, such as COBOL and FORTRAN, could run simultaneously, meaning that a variety of different programs could run at the same time without the need for any manual intervention.

The immediate benefit of this feature was improved throughput and turnaround for batch jobs. Being able to manage batch performance was one of the key requirements for systems management and the S/360 provided IT professionals many options in that regard. Individual input job classes, priority scheduling, priority dispatching, and separate output classes were some of the features that enabled technicians to better control and manage the batch environment.

The introduction of a software-based job-control language (JCL) reduced the manual changes needed to run multiple job types and increased the availability of the machine. Improving the availability of the batch environment was another key requirement of systems management. Manual changes, by their very nature, are prone to errors and delays. The more the changes are minimized, the more that costly outages and downtimes are minimized.

Referring to the last four features listed in Table E-1, we see that performance and reliability were helped in additional ways with the S/360. State-of-the-art integrated circuitry greatly decreased the cycle times of digital switches within the computer, resulting in much higher performance. At that time, cycle times were in the tens of microseconds, or one millionth of a second. Within a few years they would be reduced to nanoseconds, or one billionth of a second. This circuitry was sometimes referred to as third generation, with vacuum tubes being first generation and transistors being second. Following this came a fourth generation, based on highly integrated circuitry on chips which had become so tiny that one needed microscopic equipment to design and manufacture them.

Real Life Experience—Early Recognition of Voice Recognition

During a high school field trip in the late 1960s, I visited the Electrical Engineering (EE) department at Purdue University. A professor there showed us the research he was conducting on voice recognition. He had an old manual typewriter outfitted with small, mechanical plungers on top of each key. When he carefully spoke a letter of the alphabet into a massively wired microphone that connected to each of the 26 plungers, the corresponding plunger would activate to strike the proper key to type the correct letter. We were impressed. He had worked years on the research and this was a breakthrough of sorts. A few years later, I had the same professor for a EE course and he relished explaining how he had been able to design the electrical circuitry that could recognize speech patterns. Voice recognition is very commonplace today, but occasionally I think back to that rickety old typewriter where much of the original research began.

As previously mentioned, independent channel programs improved batch performance by allowing I/O operations such as disk track searches, record seeks, and data transfers to occur concurrently with the mainframe processing data. I/O devices actually logically disconnected from the mainframe to enable this. It was an ingenious design and one of the most advanced features of the S/360.

Real Life Experience—Quotable Quotes

In researching material for this book, I looked for some insightful quotes to include. Dr. Gary Richardson of the University of Houston provided me with the following three gems.

"I think there is a world market for, maybe, five computers."

—*Thomas Watson, Sr., Chairman of IBM, 1943*

"Computers, in the future, may weigh no more than 1.5 tons."

—*Popular Mechanics, forecasting advances in science, 1949*

"I have traveled the length and breadth of this country and talked with the best people, and I can assure you that data processing is a fad that won't last out the year."

—*Editor in charge of business books for Prentice Hall, 1957*

Another advanced feature of the system was the extensive error-recovery code that was designed into many of the operating system's routines. Software for commonplace activities—for example, fetches to main memory, reading data from I/O devices, and verifying block counts—was written to retry and correct initial failed operations. This helped improve availability by preventing potential outages to the subsystem in use. Reliability was also improved by designing redundant components into many of the critical areas of the machine.

Throughout the late 1960s, technical refinements were continually being made to boost the performance of the S/360 and improve its reliability, two of the cornerstones of systems management at the time. However, the system was not perfect by any means. Software bugs were constantly showing up in the massively complicated OS/360 operating systems. The number of Program Temporary Fixes (PTFs) issued by IBM software developers sometimes approached 1,000 a month.

> **PTF**
>
> PTF is short for Program Temporary Fix and refers to the software modifications, or patches, that software suppliers such as IBM would provide to their customers to correct minor—and occasionally major—problems with their software. PTFs usually applied to operating system software.

Nor was the hardware always flawless. The failure of integrated components tested the diagnostic routines as much as the failing component. But by and large, the S/360 was an incredibly responsive and reliable system. Its popularity and success were well reflected in its demand. To paraphrase an old saying, it might not have been everything, but it was way ahead of whatever was in second place.

Conclusion

Systems management is a set of processes designed to bring stability and responsiveness to an IT operating environment. The first commercial computers started appearing in the late 1940s. The concept of systems management began with the refinement of these early, primitive machines in the early 1950s. Throughout that decade, computers became specialized for either business or scientific applications and became prevalent in government, industry, and academia.

The specialization of computers became a two-edged sword, however, hastening their expansion but hindering their strongly desirable systems management attributes of high availability and batch throughput. These early attributes laid the groundwork for what would eventually develop into the 13 disciplines known today. Specialization led to what would become the industry's first truly general-purpose computer.

The founding father of IBM, Thomas Watson, Sr., and particularly his son, Thomas Watson, Jr., significantly advanced the IT industry. The initial systems management disciplines of availability and batch performance began in the late 1950s but were given a major push forward with the advent of the IBM System/360 in 1964. The truly general-purpose nature of this revolutionary computer system significantly improved batch performance and system availability, forming the foundation upon which stable, responsive infrastructures could be built.

Evolving in the 1970s and 1980s

The new IT products offered in the 1960s radically changed the way business was conducted. Closely linked to this phenomenon was the IBM System/360 (S/360), which was arguably the single most significant event in the advancement of IT in business and society. This new hardware and software architecture produced a truly general-purpose computing system and revolutionized the industry to a degree that is not likely to be seen again.

The popularity of general-purpose computers in the 1960s demonstrated the need for the systems management functions regarding batch performance and system availability. During the 1970s and 1980s these functions continued to evolve in both scope and sophistication. As online transaction processing—with its large supporting databases—became more prevalent, functions such as online transaction tuning, database management, and asset security were added to the responsibilities of systems management. The continued refinement and sophistication of the microchip, combined with its plummeting cost, also opened up new hardware architectures that expanded the use of digital computers. This appendix will discuss the evolution of these functions.

General Purpose Becomes General Expansion

If the 1960s were defined as a time of revolution in IT, the 1970s were a time of evolution. The Internet, though developed in the late 1960s, would not see widespread use until the early 1990s. But the decade of the 1970s would witness major changes within IT.

At this point the phenomenal success of the S/360 had stretched the limits of its architecture in ways its designers could not have foreseen. One of the most prevalent of these architectural restrictions was the amount of main memory available for application processing. This operational limitation had effectively limited growth in application sophistication and became a key redesign goal for IBM. As the cost of memory chips fell, the demand for larger amounts of main memory grew. The expensive storage chips of the 1960s—which indirectly led to the Year 2000 (Y2K) problem by prompting software developers to truncate date fields to reduce the use and cost of main memory—were replaced with smaller, faster, and cheaper chips in the 1970s.

Internal addressing and computing inside a digital computer is done using the binary number system. One of the design limitations inside the S/360 was related to the decision to use address registers of 24 **b**inary dig**its**, or *bits*, which limited the size of the addressable memory. This architectural limitation had to be resolved before the memory size could be expanded. Briefly, the binary numbering system works as described in the following paragraphs.

A binary (2 valued) number is either a 0 or a 1. The binary numbering system is also referred to as the base 2 numbering system because only 2 values exist in the system (0 and 1) and all values are computed as a power of 2. In our more familiar decimal (base 10) system, there are 10 distinct digits, 0 through 9, and all values are computed as a power of 10. For example, the decimal number 347 is actually:

$$3 \times 10^2 + 4 \times 10^1 + 7 \times 10^0 = 300 + 40 + 7 = 347$$

10^0 equals 1 because any number raised to the 0 power equals 1.

Now let's apply this formula to a base 2 number. Suppose we want to compute the decimal value of the binary number 1101. Applying the previous formula results in:

$$1 \times 2^3 + 1 \times 2^2 + 0 \times 2^1 + 1 \times 2^0 = 8 + 4 + 0 + 1 = 13$$

Using the same formula, you should be able to see that the binary number 1111 equals the decimal number 15, binary 11111 equals decimal 31, and so on.

The simple formula for computing the maximum decimal number for an n-bit binary number is $2^n - 1$. The maximum decimal value of an 8-bit binary number is:

$$2^8 - 1 = 256 - 1 = 255$$

In a similar manner, the maximum decimal value of a 24-bit binary number is approximately 16 million. The maximum number of *unique* decimal values that could be stored in an 8-bit binary field is actually 256, because 0 counts as a number. Table F-1 shows the maximum decimal values for a variety of n-bit fields, as well as some other common references and additional meanings.*

Table F-1 Maximum Values of Various Sized Bit Fields

Number of Bits	Maximum Value	Common Reference	Added Meaning
4	15	n/a	4 bits = 1 nibble*
8	255	n/a	8 bits = 1 Byte
12	4095	4k	1K = 1024 in IT
16	64K or 64KB	64KB	64KB = 64 Kilobytes
20	1,048,575	1 Meg or 1MB	1MB = 1000K in IT
24	16,777,215	16 Megs or 16MB	16MB = 16 Megabytes
28	268,435,445	256 Megs or 256MB	256MB = 256 Megabytes
30	About 1 billion	1 Gig or 1GB	1GB = 1 Gigabyte
32	About 4 billion	4 Gigs or 4GB	4GB = 4 Gigabytes
40	About 1 trillion	1 Tera or 1TB	1TB = 1 Terabyte
48	About 268 trillion	268 Teras or 256TB	256TB – 256 Terabytes

*Tongue-in-cheek programmers back in the 60's designated a 4-bit field as a nibble since it was half of an 8-bit field which was known universally as a byte. Only a seasoned IT professional can appreciate a programmer's sense of humor.

A digital computer is designed to perform all calculations in binary because most of its circuits are designed to detect only one of two states at a time. All electronic switches and gates inside a computer are designated as being either on (a binary 1) or off (a binary 0). Early computing machines were called *digital computers* for two reasons:

1. They were based on the binary system, which is a two digit, or digital, numbering scheme.
2. The name distinguished them from analog computers, which used continuous values of circuit voltage rather than the discrete values of 1 or 0 employed by their digital counterparts.

But what is the significance of all this discussion about binary numbering systems, the size of fields in bits, and the maximum quantity of unique numbers you can store in a field? Part of the answer lies in the same issue that primarily accounted for the extensive Y2K problem (the so-called millennium bug) in the late 1990s. That root issue was the cost of data storage. In this case, it specifically applied to the cost of main memory.

When IBM engineers first developed the operating system for the S/360, they had to decide how much addressable memory to design into its architecture.

The field in the operating system that would define the maximum memory size would be referenced often in the many routines managing memory and I/O. Making the fields larger than necessary would result in a costly waste of what was then expensive memory.

The expected size of programs and data also entered into the decision about maximum addressable memory. A typical S/360 programming instruction was 4 bytes in length (for example, 32 bits). An unusually large program of several thousand instructions, referencing tens of thousands of bytes of data, would still need only 20 to 30 kilobytes of memory (and that was presuming all of the data would be residing in memory, which normally was not the case).

So when designers finally decided on a 24-bit addressing scheme for the S/360, they expected a maximum addressable memory size of 16 megabytes to more than accommodate for memory requirements for a long time to come. But something interesting happened on the way to the 1970s. First, the cost and power of integrated circuits began to change dramatically in the mid-1960s. The price of manufacturing a computer chip plummeted while its relative processing power accelerated. This cost/growth phenomenon became known as Moore's Law. This growth formula has held true for the past three decades and is forecast to continue for decades to come.

Moore's Law

Moore's Law refers to the prediction Intel Corporation cofounder Gordon Moore made in 1965 when he stated that the speed and subsequent processing power of an integrated circuit will double approximately every 12 to 18 months.

The reduction of computer chip price/performance ratios meant that the cost of using more main memory was also falling. Engineers designing computers in the late 1960s were not as constrained by circuit costs as they had been in the early part of the decade. But taking advantage of inexpensive memory chips by providing vast amounts of main storage meant ensuring that an operating system could address this larger memory.

Real Life Experience—Examination Boards Wrestle with Chips

During the mid-1970s, microchips enabled electronic calculators with stored memory to arrive on the scene. Texas Instruments was especially successful with several models that could perform complex mathematical and engineering operations. These models posed a problem for examining boards, which had previously allowed simple electronic calculators to be used during testing. The boards were concerned these advanced models would compromise their ability to truly test an applicant's ability to solve complex problems. I experienced this a few years later when I took, and passed, the California State Board for Professional Engineers. The Board allowed advanced calculators to be used, but we first had to demonstrate that we had erased all available memory; this convinced proctors that there were no accessible stored programs.

As we have described, the S/360 had a maximum addressable memory of 16 megabytes. Changing the operating system to support more memory would mean millions of dollars in labor cost to redesign, code, integrate, and test all the necessary routines. Such a shift in strategic direction would require significant business justification.

Part of the justification came from IBM's customers themselves. The success and popularity of the S/360 caused many users to demand faster computers capable of running more programs concurrently. Companies started seeing the benefit of using more interactive programs that could quickly access records stored in huge corporate databases. These companies were willing to invest more capital in advanced computers as they put more and more of their business online. IBM responded to this need with an evolved version of its S/360 flagship. The new product would be called System/370, or S/370, with its name referencing the decade in which it was introduced.

Evolving S/360 Into S/370

IBM introduced S/370 in 1971. Just as S/360 was based on the complex operating system known as OS/360, the new S/370 architecture would be based on the operating system known as OS/370. One of the many unique features of OS/370 was a new memory management system called *Multiple Virtual Storage (MVS)*. Actually, MVS was the final refinement of several prior memory management schemes that included Virtual Storage 1 (VS 1), Single Virtual Storage (SVS) and Virtual Storage 2 (VS 2).

Virtual Storage

Virtual storage is an electronic memory-mapping scheme that allows very large computer programs to run in much smaller amounts of physical memory. It accomplishes this by holding only small, frequently used portions of the program in memory at a time. The operating system exploits the locality characteristic of programs to map the total number of virtual addresses in the program to the smaller number of physical addresses in main memory.

MVS was an ingenious concept that maximized the physical main memory of a computer by extending the apparent, or virtual, size of memory that would be addressable by each program. To accomplish this, MVS developers cleverly based MVS on a common but often overlooked property of most computer programs known as the *locality characteristic*. The locality characteristic refers to the property of a typical computer program in which the majority of processing time is spent executing a relatively small number of sequential instructions over and over again. Many of the other instructions in the program may be designed to handle input/output (I/O), exception situations, or error conditions and consequently are executed very infrequently.

Locality Principle

The locality characteristic refers to the property of a computer program in which the majority of processing time is spent executing a relatively small number of sequential instructions repeatedly.

This means that only a small portion of a program needs to be physically in main memory for the majority of its executing time. Portions of a program not executing, or executing infrequently, could reside on less expensive and more readily available direct access storage devices (DASD). The MVS version of OS/370 utilized these principles of locality to efficiently map a program's logical, or virtual, memory into a much smaller physical memory.

MVS accomplished this mapping by dividing a program into 4-kilobyte segments called pages. Various algorithms—such as last used, least recently used, and next sequential used—were designed into OS/370 to determine which pages of a program would be written out to DASD and which ones would be read into main memory for execution. In this way, programs could be developed with essentially no memory constraints, because MVS would allow each program to access all of the maximum 16 megabytes of memory virtually, while in reality giving it only a fraction of that amount physically. Program segments infrequently used would be stored out on DASD (said to be paged out), while frequently used segments would reside in main memory (paged in).

Real Life Experience—Victor Virtual Explains Virtual Storage

In the late 1970s, I headed up the team that would implement the virtual storage architecture for the Data Service Bureau of the City of Los Angeles. To acquaint some of our less technically oriented staff with this rather complex concept, the team placed training and awareness high on their list of tasks to do. The team made several attempts at presenting this somewhat foreign topic, but the audiences simply were not grasping it. Finally, IBM stepped in with a 15-minute video that did the trick. The video used cartoon characters—headed up by Victor Virtual—along with cartoon props to explain the relationships of such entities as main memory, physical storage, virtual storage, and program segments. To this day, it is one of the most effective presentations on virtual storage I have ever seen.

Incidentally, you may think that a software developer who designs even a moderately large program with thousands of lines of code would still need only a few 4-kilobyte pages of memory to execute his or her program. In fact, just about all programs use high-level instructions that represent dozens or even hundreds of actual machine-level instructions for frequently used routines.

In higher-level programming languages such as COBOL or FORTRAN, these instructions are referred to as *macros*. In lower-level languages such as assembler, these instructions may be machine-level macros such as supervisor calls (SVCs); I/O macros such as READ/WRITE or PUT/Fetch; or even privileged operating system macros requiring special authorizations.

Macro

A macro is a high-level instruction or command that represents a series of frequently executed, low-level instructions or commands. A macro saves programming time by eliminating the need to specify often-repeated sets of instructions or commands.

Suppose, for example, that a programmer were to write a program of 3,000 instructions. Depending on the complexity of the programming logic, this could require up to several weeks of coding and testing. By the time all the high- and low-level macros are included, the program could easily exceed 30,000 to 40,000 instructions. At roughly 4 bytes per instruction, the program would require about 160,000 bytes of memory to run, or about 40 pages of 4 kilobytes each.

But this is just a single program. Major application development efforts, such as an enterprise-wide payroll system or a manufacturing resource system, could easily have hundreds of programmers working on thousands of programs in total. As online transaction systems began being fed by huge corporate databases, the need for main memory to run dozens of these large applications concurrently became readily apparent. The MVS version of OS/370 addressed this requirement—it enabled multiple applications to run concurrently by accessing large amounts of virtual storages.

While there were many other features of S/370 that contributed to its success, the MVS concept was by far its most prominent. The S/370's expanded use of memory that helped proliferate online transaction processing (OLTP) and large databases gave way to several more disciplines of systems management.

The Impact of S/370 on Systems Management Disciplines

The impact of the S/370 in general, and of MVS in particular, on systems management disciplines was substantial. Until this time, most of the emphasis of the S/360 was on availability and batch performance. As the S/370 expanded the use of main memory and transaction processing, the emphasis on systems management began shifting from that of a batch orientation to more online systems.

Several new systems management disciplines were brought about by the proliferation of OLTP systems; the growth of huge databases; and the need to better manage the security, configuration, and changes to these expanding online environments. The online orientation also increased the importance of the already established function of availability.

The discipline of performance and tuning was one of the most obvious changes to systems management. The emphasis on this function in the 1960s centered primarily on batch systems, whereas in the 1970s it shifted significantly to online systems and to databases. Efforts with performance and tuning focused on the online systems and their transactions, on the batch programs used for mass updates, and on the databases themselves. Research in each of these three areas resulted in new processes, tools, and skill sets for this new direction of what was previously a batch-oriented function.

Real Life Experience—An Olympic-sized Challenge

The City of Los Angeles began preparing to host the 1984 Olympics at the beginning of that decade. During this time, I was the infrastructure manager for the City's Data Service Bureau, which provided data-processing services to all 55 City departments, including the departments of police, fire and transportation.

As the transportation department began running more and more traffic simulations and modeling routines to optimize traffic flows, and as the police department began analyzing more and more international crime data, I gained a new appreciation for just how valuable our computing services would become in preparing the city for one of the most successful Olympiads ever.

As databases grew in both size and criticalness, the emphasis on efficiently managing disk storage space also increased. Primary among database management concerns was the effective backing-up and restoring of huge, critical databases. This gave way to new concepts such as data retention, expiration dates, offsite storage, and generation data groups. Although the price of DASD was falling dramatically during the 1970s, disk space management still needed to be emphasized—as was the case with most IT hardware components. Fragmented files, unused space, and poorly designed indexes and directories were often the expensive result of mismanaged disk storage. All these various factors made storage management a major new function of systems management in the 1970s.

One of the systems management functions that changed the most during the 1970s was—somewhat ironically—change management itself. As we previously discussed, the majority of applications running on mainframe computers during the 1960s were batch-oriented. Changes to these programs could usually be made through a production control function in which analysts would point executable load libraries toward a revised program segment, called a *member*, instead of toward the original segment. There was nothing very sophisticated, formalized, or particularly risky about this process. If an incorrect member was pointed to, or the revised member processed incorrectly, the production control analyst would simply correct the mistake or point back to the original member and then re-run the job.

This simplicity, informality, and low risk all changed with OLTP. Changes made to OLTP systems increased in frequency, importance, and risk. If a poorly managed change caused an unscheduled outage to a critical online system, particularly during a peak usage period, it could result in hundreds of hours of lost productivity, not to mention the possible risk of corrupted data. So a more sophisticated, formal process for managing changes to production software started to emerge in the mid-to-late 1970s.

Coupled with this more structured approach to change management was a similar evolution for problem management. Help desks became a data center mainstay; these help desks initiated formal logging, tracking, and resolution of problem calls. Procedures involving escalation, prioritization, trending, and root-cause analysis started being developed in support for this process.

As more and more critical corporate data began populating online databases, the need for effective security measures also emerged. The systems management discipline of security was typically implemented at three distinct levels:

- At the operating system level
- At the application level
- At the database level.

Later on, network and physical security were added to the mix.

The final systems management discipline that came out of the 1970s was configuration management. As with many of the systems management functions that emerged from this decade, configuration management came in multiple flavors. One was hardware configuration, which involved both the logical and physical interconnection of devices. Another was operating system configuration management, which managed the various levels of the operating systems. A third was application software configuration management, which configured and tracked block releases of application software.

Significant IT Developments During the 1980s

At least four major IT developments occurred during the decade of the 1980s that had substantial influence on the disciplines of systems management:

- The continuing evolution of mainframe computers
- The expanded use of midrange computers
- The proliferation of PCs
- The emergence of client/server systems

Continuing Evolution of Mainframe Computers

A variety of new features were added to the S/370 architecture during the 1980s. These included support for higher-density disk and tape devices, high-speed laser printers, and fiber optic channels. But one of the most significant advances during this decade again involved main memory.

By the early 1980s, corporations of all sizes were running large, mission-critical applications on their mainframe computers. As the applications and their associated databases grew in size and number, they once again bumped up against the memory constraints of the S/370 architecture. Few would have believed back in the early 1970s that the almost unlimited size of virtual storage would prove to be too little. Yet by the early 1980s, that is exactly what happened.

Database

A database is a collection of logically related data, organized in such a way as to be easily retrieved by computer programs and online transactions. Gradually smaller references to a database include files, directories, indices, records, and fields.

IBM responded by extending its maximum S/370 addressing field from 24 bits to 32 bits. As shown in Table F-1, this meant that the maximum addressable memory was now extended from 16 megabytes to 4 gigabytes (4 billion bytes of memory). This new version of the S/370 operating system was appropriately named Multiple Virtual Storage/Extended Architecture, or MVS/XA.

The demand for more memory was coupled with increased demands for processing power and disk storage. This led to a more formal process for planning the capacity of CPUs, main memory, I/O channels, and disk storage. The large increase in mission-critical applications also led to a more formal process for accepting major application systems into production and for managing changes. Finally, as the availability of online systems became more crucial to the success of a business, the process of disaster recovery became more formalized.

Extended Use of Midrange Computers

Midrange computers had been in operation for many years prior to the 1980s. But during this decade, these machines flourished even more, in both numbers and importance. In the 1970s, Hewlett-Packard and DEC both thrived in the midrange market, with HP monopolizing small businesses and manufacturing companies while DEC carving out an impressive niche in the medical industry.

Contributing to this surge in midrange sales was the introduction of IBM's Advanced Systems 400, or AS/400. As more and more critical applications started running on these midrange boxes, disaster recovery now arose as a legitimate business need for these smaller computer systems; it was a natural extension of mainframe disaster recovery.

Proliferation of Personal Computers

The PC, like many technological advancements before it, was born in rather humble surroundings. But what began almost as a hobby in a San Jose garage in the late 1970s completely transformed the IT industry during the 1980s. Steve Jobs and Steve Wozniak, cofounders of Apple Computer, envisioned a huge, world-wide market. However, they were initially limited to selling mostly to hobbyists and schools, with many of the academic Apples greatly discounted or donated. Conservative corporate America was not yet ready for what many perceived to be little more than an amateur hobbyist's invention, particularly if it lacked the IBM trademark.

Eventually IBM came to embrace the PC and American business followed. Companies began to see the productivity gains of various office automation products such as word processors, spread sheets, and graphics presentation packages. Engineering and entertainment firms also saw the value in the graphics capabilities of PCs, particularly Apple's advanced Macintosh model. By the middle of the decade, both Apple and IBM-type PCs were prospering.

As the business value of PCs became more apparent to industry, the next logical extension was to network them together in small local groups to enable the sharing of documents, spreadsheets, and electronic mail (or email). The infrastructure used to connect these small clusters of PCs became known as local area networks (LANs). This growth of LANs laid the groundwork for the evolving systems management discipline of network management. The expansion of LANs also contributed to the expansion of security beyond operating systems, applications, and databases and out onto the network.

Emergence of Client/Server Systems

Toward the end of the 1980s, a variation of an existing IT architecture began to emerge. The cornerstone of this technology was a transaction-oriented operating system developed first by AT&T Bell Laboratories and later refined by the University of California at Berkeley. It was called UNIX, short for uniplexed information and computing system. The name was selected to distinguish it from the earlier mainframe operating system MULTICS, short for multiplexed information and computing system. Like midrange computers, UNIX had its origins in the late 1960s and early 1970s, but really came into its own in the 1980s.

As mini-computers—later referred to as workstation servers and eventually just servers—became more powerful and PCs became more prevalent, the merging of these two entities into a client/server (PC-server) relationship emerged. One of the outcomes of this successful merger was the need to extend storage management to client/server applications. The problems and solutions of mainframe and midrange backups and restores now extended to client/server environments.

Impact of 1980s IT Developments on New Systems Management Functions

As we have seen, the 1980s ushered in several significant advances in IT. These, in turn, necessitated several new disciplines of systems management. The continuing evolution of the S/370 highlighted the need for disaster recovery, capacity planning, change management, and production acceptance. The proliferation and interconnection of PCs necessitated the need for formal network management.

Just as it is difficult to define the exact date of the origin of the computer, it is similarly difficult to pinpoint the beginning of some of the disciplines of systems management. I believe that the timing of these new systems management disciplines is closely linked to the major events in the progression of IT.

Real Life Experience—Value of Networking, Technical and Otherwise

In addition to preparing for the 1984 Olympics, the City of Los Angeles Data Service Bureau also was involved in implementing the region's first 911 emergency calling system. To me, the most striking aspect of this mammoth telecommunications undertaking was not the complexity of the networks or the software that would help route and track the millions of calls expected. The most significant lesson learned for me was seeing how the political battles that ensued over who would have overall jurisdiction for the system totally superseded the technical challenges. Southern California is a vast, diverse collection of local departments of law enforcements, fire departments, emergency medical response units, and public safety agencies. It took almost two additional years to sort out how all the various authorities would work for and with each other. As a manager, it just reinforced the notion that people issues always need to be addressed ahead of the technical ones.

Impact of 1980s IT Developments on Existing Systems Management Functions

Just as new systems management disciplines resulted from the IT developments of the 1980s, existing systems management processes were impacted by those same IT developments. This included security, which now extended beyond batch applications, online systems, and corporate databases, to now include the network arena.

It also included the function of storage management, which now extended beyond the mainframe and midrange environments to that of client/server systems. As more and more critical applications began running on these platforms, there was a genuine need to ensure that effective backups and restores were performed on these devices.

Conclusion

The growth of online systems with huge corporate databases, coupled with falling prices of memory chips, exposed the limited memory of the otherwise immensely successful S/360. IBM responded with an evolved architecture called S/370, which featured a memory mapping scheme. The MVS memory mapping scheme essentially gave each application access to the full 16 megabytes of memory available in OS/370.

MVS helped proliferate OLTP systems and extremely large databases. These, in turn, shifted the emphasis of performance and tuning away from a batch orientation to that of online transactions and databases. Five other systems management functions also became prominent during this time:

- Storage management
- Change management
- Problem management
- Security
- Configuration management

Four of the key IT developments of the 1980s that helped advance the field of systems management were the evolution of mainframe computing, the expanded use of midrange computers, the proliferation of PCs, and the emergence of client/server systems.

The continuing evolution of mainframe computers helped formalize capacity planning, production acceptance, change management, and disaster recovery. The expanded use of midrange computers encouraged the refinement of disaster-recovery processes.

The proliferation of PCs brought the discipline of network management into the forefront. Finally, the 1980s saw the coupling of two emerging technologies: the utility of the workstation server merged with the power of the desktop computer to usher in the widespread use of client/server computing. Among the many offshoots of client/server computing was the refinement of the storage management function.

Into and Beyond the New Millennium

This appendix concludes our historical look at systems management by presenting key IT developments in the decade of the 1990s along with a few predictions for the new millennium. This is worth reviewing because the future direction of IT is where many of us will spend much of our professional lives.

The proliferation of interconnected PCs led to critical emphasis on the performance and reliability of the networks that connected all these various clients to their servers. As a result, capacity planning expanded its discipline into the more widespread area of networks, with multiple distributed computing resources of various architectures.

Undoubtedly the most significant IT advancement in the 1990s was the world-wide explosion of the Internet. In the span of a few short years, companies went from dabbling in limited exposure to the Internet to becoming totally dependent on its information resources. Many firms have spawned their own intranets and extranets. Security, availability, and capacity planning are just some of the disciplines touched by this incredibly potent technology.

No discussion of the new millennium would be complete without mention of the ubiquitous Y2K computer problem (the so-called millennium bug). Many IT observers predicted that this fatal software flaw would bring down virtually every non-upgraded computer at midnight on December 31, 1999. Although the problem was identified and addressed in time to prevent widespread catastrophic impacts, its influence on a few of the systems management disciplines is worth noting.

Re-Inventing the Mainframe

The 1990s saw the world of mainframes come full circle. During the 1970s, many companies centralized their large processors in what became huge data centers. Favorable economic growth in the 1980s allowed many businesses to expand both regionally and globally. Many of the IT departments in these firms decentralized their data centers to distribute control and services locally. Driven by the need to reduce costs in the 1990s, many of these same companies now recentralized back into even larger data centers. This is a pattern that continues to repeat every few years as companies grow, split off, merge, acquire, or sell other business entities.

Automated Tape Library

An automated tape library is a mechanical apparatus in which a centralized, robotic arm retrieves cartridges or cassettes of stored magnetic tape, feeds them into a tape drive for use, and then places them back into their assigned slot after use. The system uses sophisticated software and lasers to ensure the proper tape is retrieved and loaded into the proper drive.

As the mainframe architectures migrated back to major data centers, managers felt increased pressure to improve the overall efficiency of their operating environments. One method employed to accomplish this was to automate parts of the computer operations organization. Terms such as *automated tape libraries*, *automated consoles*, and *automated monitoring* started becoming common in the 1990s.

Automated Console

An automated console is a desktop monitor loaded with software to automatically display and respond to commands that would normally be performed by computer operators.

Automated Monitoring

Automated monitoring is the use of computer and network software to constantly sample the hardware, software, and physical environment of a data center and to send alert messages to designated recipients whenever some exception threshold is reached.

As data centers gradually began operating more efficiently and more reliably, so did the environmental functions of these centers. Environmental controls for temperature, humidity, and electrical power became more automated and integrated into the overall management of the data center. The function of facilities management had certainly been around in one form or another in prior decades. But during the 1990s it emerged and progressed as a highly refined function for IT operations managers.

Mainframes themselves also went through some significant technical refinements during this time frame. One of the most notable advances again came from IBM. An entirely new architecture that had been in development for over a decade was introduced as System/390 (S/390), with its companion operating system OS/390. Having learned their lessons about memory constraints in years past, IBM engineers planned to stay ahead of the game by designing a 48-bit memory addressing field into the system. This would eventually provide the capability to address up to approximately 268 trillion bytes of memory. Will this finally be enough memory to satisfy the demands of the new millennium? Only time will tell, of course. But there are systems already announced, such as Windows 7, with 64-bit addressing schemes. In all likelihood, the 48-bit memory addressing will not be the next great limiting factor in IT architectures; more probably it will be either the database or network arenas that will apply the brakes.

Real Life Experience—Executives Seek to Solve Titanic Problem

In December 1997, 20th Century Fox and Paramount Studios released the motion picture Titanic amid much speculation that the picture would flop. After all, it was grossly over budget, six months behind schedule, in a genre of disaster movies which notoriously perform poorly at the box office during the Christmas holidays, its cast contained no blockbuster stars, and it was a story about which everyone knew the ending.

So it was more than a little surprising when the picture started setting box office records right from the start. For 15 consecutive weeks, it was the No. 1 movie in America. As the infrastructure manager at Fox at the time, I witnessed all this reaction first-hand. I especially remember the morning some executives from marketing came down to question me as to whether the programs generating the box office predictions and results were running properly. They simply could not believe the number they were seeing and actually thought for a moment that perhaps the software had changed and become faulty; that's how far off the charts the numbers were. I assured them that software had not been changed and was running as designed. They later attributed part of the phenomenal success of Titanic to what they called the Leo Factor: millions of girls in their early teens going to see the movie 8, 10, even 15 times to watch the romantic tragedy of the movie's leading man, Leonardo DiCaprio.

IBM's new architecture also introduced a different process technology for its family of processors. It is based on complimentary metal-oxide semiconductor (CMOS) technology. While not as new or even as fast as other circuitry IBM has used in the past, it is relatively inexpensive and extremely low in heat generation. Heat has often plagued IBM and others in their pursuit of the ultimate fast and powerful circuit design. CMOS also lends itself to parallel processing, which more than compensates for its slightly slower execution speeds.

CMOS

CMOS is short for complimentary metal-oxide semiconductor. CMOS technology uses both negatively charged and positively charged transistors in a complimentary manner for improved current flow. Unlike other semiconductors, CMOS uses no power when not in use and generates almost no heat.

Other features were designed into the S/390 architecture that helped prepare it for some of the emerging technologies of the 1990s. One of these was the more robust use of high-speed, fiber-optic channels for I/O operations. Another was the integrated interface for IBM's version of UNIX, which it called AIX (for advanced interactive executive). A third noteworthy feature of the S/390 was its increased channel port capacity. This was intended to handle anticipated increases in remote I/O activity primarily due to higher Internet traffic.

Fiber-Optic Channels

Fiber-optic channels are tiny glass fibers rather that metal cables to transmit information digitally through pulses of light. Fiber-optic channels are thinner and lighter than metal cables and can transmit large amounts of data at very high speeds with virtually no electric or magnetic interference. Their drawbacks are their expensive costs, their fragility, and the difficulty of splicing them.

The Evolving Midrange and Client/Server Platforms

The decade of the 1990s saw many companies transforming themselves in several ways. Downsizing and rightsizing became common buzzwords as global competition forced many industries to cut costs and become more productive. Acquisitions, mergers, and even hostile takeovers became more commonplace as industries as diverse as aerospace, communications, and banking endured corporate consolidations.

The push to become more efficient and streamlined drove many companies back to centralizing their IT departments. The process of centralization forced many IT executives to take a long, hard look at the platforms in their shop. This was especially true when merging companies attempted to combine their respective IT shops. This recognition highlighted the need for a global evaluation to identify which types of platforms would work best in a new consolidated environment and which kinds of operational improvements each platform type offered.

By the early 1990s, midrange and client/server platforms both had delivered improvements in two areas:

1. The volumes of units shipped, which had more than doubled in the past 10 years.
2. The types of applications now running on these platforms.

Companies that had previously run most all of their mission-critical applications on large mainframes were now migrating many of these systems onto smaller midrange computers, or more commonly onto client/server platforms.

The term *server* itself was going through a transformation of sorts about this time. As more data became available to clients—both human and machine—for processing, the computers managing and delivering this information started being grouped together as servers, regardless of their size. In some cases, even the mainframe was referred to as a giant server.

As midrange computers became more network-oriented, and as the more traditional application and database servers became more powerful, the differences in terms of managing the two types began to fade. This was especially true in the case of storage management. Midrange and client/server platforms by now were both running mission-critical applications and enterprise-wide systems. This meant the backing up of their data was becoming just as crucial a function as it had been for years on the mainframe side.

The fact that storage management was now becoming so important on such a variety of platforms refined the storage management function of systems management. The discipline evolved into an enterprise-wide process involving products and procedures that no longer applied just to mainframes but to midrange and client/server platforms as well. Later in the decade, Microsoft introduced its new, 32-bit NT architecture that many in the industry presumed stood for New Technology. As NT became prevalent, storage management was again extended and refined to include this new platform offering.

Real Life Experience—A New Technology by Any Other Name

During the late 1990s, Microsoft announced its plans for a new, advanced operating system that they referred to as NT. My CIO at the time was not a strong supporter of Microsoft, but reluctantly agreed to have us evaluate the merits of NT. Time and again, Microsoft kept pushing back the date of when a copy would be made available for us to test.

At a subsequent staff meeting, I reported on the delayed status of our evaluation. One of my coworkers asked what NT stood for and before I could respond, my CIO, in a rather irritated tone, said, "It stands for Not There; at this rate, I'm not sure it will ever be." Six months later, Microsoft delivered their new operating system to us, which we tested to our satisfaction.

Just as NT began establishing itself as a viable alternative to UNIX, a new operating system arrived on the scene that was radically different in concept and origin. In 1991, Linus Torvald, a 21-year-old doctorial student at Helsinki University in Finland, wrote his own operating system (called Linux). It was to be an improved alternative to the well-established but flawed UNIX system and to the unproven and fledgling NT system. More importantly, it would be distributed free over the Internet with all of its source code made available to users for modification. Thus began a major new concept of free, open source code for a mainstream operating system in which users are not only allowed to improve and modify the source code for their own customized use, they are encouraged to do so. As of 2006, less than 2 percent of the current Linux operating system has Torvald's original code in it.

The Growing Use of PCs and Networks

By the time the last decade of the 20th century rolled around, PCs and the networks that interconnected them had become an ingrained part of everyday life. Computer courses were being taught in elementary schools for the young, in senior citizen homes for the not so young, and in most every institution of learning in between.

Not only had the number of PCs grown substantially during these past 10 years, but so had their variety. The processing power of desktop computers changed in both directions. Those requiring extensive capacity for complex graphics and analytical applications evolved into powerful—and expensive—PC workstations. Those needing only minimal processing capability (such as for data entry, data inquiries, or Internet access) were offered as less-expensive network computers.

Thin Client

A thin client refers to a desktop PC with minimal processing and storage capability for use primarily as a data- or order-entry device, for data inquiries, or for Internet access. Data for these applications are typically stored in the server rather than on the client.

These two extremes of PC offerings are sometimes referred to as fat clients and thin clients, with a wide variation of choices in between. Desktop models were not the only offering of PCs in the 1990s. Manufacturers offered progressively smaller versions commonly referred to as laptops (for portable use), palmtops (for personal scheduling—greatly popularized by the Personal Digital Assistant *Palm Pilot* and the *BlackBerry*, which is shown in Figure G-1), and thumbtops (an even smaller, though less popular offering). These models provided users with virtually any variation of PC they required or desired.

Figure G-1   BlackBerry Pearl Model 8220

Fat Client

A fat client refers to a desktop PC with extensive processing and storage capability for use with applications that are downloaded from a server to run in real-time on the desktop. Data for these applications are typically stored in the client rather than the server. Fat client applications usually require substantial processing capability, such as for multi-media, high-resolution graphics, or numerical analysis.

Laptop computers alone had become so popular by the end of the decade that most airlines, hotels, schools, universities, and resorts had changed policies, procedures, and facilities to accommodate the ubiquitous tool. Many graduate schools taught courses that actually required laptops as a pre-requisite for the class.

As the number and variety of PCs continued to increase, so also did their dependence on the networks that interconnected them. This focused attention on two important functions of systems management: availability and capacity planning.

Availability now played a critical role in ensuring the productivity of PC users in much the same way as it did during its evolution from mainframe batch applications to online systems. However, the emphasis on availability shifted away from the computers themselves because most desktops had robust redundancy designed into them. Instead, the emphasis shifted to the availability of the LANs that interconnected all these desktop machines.

The second discipline that evolved from the proliferation of networked PCs was capacity planning. It, too, now moved beyond computer capacity to that of network switches, routers, and especially bandwidth.

The Global Growth of the Internet

Among all the numerous advances in the field of IT, none has had more widespread global impact than the unprecedented growth and use of the Intranet.

What began as a relatively limited-use tool for sharing research information between Defense Department agencies and universities has completely changed the manner in which corporations, universities, governments, and even families communicate and do business.

The commonplace nature of the Internet in business and in the home generated a need for more stringent control over access. The systems management function of strategic security evolved as a result of this need by providing network firewalls, more secured password schemes, and effective corporate policy statements and procedures.

As the capabilities of the Internet grew during the 1990s, the demand for more sophisticated services intensified. New features such as voice cards, animation, and multimedia became popular among users and substantially increased network traffic. The need to more effectively plan and manage these escalating workloads on the network brought about additional refinements in the functions of capacity planning and network management.

Lingering Effects of the Millennium Bug

By 1999 there were probably few people on the planet who had not at least heard something about the Y2K computer problem. While many are now at least somewhat aware of what the millennium bug involved, this section describes it once more for readers who may not fully appreciate the source and significance of the problem.

As mentioned earlier, the shortage of expensive data storage, both in main memory and on disk devices, led application software developers in the mid-1960s to conserve on storage space. One of the most common methods used to save storage space was to shorten the length of a date field in a program. This was accomplished by designating the year with only its last two digits. The years 1957 and 1983, for example, would be coded as 57 and 83, respectively. This would reduce the four-byte year field down to two bytes.

Taken by itself, a savings of two bytes of storage may seem relatively insignificant. But date fields were very prevalent in numerous programs of large applications, sometimes occurring hundreds or even thousands of times. An employee personnel file, for example, may contain separate fields for an employee date of birth, company start date, company anniversary date, company seniority date, and company retirement date—all embedded within each employee record. If the company employed 10,000 workers, the firm would store 50,000 date fields in its personnel file. The two-byte savings from the contracted year field would total 100,000 bytes, or about 100 kilobytes of storage for a single employee file.

Real Life Experience—Unprepared for this Type of Y2K Problem

One of the major projects I headed up while serving as the Director of Operations for 20th Century Fox was to outsource their mainframe operations. We completed the outsourcing successfully in February 1996 and enjoyed a very professional relationship with the outsourcing company for several years. In the summer of 1998, a larger company acquired the outsourcing company. This larger company focused much of its energy on preparing to bail companies out of major Y2K disasters that the company was sure would occur. In fact, the company banked most all of its future business on the premise that Y2K catastrophes would befall any number of large corporations and that this company would be there to save the day. As we all know now, there were no major calamities resulting from Y2K. This company barely avoided bankruptcy. The outsourcing part of the company continued to operate successfully.

Consider an automotive or aerospace company that could easily have millions of parts associated with a particular model of a car or an airplane. Each part record may have fields for a date of manufacture, a date of install, a date of estimated life expectancy, and a date of actual replacement. The two-byte reduction of the year field in these inventory files could result in millions of bytes of savings in storage.

But a savings in storage was not the only reason that a 2-byte year field in a date record was used. Many developers needed to sort dates within their programs. A common scheme used to facilitate sorting was to comprise the date in a *yy-mm-dd* format. The two-digit year gave a consistent, easy-to-read, and easy-to-document form for date fields, not to mention slightly faster sort times due to fewer bytes that must be compared.

Perhaps the most likely reason that programmers were not worried about concatenating their year fields to two digits was that few, if any, thought that their programs would still be running in production 20, 30 and even 40 years later. After all, the IT industry was still in its infancy in the 1960s, when many of these programs were first developed. IT was rapidly changing on a year-to-year and even a month-to-month basis. Newer and more improved methods of software development—such as structured programming, relational databases, fourth-generation languages, and object-oriented programming—would surely replace these early versions of production programs.

Of course, hindsight is often 20/20. What we know now but did not fully realize then was that large corporate applications became mission-critical to many businesses during the 1970s and 1980s. These legacy systems grew in such size, complexity, and importance over the years that it became difficult to justify the large cost of their replacements.

The result was that countless numbers of mission-critical programs developed in the 1960s and 1970s with two-byte year fields were still running in production by the late 1990s. This presented the core of the problem, which was that the year 2000 in most of these legacy programs would be interpreted as the year 1900, causing programs to fail, lock up, or otherwise generate unpredictable results.

A massive remediation and replacement effort began in the late 1990s to address the Y2K computer problem. Some industries, such as banking and airlines, spent up to four years correcting their software to ensure it ran properly on January 1, 2000. These programming efforts were, by and large, successful in heading off any major adverse impacts of the Y2K problem.

There were also a few unexpected benefits from the efforts to address the millennium bug. One was that many companies were forced to conduct a long-overdue inventory of their production application profiles. Numerous stories surfaced about IT departments discovering from these inventories that they were supporting programs no longer needed or not even being used. Not only did application profiles become more accurate and current as a result of Y2K preparations, the methods used to compile these inventories also improved.

A second major benefit of addressing the Y2K problem were the refinements it brought about in two important functions of systems management. The first was in change management. Remedial programming necessitated endless hours of regression testing to ensure that the output of the modified Y2K-compliant programs matched the output of the original programs. Upgrading these new systems into production often resulted in temporary back-outs and then re-upgrading. Effective change management procedures helped to ensure these upgrades were done smoothly and permanently when the modifications were done properly; they also ensured that the back-outs were done effectively and immediately when necessary.

The function of production acceptance was also refined as a result of Y2K. Many old mainframe legacy systems were due to be replaced because they were not Y2K compliant. Most of these replacements were designed to run on client/server platforms. Production acceptance procedures were modified in many IT shops to better accommodate client/server production systems. This was not the first time mission-critical applications were implemented on client/server platforms, but the sheer increase in numbers due to Y2K compliance forced many IT shops to make their production acceptance processes more streamlined, effective, and enforceable.

Major Events of the New Millennium

A number of major events helped shape the IT environment during the outset of the new millennium. Some of these events combined the forces of technology, economics, and politics. For example, a number of technology companies purchased other firms in a series of high-profile, mega-billion (U.S. dollar) acquisitions (see Table G-1). Many of these mergers put additional strain on their IT infrastructures in attempting to integrate dissimilar platforms, products, and processes.

Table G-1   Sampling of Major Corporate Acquisitions

Year	Acquiring Company	Company Acquired	Cost in Billions (USD)
1998	Compaq	DEC	$9.6
2002	HP	Compaq	$25
2002	Sungard	Comdisco	$10
2004	Cingular	AT&T Wireless	$41
2005	SBC	AT&T	$16

Toward the end of the 1990s and beyond, many companies worldwide scrambled to provide a presence on the Web. This resulted in many hastily designed websites with little regard for security. Almost overnight, cyberspace became the playground of hackers and crackers, some merely wanting to pull off pranks but many others with malicious intents. New legislation, prosecutions, and jail time heightened the awareness of how vulnerable the Internet could be and greatly increased the emphasis on network and data security.

Companies also began using the Internet for e-commerce. This impacted not only security but other IT functions, such as availability and capacity. The giant toy retailer *Toys-R-Us* experienced this first-hand when the capacity of their network and website could not handle the huge amount of pre-Christmas traffic in 1999, leaving many a child without toys on Christmas morning.

The emotional, political, and economical effects of the 9/11 attacks on the World Trade Centers are still being felt and assessed. One of the results was greater concern and emphasis on disaster recovery and business continuity. This obviously impacts several other infrastructure processes such as availability, security, and facilities management.

What the Future May Hold

The next 10 to 20 years will be very exciting times for IT infrastructures. A number of currently emerging technologies will be refined and made commonplace. Wireless technology will continue to evolve mobility and portability beyond its present state of emails and the Internet to possibly include full-scale application access and processing. Similarly, bio-metrics and voice recognition may well advance to such sophisticated levels that identify theft becomes a crime of the past. Researchers are already working on implanted chips that combine personal identification information with DNA characteristics to verify identities.

The manufacturing of computer chips will also drastically change in the next few years. Scientists are now experimenting with re-programmable chips that can re-configure themselves depending on the type of tasks they are required to perform. Improvements in power and miniaturization will continue, enabling tiny devices to process millions of operations almost instantaneously. The integration of technologies will continue accelerating beyond today's ability to combine the functions of a telephone, camera, laptop computer, music player, geo-positioning satellite, and dozens of other functions yet to be developed. These various functions will all need to be controlled and managed with robust infrastructure processes.

Without question, the Internet will continue expanding and improving in performance and functions. Current concerns about capacity and network bandwidth are already being addressed. Improvements to security are enabling the proliferation of wireless technologies. Researchers are investing technologies today that will enable tomorrow's next generation of the Internet to increase its speed, power, and capacity by tenfold. This blinding speed could enable companies and users to utilize and integrate more powerful applications on the Web, and will greatly enhance streaming video, Web TV, and large-scale video conferencing.

Regardless of the number of technical advances and the usefulness that they offer, there will always be the need to design their use appropriately, to implement their features properly, and to manage their results responsibly. Issues of security, availability, performance, and business continuity will always be present and need to be addressed. This is where the prudent execution of IT systems management becomes most valuable.

Timelining the Disciplines of Systems Management

Table G-2 summarizes these timelines and shows for which systems the disciplines emerged and evolved.

Table G-2   Emergence and Evolution of Systems Management Disciplines

Discipline	1960s	1970s	1980s	1990s	2000s
Availability management	Emerged (for batch)	Evolved (for onlines)	Evolved (for networks)		
Performance and tuning	Emerged (for batch)	Evolved (for onlines)	Evolved (for networks)		
Storage management		Emerged		Evolved (for client/server)	
Change management		Emerged			
Service desk		Emerged			
Problem management		Emerged			
Security management		Emerged	Evolved (for networks)	Evolved (for Internet)	
Configuration management		Emerged			
Network management			Emerged		
Production acceptance			Emerged	Evolved (for client/server)	Evolving (for RAID)
Disaster recovery			Emerged	Evolved (for mid-r&c-svr)	Evolving (for networks)
Capacity planning			Emerged	Evolved (for networks)	
Facility management				Emerged	Evolving (for auto ops)

Conclusion

The trend to centralize back and optimize forward the corporate computer centers of the new millennium led to highly automated data centers. This emphasis on process automation led to increased scrutiny of the physical infrastructure of data centers, which, in turn, led to a valuable overhaul of facilities management. As a result, most major computer centers have never been more reliable in availability, nor more responsive in performance. Likewise, most have never been more functional in design nor more efficient in operation.

The 1990s saw the explosive and global growth of the Internet. The wide-spread use of cyberspace led to improvements in network security and capacity planning. Midrange computers and client/server platforms moved closer to each other, technology-wise, and pushed forward the envelope of enterprise-wide storage management. The popularity of UNIX as the operating system of choice for servers, particularly application and database servers, continued to swell during this decade. IBM adapted its mainframe architecture to reflect the popularity of UNIX and the Internet. Similarly, Microsoft refined its NT operating system and Internet Explorer browser to improve the use of the Internet and to aggressively compete against the incumbent UNIX and the upstart Linux.

PCs proliferated at ever-increasing rates, not only in numbers sold but in the variety of models offered. Client PCs of all sizes were now offered as thin, fat, laptop, palmtop, or even thumbtop. The interconnection of all these PCs with each other and with their servers caused capacity planning and availability for networks to improve as well.

The final decade of the second millennium concluded with a flurry of activity surrounding the seemingly omnipresent millennium bug. As most reputable IT observers correctly predicted, the problem was sufficiently addressed and resolved for most business applications months ahead of the year 2000. The domestic and global impacts of the millennium bug proved to have been relatively negligible. The vast efforts expended in mitigating the impacts of Y2K did help to refine both the production acceptance and the change management functions of systems management.

This appendix and the previous two appendices collectively presented a unique historical perspective of some of the major IT developments that took place during the latter half of the 20th century and the first decade of this century. These developments had a major influence on initiating or refining the disciplines of systems management. Table G-2 summarized a timeline for the 12 functions that are described in detail in Part Two of this book.

Answers to Selected Questions

Chapter 1

A2—False

A4—customers

Chapter 2

A2—True

A4—owner

Chapter 3

A3—ability

Chapter 4

A1—False

A4—1990s

Chapter 5

A1—True

A2—False

Chapter 6

A2—False

A4—ISO20000

Chapter 7

A1—False

A2—True

Chapter 8

A1—True

A3—encryption codes

A4—buffers

Chapter 9

A2—True

A4—applications development

Chapter 10

A4—emergency changes

Chapter 11

A1—True

A3—closed

Chapter 12

A2—False

A4—logical backup

Chapter 13

A1—True

Chapter 14

A1—False

A4—expense

Chapter 15

A2—False

A4—documentation and capacity planning

Chapter 16

A1—True

A2—False

Chapter 17

A4—recovery strategies

Chapter 18

A1—True
A3—backup tape library

Chapter 19

A2—True
A3—response times of transactions

Chapter 20

A1—False
A3—value and quality

Chapter 21

A2—True
A3—change managementA4—integration

Chapter 22

A2—False
A4—storage arrays

Bibliography

Adams, Michael J. (1993). *Big Blues,* Wall Street Journal Press

Adzema, J., and Schiesser, R. (July/August 1997). *Establishing a Customer Service Center,* Enterprise Management Issues Magazine

Hallbauer, J., and Schiesser, R. (July/August 1998). *Capacity Planning for Open Systems Environments,* Enterprise Management Issues Magazine

Humphrey, W. (1999). *The Meeting Behind Making of IBM 360,* USA Today

Kern, H., and Johnson, R. (1994). *Rightsizing the New Enterprise: The Proof, Not the Hype,* Sun Microsystems Press/Prentice Hall

Kern, H., Johnson, R., Hawkins, M., Lyke, H., Kennnedy, W., and Cappel, M. (1995). *Networking the New Enterprise: The Proof, Not the Hype,* Sun Microsystems Press/Prentice Hall

Kern, H., Johnson, R., Hawkins, M., and Law, A. (1996). *Managing the New Enterprise: The Proof, Not the Hype,* Sun Microsystems Press/Prentice Hall

Kovar, J. (1999). *Sun To Release New Fibre Channel RAID,* Computer Reseller News

Lee, J., and Winkler, S. (1995). *Key Events in the History of Computing;* Institute of Electrical and Electronic Engineers (IEEE) Computer Society, November 5, 1995

Maney, K. (1999). *Computer Giant Tries to Repeat Success of 360,* USA Today

Robbins, G. (1999). *Good Quotations by Famous People,* Department of Computer Science, University of Virginia

Royster, H., and Schiesser, R. (January/February 1998). *Disaster Recovery In The AS/400 Arena,* Enterprise Management Issues Magazine

Schiesser, R. (March/April 1994). *Applying Baldrige To Computer Operations,* The Computer Operations Manager

Schiesser, R. (March/April 1998). *The Effective Use of Consultants,* Enterprise Management Issues Magazine

Troppe, S. (1983). *IBM and the Growth of Computer Technology: Teaching History in Computer Education,* Yale-New Haven Teachers Institute

Index

SECOND EDITION

IT Systems Management

RICH SCHIESSER

FREE Online Edition

Your purchase of **IT Systems Management** includes access to a free online edition for 45 days through the Safari Books Online subscription service. Nearly every Prentice Hall book is available online through Safari Books Online, along with more than 5,000 other technical books and videos from publishers such as Cisco Press, Exam Cram, IBM Press, O'Reilly, Addison-Wesley Professional, Que, and Sams.

SAFARI BOOKS ONLINE allows you to search for a specific answer, cut and paste code, download chapters, and stay current with emerging technologies.

Activate your FREE Online Edition at
www.informit.com/safarifree

> **STEP 1:** Enter the coupon code: HYNZYBI.

> **STEP 2:** New Safari users, complete the brief registration form.
> Safari subscribers, just log in.

If you have difficulty registering on Safari or accessing the online edition,
please e-mail customer-service@safaribooksonline.com

Safari
Books Online

Addison Wesley   AdobePress   ALPHA   Cisco Press   FT Press   IBM Press   lynda.com   Microsoft Press   New Riders

O'REILLY   Peachpit Press   PRENTICE HALL   QUE   Redbooks   SAMS   SAS Publishing   Sun microsystems   WILEY